CW00344573

British Elections & Parties Review
VOLUME 8

BRITISH ELECTIONS & PARTIES REVIEW

VOLUME 8

The 1997 General Election

EDITED BY
David Denver • Justin Fisher
Philip Cowley • Charles Pattie

FRANK CASS
LONDON • PORTLAND,OR

First published in 1998 in Great Britain by
FRANK CASS PUBLISHERS
Newbury House, 900 Eastern Avenue, London IG2 7HH

and in the United States of America by
FRANK CASS PUBLISHERS
c/o ISBS, 5804 N.E. Hassalo Street
Portland, Oregon 97213-3644

Website http://www.frankcass.com

Copyright © 1998 Frank Cass & Co. Ltd.
D. Denver, J. Fisher, P. Cowley, C. Pattie

British Library Cataloguing in Publication Data

British elections & parties review
Vol. 8: The 1997 General Election
1. Elections – Great Britain 2. Political parties – Great
Britain 3. Great Britain – Politics and government – 1997–
I. Denver, D. T., 1944–
324.9'41'0859
ISBN 0 7146 4466 8

ISBN 0 7146 4909 0 (cloth)
ISBN 0 7146 4466 8 (paper)
ISSN 1368 9886

Library of Congress Cataloging-in-Publication Data
applied for

*All rights reserved. No part of this publication may be reproduced, stored in or
introduced into a retrieval system, or transmitted, in any form or by any means,
electronic, mechanical, photocopying, recording or otherwise, without the prior
written permission of the publisher of this book.*

Printed in Great Britain by
Antony Rowe Ltd., Chippenham, Wilts.

CONTENTS

PREFACE

This is the eighth annual volume published under the auspices of the Elections, Public Opinion and Parties (EPOP) specialist group of the Political Studies Association. The first six volumes were published under the title *British Elections and Parties Yearbook*, but from last year we have substituted 'Review' for 'Yearbook' as that more accurately describes the contents and the aims and scope of the volumes. From now on the *Review* will be conceived of, and marketed as, an annual series under the general editorship of David Denver.

This edition contains a selection of articles originally presented as papers at EPOP's annual conference at the University of Essex in September 1997. It is worth emphasizing, however, that – as in all previous volumes – the papers have been substantially revised and the articles finally published have all been independently and extensively refereed.

As is now traditional at post-election EPOP conferences, the programme included contributions from representatives of the political parties and pollsters as well as academic papers. This volume is drawn from the latter, and all of the articles published here are concerned with the 1997 general election. In addition to the articles, the reference section provides details of the general election results, as well as a chronology of the year, results of local elections and parliamentary by-elections, and opinion polls and so on.

A second volume arising out of the conference will also be published by Frank Cass. This is the latest in the Political Communications series – *Political Communications: Why Labour Won the 1997 General Election* – edited by Ivor Crewe, Brian Gosschalk and John Bartle. In addition to academic analyses, this will include reflections on the 1997 election campaign by politicians and party strategists.

We are grateful to the authors of the articles included here for revising their original papers and responding so positively to our requests for amendments (usually involving a reduction in length!). We know how hectic life is in British universities and are grateful that our colleagues found time to cope with tight deadlines. We would also like to acknowledge the financial and other support given to the EPOP conference by the Economic and Social Research Council, the Arthur McDougall Trust, the University of Essex and the Political Studies Association. Finally, we are grateful to Frank Cass publishers and to Cathy Jennings in particular who continues to be a source of support, encouragement and invaluable advice to the editors.

David Denver   Justin Fisher   Philip Cowley   Charles Pattie

April 1998

NOTES ON CONTRIBUTORS

Michael Billig is Professor of Social Science in the Department of Social Sciences, Loughborough University.

Harold D. Clarke is Regents Professor of Political Science, University of North Texas. His research focuses on voting, elections and the political economy of party support in Anglo-American democracies. His articles have appeared in journals such as the *American Political Science Review, American Journal of Political Science, British Journal of Political Science,* and *Journal of Politics.* Current projects include studies of voting behaviour in the 1995 Quebec referendum and the dynamics of party support in Britain.

Philip Cowley is a lecturer in the Department of Politics at the University of Hull and research secretary of the Centre for Legislative Studies. He is editor of *Conscience and Parliament* (Frank Cass, 1998), as well as the author of articles in a range of journals, including the *British Journal of Political Science, Political Studies, Party Politics,* and *Journal of Legislative Studies.*

John Curtice is Deputy Director of the ESRC Centre for Research into Elections and Social Trends (CREST), Co-Director of the British Election Study, and Professor of Politics at Strathclyde University. He is co-author/editor of *How Britain Votes, Understanding Political Change, Labour's Last Chance?* and of numerous British Social Attitudes reports, and is a regular commentator on elections for newspapers and television.

David Deacon is a lecturer in Communication and Media Studies in the Department of Social Sciences at Loughborough University.

David Denver is Professor of Politics at Lancaster University. He is co-convenor of the Elections, Public Opinion and Parties specialist group of the PSA and has published extensively on elections and voting behaviour.

Daniel Dorling is a lecturer in Geography at the University of Bristol.

Patrick Dunleavy is Professor of Government at the London School of Economics and Political Science.

Geoffrey Evans is a Fellow of Nuffield College, Oxford. A member of the British Election Study team since 1987, he has also directed ESRC- and EU-funded studies of political attitudes and behaviour in 13 post-communist societies and an election study in Northern Ireland. He is co-author of *Understanding Political Change*, and has published numerous articles on voting behaviour, comparative political sociology and democratization.

David M. Farrell is a senior Jean Monnet lecturer at the University of Manchester. Co-editor of the journals *Party Politics* and *Representation*, his recent publications include: *Comparing Electoral Systems* (Prentice-Hall, 1997), and *Party Cohesion, Party Discipline and the Organization of Parliaments* (co-editor, Ohio State University Press, 1998). In 1997 he was a fellow at the Shorenstein Center on the Press, Politics and Public Policy at the John F. Kennedy School of Government, Harvard University.

Justin Fisher is Senior Lecturer in Political Science at London Guildhall University. He is the author of *British Political Parties* (Prentice Hall), has co-edited previous editions of the *British Elections and Parties Review* (Frank Cass) and published numerous articles on party and political finance.

Peter Golding is Professor of Sociology in the Department of Social Sciences at Loughborough University.

Gordon Hands is Senior Lecturer and head of the Department of Politics at Lancaster University. He has co-authored *Modern Constituency Electioneering* (Frank Cass, 1997) and is currently completing research on local campaigning at the 1997 election.

Anthony Heath, FBA, is an official fellow of Nuffield College, Oxford, and Professor of Sociology at the University of Oxford. He is Co-Director of CREST and of the 1997 British Election Study, and co-author of the three books resulting from these studies: *How Britain Votes* (1985), *Understanding Political Change* (1991) and *Labour's Last Chance?* (1994).

Simon Henig is a lecturer in Politics at the Centre for Contemporary Political Issues at the University of Sunderland. He has written on regional voting behaviour in Britain and the Labour Party, and is currently working on a study of women's political participation throughout Europe.

Ron Johnston is Professor of Geography at the University of Bristol.

Roger Jowell is Director of Social and Community Planning Research, London, Co-Director of the British Attitudes Survey series, and visiting

Professor at the London School of Economics and Political Science. He is Co-Director of CREST and of the 1997 British Election Study, and co-author of the three books resulting from these studies: *How Britain Votes* (1985), *Understanding Political Change* (1991) and *Labour's Last Chance?* (1994).

Helen Margetts is a lecturer in Public Policy at the Department of Politics and Sociology at Birkbeck College, London.

Ian McAllister is Director of the Research School of Social Sciences at the Australian National University. He is the author of *Political Behaviour* (1992), *Dimensions of Australian Society* (1995, co-author), *The Australian Political System* (1995, co-author) and *Russia Votes* (1996, co-author). His research interests are in the areas of comparative political behaviour, political parties, voters and electoral systems.

Iain D. MacAllister is a research assistant in Geography at the University of Bristol.

Pippa Norris is Associate Director of the Joan Shorenstein Center on the Press, Politics and Public Policy and lectures at the John F. Kennedy School of Government, Harvard University. Her recent books on voting behaviour include *Electoral Change Since 1945* (Blackwell, 1997), *Britain Votes 1997* (Oxford University Press, 1997) and *Elections and Voting Behaviour* (Ashgate, 1998).

Brendan O'Duffy is a lecturer in Politics at Queen Mary and Westfield College, London.

Charles J. Pattie is Senior Lecturer in Geography at the University of Sheffield.

Colin Rallings is Professor of Politics at the University of Plymouth. He is the co-author, with Michael Thrasher, of *Local Elections in Britain* (Routledge) and of numerous journal articles on aspects of local electoral politics.

David Rossiter is Research Fellow in Geography at the University of Bristol.

David Sanders is Professor of Government and Pro-Vice Chancellor at the University of Essex.

Patrick Seyd is Professor and Chairman of the Department of Politics, University of Sheffield. He is the co-author with Paul Whiteley of *Labour's Grass Roots: The Politics of Party Membership* (Oxford University Press, 1992) and with Paul Whiteley and Jeremy Richardson of *True Blues: The Politics of Conservative Party Membership* (Oxford University Press, 1994).

Marianne C. Stewart is Professor in the School of Social Sciences, University of Texas at Dallas. Her research interests concern the impact of economic evaluations and party leader images on voting behaviour and party identification in Canada, Great Britain and the United States. She has published in journals such as *American Political Science Review, American Journal of Political Science, European Journal of Political Economy, European Journal of Political Research,* and *Journal of Politics.*

Donley T. Studlar is Eberly Family Distinguished Professor of Political Science at West Virginia University. Author of *Great Britain: Decline or Renewal?* (Westview Press, 1996), he has written many articles on British politics. He serves as executive secretary of the British Politics Group and on the editorial board of the *Journal of British Politics and International Relations.*

Bridget Taylor is Research Officer in CREST at Nuffield College, Oxford. She is joint editor of *Understanding Change in Social Attitudes* (1996).

Katarina Thomson is Research Director at SCPR and Co-Director of the British Social Attitudes Survey series. She is joint editor of *Understanding Change in Social Attitudes* (1996).

Michael Thrasher is Professor of Politics and Co-Director, with Colin Rallings, of the Local Government Chronicle Elections Centre at the University of Plymouth. The centre has recently begun work on a Leverhulme Trust-funded study of the process and consequences of local electoral re-districting in England.

Helena Tunstall is a research assistant in Geography at the University of Bristol.

Stuart Weir is Senior Research Fellow in the Centre for Human Rights in the Department of Law at the University of Essex.

Paul Whiteley is Professor of Politics at the University of Sheffield. His research interests include the causes and consequences of party activism, political participation in Britain and other mature democracies, and the political economy of party support. He has published several books and his articles have appeared in journals such as the *British Journal of Political Science, European Journal of Political Research, Journal of Politics, Political Research Quarterly*, and *Political Studies*.

ABSTRACTS OF ARTICLES

Political Change and Party Choice: Voting in the 1997 General Election

Harold D. Clarke, Marianne C. Stewart and Paul Whiteley

In their commentaries on the 1997 general election many observers have been very guarded about the influence of Tony Blair and other party leaders. Their caution is unfounded. Time-series and cross-sectional analyses of national survey data gathered between January 1992 and April 1997 demonstrate that party leader images and party identification subjugated all other influences on party support, including those exerted by personal economic expectations (the 'feel good factor') and other kinds of economic evaluations. The weakness of prospective economic judgements relative to retrospective ones in 1997 is explicable in terms of a 'responsibility for the future' conjecture that recognizes that many voters had concluded that Labour would win the 1997 election, but differed regarding their attributions of praise or blame to present and future governments for their economic futures.

New Labour Landslide – Same Old Electoral Geography?

R. J. Johnston, C. J. Pattie, D. F. L. Dorling, D. J. Rossiter, H. Tunstall and I. D. MacAllister

After years in the political wilderness, Labour won the 1997 general election by a landslide majority of seats. Its winning share of the vote, while impressive by the standards of the party's performance in recent elections, was not exceptional, however. A large part of the key to Labour's success can be traced to the changing geography of the vote between 1992 and 1997. Labour not only improved its position in its heartland constituencies, but also made (larger) inroads in the seats it had to win from the Conservatives. The article assesses the contributions of constituency socio-economic conditions, campaign strategy, and electoral redistribution to Labour's victory.

New Labour, New Tactical Voting? The Cause and Consequence of Tactical Voting in the 1997 General Election

Geoffrey Evans, John Curtice and Pippa Norris

In the 1997 election Labour secured a landslide and the Liberal Democrats a revival, in terms of seats, but not in votes. One reason appears to have been an increased incidence of anti-Conservative tactical voting. This article examines both the election results and British Election Study survey data to estimate how much tactical voting increased in 1997 and why. Both sources suggest that there was a small but significant increase in anti-Conservative tactical voting. This happened primarily because of changes in the appeal of the parties to voters rather than because of changes in the motivations of voters. In particular, compared with 1992, Liberal Democrat supporters were more likely to favour Labour and dislike the Conservatives, making them more willing to lend tactical support to Labour.

Sex, Money and Politics: Sleaze and the Conservative Party in the 1997 Election'

David M. Farrell, Ian McAllister and Donley T. Studlar

Sleaze emerged as a major issue in British politics in the mid-1990s. This article considers its effects on the 1997 re-election prospects of the Conservative Party in two respects. First we explore its influence on individual constituency results, by focusing on two key aspects, sex and money. We show that four Conservative losses can be directly attributable to the issue of sleaze. Second, we test for the effects of sleaze on Conservative support generally, concluding that a further 15 seats were probably affected. In a close election, such losses could have been highly significant. The article finishes with some discussion of how the British experience of sleaze compares with that in the USA.

Euroscepticism and the Referendum Party

Anthony Heath, Roger Jowell, Bridget Taylor and Katarina Thomson

This article uses the 1992–7 British Election Panel Study to study the sources and motivations of the Referendum Party's vote. As might be expected, just under two-thirds of people who voted for the Referendum Party in 1997 had supported the Conservatives in 1992. They were, moreover, extremely eurosceptic and this scepticism was long-standing, going back at least until 1992. However, analysis of the panel study shows that their disillusion with the Conservative party was also long-standing and was already evident at the European elections of 1994. In almost all respects, other than their attitudes to Europe, the eventual Referendum Party voters were remarkably similar to other defectors from the Conservatives. The formation of the Referendum Party, therefore, probably had little impact on the Conservative share of votes or seats but simply redistributed the anti-Conservative vote away from the centre-left parties.

Split-Ticket Voting at the 1997 British General and Local Elections: An Aggregate Analysis

Colin Rallings and Michael Thrasher

The synchronous general and local elections of May 1997 provided a rare opportunity to examine how electors behave when faced with making almost simultaneous voting decisions in different types of contest. This article uses the results of the two elections in 76 English constituencies where local elections were held, and where the boundaries of local electoral divisions and parliamentary seats coincide, to seek evidence of the existence and extent of split-ticket voting. With few significant differences in participation at the two elections, it is clear that many individuals cast their available votes for different parties. The Conservative and Labour parties fared better on average at the general election; the Liberal Democrat vote was consistently higher in the local elections. The overall level of split-ticket voting appears to have been higher than in 1979, the last occasion on which a general election was held on local election day.

Between Fear and Loathing: National Press Coverage of the 1997 British General Election

David Deacon, Peter Golding and Michael Billig

This article examines the political realignment of the British press during the 1997 general election. It argues that although the party affiliations of many papers shifted in comparison with previous elections, it is a mistake to overestimate the change that occurred. For many national newspapers, the 1997 campaign was as much about political disorientation as it was about reorientation.

Does Negative News Matter? The Effect of Television News on Party Images in the 1997 British General Election

David Sanders and Pippa Norris

It is widely assumed that British voters obtain a considerable amount of their political information from television and that television news plays an important part in shaping their political and economic perceptions. This study uses an experimental research design to assess the extent to which the political perceptions of a sample of 1125 UK voters, tested during the 1997 general election campaign, were affected by 'positive' and 'negative' party images presented in television news programmes. As well as being of intrinsic importance to debates about the effects of television news, this focus on positive and negative news has more than passing relevance for the kinds of campaigning that political parties adopt. The evidence reported in the article

BRITISH ELECTIONS AND PARTIES REVIEW

shows that voters' views about the political parties can be swayed quite markedly by the content of television news. In particular, the analysis indicates that positive news images exert far more powerful effects on voters' perceptions than negative news.

Triumph of Targeting? Constituency Campaigning in the 1997 Election

David Denver, Gordon Hands and Simon Henig

In the 1997 election all three major parties put a greater effort than ever before into targeting their local campaigns . In the case of the Conservatives and Labour this involved targeting not only constituencies but also individual voters, who had been identified for the purpose by extensive organizational efforts during the pre-election period. Analysis of responses to a survey of local campaign organizers shows that local campaigning was more intensive in target seats than it was in other comparable seats (i.e., seats that were neither hopeless nor very safe but were not targeted). The extra campaign effort appears to have had significant effects. Turnout was clearly higher in target seats and, after other factors are taken into account, the Liberal Democrats gained a clear electoral bonus from targeted campaigning while Labour obtained a smaller but still significant benefit. The effect of targeted campaigning by the Conservatives is less clear.

Labour's Grassroots Campaign in 1997

Paul Whiteley and Patrick Seyd

The Labour party organized a targeting campaign strategy which focused on the key marginals and was linked to a long-term campaign of recruiting new members and revitalizing the party organization. However, the election results suggest that turnout and swings were not appreciably different in target seats as compared with other types of seats. This has been interpreted by some observers as evidence that grassroots campaigning does not influence the vote. However, the results of a new survey of Labour party members conducted after the 1997 election shows that while the average Labour party member was fairly active during the campaign, few members campaigned extensively outside their own constituencies. While members were aware of the targeting strategy, they did not actually implement it at the grassroots level. Thus Labour did well in all types of seats, because it campaigned extensively in all types of seats. The survey also showed that significant differences in activism existed between those members who joined the party since Tony Blair became leader in 1994, and those who joined earlier. If this situation persists in future the grassroots party will progressively 'de-energize' over time.

Remodelling the 1997 General Election: How Britain Would Have Voted under Alternative Electoral Systems

Patrick Dunleavy, Helen Margetts, Brendan O'Duffy and Stuart Weir

This article simulates detailed outcomes for the 1997 general election under a range of different voting systems. With any system taking account of voters' second or subsequent preferences, the Conservatives would have fared worse than under the existing first-past-the-post electoral system. Under the supplementary vote (SV) or alternative vote (AV) Labour's overall majority would have been greater than with first-past-the-post. Even under the single transferable vote (STV) Labour would have had a comfortable working majority over all other parties. Only with a 'classic' version of the Additional Member System (AMS) or (some forms of) List PR would Labour have fallen short of an overall majority. The Liberal Democrats would nearly double their number of seats under any alternative electoral system, and triple it under STV. In 1997 and 1992 the most clearly and consistently proportional voting method was 'classic' AMS. STV did not achieve any close fit between parties' seats and their first preference votes in 1997. SV and AV were markedly *less* proportional than first-past-the-post in 1997, seeming to rule them out as options in the promised voting systems referendum.

Introduction:
The British General Election of 1997

Philip Cowley, David Denver, Justin Fisher and Charles Pattie

On 17 March 1997 the Prime Minister, John Major, went to Buckingham Palace to request a dissolution of Parliament and thereby inaugurated the longest general election campaign of the post-war era. Polling took place more than six weeks later on 1 May.

Throughout the intervening period, every published opinion poll indicated that Labour would win the election (see Tables 4.3 and 4.4 in the reference section of this volume) and, indeed, most pointed to a landslide victory. All but two of the polls published during the campaign pointed to a Labour majority of over 100; all but four implied a majority of over 150. Commentators and academic experts were cautious in their predictions, however, as they were fearful of having their fingers burned, as in 1992, through placing too much reliance on poll results. Labour too tried to downplay their chances – throughout the campaign, Labour's stock response to any question about the potential size of their majority was that 'Britain is not a landslide country'. A majority of around 30 was the best that Labour spokespeople would publicly consider, and then only grudgingly. Such a response was doubtless sensible politics, arising from caution about the accuracy of the polls and a concern not to be seen to be arrogant. Conservative strategists soon realized that they were heading for defeat and Conservative politicians could only repeat the line about 'the only poll that matters' being on 1 May.

When the results started to come in on election night it quickly became apparent that although the final predictions of the polls were less accurate than they might have been, they were closer to what transpired than the expectations of many commentators. The 1997 election turned out to be a truly remarkable election. Table 1 summarizes the results for the United Kingdom as a whole (further details are given in section 2 of the reference section).

TABLE 1
GENERAL ELECTION RESULTS 1992 AND 1997 (UK)

	1992		1997	
	Votes (%)	Seats	Votes (%)	Seats
Conservative	41.9	336	30.7	165
Labour	34.4	271	43.2	418
Liberal Democrat	17.8	20	16.8	46
SNP/PC	2.4	7	2.5	10
N. Ireland	2.3	17	2.5	18
Others	1.2	0	4.3	2
Turnout	77.7		71.4	

Sources: Rallings and Thrasher, 1993, 1998.
Note: The Speaker is counted as an 'other' in 1997.

These data show the scale of the change between 1992 and 1997. The Conservative share of the vote plummeted by 11.2 percentage points while Labour's increased by 8.8 points (the resulting swing of 10 per cent being a post war record). The share of votes received by 'others' (the most significant of these being the Referendum Party) more than tripled. Turnover of seats was even more dramatic. The number of Conservative MPs after 1 May was less than half of what it had been after the 1992 election; the number of Labour seats leapt to 418 giving them an unprecedented majority of 178 over all other parties. Despite a fall in their vote share, the number of Liberal Democrat MPs more than doubled to 46 and, for the first time since 1945, an non-party Independent (Martin Bell) was elected. In terms of seats won there was unquestionably an anti-Conservative landslide. On 1 May 1997, as William Hague later admitted, 'the Conservative Party was not merely defeated. It was humiliated'. As the table shows, all of this happened on a sharply reduced national turnout – down from 77.7 per cent in 1992 to 71.4 per cent in 1997, the lowest turnout of any post-war election.

Although the results presented in Table 1 are remarkable enough they do not convey just how remarkable the 1997 election was. In the words of Pippa Norris (1997: 1), 'the record books of modern British politics were less broken than smashed and overturned' and Anthony King lists no less than 19 electoral records that were broken in 1997 (King, 1997b: 7-10). In addition to those already mentioned, the election saw the end of the longest period of one-party rule since the beginning of the nineteenth century. The Conservative vote share was the party's smallest since 1832 and the number of Conservative MPs was the smallest since 1906. In both Scotland and Wales the Conservatives failed to win a single seat. The Labour share of the vote exceeded 40 per cent for the first time since 1970. Labour's majority over all other parties was the largest enjoyed by one party in Britain in the twentieth century.

Nor were the records confined to the major parties The election saw a record number of candidates (3,717); Liberal Democrat representation increased to 46, the largest number of centre-party MPs since 1929; and the election saw the newly-launched Referendum Party gain almost three per cent of the vote, the strongest-ever performance by a fringe party. (Details of minor party candidates and votes are given in the reference section, Tables 2.1 to 2.4.) In addition, the number of women MPs doubled to 120 (another new record) while a new high of nine ethnic-minority MPs (all Labour) were returned.

Not unexpectedly, the election results were hailed as a 'triumph' for New Labour – not just by the Labour Party itself but also by academic commentators (King, 1997a). It might be noted, however, that the very low turnout hardly constitutes a ringing endorsement and that Labour's vote share (43.2 per cent) was smaller than in any election between 1945 and 1966. Moreover, Labour's landslide was achieved with the support of just 30.8 per cent of the eligible electorate – a figure bettered by the Conservatives in three of their four victories from 1979 to 1992. Similarly, although the Liberal Democrats achieved a significant increase in their representation at Westminster, the vote share of the centre party (or parties) declined for the third election in a row.

TABLE 2
THE FLOW OF THE VOTE 1992–7

1992 Vote

1997 Vote	Too Young %	Did Not Vote %	Con %	Lab %	Lib Dem %
Con	20	20	71	1	6
Lab	57	55	14	90	23
Lib Dem	18	20	10	7	66
Other	5	5	4	2	6
(N)	116	148	863	729	268

Source: NOP/BBC exit poll.

Nonetheless, the flow of votes away from the Conservatives was dramatic. Table 2, derived from the BBC/NOP exit poll, compares party choice in 1997 with reported vote in 1992. Almost 30 per cent of 1992 Conservatives defected to other parties. In the nature of things an exit poll cannot measure changes from voting to non-voting and when that flow is taken into account it would seem that the Conservatives – at a minimum – lost a third of their 1992 vote while recruiting poorly among previous non-voters and first-time voters. Labour's only significant loss was to the Liberal Democrats and there was a lot of switching from the Liberal Democrats to Labour – in both cases tactical voting probably played an important part in this.

These changes are even more impressive if one recalls the judgements made after the 1992 election. The Conservatives were said to have become a 'Super Party' (King, 1992), and the future painted for the opposition parties was irredeemably bleak. Britain, it was argued, had become a *de facto* one-party state (King, 1993; Margetts and Smyth, 1993; Heywood, 1994). The electoral pendulum, it appeared, had simply stopped swinging.

There are two separate main questions to be asked and answered about the 1997 general election. The first is 'Why did the distribution of support for the parties change so much from 1992?' and the second, 'Why did the distribution of votes result in a landslide victory for Labour in terms of seats in the House of Commons?'

A good deal of work dealing with these and other questions has already been published, of course. As well as the 'Nuffield' study (Butler and Kavanagh, 1997), a feature of every general election since 1945, the election has already spawned three other edited collections (Geddes and Tonge, 1997; King, 1997a; Norris and Gavin, 1997), an account of the campaign by one of the BBC's journalists (Jones, 1997), and a fair amount of hagiography (see for example, Williams, 1997). The four academic accounts are excellent in their different ways. Inevitably, however, the analyses that they contain were produced very speedily after the election. In addition, they are generally directed towards a non-specialist audience that is assumed to be relatively unsophisticated in terms of statistical and methodological understanding or concern.

The aim of this volume – as of its predecessors – is to publish research which is at the cutting edge of electoral studies, and hence the articles in this volume analyse aspects of the 1997 election in more depth and with greater methodological sophistication than is usually possible in works intended for a more general market. In addition, the passage of time has allowed for more reflection on the part of researchers and has also allowed the use of data not previously available. We include here, for example, articles using data on the campaign activism of Labour Party members and on constituency campaigning, as well as some of the first published findings from the 1997 British Election Study (BES), none of which were previously available.

Almost as soon as academics and others had concluded after the 1992 election that the Conservatives were almost invincible, the government sunk to record lows in the opinion polls. Their ratings did slowly improve as the 1997 election approached but in the first week of the campaign the polls, on average, still put the Conservatives at less than 30 per cent of voting intentions. Nicholas Jones's book on the election campaign (*Campaign 1997*) is subtitled *How The General Election Was Won and Lost*, but Jones is forced to admit that anyone trying to explain the Conservatives' defeat in the 1997 election needs to begin their search for explanations further back in time than the campaign itself. Why did support for the Conservatives slump so dramatically after the 1992 election? And why, contrary to the widespread belief that a relatively successful economy will ensure a government's re-election, did the performance of the economy not rescue them? These questions are tackled in the article by Clarke, Stewart and Whiteley, which examines the levels of support for the parties throughout the inter-election cycle between 1992 and 1997 and, paying particular attention to the role of party leaders and the economy, seeks to explain both the remarkable collapse in Conservative support and its failure to recover sufficiently to be a serious threat to Labour in the election.

The role and impact of the media in election campaigns is frequently and hotly disputed. One of the earliest events of the campaign proper in 1997 was the decision of the *Sun* newspaper – the largest-selling daily in Britain and virulently pro-Conservative in previous elections – to back the Labour Party (or, more accurately, to 'back Blair', the paper still having its doubts about the party *per se*). The *Sun*'s decision was emblematic of a wider desertion of the Conservative Party by usually supportive papers, a process which began long before the election campaign got under way. Deacon, Golding and Billig examine the nature of that desertion. The *Sun*'s defection was (understandably) dismissed by John Major, who said that he didn't think that 'up and down the country, in the Dog and Duck or at number 10 Acacia Avenue, they are going to say "Gosh, the *Sun*'s backing Labour, and therefore, I must change my mind"'. In his own way, Major had hit on the great unanswered question of media studies and political communication: does it actually matter what the media say? The article by Sanders and Norris reports an attempt to answer that question in respect of television news by use of an innovative methodological experiment attempting to measure voters' reactions to news about the parties.

Much of the media coverage during the election campaign – and especially in the first two weeks – focused on one issue: 'sleaze'. The term 'sleazy' was formerly used to refer to 'disorderly houses, illicit liquor or drug dens, low dives, questionable night clubs and other disreputable premises' (Smith, 1995: 3). For much of the 1990s, however, it was used about politicians, especially Conservative politicians. That the Conservative Party came to be widely considered as 'sleazy and disreputable' is not contested (Mortimore, 1995). Farrell, McAllister and Studlar consider whether that perception cost the Conservatives votes.

We noted above that the fact that any account of the 1997 election would have to explain why Labour won 63 per cent of the seats with only 43 per cent of the votes. This draws attention to the electoral system. Until now interest in reform of the British electoral system has been a minority concern (although a passion for some) and the question of reform has been largely hypothetical. With the election of the new government, however, the issue is firmly on the agenda and a commission has been established to investigate alternatives. The article by Dunleavy and his colleagues analyses the operation of the current electoral system in 1997 and goes on to consider – on the basis of a large-scale survey of electors – how Britain would have voted under alternative electoral systems.

The nature and operation of the electoral system is only one element in determining the translation of votes into seats, however. Just as crucial is the relationship between the electoral system and the electoral geography of the country. How a party's support is distributed matters almost as much as how much support it has. When newspapers carry opinion poll results they frequently provide 'projected' figures detailing the number of seats that such a distribution of party support would yield. The problem with such projections is that they assume a uniform swing across the country as a whole. These days uniform swing simply does not happen, however. Changes in party support can, and do, vary dramatically, as a result of regional differences, or due to a variety of local constituency-level factors, such as the performance or attributes of the local candidates, the quality and vitality of the local campaign, or the tactical situation in the constituency. Indeed, it was only these sorts of variation that resulted in projections of seats based on opinion poll results in 1997 appearing fairly accurate (see, for example, Cooper, 1997).

This volume contains six articles which, in whole or in part, examine the reasons for the variations in election outcomes across constituencies. Ron Johnston and his colleagues outline the new electoral geography of Britain, distinguishing regional, inter-constituency and local factors which help to explain the election outcome. Five other articles concentrate on four key aspects of this geography in more detail, looking at the effect of sleaze allegations against individual candidates, tactical voting, the impact of the Referendum Party, and the nature and efficacy of local campaigning. The article by Farrell, McAllister and Studlar investigates whether sleaze may have had localized as well as national implications. It examines the fate of those Conservative candidates who went into the election under allegations of 'sleaze' and assesses whether they fared worse than their colleagues who did not. Tactical voting – where electors vote for a party other than their preferred party in order to achieve a desired outcome – has been much commented on since the 1983 election. The pattern of election results in 1997 suggested that it was more widespread than ever before and that it was decisively anti-Conservative. Evans, Curtice and Norris use 1997 BES survey data to measure the level of tactical voting and go on to offer an explanation for the increased willingness of the electorate to vote tactically.

The Referendum Party was a new actor in the 1997 election drama and one of some potential significance. The party was formally launched in October 1995 to campaign for a referendum on Britain's membership of the

EU. Funded by the millionaire businessman Sir James Goldsmith, it spent around £20 million and put forward candidates in 547 constituencies. It polled 2.7 per cent of the votes in Great Britain and it has been widely assumed that most of these came from voters who had previously voted Conservative. In 19 seats the Referendum Party vote was larger than the margin by which the Conservative candidate lost and it has been suggested (not least by Conservative politicians) that the 'intervention' of the new party cost the Conservatives these seats. These assumptions are considered (and contested) by Anthony Heath and his colleagues in an analysis which is again based on BES survey data.

Two articles focus on campaigning at the local level. Such campaigning has been largely discounted in the past, often being thought to be little more than a meaningless ritual. In recent elections, however, innovative research has suggested that local campaigning can have a significant impact on election outcomes. Here, Denver, Hands and Henig explain how party headquarters made efforts to target their local campaigning in 1997 and compare the parties' performances in their target and non-target seats. Whiteley and Seyd present evidence about the role of Labour party members in local campaigning and suggest that newer recruits were significantly less active in this respect than were long-standing members – a development which has important implications for the future organizational health of the party.

Largely unremarked on in the national media, the 1997 general election coincided with local elections in English shire counties and some unitary authorities. In the words of Rallings and Thrasher, this provides something of an 'analytical feast' for election specialists. They analyse the extent to which voters 'split' their votes – voted for a different party in the local and national elections – and their results put yet another nail into the coffin of the view of the British electorate as inexorably wedded to one party or another.

On 2 May Tony Blair was driven through a sun-drenched London, first to Buckingham Palace and then to Downing Street which was packed with flag-waving crowds. Throughout the country, non-Conservatives were elated and a sense of relief that things had changed was almost palpable. Even Conservative supporters appeared to be relieved that the party was to be released from the torments of the previous five years. Although it remains to be seen how long these reactions to the election persist, the articles in this book focus on how and why the change occurred and offer a variety of insights into what may prove to be a major turning point in British electoral history.

REFERENCES

Butler, David and Dennis Kavanagh (1997) *The British General Election of 1997*. Basingstoke: Macmillan.

Cooper, Andrew (1997) *Wrong Again. The Opinion Polls and the 1997 General Election*. London: Conservative Political Centre.

Geddes, Andrew and Jonathan Tonge (eds) (1997) *Labour's Landslide*. Manchester: Manchester University Press

Heywood, Andrew (1994) 'Britain's dominant-party system', in L. Robins, H. Blackmore and R. Pyper (eds), *Britain's Changing Party System*, pp.10–25. Leicester: Leicester University Press.

Jones, Nicholas (1997) *Campaign 1997. How the General Election Was Won And Lost*. London: Indigo.

King, Anthony (1992) 'Tory "Super-Party" Born out of Last-Minute Switching', *Daily Telegraph*, 13 April.

King, Anthony (1993) 'The Implications of One-Party Government', in A. King *et al.*, *Britain at the Polls 1992*, pp.223–48. Chatham, NJ: Chatham House.

King, Anthony (1997a) *New Labour Triumphs: Britain At The Polls*. Chatham NJ: Chatham House.

King, Anthony (1997b) ' The Night Itself' in A. King (ed) *New Labour Triumphs: Britain At The Polls*. Chatham NJ: Chatham House.

Margetts, Helen and Gareth Smyth (eds) (1993) *Turning Japanese?* London: Lawrence and Wishart.

Mortimore, Roger (1995) 'Politics and Public Perceptions', in F.F. Ridley and Alan Doig (eds) *Sleaze: Politicians, Private Interests and Public Reaction*, pp.29–41. Oxford: Oxford University Press.

Norris, Pippa (1997) 'Anatomy of a Labour Landslide' in P. Norris and N. Gavin (eds) *Britain Votes 1997* pp.1–33. Oxford: Oxford University Press.

Norris, Pippa and N. Gavin (eds) (1997) *Britain Votes 1997*. Oxford: Oxford University Press.

Rallings, Colin and M. Thrasher (1993) *Britain Votes 5*. Aldershot: Dartmouth.

Rallings, Colin and M. Thrasher (1993) *Britain Votes 6*. Aldershot: Ashgate Publishing.

Smith, Trevor (1995) 'Causes, Concerns and Cures', in F.F. Ridley and Alan Doig (eds), *Sleaze: Politicians, Private Interests and Public Reaction*, pp. 3–13. Oxford: Oxford University Press.

Williams, John (1997) *Victory*. London: Bookman.

Political Change and Party Choice: Voting in the 1997 General Election

Harold D. Clarke, Marianne C. Stewart and Paul Whiteley

Labour's victory in the 1997 general election illustrates the point that party fortunes are often unrelated to political forecasts. In the wake of its 1992 defeat, some observers pondered the question of whether Labour had squandered its 'last chance' (Heath *et al.*, 1994). Subsequently, even after Labour's stock in public opinion polls soared, and the Conservatives repeatedly demonstrated their apparent determination to dissipate their remaining political capital, few media pundits or academic commentators dared to predict an outright Labour victory. Caution about Labour's prospects persisted even as its new leader, Tony Blair, prepared the party to take advantage of its best opportunity in years. In the event, Labour scored the largest triumph for a party in any general election since World War Two. Although post-election analysts have quickly catalogued many factors that might be responsible for this remarkable reversal of political fortune (see, for example, Geddes and Tonge, 1997; Norris and Gavin, 1997; King, 1998a), we contend that a proper starting point for understanding Labour's landslide should be voters' evaluations of the parties, their leaders, and their policies. These evaluations help us to understand the choices that voters made on 1 May, and the gales of political change that blew the Conservatives out of office after nearly two decades in power.

Although the key evaluative variables in models of political change and party choice are well known, there is no agreement concerning which of them deserves the title of best predictor. Moreover, how these variables performed in the context of such events as the major electoral upheaval of 1997 remains to be documented. Accordingly, the beginning of this article reintroduces the reader to debates about party identification, leader assessments, and economic judgements. We then turn to aggregate time series analyses of public support for both major parties over the period from January 1992 to April 1997. The results of these analyses show that Labour's new beginnings in the polls took shape only a few months after its fourth consecutive defeat, and that the party was the likely winner in the next election, whenever that contest should be held. Models of the dynamics of party support are then constructed and estimated. We next examine cross-sectional survey data to assess how party identification, best prime minister judgements and economic evaluations affected the probabilities of voting Labour and Conservative. Finally, we consider and offer an explanation for the weakness of the 'feel-good factor' in the set of forces affecting electoral choice in 1997. The conclusion recapitulates the principal arguments and major findings.

Change, Choice and Controversy

Research on voting behaviour and conceptualizations of party identification have been bound together in older social-psychological and newer 'economic-rational' models of party support (Dalton and Wattenberg, 1993). The earliest model was developed at the University of Michigan in the 1950s and employs reference- and small-group theory (Campbell *et al.*, 1960; see also Miller and Shanks, 1996). The central component in this model is party identification, i.e., 'an individual's affective orientation to an important group-object in his environment' (Campbell *et al.*, 1960: 121). According to this conceptualization, a party identification is typically inherited by children from their parents and, once formed, tends to be directionally stable and to strengthen in intensity over time (Converse, 1976). Party identification acts on voting behaviour both directly as a powerful long-term force, and indirectly by affecting perceptions of parties, candidates, and issues. It thus is an 'unmoved mover' in political psychology as declared by its creators and defended by their successors.

For a number of years, the Michigan model dominated thinking about electoral choice in the Anglo-American and other democracies. In Britain prior to the 1970s, it was argued that simple but powerful links existed among class position, party identification, and voting behaviour (Butler and Stokes, 1976; see also Heath *et al.*, 1985, 1991). Not surprisingly, a model that emphasizes long-term forces generated by a social class cleavage gives short shrift to short-term ones. Thus, the effects, if any, of leader images on voting could be dismissed as 'embellishment and detail' (Pulzer, 1967: 98). Moreover, leader images are very much subordinate to evaluations of parties' issue competence, and they are subsumed under more general party images that were said to determine individual voting and election outcomes (see, for example, Butler and Stokes, 1976: ch.16; Sarlvik and Crewe, 1983: 132–3; Crewe, 1985: 183; Rose and McAllister, 1990: 132–42).

Although the social-psychological construction of partisanship and voting has numerous adherents, other models have attracted sizeable followings as well. One of these alternatives accentuates 'economic' or 'rational' aspects of party-support decisions (Downs, 1957; Key, 1968; Fiorina, 1981). According to Key, 'many persons bring parties to their service by a mental shortcut' (1967: 442). Although people could form an identification which leads them to adopt the preference of their party, they also can develop a preference which influences an identification (Key, 1967: 443). In keeping with the latter possibility, '[l]ike or dislike of a political personality or a party policy and many other factors bring shifts in party identification' (Key, 1967: 298–9). Newer versions of the economic-rational model are recognizable descendants of the theories of Downs and Key. In these models, partisanship is conceptualized as a summary 'running tally' of current and (discounted) previous party performance evaluations (Fiorina, 1981: ch.5). Thus, partisanship is updated over time as utility-maximizing or -satisficing voters acquire new information about the performance of political parties and their leaders (see, for example, Franklin, 1992; MacKuen, Erikson and Stimson, 1989).

Models which acknowledge the possibility of partisan change are compatible with the growing evidence of it during the past three decades. In Britain, survey data show that the class-vote nexus, the size of the cohort of Labour identifiers, and the strength of major-party identification declined in the 1970s (Crewe, Sarlvik and Alt, 1977). These patterns continued in the 1980s (Clarke and Stewart, 1984). However, until recently, the absence of aggregate-level time series data has prevented resolution of disagreements over the extent of partisan (in)stability, and the utility of specifying party identification variables in vote models (see, for example, Budge, Crewe and Farlie, 1976; Crewe, Sarlvik and Alt, 1977; Heath et al., 1985, 1991; Heath and McDonald, 1988; Heath and Pierce, 1992; Sarlvik and Crewe, 1983). This situation has changed, as one study now employs the standard British Election Study (BES) party identification question sequence in monthly surveys conducted by the Gallup organization.[1] Using the BES battery avoids the question-wording controversy that has bedevilled research on 'macropartisanship' in the United States (see, for example, MacKuen et al., 1992; Abramson and Ostrom, 1991; Bishop et al., 1994). The new time series data strongly indicate that aggregate-level partisanship was highly unstable during the months bracketed by the 1992 and 1997 general elections (Clarke, Stewart and Whiteley, 1997a, 1997b).

In Britain and elsewhere, partisan instability has been accompanied by the increasing importance of issues, notably economic ones, and party leader images in the set of forces affecting voting decisions. With respect to economic influences, objective indicators such as inflation and unemploy-ment rates traditionally occupied central roles in models of the dynamics of party support. However, during the past decade, subjective economic evaluations have been employed to improve understanding of how the economy affects voters' decisions. In one such model, personal retrospections (PR) retain the 'pocketbook' emphasis of 'reward-punishment' explanations of electoral choice. However, both PR and its national retrospective (NR) mate (see, for example, Key, 1968; Fiorina, 1981; Norpoth, 1992) have been challenged by the personal prospective (PP) and national prospective (NP) models. The PP or 'Essex' model proposes that fluctuations in interest rates propel movements in personal expectations (the feel-good factor), which, in turn, activate the dynamics of governing party support (see, for example, Sanders, 1991, 1993). Although the NP or 'Bankers' model has not claimed many adherents in Britain, in the United States its proponents have argued that expectations about the national economy drive presidential approval ratings (MacKuen, Erikson and Stimson, 1992, 1996).

In the case of leader variables, they too display sizeable effects on party choice during elections (Miller *et al.*, 1990: ch.7; Stewart and Clarke, 1992; Crewe and King, 1994), and between them (Norpoth, 1992; Clarke and Stewart, 1995; Nadeau, Niemi and Amato, 1996; Clarke, Stewart and Whiteley, 1997a, 1997b). Leaders matter for at least three reasons. First, they have concrete presence, i.e., they can be seen and heard, which is instrumental to depicting other, more abstract, objects to the public. Such objects include party issue positions, platforms, and performance in economic and other policy areas. Second, a leader's convictions, experience, and personality can define a position, a platform, and performance, as well as the character of the party organization, in the public mind. Third, an American-style 'presidentialization' of the office of the prime minister (see Mughan, 1997) has encouraged, and been encouraged by, growing media coverage of the PM and, to a lesser extent, opposition party leaders. Their increasing importance is obvious in their dominance of the parties' election campaigns (see, for example, Semetko, Scammell and Goddard, 1997: 599) and their influence on voting behaviour. However, the strength of prime minister or opposition leader effects on party support varies from one incumbent to another (Clarke, Ho and Stewart, 1997). In sum, people form structured perceptions of party leaders (Stewart and Clarke, 1992), and they use these perceptions to decide who is best suited to govern (Miller, Wattenberg and Malanchuk, 1986).

The Dynamics of Party Support

Soon after the April 1992 election, the percentages of persons stating that they would vote Conservative or Labour, regarded the Conservative or Labour leader as making the best prime minister, and identified with one party or the other, changed markedly.[2] The most dramatic movements occurred at the time of the currency crisis in September 1992 when the popularity of the Conservatives and Prime Minister Major dropped precipitously (Figure 1). Viewed more generally, the Tories' 1992 general election vote (42 per cent) provides a benchmark for gauging subsequent movements in their support. The party's lowest vote intention percentage (15 per cent) was recorded in January 1995 and, although a modest upward trend occurred in the run-up to the general election, in April 1997 only 29 per cent reported that they intended to cast a Conservative vote. The downward dynamics of Tory vote intentions were accompanied by a very substantial erosion in the percentage of persons who thought that John Major would make the best prime minister. In fact, Gallup surveys show that his strong position (51 per cent) just two months after the 1992 election was quartered (12 per cent) by January 1995. The Conservative's share of party identifiers suffered as well, falling from 36 per cent in April 1992 to only 19 per cent in July 1994. In mid-April 1997, 32 per cent stated that they were Tory identifiers.

FIGURE 1
THE DYNAMICS OF CONSERVATIVE SUPPORT, JAN. 1992–APR. 1997

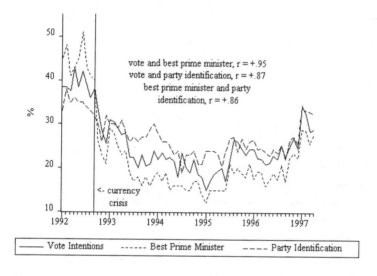

Labour also experienced considerable change in its support (Figure 2). In April 1992, 35 per cent of the British electorate voted Labour, whereas four years later (April 1996) fully 55 per cent stated that they would vote Labour in a forthcoming general election. In the event, over 44 per cent cast a Labour ballot in 1997. The party also enjoyed handsome increases in the number of people who believed that its leader would make the best prime minister. In the month after the 1992 election, only 18 per cent regarded Neil Kinnock as best suited to be prime minister. As noted, party leader perceptions shifted markedly at the time of the currency crisis, and afterwards, the Labour leaders (Smith, Blair) consistently led their Conservative and Liberal Democrat rivals by substantial margins. Although Labour's share of party identifiers increased less than its share of vote intentions or best prime minister judgements, it moved upward as well. Thus, the percentage of Labour partisans climbed from 34 per cent in April 1992 to 47 per cent in December 1994. The latter figure represented a high-water mark, and Labour partisanship drifted downward to 40 per cent in April 1997.

FIGURE 2
THE DYNAMICS OF LABOUR SUPPORT, JAN. 1992–APR. 1997

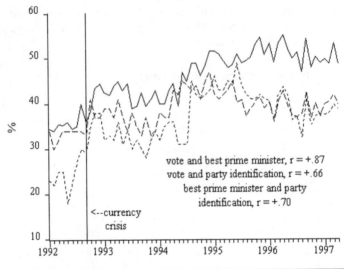

The dynamics of vote intentions, best prime minister judgements, and party identification were closely interrelated for both parties. For the Conservatives, each of the three correlations was +0.86 or higher, with the correlation (r) between vote intentions and best prime minister assessments being fully +0.95. The comparable Labour correlations were somewhat weaker, but nonetheless impressive. Thus, although Labour's vote percentage stood above its partisan share throughout the 1992–7 period, these two series were strongly interrelated (r = +0.66). As in the Conservative case, perceptions of the Labour leader as best prime minister also moved in tandem with vote intentions and party identifier share (r = +0.70). For both parties, the very similar movements among the three series suggest that important causal relationships exist among them. These relationships are analysed in the next section.

The Determinants of Party Support

In previous studies (Clarke, Stewart and Whiteley, 1997a, 1997b), we have discussed the utility of error correction models for analysing the long- and short-term dynamics of party support. In these models, the long-term component is established via the specification of an error correction mechanism (ECM) involving the hypothesized dependent variable and one or more independent variables.[3] We will not repeat the technical aspects of these discussions here, but the reader should note that empirical warrant for an ECM specification is provided by demonstrating that variables of interest are nonstationary and cointegrate (see, for example, Hendry, 1995: ch.4). In this respect, unit-root tests (not shown) using the January 1992–April 1997 Gallup monthly time series data demonstrate that Labour vote intentions, perceptions that the Labour leader would make the best prime minister, and Labour party identification all are nonstationary. The same is true of Conservative vote intentions, perceptions that John Major would be the best prime minister, and Conservative party identification. In both the Labour and Conservative cases, regressing vote intentions on party leader perceptions and party identification indicates that the variables cointegrate. Leader perceptions and party identification have strong, statistically significant, effects on Labour and Conservative vote intentions and, as is required for cointegration, regression residuals constitute stationary series (Table 1).

TABLE 1
COINTEGRATING REGRESSIONS

Panel A: Labour Vote Intentions, Labour Leader as Best Prime Minister and Labour Party Identification, 1992–7

Regressor Variables	β	s.e.
Labour leader	0.635	0.083
Labour party identification	0.585	0.078
	$R^2 = 0.709$	

Unit root test for residuals = -3.59, rejects null hypothesis of nonstationarity at .05 level (critical value = -3.44).

Panel B: Conservative Vote Intentions, Conservative Leader as Best Prime Minister and Conservative Party Identification, 1992–7

Regressor Variables	β	s.e.
Conservative leader	0.474	0.038
Conservative party identification	0.543	0.034
	$R^2 = 0.911$	

Unit root test for residuals = -6.65, rejects null hypothesis of nonstationarity at .05 level (critical value = -3.44).

The error-correction mechanisms implied by these analyses are:

Labour: LABV -.635*LLEAD - .585*LPID = ECML   (1)
Conservative: CONV - .474*CLEAD - .543*CPID = ECMC   (2)

where: LABV = Labour vote intentions; LLEAD = perceptions that the Labour leader would make the best prime minister; LPID = Labour party identification, ECML = Labour error correction mechanism; CONV = Conservative vote intentions; CLEAD = perceptions that John Major would make the best prime minister; CPID = Conservative party identification; ECMC = Conservative error correction mechanism. Substantively, these equations indicate that vote intentions travel together in the long run with party leader images and a party's share of identifiers in the electorate. The absence of constants in the ECM equations means that, *ceteris paribus*, if no one in the electorate believes that a party's leader is best suited to be prime minister and no one identifies with the party, that party's vote intention share would fall to zero in the long run. Short-run dynamics in vote intentions are affected by the ECM as well. If, for whatever reason, a (positive or negative) political or economic shock to vote intentions occurs, the error correction mechanism causes that shock to decay in subsequent time-periods. The rate of decay is estimated as part of the more general analysis of the dynamics of the party's vote intention share.

Our specification of those dynamics is guided by the theoretical discussion in the preceding section. The Labour voting intention model is:

$$\Delta LABV_t = \beta_0 + \beta_1 \Delta LLEAD_{t-i} + \beta_2 \Delta LPID_{t-i} + \beta_3 \Delta ECEVAL_{t-i} +$$
$$\beta 4 \, \Delta INTR_{t-i} + \Sigma \beta_{5-j} \Delta IMPIS_{t-i} + \Sigma \beta_{6-k} EVENTS_{t-i} + \alpha ECML_{t-1} + \varepsilon_t \quad (3)$$

where: LABV, LLEAD and LPID are as above; ECEVAL = subjective economic evaluations (either personal prospective, personal retrospective, national retrospective, or national prospective); INTR = interest rates; IMPIS = perceptions of most important issues facing the country; EVENTS = miscellaneous political and economic events; ECML = error correction mechanism (measured as the residuals of the Labour vote intention cointegrating regression (1)) ε = Gaussian error term ($\sim N(0, \sigma^2)$); β = regression coefficient; α = adjustment coefficient for error correction mechanism. Consonant with the existence of a (stable) negative feedback process implied by the error correction mechanism, the coefficient (α) accompanying the ECM is expected to be negatively signed and less than 1.0 in value. *Mutatis mutandis*, the Conservative vote intention model is very similar. Parameter estimates are obtained via OLS regression, with separate Labour and Conservative models being estimated for each of the four different types of subjective economic evaluations.

Tables 2 and 3 summarize the effects of the party leader, party identification and economic evaluation variables in these vote intention models.[4]
Perceptions that a party's leader would make the best prime minister, and party

TABLE 2
ERROR CORRECTION MODELS OF LABOUR VOTE INTENTIONS 1992 (APR.)–1997 (APR.)

	Models			
	PP	PR	NR	NP
Predictor Variable	β	β	β	β
Constant	0.47c	0.47c	0.47c	0.45c
Best prime minister (t)	0.27a	0.29a	0.28a	0.29a
Labour party identification (t-2)	0.19c	0.16c	0.16c	0.16c
Error correction mechanism (t-1)	-0.15c	-0.14c	-0.14c	-0.14c
Economic Evaluations:				
Personal expectations (t)	-0.08c	X	X	X
Personal retrospections (t)	X	-0.04	X	X
National retrospections (t)	X	X	-0.02	X
National expectations (t)	X	X	X	-0.02
Interest rates (t)	1.40d	1.43d	1.35d	1.31d
Model Diagnostics				
Adjusted R^2	0.67	0.65	0.65	0.65
Standard error of estimate	1.74	1.79	1.80	1.79
Durbin-Watson	2.14	2.29	2.26	2.25
Serial correlation (12 lags)	16.10	17.10	18.28	18.06
Functional form	2.02	0.81	0.91	0.90
Normality	4.65	3.24	3.39	3.72
General heteroskedasticity	25.57	20.03	23.01	22.67
ARCH (1)	0.07	0.22	0.29	0.19

Note: a - $p \le .001$; b - $p \le .01$; c - $p \le .05$; d - $p \le .10$; one-tailed test. Dependent variable is first-
differenced.

identification, both significantly influence Labour and Conservative vote
intentions. These effects are such that a 10 per cent change in the group of
persons judging that the Labour leader would make the best prime minister
causes a 2.7 to 2.9 per cent change in the Labour vote intention share (Table 2).
Leader influences in the Conservative models are virtually identical (Table 3).
Party identification effects are very similar for Labour and the Conservatives as
well – a 10 per cent change in the number of Labour identifiers alters that
party's vote share by 1.6 to 1.9 per cent, and the comparable figure for the Tory
vote share is 1.8 to 1.9 per cent. In fact, the percentages of persons selecting the
Labour leader as best prime minister and declaring themselves to be Labour
identifiers increased by 31 per cent and 17 per cent, respectively, between the
1992 and 1997 general elections, while the comparable Tory percentages fell
by 39 per cent and 19 per cent. These substantial movements indicate that party
leader images and party identifications had decidedly non-trivial effects on
electoral support for the two parties.

The ECM specification signifies that there were important *long-run*

TABLE 3
ERROR CORRECTION MODELS OF CONSERVATIVE VOTE INTENTIONS 1992 (APR.)–1997 (APR.)

	Models			
	PP	PR	NR	NP
Predictor Variables	β	β	β	β
Constant	-0.29c	-0.34c	-0.35c	-0.30c
Best prime minister (t)	0.28a	0.29a	0.30a	0.29a
Cons. party identification (t)	0.18c	0.19b	0.19c	0.18c
Error correction mechanism (t-1)	-0.71a	-0.72a	-0.73a	-0.76a
Economic Evaluations:				
Personal expectations (t-1)	-0.08b	X	X	X
Personal retrospections (t-1)	X	0.13a	X	X
National retrospections (t-1)	X	X	0.05c	X
National expectations (t-1)	X	X	X	0.04c
Interest rates (t)	-1.79a	-1.83a	-2.03a	-1.84a
Model Diagnostics				
Adjusted R^2	0.85	0.86	0.85	0.85
Standard error of estimate	1.66	1.13	1.18	1.17
Durbin-Watson	2.36	2.32	2.26	2.21
Serial correlation (12 lags)	14.79	18.91	16.48	13.90
Functional form	0.02	1.40	0.66	0.23
Normality	4.40	3.75	5.54	2.21
General heteroskedasticity	20.03	16.20	16.43	22.62
ARCH (1)	2.01	0.27	0.45	0.00

Note: a - $p \leq .001$; b - $p \leq .01$; c - $p \leq .05$; d - $p \leq .10$; one-tailed test. Dependent variable is first-differenced.

components to these effects. In both the Labour and Conservative cases, the coefficients for the ECM variables behave as anticipated, i.e., they are statistically significant and negatively signed. However, there are large differences in their magnitudes. Labour's ECM coefficients vary from -0.14 to -0.15 (Table 2), thereby indicating that, although leader perceptions and party identification formed a long-run cointegrating system with Labour voting intentions, that system had considerable play. A shock to Labour vote intentions, from whatever source, was adjusted by the error correction mechanism at a rate of only about 15 per cent per month. In sharp contrast, the Conservative system was very tightly wrapped, with ECM coefficients ranging from -0.71 to -0.76 (Table 3). A shock to Tory vote intentions was quickly re-equilibrated by the party leader-party identification ECM, with nearly three-quarters of the shock's initial impact evaporating in the month after it occurred. These differences suggest that, although Labour enjoyed very favourable positions in terms of party leader images and party identification in the run-up to the 1997 election, these advantages could have been negated in the short-run by one or more strong negative shocks. The decision of Labour strategists to run a closely controlled long campaign (see, for example, Fielding, 1997; Kavanagh, 1997; Seyd, 1998) was thus well advised. The Tories' situation was different. Without major Labour gaffes, any lasting upturn in their electoral prospects was heavily predicated on a very substantial improvement in their leader's image and the return of large numbers of erstwhile partisans. In the event, the party was unable to engineer either of these conditions – Mr. Major remained very unpopular and the ranks of Tory identifiers remained depleted.

Net of the several effects discussed above, economic variables affected both parties' vote intention shares. As anticipated, interest rates had a negative influence on Conservative support, and a positive one on Labour support. Subjective judgements about national and economic conditions were influential as well. In the Labour case, personal economic expectations – the much discussed feel-good factor – is the only type of economic evaluation to achieve statistical significance. As anticipated, the impact is negative (-0.08); as voters' perceptions of their economic prospects became more sanguine, the likelihood that they would cast a Labour ballot declined (Table 2). The personal economic expectations coefficient is identical in magnitude, but oppositely signed, in the Conservative model (Table 3). However, other economic evaluations are also significant in the Conservative analyses, and, in every case, they carry the appropriate (positive) sign.

Contrary to interpretations offered by some observers in the immediate aftermath of the Conservatives' election debacle, these results indicate that economic variables influenced support for both major parties in predictable ways over the 1992–7 period. Additional time series analyses of the determinants of perceptions of prime ministerial performance, which party leader would make the best prime minister, and party identification (Clarke, Stewart and Whiteley, 1997a, 1997b) lend force to this conclusion. These analyses (not shown) reveal that interest rates, personal economic expectations and other types of economic evaluations exerted *indirect* influences via their effects on party leader perceptions and party identification. As demonstrated above, the latter variables affected the short- and long-run evolution of Labour and Conservative vote intentions. The impact of the September 1992 currency crisis in these party leader and party identification analyses also merits note. Although 'Black Wednesday' did not have a *direct* effect on the parties' vote intention shares, it did exercise *indirect* effects via large, negative influences on impressions of Prime Minister Major's competence and the Conservative share of party identifiers (Clarke, Stewart and Whiteley, 1997a). The crisis also (positively) influenced the dynamics of public evaluations of the Labour leader and Labour's portion of party identifiers (Clarke, Stewart and Whiteley, 1997b).

In sum, the error correction models of Conservative and Labour vote intentions, in conjunction with analyses of party leader perceptions and party identification, tell a simple, straightforward story of the forces that set the stage for Labour's 1997 triumph. Principal players in the drama were perceptions of the party leaders and party identification. Substantial differences in the images of the Conservative prime minister and his Labour rivals combined with a sizeable shift in the balance of party identifiers between the two parties to create the basis for a massive reversal of electoral fortune. As just observed, these leader and party forces assumed the configurations they did *in part* because of the impact of the ERM fiasco. But, as Denver (1998) has emphasized (see also Norton, 1998; Sanders, 1998), other factors were at work as well. The image of the prime minister and his party were repeatedly tarnished by internecine strife about the desirability of Britain's adoption of the single European currency and other aspects of Britain's relationship with the European Union. These intra-party conflicts, together with an ongoing series of scandals involving Tory ministers and back-bench MPs, created the impression that the Conservatives were disunited, incompetent and sleazy. Labour, in sharp contrast, had its 'act' very much together. It had set aside the ideological battles of the 1980s and united behind Tony Blair, whose 'New Labour' project was designed to give the party an image of competence, moderation and trustworthiness. Given these potent forces, it was little wonder that an improving economy and the relatively favourable economic evaluations that it stimulated could not save the embattled Tories.

Political Choice

The preceding analyses indicate that party leader images, party identification and evaluations of economic conditions all behaved as hypothesized in our time series models of the dynamics of Conservative and Labour vote intentions over the period from January 1992 to April 1997. But some analysts (for example Bartle, Crewe and King, 1997) have argued that leader images had only minor effects on the vote itself and, as noted, others have concluded that the feel-good factor was a casualty of the sea-change in public perceptions of the parties' competence to manage the economy (see, for example, Gavin and Sanders, 1997: 631; King, 1998b: 187). Although the 1997 British Election Study survey data are not available at the time of writing, our April 1997 Gallup survey enables us to study voting intentions expressed immediately prior to the election.

The vote model is a cross-sectional analogue to the time series one (3) presented above. Vote intentions are a function of perceptions of which party leader will make the best prime minister,[5] party identification[6] and subjective economic evaluations. Paralleling the time series analyses, the effects of four different kinds of evaluations are considered.[7] An additional analysis uses an overall index to summarize the effects of all four types of economic evaluations.[8] Also, because an error correction mechanism is not applicable in the context of analysing cross-sectional data, we control for long-term forces on the vote by including three demographic variables – age, gender and social class.[9] Since voters could choose among several parties, multinomial logit is utilized for estimation purposes (Long, 1997: ch. 6). Treating Conservative voting as the reference category, the voting categories are: Labour, Liberal Democrat, and 'other parties.' We conduct a separate binary logit (Long, 1997: ch. 3) to shed additional light on Conservative support, dichotomizing voting behaviour as Conservative = 1 and other parties = 0.

The results for the model incorporating the overall economic evaluations index are displayed in Table 4. Perceptions of which party leader is best suited to be prime minister have a variety of statistically significant effects. As anticipated, persons believing that John Major had the 'right stuff' were more likely to vote Conservative, and less likely to vote for one of the opposition parties. Similarly, those favourably impressed by Tony Blair's or Paddy Ashdown's qualifications were more likely to cast a Labour or Liberal Democrat ballot, respectively, and less apt to vote for other parties. The influence of party identification is consistent as well and, once more, all significant coefficients are signed appropriately – for example, Labour

TABLE 4

LOGIT AND MULTINOMIAL LOGIT MODELS OF VOTING INTENTIONS IN THE 1997 GENERAL ELECTION

Voting Intentions

Predictor Variables	Conservative	Labour	Lib Dem	Others
Constant	-1.59c	-0.120	0.29	1.20
Party Identification:				
Conservative	2.17a	-2.39a	-1.90a	-2.13a
Labour	-2.86a	3.49a	1.38d	1.02
Liberal Democrat	-2.34b	2.04b	3.19a	0.91
Other	-1.37c	0.94	0.07	2.36b
Best Prime Minister:				
Major	1.50a	-1.79a	-1.66a	-1.11c
Blair	-1.27b	1.91a	0.85d	-0.45
Ashdown	-1.37b	1.02c	1.93a	0.81
Economic Evaluations Index	0.90b	-0.82b	-0.52d	-1.44a
Age	-0.00	0.02c	-0.01	-0.01
Gender	0.49d	-0.67c	-0.16	-0.65d
Social Class	-0.02	-0.10	0.25	-0.06
Estimated R^2	0.72		0.58	

Note: a - $p \leq .001$; b - $p \leq .01$; c - $p \leq 05$; d - $p \leq .10$. The analysis of Conservative voting intentions is a binary logit (Conservative v. other parties). The analysis of Labour, Liberal Democrat and other parties voting intentions is a multinomial logit with Conservative voting as the reference category.

identification enhanced the probability of a Labour vote, and Conservative and Liberal Democrat identifications diminished it. The summary economic evaluation index also behaves as anticipated; persons with high scores on the index were more likely to vote Conservative, and those with low scores were more likely to vote for an opposition party. Net of these several leader, partisan and economic evaluation effects, social class did not exert a significant impact; age did so only in the Labour case, and women were more likely to vote Conservative and less likely to choose Labour or one of the other parties.

Replication of the analyses using each of the four economic evaluation variables in turn shows that personal retrospections, i.e., judgements about the financial situation of oneself and one's family over the past year, have the most consistent effects (Table 5). Such judgements have the expected positive impact on the likelihood of voting Conservative, and a negative impact on the likelihood of voting for Labour or other opposition parties. Other types of evaluations do not behave as consistently but, when significant, their effects are sensible. Thus, national retrospective and national prospective judgements are negatively associated with Labour and 'other party' voting, respectively. Personal economic expectations have the anticipated positive relationship with Conservative voting and, although effects on opposition party voting are negative, they are significant only for the miscellaneous 'other parties' category. Overall, then, there is evidence that economic judgements *were* operative in 1997, and that assessments of personal rather than national conditions had the strongest influence. However, consonant with claims about the weakened impact of the feel-good factor, personal retrospections, not personal prospections, were what counted most.

TABLE 5
EFFECTS OF SUBJECTIVE ECONOMIC EVALUATIONS IN LOGIT AND MULTINOMIAL LOGIT
MODELS OF VOTING INTENTIONS IN THE 1997 GENERAL ELECTION

		Voting Intentions		
			Lib	Other
Economic Evaluations	Conservative	Labour	Dem	Parties
Personal Prospective	0.31c	-0.14	-0.10	0.75a
Personal Retrospective	0.59a	-0.59a	-0.55b	-0.66a
National Prospective	0.17	0.10	-0.07	-0.54c
National Retrospective	0.17	-0.32c	0.03	-0.18
Economic Evaluation Index	0.90	-0.82b	-0.52d	-1.44a

Note: a - $p \leq .001$; b - $p \leq .01$; c - $p \leq .05$; d - $p \leq .10$; one-tailed test.

It bears emphasis that the logit results gainsay claims that leader images and economic evaluations did not matter in 1997. Perhaps those who argue that leaders and the economy did not matter *much* are on better ground – the effects in question may be statistically significant, but substantively trivial. In this regard, since the logit function form is non-linear, the coefficients in Tables 4 and 5 cannot be easily interpreted. Although there are various methods that one might employ to facilitate interpretation (see, for example, Long, 1997: 61–78; 164–77), the most straightforward approach is to construct scenarios in which the values of variables of interest are manipulated while the values of other variables are held constant. We first focus on how changes in party identification and party leader preferences affected the probability of voting Labour. Other variables in the model are fixed at their mean values.

These scenarios demonstrate that, regardless of voters' party identifications, changes in their perceptions of which leader would make the best prime minister had a large impact on the probability of casting a Labour ballot. Among Conservative identifiers, persons favouring John Major as prime minister had only 0.02 probability of voting Labour (Figure 3). This figure climbed to 0.41 among those favouring Tony Blair. Among Liberal

FIGURE 3
PROBABILITY OF VOTING LABOUR BY PARTY IDENTIFICATION AND BEST PRIME MINISTER

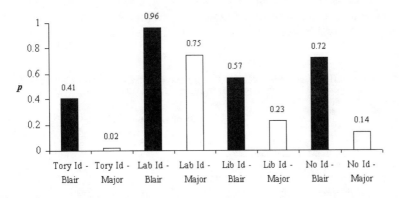

identifiers and voters without a party identification, the comparable increases were from 0.23 to 0.57, and from 0.14 to 0.72, respectively. Even among those who were Labour partisans, best prime minister perceptions were consequential. The probability of a Labour vote among such persons climbed from 0.75 to 0.96 if they preferred Blair rather than Major. Party identification itself was very important as well. For example, among voters preferring Tony Blair as prime minister, the probability of a Labour vote moved from 0.41 among Tory identifiers to 0.57 among Liberal identifiers, to 0.72 among non-identifiers, and to 0.96 among Labour identifiers. The Labour vote scenarios in Figure 3 thus bolster the argument that Labour's advantages in terms of leader images and partisanship did much to produce its 1997 victory.

Next, we consider scenarios that assess the impact of economic evaluations. For this purpose, we utilize the overall economic evaluations index. We compute voting probabilities allowing scores on the index to vary from two standard deviations below the index mean to two standard deviations above it. Since most research on the impact of economic evaluations has concentrated on support for governing parties, we focus on probabilities of voting Conservative. Probabilities of casting a Tory ballot are computed for groups of voters who differed in terms of party identification and their view of which leader would make the best prime minister. Other variables are set at their mean values.

As Table 6 shows, the results are decidedly mixed. For Conservative identifiers (Panel A), changes in economic evaluations had large effects on the probability of a Tory vote, regardless of which leader was preferred as prime minister. For example, among Conservative partisans who preferred Blair or were undecided about who was the most capable party leader, the probabilities of a Tory vote climbed from 0.44 to 0.86, and from 0.18 to 0.64, respectively, as economic evaluations moved from very negative (minus two standard deviations) to very positive (plus two standard deviations). Even among Conservative identifiers believing Major to be the best prime minister, economic judgements made a difference, as the probability of a Conservative ballot increased from 0.78 among voters making very negative assessments to

TABLE 6
PROBABILITY OF VOTING CONSERVATIVE BY ECONOMIC EVALUATIONS, BEST PRIME
MINISTER AND PARTY IDENTIFICATION

	Economic Evaluation Index			
	+2 S.D.	+1 S.D.	-1 S.D.	-2 S.D.
A. Conservative Identifiers				
Best Prime Minister:				
Major	0.97	0.94	0.86	0.78
Undecided	0.86	0.79	0.57	0.44
Blair	0.64	0.51	0.27	0.18
B. Labour Identifiers				
Best Prime Minister:				
Major	0.16	0.10	0.04	0.02
Undecided	0.04	0.02	0.01	0.01
Blair	0.01	0.01	0.00	0.00
C. Liberal Democrat Identifiers				
Best Prime Minister:				
Major	0.24	0.19	0.07	0.04
Undecided	0.07	0.04	0.01	0.01
Ashdown	0.02	0.01	0.00	0.00
D. Non-identifiers				
Best Prime Minister:				
Major	0.77	0.66	0.40	0.29
Undecided	0.42	0.30	0.13	0.08
Blair	0.17	0.11	0.04	.02

fully 0.97 among those making very positive ones. Differing economic evaluations also had large effects on the likelihood of a Conservative vote among non-identifiers, provided such persons preferred Major or were undecided about who was best suited to be prime minister. In sharp contrast, economic evaluations had little influence on the probability of a Conservative vote among Liberal Democrat identifiers (Panel C), unless they liked Major as prime minister and, even in this case, the maximum probability was only 0.24. For Labour identifiers (Panel B), the patterns are similar, with the probability of casting a Tory ballot reaching a maximum of only 0.16 among those who both preferred Major as prime minister and made very positive economic evaluations.

Economic evaluations thus had important direct effects on some, but not all, voters in 1997. Among the groups who were either Labour (40 per cent) or Liberal Democrat (11 per cent) identifiers, economic judgements mattered little. Time series analyses (see above) indicate that such judgements enhanced the size of the Labour identifier group. But, these effects occurred well before the official campaign began. However, despite substantial erosion, the Conservative partisan cohort remained sizeable (32 per cent) as polling day approached. And it was among this group that economic evaluations had large impacts on the probability of a Tory vote. As discussed above, the most influential of those assessments were personal retrospective ones. Personal prospections – the feel-good factor – were less important. Despite an improving economy and strenuous Tory efforts on the hustings to convince voters that Britain was booming, the feel-good factor apparently lost much of its power to deliver votes.

Feeling Bad about the Feel-Good Factor

A number of commentators (for example, Denver, 1998; Gavin and Sanders, 1997; King, 1998b; Sanders, 1998; Wickham-Jones, 1997) have attempted to account for what went wrong with the feel good factor in 1997. The consensus is that confidence in the Conservatives' ability to manage the economy was irreparably damaged when Britain withdrew from the ERM in September 1992. This explanation is plausible, and responses to a Gallup question about whether the Conservatives led by Major or Labour led by Kinnock/Smith/Blair could best handle economic difficulties show a sharp, permanent shift in favour of Labour at that time (Gavin and Sanders, 1997: 633). Lacking confidence in the Tories after their mishandling of the currency crisis, voters refused to credit them for the pre-election economic upswing. If the economy had improved, it was not because of the Conservatives' managerial acumen, the lack of which they had demonstrated in a most glaring fashion. A key link in the causal chain of the political business cycle, which had served the Conservatives well in previous elections, had been snapped.

Yet, there are reasons to doubt that this is the whole story. If one defines the 'feel-good correlation' as the percentage difference in Conservative vote intentions among persons with positive as opposed to negative personal economic expectations, its mean value for the January–September 1992 monthly surveys is 33 per cent. The mean post-currency-crisis value (i.e., for the period from October 1992 to April 1997) is lower but still substantial – 22 per cent. Thus, the feel-good correlation may have been eroded, but it was not obliterated, by Black Wednesday. However, the correlation was much diminished (only 9 per cent) in the April 1997 Gallup survey. What happened? Analogous correlations for other types of economic evaluations provide a clue. In the April survey, the correlations for personal and national *retrospective* economic judgements were 36 per cent and 44 per cent, respectively, whereas the correlation for national *prospective* economic judgements was only 8 per cent. The two retrospective correlations were strong; the two prospective ones – not just the feel-good correlation – were weak.

The 'Responsibility for the Future' Conjecture

The above pattern suggests that there is something about *prospective* judgements that results in weaker correlations with support for the governing party. We conjecture that the 'something' involves recognition by a substantial number of voters that the opposition Labour Party was likely to win the forthcoming general election. This, in turn, creates a situation where differing assumptions about which party is responsible for future economic well-being weaken the correlation between prospective economic evaluations and governing party support. Voters believing that the current government, i.e., the Conservatives, are responsible for the future will support the Tories if they believe that their economic future is rosy. This will be true regardless of voters' beliefs about which party will win the election. However, if voters believe that Labour will win, their future economic prospects are good, and a *future* government will determine these prospects, then they will support Labour. But, since it is plausible that some of the economic optimists who believe Labour will win attribute responsibility for their economic futures to actions of the *present* government, they will support the Conservatives.

This 'responsibility for the future' conjecture thereby suggests that the feel-good correlation should vary in strength depending upon which party voters believe will win the general election. It should be weaker among that group who believe an opposition party will form the next government. Unfortunately, we cannot test this hypothesis at the individual level with our April 1997 Gallup survey since a question soliciting opinions regarding which party would win the election was not included. However, this question was asked in a survey conducted in the month (March) before the 1992 general election. At that time, 39 per cent stated that they thought the Conservatives would win, and 35 per cent thought Labour would do so. For the 'Tories will win' group, the feel-good correlation is 27 per cent. As hypothesized, however, it is much weaker – only 3 per cent – for the 'Labour will win' group.

Additional evidence regarding the conjecture can be brought to bear by using time series data on the likely winner question. Consistent with expectations, the correlation between the percentage who believe the opposition Labour Party will win and the strength of the feel-good correlation for the period from January 1992 to April 1997 is fully -0.67. Also, as Figure 4 reveals, the feel good correlation series does not collapse after September 1992, but rather trends downward, albeit erratically, as the percentage of persons believing Labour will win the next election moves upward. The evident nonstationarity in the two series is confirmed by unit-root tests,[10] and a test for cointegration indicates that the series share a long-run relationship.[11]

Given these results, we model the relationship between the strength of the feel-good correlation and perceptions that Labour will win in error correction form. We also include a dummy variable for the currency crisis to assess its impact on the strength of the relationship between personal economic expectations and governing party support. A second dummy variable for the 1992 election also is included to control for the surge in the strength of the feel-good correlation that occurred immediately after the Tories' 1992 victory (see Figure 4). Model estimates (Table 7) reveal that the percentage believing

FIGURE 4
PERCENTAGES BELIEVING LABOUR WILL WIN NEXT ELECTION AND 'FEEL-GOOD'
CORRELATION, JAN. 1992-APRIL 1997

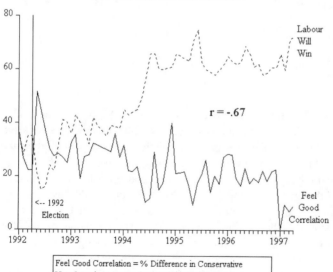

that Labour would win a forthcoming election has significant short- and long-run effects on the strength of the feel-good correlation. As indicated by the coefficient (-0.70) for the ECM, the long-run relationship is strong – *ceteris paribus*, any shock to the feel-good correlation is eroded by the cointegrating relationship between that correlation and perceptions of which party will win the next election at the rate of 70 per cent per month. Net of these effects, the currency crisis did not influence the feel-good correlation; its coefficient is negative (-5.8), but insignificant ($p \geq .10$). However, the 1992 election did matter; it permanently boosted the feel-good correlation by nearly 20 points.

TABLE 7
ERROR CORRECTION MODEL OF THE STRENGTH OF THE FEEL-GOOD CORRELATION, JAN.
1992–APR. 1997

	β	s.e.	t
Predictor Variables			
Constant	-0.361	0.808	-0.447
Δ Labour Will Win (t)	-0.375	0.173	-2.175c
Error Correction Mechanism (t-1)	-0.700	0.126	-5.569a
1992 Election (t)	19.481	6.862	2.839b
Currency Crisis (t)	-5.835	6.291	-0.928
Model Diagnostics			
Adjusted R^2		0.450	
Standard error of estimate		6.180	
Durbin-Watson		1.932	
Serial correlation (12 lags)		10.738	
Functional Form		0.515	
Normality		4.291	
General heteroskedasticity		3.482	
ARCH (1)		0.022	

Note: a - $p \leq .001$; b - $p \leq .01$; c - $p \leq .05$; d - $p \leq .10$; one-tailed test. Dependent variable is first-differenced.

The credibility of these estimates is bolstered by the fact that the model passes an extensive battery of diagnostic tests. Additional confidence is derived from the behaviour of the feel-good correlation in the period after the 1997 election. Labour's huge victory should have left no doubt in the voters' minds about who the government will be for several years to come, and one would expect, therefore, that the feel-good correlation would have snapped back immediately after the election. This is exactly what happened. In the May–October 1997 Gallup surveys, the average value of the feel-good correlation is fully 41 points, with persons believing that their economic futures would be bright being much more likely to support the governing party (Labour) than those who thought otherwise. Overall, then, these findings suggest that much of the weakness of the feel-good correlation in data from surveys conducted in the run-up to the 1997 election reflects the fact that a large majority of voters believed that an opposition party would win the election while differing in their attributions of responsibility for their economic futures. Black Wednesday did have an important negative effect on Conservative re-election prospects, but it was not a proximate cause of the failure of the feel-good factor to exert a powerful influence on party support at the time of the 1997 election.

Conclusion: Change and Choice

In their discussions of the factors affecting voting behaviour in 1997, many commentators have been very guarded in their attributions of influence to Mr Blair or his Conservative and Liberal Democrat counterparts. They need not be. Time series and cross-sectional analyses presented above are consistent with models that recognize the importance of short-term forces operating on party choice. Thus, the analyses demonstrate that perceptions of party leaders exerted significant effects on party support throughout the 1992–7 period. Together with party identification, leader images formed cointegrating relationships with Labour and Conservative vote intentions that subjugated all other influences on party support, including those exerted by personal economic expectations and other kinds of subjective economic evaluations. Shocks to vote intentions, from whatever source, were eroded by the long-term equilibriating influences of party leader images and party identification. In the Conservative case, these influences were very strong – without large increases in the percentage of persons judging Mr. Major best suited to be prime minister and their share of party identifiers, the Tories were forced to depend on the decay of Labour support to boost their election chances. Such a decay was technically possible; although Labour vote intentions marched in tandem with public perceptions of the leadership qualities of Labour leaders and the party's share of identifiers, economic and political shocks could exert sizeable, and potentially electorally consequential, short-run influences.

In the event, translating technical possibilities into political realities proved an impossible task for the Conservatives. The economy was on an up-swing in the year before the election, and Conservative campaign strategists tried desperately to persuade voters that the Prime Minister and his party were responsible for this happy state of affairs. Although Britain may have been booming, the Conservatives were unable to reap sizeable political profits, as many voters were apparently unwilling to credit them for the situation. In their post-election commentaries, numerous observers have argued that the Tories' failure to translate a healthy economy into an election victory was due to their inept handling of the currency crisis in September 1992. Our analyses suggest that this interpretation has some merit; the currency crisis was influential. However, it affected Conservative vote intentions indirectly by diminishing public confidence in John Major and eroding the group of Tory party identifiers. Operating in conjunction with a series of scandals and acrimonious intra-party conflicts over a common currency and other aspects of Britain's membership in the European Union, Black Wednesday set the stage for the Conservatives' electoral defeat.

Moreover, it is worth re-emphasizing that economic effects on party choice were operative throughout the 1992–97 period. Time series analyses demonstrate that subjective economic evaluations affected the dynamics of vote intentions directly, as well as indirectly, by influencing voters' judgements about party leaders and their party identifications. Cross-sectional analyses complement these findings by revealing that economic evaluations continued to affect party support in the days immediately preceding the election. But, consonant with hypotheses advanced in post-election commentaries, our analyses show that personal economic expectations – the feel-good factor – was not a powerful influence on electoral choice. The effects of personal retrospective economic judgements were much stronger. We have argued that the relative strength of retrospective economic evaluations in 1997 can be understood in terms of variations in voters' assumptions about who bears responsibility for the future. In a situation where a large number of voters believe that an opposition party will win a forthcoming election, statistical relationships between prospective economic judgements and voting intentions will be attenuated to the extent that voters differ in their attributions of responsibility to present and future governing parties for future economic conditions. As shown above, there is considerable statistical evidence to suggest that this hypothesis does much to explain the weakness of the correlation between personal expectations and party support in surveys conducted in the run-up to the 1997 election, and the strong rebound in this correlation in post-election surveys.

In the afterglow of his party's triumph, Tony Blair declared: 'We have been elected as New Labour and we will govern as New Labour' (King, 1998c: 7). The first part of this statement is only partially true. Undoubtedly, the transformation of Labour into New Labour did much to reassure many voters that their futures could be entrusted to Mr Blair and his colleagues. But, many of these people would not have considered a Labour alternative – old or new – had Mr Major and the Conservatives not made such a terrible botch of their mandate. By so doing, the Prime Minister's image was severely tarnished and the Conservative cohort of party identifiers was substantially reduced. Since party leader images and party identification are critical elements in the skein of forces affecting electoral choice, the prospect that the Tories would be trounced in a forthcoming election was apparent long before voters went to the polls on 1 May. The economy was not irrelevant in 1997, but it was subordinated to a powerful combination of anti-Conservative and pro-Labour political factors. These factors were products of Labour's very astute long campaign to win power, and the Conservatives' seeming determination to lose it at all costs. Both parties bear heavy responsibilities, albeit very different ones, for bringing New Labour to power.

NOTES

1. The study covered the January 1992–April 1997 period and was supported by National Science Foundation grants SES-9309018 and SES-9600018. Fieldwork was conducted by the British Gallup Organization. The authors thank Robert Wybrow, Rory Fitzgerald, Shari Weber and the Gallup Organization for their assistance with this project. Neither NSF nor Gallup is responsible for the analyses and interpretations of the data presented in this article.

2. The *vote intention* questions are: (a) 'If there were a general election tomorrow, which party would you support?;' (b) [If 'don't know'] 'Which party would you be most inclined to vote for?' Labour support in the electorate is calculated as the sum of the percentages of persons responding 'Labour' to (a) or (b) with refusals and declared non-voters excluded. The *best prime minister* question is: 'Who would make the best Prime Minister, Mr Major, Mr Kinnock/Smith/Blair, or Mr Ashdown?' *Party identification* is measured using responses to the first question in the standard BES sequence: 'Generally speaking, do you think of yourself as Conservative, Labour, Liberal Democrat, or what?' The SNP and Plaid Cymru also are mentioned in Scotland and Wales, respectively. The *economic evaluation* questions are: (a) 'How do you think the financial situation of your household will change over the next 12 months?' (personal prospections); (b) 'How does the financial situation of your household now compare with what it was 12 months ago?' (personal retrospections); (c) 'How do you think the general economic situation in this country will develop over the next 12 months?' (national prospections); (d) 'How do you think the general economic situation in this country has changed over the last 12 months?' (national retrospections). The response categories for these questions are: 'get/got a lot better,' 'get/got a little better,' 'stay the same,' 'get/got a little worse,' 'get/got a lot worse.' The economic evaluation variables are constructed by subtracting the percentage offering negative responses from the percentage offering positive ones.

3. Tests for weak exogeneity indicate that a single-equation system is appropriate for estimating the parameters in the error correction models. See Clarke, Stewart and Whiteley (1997a, 1997b).

4. Since our analyses focus on the influence of party leader images, party identification and subjective economic evaluations, we do not display coefficients for various political and economic interventions in Tables 2 and 3. For discussions of the effects of these interventions, see Clarke, Stewart and Whiteley (1997a, 1997b).

5. The best prime minister variables are a series of 0-1 dummy variables, with persons who responded 'undecided' or 'don't know' constituting the reference group.

6. The party identification variables are a series of 0-1 dummy variables, with persons who state that they did not identify with a party constituting the reference group.

7. Responses to each of the subjective economic evaluation questions (see note 2 above) are scored: lot better = 2, little better = 1, same/don't know = 0, little worse = -1, lot worse = -2.

8. The economic evaluation index is the average score on the four economic evaluation variables (see note 7).

9. Age is measured in years; gender is scored: women = 1, men = 0; social class is a dichotomy: class groups A, B, C1 are scored 1, and groups C2, D, E are scored 0.

10. The Dickey Fuller (1979) test statistics for the percentage believing that Labour would win the next general election and the feel good correlation are -1.09 and -1.23 (augmented test), respectively. The MacKinnon (1991) critical value of the test ($p \leq .05$) is -2.91.

11. The Dickey Fuller (1979) test statistic for the cointegration test is -6.05. The MacKinnon (1991) critical value of the test ($p \leq .05$) is -3.47.

REFERENCES

Abramson, Paul R. and Charles W. Ostrom (1991) 'Macropartisanship: An Empirical Assessment', *American Political Science Review* 85: 181–92.

Bartle, John, Ivor Crewe and Anthony King (1997) 'Was It Blair Wot Won It? Leadership Effects in the 1997 British General Election'. Paper presented at the Annual Conference of the American Political Science Association, Washington, DC.

Bishop, George F., Alfred J. Tuchfarber and Andrew E. Smith (1994) 'Question Form and Context Effects in the Measurement of Partisanship: Experimental Tests of the Artifact Hypothesis', *American Political Science Review* 88: 945–58.

Budge, Ian, Ivor Crewe and Dennis Farlie (eds) (1976) *Party Identification and Beyond: Representations of Voting and Party Competition,* New York: John Wiley & Sons.

Butler, David and Donald E. Stokes (1976) *Political Change in Britain*, 2nd College Edition. New York: St. Martin's Press.

Campbell, Angus, Philip E. Converse, Warren E. Miller and Donald E. Stokes (1960) *The American Voter,* New York: John Wiley & Sons.

Clarke, Harold D., Karl Ho and Marianne C. Stewart (1997) 'Major's Lesser (Not Minor) Effects: Prime Ministerial Approval and Governing Party Support Since 1979', unpublished manuscript., Department of Political Science, University of North Texas.

Clarke, Harold D. and Marianne C. Stewart (1984) 'Dealignment of Degree: Partisan Change in Britain, 1974–83', *Journal of Politics* 46: 689–718.

Clarke, Harold D., Marianne C. Stewart and Paul Whiteley (1997a) 'Tory Trends: Party Identification and The Dynamics of Conservative Support Since 1992', *British Journal of Political Science* 26: 299–318.

Clarke, Harold D., Marianne C. Stewart and Paul Whiteley (1997b) 'Error Correction Models of Party Support: The Case of New Labour', in Charles Pattie, David Denver, Justin Fisher and Steve Ludlam (eds) *British Elections & Parties Review Volume 7*, pp.145–67. London and Portland OR: Frank Cass.

Converse, Philip E. (1976) *The Dynamics of Party Support: Cohort-Analysing Party Identification.* Beverly Hills: Sage.

Crewe, Ivor (1985) 'How to Win a Landslide Without Really Trying: Why the Conservatives Won in 1983', in Austin Ranney (ed) *Britain at the Polls 1983,* pp.155–96. Durham, NC: Duke University Press.

Crewe, Ivor and Anthony King (1994) 'Did Major Win? Did Kinnock Lose?: Leadership Effects in the 1992 British General Election', in Anthony Heath, Roger Jowell and John Curtice (eds) *Labour's Last Chance? The 1992 Election and Beyond,* pp.125–48. Aldershot: Dartmouth.

Crewe, Ivor, Bo Sarlvik and James E. Alt (1977) 'Partisan Dealignment in Britain, 1964–1974', *British Journal of Political Science* 7: 129–90.

Dalton, Russell J. and Martin P. Wattenberg (1993) 'The Not So Simple Act of Voting', in Ada W. Finifter (ed.) *Political Science: The State of the Discipline II,* Washington, DC: American Political Science Association.

Denver, David (1998) 'The Government That Could Do No Right', in Anthony King (ed) *New Labour Triumphs: Britain at the Polls,* pp.15–48. Chatham, NJ: Chatham House.

Dickey, D. A. and Wayne A. Fuller (1979) 'Distribution of the Estimators for Autoregressive Series With a Unit Root', *Journal of the American Statistical Association* 74: 427–31.

Downs, Anthony (1957) *An Economic Theory of Democracy*. New York: Harper & Row.

Fielding, Steven (1997) 'Labour's Path to Power', in Andrew Geddes and Jonathan Tonge (eds) *Labour's Landslide: The British General Election 1997,* pp.23–35. Manchester: Manchester University Press.

Fiorina, Morris P.(1981) *Retrospective Voting in American National Elections,* New Haven, CT: Yale University Press.

Franklin, Charles H. (1992) 'Measurement and the Dynamics of Party Identification', *Political Behavior,* 4: 297–310.

Gavin, Neil T. and David Sanders (1997) 'The Economy and Voting', *Parliamentary Affairs* 50: 631–40.

Geddes, Andrew and Jonathan Tonge (eds) (1997) *Labour's Landslide: The British General Election 1997*. Manchester: Manchester University Press.

Heath, Anthony, Roger Jowell and John Curtice (1985) *How Britain Votes*. Oxford: Pergamon Press.

Heath, Anthony, John Curtice, Roger Jowell, Geoff Evans, Julia Field and Sharon Witherspoon (1991) *Understanding Political Change: The British Voter 1964–1987*. Oxford: Pergamon Press.

Heath, Anthony, Roger Jowell and John Curtice (eds) (1994) *Labour's Last Chance?* Aldershot: Dartmouth.

Heath, Anthony and Sarah-K. MacDonald (1988) 'The Demise of Party Identification Theory?', *Electoral Studies* 7: 95–108.

Heath, Anthony and Roy Pierce (1992) 'It was Party Identification all Along: Question Order Effects on Reports of Party Identification in Britain', *Electoral Studies* 11: 93–105.

Hendry, David (1995) *Dynamic Econometrics*, Oxford: Oxford University Press.

Kavanagh, Dennis (1997) 'The Labour Campaign', *Parliamentary Affairs* 50: 533–42.

Kellner, Peter (1997) 'Why the Tories Were Trounced', *Parliamentary Affairs* 50: 616–31.

Key, V.O. (1967) *Public Opinion and American Democracy*. New York: Alfred A. Knopf.

Key, V.O. (1968) *The Responsible Electorate: Rationality in Presidential Voting, 1936–1960*. New York: Vintage Books.

King, Anthony (ed) (1998a) *New Labour Triumphs: Britain at the Polls,* Chatham, NJ: Chatham House.

King, Anthony (1998b) 'Why Labour Won – At Last', in Anthony King (ed) *New Labour Triumphs: Britain at the Polls,* pp.177–209. Chatham, NJ: Chatham House.

King, Anthony (1998c) 'The Night Itself', in Anthony King (ed) *New Labour Triumphs: Britain at the Polls,* pp.1–14. Chatham, NJ: Chatham House.

Long, J. Scott (1997) *Regression Models for Categorical and Limited Dependent Variables*. Thousand Oaks, CA: Sage.

MacKinnon, James (1991) 'Critical Values for Cointegration Tests', in Robert F. Engle and Clive W. J. Granger (eds) *Long-Run Economic Relationships: Readings in Cointegration,* pp.267–76. Oxford: Oxford University Press.

MacKuen, Michael B., Robert S. Erikson and James A. Stimson (1989) 'Macropartisanship', *American Political Science Review* 83: 1125–42.

MacKuen, Michael B., Robert S. Erikson and James A. Stimson (1992) 'Peasants or Bankers? The American Electorate and the US Economy', *American Political Science Review* 86: 597–616.

MacKuen, Michael B., Robert S. Erikson and James A. Stimson (1996) 'Comment', *Journal of Politics* 58: 793–801.

MacKuen, Michael B., Robert S. Erickson and James A. Stimson (1992) 'Controversy: Question Wording and Macropartisanship', *American Political Science Review* 86: 475–86.

Miller, Arthur H., Martin P. Wattenberg and Oksana Malanchuk (1986) 'Schematic Assessments of Presidential Candidates', *American Political Science Review* 80: 521–40.

Miller, Warren E. and J. Merrill Shanks (1996) *The New American Voter*. Cambridge, MA: Harvard University Press.

Miller, William L., Harold D. Clarke, Martin Harrop, Lawrence Leduc, Paul Whiteley (1990) *How Voters Change: The 1987 British Election Campaign in Perspective*. Oxford: Oxford University Press.

Mughan, Anthony (1997) 'Party Leaders and The Presidentialization of British Politics', unpublished manuscript, Department of Political Science, Ohio State University.

Nadeau, Richard, Richard G. Niemi and Timothy Amato (1996) 'Prospective and Comparative or Retrospective and Individual? Party Leaders and Party Support in Great Britain', *British Journal of Political Science* 26: 245–58.

Norpoth, Helmut (1992) *Confidence Regained: Economics, Mrs Thatcher, and the British Voter*. Ann Arbor, MI: University of Michigan Press.

Norris, Pippa and Neil T. Gavin (eds) (1997) 'Britain Votes 1997', *Parliamentary Affairs,* 50.

Norton, Philip (1998) 'The Conservative Party: "In Office but Not in Power"', in Anthony King (ed) *New Labour Triumphs: Britain at the Polls,* pp. 75–112. Chatham, NJ: Chatham House.

Pulzer, Peter G. (1967) *Political Representation and Elections in Britain.* London: Allen & Unwin.
Rose, Richard and Ian McAllister (1990) *The Loyalties of Voters: A Lifetime Learning Model.*
    London: Sage.
Sanders, David (1991) 'Government Popularity and the Next General Election', *Political
    Quarterly* 62: 235–61.
Sanders, David (1993) 'Why the Conservatives Won – Again', in Anthony King (ed) *Britain at
    the Polls 1992*, pp.172–222. Chatham, NJ: Chatham House.
Sanders, David (1998) 'The New Electoral Battleground', in Anthony King (ed) *New Labour
    Triumphs: Britain at the Polls,* pp.209–48. Chatham, NJ: Chatham House.
Sarlvik, Bo and Ivor Crewe (1983) *Decade of Dealignment: The Conservative Victory of 1979
    and Electoral Trends in the 1970s.* Cambridge: Cambridge University Press.
Semetko, Holli A., Margaret Scammell and Peter Goddard (1997) 'Television', *Parliamentary
    Affairs* 50: 609–615.
Seyd, Patrick (1998) 'Tony Blair and New Labour', in Anthony King (ed) *New Labour Triumphs:
    Britain at the Polls,* pp.49–74. Chatham, NJ: Chatham House.
Stewart, Marianne C. and Harold D. Clarke (1992) 'The (Un)Importance of Party Leaders:
    Leader Images and Party Choice in the 1987 British Election', *Journal of Politics* 54:
    447–70.
Wickham-Jones, Mark (1997) 'How the Conservatives Lost the Economic Argument', in Andrew
    Geddes and Jonathan Tonge (eds) *Labour's Landslide: The British General Election 1997,*
    pp.100–18. Manchester: Manchester University Press.

New Labour Landslide – Same Old Electoral Geography?

R.J. Johnston, C.J. Pattie, D.F.L. Dorling,
D.J. Rossiter, H. Tunstall and I.D. MacAllister

Great Britain has a well-established electoral geography. Using the terminology developed by Key (1955) for the study of American elections, this has produced a long series of 'normal' elections, with none that can be identified as 'deviating', let alone 'critical'. Once established, the geography has remained largely stable in a relative sense, though not in an absolute one: the electoral map is similar to a topographic surface whose relative morphology remains constant but whose elevation changes (occasional periods of uplift punctuated by depression, and sometimes of tilting too). The 1997 general election continued that overall sequence, though with some interesting variations which point to the possible beginning of a new era of micro-geography within the same overall pattern. We illustrate that here by decomposing the map into three separate spatial scales – regional, inter-constituency and local.

Decomposing the Map: The Scale Components of British Electoral Geography

The dominating feature of Great Britain's electoral geography has been the inter-constituency component. It reflects the basic social cleavage that has dominated British electoral politics throughout the twentieth century – socio-economic class. Other socio-economic factors in addition to class also help create inter-constituency variations in electoral support so that the party preferences of people living in a constituency are highly predictable from knowledge of a small number of aggregate features of its population, although those preferences tend to be skewed towards the majority view. Thus, pro-Labour areas tend to give more support to that party than the population composition would imply (see Miller, 1977; Johnston *et al.*, 1988). To a considerable extent, therefore, and as some critics have stressed (McAllister and Studlar, 1992), British electoral geography is nothing more than a mirror image of the country's socio-economic geography, with each election providing a slightly different distortion of that image.

Overlaid on this inter-constituency pattern, however, is a regional geography. Holding constant individual voter characteristics, there are – and always have been – significant inter-regional differences in propensity to vote in certain ways, as illustrated by the relative strength of Labour in the northern conurbations and in south Wales, and the strong Liberal traditions in parts of rural Wales and south-west England. Bogdanor's comment that 'an elector in Cornwall would tend to vote the same way as an elector from a similar class in Glasgow' (1983: 53) is misleading. From the 1950s on, and especially from 1970 on, these regional differences were accentuated, as shown in Curtice and Steed's seminal paper (1982): the north–south and urban–rural divides were both intensified, with the Conservative party dominating the 'south' and the 'rural' (including the small towns, suburbia, and the rural areas) and Labour extending its hegemony in the 'north' and in the large cities. These divides became even greater during the Thatcher years and the elections of 1983 and 1987 saw a very polarized situation (Johnston *et al.*, 1988): they remained a major feature in 1992 (Pattie *et al.*, 1993), and there is evidence that they opened up slightly in the run-up to that election, contributing to John Major's majority of 21 seats (Russell *et al.*, 1996).

The reasons for these differences have been the focus of considerable research and debate. To some extent, Curtice and Steed argued, they reflect changes in the inter-constituency geography of population characteristics, consequent on economic restructuring and inter-regional migration, plus the growing strength of 'third parties' in some areas. Holding these constant, however – and contrary to the view of McAllister and Studlar (1992: 191) that 'people react in similar ways in different regions according to their individual characteristics' – the inter-regional differences remain (Pattie and Johnston, 1998). They reflect spatial variations in the 'feel-good factor' (see Sanders *et al.*, 1987; Price and Sanders, 1995; Sanders, 1994). Those feeling good, both personally and about the national economy, are more likely to reward the incumbent government than those feeling less optimistic about both the national and their personal economic circumstances, and to the extent that optimism and pessimism are regionally variable, the pattern of voting follows (Johnston and Pattie, 1997a). In addition, people separately evaluate not only their personal and the national situations but also the relative condition of their regional economy, and all three impact upon their propensity to reward or punish the incumbent government (Pattie and Johnston, 1995, 1998).

Economic voting, and voters' perceptions of government economic competence, was a factor in the 1997 election. The Conservative government's popularity tumbled soon after the 1992 general election, and its reputation for the management of the economy suffered a major blow with the withdrawal from the European ERM in September 1992, from which it never recovered during the succeeding five years, despite economic recovery later in the period (Kellner, 1996). An asymmetrical relationship developed, whereby economic optimists who had voted Conservative in 1992 tended to give the party continued strong support, whereas those who became pessimistic deserted it, but optimists who were supporting other parties did not transfer their allegiance to the incumbents to anything like the extent that they are assumed to have done in the 1980s (Johnston and Pattie, 1998). Furthermore, there remained an autonomous regional dimension to their partisan preferences: those who lived in the north in 1996 and felt good about the trend of their regional economy were less likely to reward the government with their voting intentions than were those who lived in the south and felt the same way (Johnston and Pattie, 1997b).

The third, local element of the electoral geography of Great Britain operates at the scale of one or a few constituencies only. Some parts of it may be relatively long-lived, such as the weaker support given to the Labour party in the Dukeries coalfield of north Nottinghamshire, compared to that in adjacent South Yorkshire (Johnston, 1991; Jones, Johnston and Pattie, 1992), whereas others may reflect local situations of immediate concern only – such as the race issue in the Wolverhampton area in 1964 and Enoch Powell's advice a decade later to his former constituents there that they should vote Labour on the sovereignty issue related to membership of the (then) EEC (Taylor and Johnston, 1979: 294–300). The popularity (or otherwise) of a candidate can cause the voting in one constituency to deviate from the general trends, as analyses of voters' reactions to rebel MPs have shown (Pattie *et al.*, 1994). Finally, the intensity of local campaigning can have a significant impact on the outcome in a constituency (Pattie *et al.*, 1995), especially where it involves canvassing for tactical voting (Johnston and Pattie, 1991).

From 1992 to 1997

The following sections analyse the outcome of the 1997 general election in Great Britain, with special reference to change between 1992 and 1997, in the context of the above three-component model. In these analyses of change, we have not used the traditional indicator – two-party (Conservative–Labour) swing – because of its disadvantages when more than two parties are in contention. Our preferred measures of change in detailed analyses at the local scale are the individual cells in constituency flow-of-the-vote matrices, since these allow us to examine how voters were shifting their support in some detail. But less detail is required for the regional and inter-constituency analyses and in this case we use a single absolute measure, the change in the percentage of the votes cast for a party between two elections.[1]

The Regional Scale

Table 1 shows inter-regional variations in voting at the 1992 and 1997 general elections according to a 22-region division of the country used in many of our earlier analyses (see Johnston *et al.*, 1988, for full details). The table shows very substantial inter-regional differences in party support (statistically significant, using ANOVA tests) at both dates. The Conservatives were strongest, and Labour weakest, in the southern regions plus the more rural areas of the north ; the Liberal Democrats were strongest in the south-west and Wessex, in the area around London and in the rural areas; and abstentions were greatest in the conurbations (especially Inner London).

TABLE 1

REGIONAL VARIATIONS IN THE PERCENTAGE OF THE VOTES CAST WON BY EACH PARTY AND IN THE PERCENTAGE OF THE ELECTORATE WHO ABSTAINED.

	Conservative		Labour		Liberal		SNP/PC Democrat		Abstain	
	92	97	92	97	92	97	92	97	92	97
Strathclyde	20	13	51	58	8	7	20	20	26	30
EC Scotland	25	17	43	51	11	10	20	20	24	27
Rural Scotland	31	22	21	28	22	22·	25	26	27	28
Rural Wales	32	22	34	42	17	15	16	18	21	25
South Wales	25	17	60	64	10	11	5	5	22	28
Rural north	46	34	33	43	21	20			22	28
Industrial NE	29	18	56	67	14	11			25	32
Merseyside	28	19	52	63	17	14			26	32
Gtr Manchester	35	24	47	56	16	16			25	32
Rest of NW	41	31	43	54	14	12			20	27
W Yorkshire	37	28	46	55	15	13			24	31
S Yorkshire	26	16	58	63	15	16			28	36
W Midlands Con	42	30	44	54	12	11			25	32
Rest W Midlands	47	37	34	43	18	16			20	26
E Midlands	46	34	38	48	15	14			20	27
East Anglia	51	39	28	39	19	18			20	25
South-west	46	35	18	23	34	35			19	25
Wessex	48	37	20	28	30	29			19	25
Outer south-east	53	40	20	32	25	23			21	26
Outer metropolitan	56	42	22	33	21	20			20	26
Outer London	49	34	33	47	16	15			24	30
Inner London	35	24	47	58	15	13			32	37

Note: Because of minor party involvement, especially in 1997, percentages may not sum to 100 per cent.

But what of changes between the two elections? On average, the Conservative share of the votes cast fell by 11.4 per cent (Table 2). Nine regions experienced an even greater average decline – all but three (Rural north, Greater Manchester and West Midlands Conurbation) are in southern England, and only the south-west and Wessex of the southern regions experienced a below-average loss. In general terms, therefore, as a comparison of Tables 1 and 2 shows, the Conservative performance was worst in the regions where they performed best in 1992 – the non-Conservative vote increased by almost 15 percentage points in outer London and the adjacent inner Home Counties ring (outer metropolitan), compared to only around 10 percentage points in the urban areas of Scotland and Wales.

TABLE 2
REGIONAL VARIATIONS IN THE CHANGE IN THE PERCENTAGE OF THE VOTES CAST WON BY EACH PARTY AND IN THE CHANGE IN THE PERCENTAGE OF THE ELECTORATE WHO ABSTAINED.

	Conservative	Labour	Liberal Democrat	Abstain
Strathclyde	-7.0	6.4	-1.0	4.7
EC Scotland	-8.1	7.8	-0.2	3.4
Rural Scotland	-9.7	7.0	0.4	1.6
Rural Wales	-9.9	7.6	**-1.7**	4.4
South Wales	-8.6	4.1	0.8	4.9
Rural north	**-12.2**	**9.9**	1.0	**6.2**
Industrial NE	-11.0	**10.8**	**-2.9**	**6.5**
Merseyside	-9.3	**10.6**	**-2.6**	5.7
Gtr Manchester	**-11.5**	9.1	0.4	**6.9**
Rest of NW	-10.9	**10.5**	**-2.1**	**7.1**
W Yorkshire	-9.6	8.7	**-2.1**	**6.4**
S Yorkshire	-9.4	4.8	0.7	**7.8**
W Midlands Con	**-11.9**	9.6	0.6	**6.9**
Rest W Midlands	-10.2	9.3	**-2.0**	**6.3**
E Midlands	**-12.1**	**10.7**	**-1.7**	**7.0**
Anglia	**-12.5**	**10.6**	**-1.7**	5.3
South-west	-11.3	5.8	1.2	**6.0**
Wessex	-10.9	8.2	-0.8	5.7
Outer south-east	**-13.0**	**11.3**	**-2.5**	5.5
Outer metropolitan	**-13.4**	**11.4**	**-1.7**	**6.4**
Outer London	**-15.4**	**13.8**	1.0	5.3
Inner London	**-11.8**	**10.3**	-0.1	5.1
Mean	-11.4	9.6	-1.3	5.8
R^2	*0.37*	*0.24*	*0.07*	*0.24*

Note: Changes greater than the national figure are in bold.

The changing geography of Labour support is not a mirror image of Conservative decline, however, and its performance at winning over more converts from the 1992 non-Labour-voting electorate was above average in some of the regions where the Conservatives also performed relatively well (or, more accurately, not as badly as their national average) – notably in north-east and north-west England. But elsewhere Labour benefited from Tory discomfort. The Tory performance was particularly bad in its south-eastern 'heartlands' and Labour's vote share increased by an above average amount there.

The Liberal Democrats' share of the vote fell by 1.3 percentage points on average between 1992 and 1997. They were net gainers in some regions, however: in Rural Scotland, South Wales, Rural North, Greater Manchester, the West Midlands conurbation, South Yorkshire, the Southwest and Inner London. These regions are very different in their nature, and suggest concentrations of support for the Liberal Democrats reflecting the operation of very localized influences.

Finally, with regard to abstentions, the percentage not voting increased by 5.8 percentage points overall. The change was less than the average in two main blocks of regions, however: Scotland and Wales, and southern England (excluding outer metropolitan); the growth in abstentions was greater than average in the English northern conurbations and Midlands.

All of these differences by region are statistically significant (at the 0.05 level or better) according to ANOVA tests. The associated R2 values are not very high in most cases , however, accounting for less than 25 per cent of the variation in all cases except those involving the Conservative party: intra-regional variation is substantial. The 'best fits' at the regional scale are for Conservative net change, suggesting that its performance had a substantial regional component – much more so than the performance of either of its opponents (especially the Liberal Democrats) or abstentions.

The overall pattern which emerges from Table 2 is that the regional geography of the vote became less pronounced between 1992 and 1997: spatial polarization decreased somewhat in absolute terms. This conclusion applies particularly to the geographies of support for Conservative and Labour: Conservative vote share fell most where it was strongest, and was countered in most of those areas by an above-average increase in support for Labour. The regional geography of the Liberal Democrat vote did not change in a uniform way, however: it became even more varied – not only between regions but also within them. Finally, the geography of abstentions changed: the fall in turnout was smaller among the Scots and Welsh than in many parts of England, for example, and there were intriguing regional variations within England although, as with the changing geographies of Liberal Democrat support, there was very considerable intra-regional variation too.

The regional patterns are significant in themselves, and of considerable interest, but they are only the start of the analysis, for two reasons. First, and following the critiques of McAllister and others, it may be that they are mere artefacts of inter-constituency and local scale differences and we can only conclude that they are 'real' once those have been held constant. Secondly, the regional differences, although significant, conceal more than they reveal (as the R^2 values in Table 2 indicate): there is much more to the geography of New Labour's landslide which needs to be explored.

The Inter-constituency Scale

At the inter-constituency scale, rather than treating constituencies as homogeneous geographical groupings – defined by regional location – we treat each constituency as a separate unit and look for continuous rather than discrete variations over space, in the manner typical of ecological analyses. At the first stage of this analysis, we employ eleven variables taken from the 1991 Census (for a key to the variables, see Table 3): these reflect what are widely taken as the main socio-economic correlates of variations in voting behaviour across Great Britain, and represent the continuity in the country's electoral geography. We then add further variables relating to the geography of the country's labour markets between 1992 and 1997, before finally adding the regional variables to see if there are differences between parts of the country which cannot be associated with the ecological relationships. All of the analyses reported in this section use multiple linear regression.

For the labour market analyses we use unemployment data taken from the NOMIS database. Two variables are included, as indicated in Table 3, to indicate the level of unemployment in the constituency (the number of registered unemployed in '00s) and the change in the number of unemployed between January 1996 (the earliest date on which data were available for the new constituencies) and April 1997.

There are considerable collinearities between the 11 census-based variables and the two indicating recent labour market performance, and so principal components analyses were undertaken to obtain interpretable independent variables. Five components with eigenvalues exceeding 1.0 were extracted, and the loadings on the structure matrix (oblimin rotation) are given in Table 3. The first four of the five components are readily interpreted, the fifth less so.

I. *Financial Britain*: The high positive loadings on EMPM, EDUC and FINA and the high negative loading for MANU contrast the areas dominated by white-collar, well-educated people employed in service industries with those dominated by manufacturing – the high negative loading for long-term illness indicates the concentration of those individuals in Britain's manufacturing areas. Constituencies with high positive scores on the component are therefore areas with high employment in financial services and in the professions and management; constituencies with high negative scores are manufacturing areas.

II. *Suburban Britain*: The negative loadings for UNAP and UNCH indicate that the constituencies with the smallest numbers unemployed were also those with relatively small changes in that number over the period immediately preceding the 1997 election; the high positive loading for OWNE indicates that unemployment was lowest, and falling most, where owner-occupation was greatest (i.e. the more affluent

TABLE 3
THE INDEPENDENT VARIABLES (AND THEIR MNEMONICS) USED IN THE
INTER-CONSTITUENCY SCALE ECOLOGICAL REGRESSION ANALYSES

EMPM   % economically-active population who are employers or managers;
ENWA   % economically-active population employed in the energy and water industries;*
EDUC   % population aged over 18 with a higher educational qualification;
AGRI   % economically-active population employed in agriculture, forestry or fishing;
FINA   % economically-active population employed in financial services;
FORC   % economically-active population in the armed forces;
LONG   % population aged over 16 with long-term illnesses;
MANU   % economically-active population employed in manufacturing industry;
NONW   % population aged over 16 with (self-assigned) non-white ethnicity;
OWNE   % population aged over 16 living in owner-occupied properties;
PENS   % population aged over 16 who are of pensionable age;
UNAP   number of unemployed (in '00s) in April 1997
UNCH   % change in the number of unemployed – January 1996 to April 1997

* This employment category (which includes all mining and quarrying, the oil industry and the
nuclear power industry as well as water) is the best available for identifying the country's mining
constituencies.

Structure Matrix: Rotated Factor Analysis

	I	II	III	IV	V
EMPM	0.85	0.56	–	–	–
EDUC	0.87	–	–	–	–
FINA	0.84	–	–	–	–
LONG	-0.69	-0.46	0.47	–	–
MANU	-0.72	–	–	0.31	–
OWNE	–	0.75	–	–	0.31
UNAP	–	-0.75	–	0.30	–
UNCH	–	-0.71	–	–	–
PENS	–	–	0.95	–	–
AGRI	–	0.26	0.41	-0.69	–
FORC	–	–	–	-0.81	–
ENWA	–	–	–	–	0.84
NONW	–	-0.39	-0.46	–	-0.63

areas), an interpretation strengthened by the small positive loading for EMPM, whereas the negative loadings for LONG and NONW suggest the concentration of unemployment in the areas where relative disadvantage is concentrated. High positive scores on the component therefore reflect the more suburban areas.

III. *Retirement Britain*: The single high positive loading on PENS scales constituencies according to their percentages of old people, and the smaller loadings indicate that they are to some extent concentrated in the areas with most long-term ill and in rural areas, and with few non-white residents.

IV. *Urban Britain*: The two high negative loadings indicate that Britain's rural areas are where the country's armed forces are concentrated: the more positive a constituency's score on this component, the less rural, and the more urban it is.

V. *Coalfields Britain*: The two high loadings indicate that non-white residents are relatively absent from those parts of the country with high percentages employed in the energy and water industries. Many non-whites live in relatively deprived inner city areas (high unemployment, few old people). High positive scores on the component therefore reflect mainly coalfield areas (hence the name): high negative scores indicate inner city areas.

The results of the ecological regressions of three dependent variables for each party and for abstentions – the 1992 and 1997 patterns and percentage change between those two dates – using the five factors as independent variables are in Table 4.[2] The geographies of Conservative and Labour support and of abstentions are very predictable at this scale (as indicated by the high R2 values), in both 1992 and 1997; those of the Liberal Democrats are much less so.

The Conservative share of the vote in 1992 was significantly related to only two of the components – Financial Britain and Suburban Britain; in 1997 it was also linked to Retirement Britain. As shown by many other analyses, the Conservatives won most support in the parts of the country dominated by the new service economy, and in the areas where older people were concentrated. The much lower constant value in 1997 than 1992 indicates the general decline in the party's standing in all areas, however, a finding buttressed by the smaller regression coefficients too. For change between 1992 and 1997, the negative coefficients for the first two components indicate that the Conservative share of the vote fell most in the areas dominated by the service industries and in the suburbs (i.e. the party's heartlands). The significant coefficients for the third and fourth factors show that the

Conservative vote held up relatively well in constituencies with older populations and in the rural areas (both areas where the party traditionally does well), whereas that for the fifth indicates that the 1997 Conservative vote did not drop by as much, other things being equal, in coalfield areas as elsewhere.

Labour's performance and changing performance are related to all of the components, with 14 out of 15 regression coefficients significant. In both 1992 and 1997 it performed best in the old manufacturing areas (I), the areas of high unemployment and relatively small decline in unemployment (II), the areas with relatively few residents of pensionable age (III) and the areas with few people employed in agriculture and in the armed forces (IV): in addition it performed better in 1997 the greater the proportion of non-whites in the population (V). Between 1992 and 1997, Labour's share of the vote increased less in the more rural areas (IV), the coalfields (V), and the areas with more

TABLE 4
INTER-CONSTITUENCY SCALE REGRESSIONS OF PERCENTAGE OF THE VOTES CAST WON BY EACH PARTY, THE PERCENTAGE OF THE ELECTORATE WHO ABSTAINED, THE CHANGE IN EACH PARTY'S VOTE SHARE, AND THE CHANGE IN THE PERCENTAGE OF THE ELECTORATE WHO ABSTAINED, 1992–97.

	Conservative			*Labour*		
	92	97	C	92	97	C
Factor						
Financial	**7.02**	**6.04**	**-0.97**	**-10.07**	**-9.62**	**0.45**
Suburban	**7.47**	**6.82**	**-0.65**	**-7.06**	**-6.56**	**0.49**
Retirement	0.23	**0.57**	**0.34**	**-3.48**	**-4.36**	**-0.87**
Urban	0.01	**-0.40**	**-0.41**	**4.57**	**5.21**	**0.64**
Coalfields	-0.53	**-0.24**	**0.29**	-0.47	**-0.85**	**-0.39**
Constant	**41.56**	**30.17**	**-11.38**	**36.19**	**45.81**	**9.62**
R^2	*0.65*	*0.66*	*0.17*	*0.73*	*0.69*	*0.08*

	Liberal Democrat			*Abstention*		
	92	97	C	92	97	C
Factor						
Financial	**3.34**	**3.87**	**0.53**	**-0.93**	**-1.62**	**-0.69**
Suburban	**1.99**	**1.97**	-0.02	**-3.41**	**-3.09**	**0.32**
Retirement	**2.70**	**2.95**	0.25	-0.29	**-0.57**	**-0.28**
Urban	**-2.31**	**-2.28**	0.03	-0.15	**0.31**	**0.46**
Coalfields	-0.13	0.18	**0.31**	**-1.67**	**-1.68**	-0.02
Constant	17.98	**16.68**	**-1.31**	**22.77**	**28.54**	**5.76**
R2	*0.34*	*0.32*	*0.02*	*0.61*	*0.59*	*0.13*

Note: C = change. Coefficients significant at the 0.05 level or better are in bold.

pensioners (III), but more in the service industry (I) areas, and the suburbs (II). Labour invaded some Conservative heartlands.

The inter-constituency geography of support for the Liberal Democrats was very similar in both 1992 and 1997: relative strength in Financial Britain, the suburbs, Retirement Britain, and the rural areas. Compared to the regressions for Conservative and Labour, however, the R^2 values were relatively low. Between 1992 and 1997, the only significant links to the geography of change in Liberal Democrat support were the party's better performances in Financial Britain (a further invasion of the Tory heartlands), and in coalfield areas.

Finally, abstentions were greatest in both years in the older manufacturing areas, the unemployment concentrations, the areas with relatively few pensioners, and the inner cities. Where Labour did well larger numbers abstained and abstentions tended to increase most where Labour did relatively well also.

The Local Scale

At this final scale, we treat each constituency as a separate spatial unit with its own peculiar features which influenced the outcome there in 1997 relative to 1992. Many of the relevant features relate to the electoral context in the constituencies: whether they are considered marginal or safe by the parties; whether they are targeted by one party or more for intensive campaigning and canvassing; and the political composition of the local authority. Those which are explored here are:

1. Constituency marginality;
2. The strength of the parties in the local milieux (notably in local government); and
3. The nature of the local campaign and tactical voting.[3]

Marginality and the Local Milieux

The regional analyses showed that the Conservative vote fell most where it was strongest in 1992 whereas the Labour vote increased most where it was relatively weak. To explore this broad generalization further, we look at the relationship between our change variables and marginality, according to the nature of the constituency contest – defined by the parties in first and second place in the estimated 1992 results. Of the 639 constituencies, 226 were Labour–Conservative contests (i.e. Labour occupied first place and the Conservative second), 187 were Conservative–Labour, 157 were Conservative–Liberal Democrat, and 31 were Labour–Nationalist; the other 38 were spread across the remaining contest types, and were too few to allow statistical analysis.

Three independent variables were included in all of the analyses:

> *Margin:* defined as the difference in percentage points between the share of the votes 'won' by the first- and second-placed parties in the 1992 estimated results;

> *By-election:* a dummy variable indicating whether a by-election had been held in the constituency (or a major part of it) between 1992 and 1997 (1= by-election held; 0 = otherwise); and

> *Third/second:* the ratio of the share of the votes 'won' by the third- and second-placed parties in the 1992 estimated results (the larger the ratio, the smaller the gap between the two).

In addition, for contests involving the Liberal Democrats a dummy variable was included to indicate whether the seat was one of the 34 identified by the party as its major campaigning targets.

> *LibDem Target:* a dummy variable (1 = target; 0 = otherwise) indicating whether the seat was on the Liberal Democrats' target list.[4]

It is widely accepted that one of the problems faced by the Liberal Democrats when contesting Parliamentary constituencies is the party's lack of experience of government. To counter this, the party stressed during the 1997 campaign that it was involved in running more local governments than the Conservatives. Where the party was in power locally, therefore, voters could evaluate its 'governing potential' – with the implication that the stronger the Liberal Democrat presence in a local government, the better would be performance. To test this, we calculated for each constituency the percentage of the seats held by the Liberal Democrats in the main local council.[5] The following variable was included in all the equations.

> *LibDem Council:* the percentage of council seats held by the Liberal Democrat party immediately prior to the 1997 general election was included in all of the equations.

In addition, much recent work has demonstrated the importance of the local campaign in accounting for the constituency vote (see e.g. Pattie *et al.*, 1995; Denver and Hands, 1997; Seyd and Whiteley, 1992). An effective local campaign boosts the share of the vote for one's own party, and reduces the vote share of one's rivals. To measure the intensity of the local campaign, we have employed local parties' reports of how much they spent on the campaign, as a percentage of the legally permitted maximum expenditure in each seat. This is a surrogate for actual campaign intensity, but it correlates well with other measures of local campaigning (Pattie *et al.*, 1994: Denver and Hands, 1997). Three variables were available for each of 572 seats:

> *ConSpend:* the amount spent by the local Conservative party in 1997 as a percentage of the legal maximum;

LabSpend: the amount spent by the local Labour party in 1997 as a percentage of the legal maximum;

LibDemSpend: the amount spent by the local Liberal Democrat party in 1997 as a percentage of the legal maximum.

Marginality is significantly related to the volume of change in six out of the eight regressions relating to *Conservative–Labour* and *Labour–Conservative* contests (Table 5). In the former, the wider the margin, the greater the loss of votes by the incumbent Conservative party (recall that the change values for Conservative are almost all negative): the Conservatives lost votes in greatest number where their hold was relatively safe. The Liberal Democrat share of the vote increased most where the Labour party had the least chances of winning (i.e. the margin was widest). Where Labour was challenging the Conservatives from second place, therefore, the incumbents retained more of their support, the closer the contest. Labour's gains were also greater the less secure it was in second place, as shown by the positive coefficient for third/second, whereas the Liberal Democrats picked up most additional votes where the gap between their third-placed candidate and the Labour runner-up was largest: holding margin constant, the closer the contest between Labour and the Liberal Democrats in these Conservative-held seats, the better the Labour performance and the poorer its opponents'. Abstentions, too, increased more in safer Conservative seats than in the more marginal ones. In the *Labour–Conservative* contests, the wider the margin between the two front-runners the smaller the net decline in both the Conservative and Liberal Democrat vote: the Conservatives also performed relatively well where they were strongly placed relative to the third-placed Liberal Democrats (with the reverse being the case for the latter party). Labour's support, meanwhile, was related to marginality in these seats: the wider Labour's lead over the Conservatives, the smaller the increase in its share of the vote.

Marginality was significant in three of the regressions for the *Conservative–Liberal Democrat* contests. For the Conservatives and Labour, the wider the margin the greater the net loss (or, for Labour, often, the smaller the net gain) of votes, but for the Liberal Democrats, the narrower the margin, the greater the gain in votes. LibDem target was a crucial variable, however: in those seats where the party focused its campaigning resources, the Conservative vote fell more than it did in the untargeted seats, while the Labour net increase was less than average and the Liberal Democrat growth substantially greater, representing a considerable return to the second-placed party for its focused investment. (Abstentions also increased less in those targeted seats.) Finally, constituencies where there were by-elections between 1992 and 1997 saw significant falls in the Conservative net share of the vote, relative to those not contested between the two general elections. These

TABLE 5
REGRESSIONS OF THE IMPACT OF CONTEST TYPE ON CHANGES IN THE PERCENTAGE OF
THE VOTES CAST WON BY EACH PARTY AND CHANGES IN THE PERCENTAGE OF THE
ELECTORATE WHO ABSTAINED, 1992–97.

	Conservative	Labour	Liberal Democrat	Abstain
Con–Lab Contests				
Margin	**-0.14**	0.02	**0.12**	**0.05**
By-election	-0.75	-0.59	1.22	1.88
Third/second	**4.69**	**6.80**	**-13.10**	**-2.51**
LibDem council	0.08	-0.01	0.01	0.04
ConSpend	**0.04**	-0.03	-0.01	-0.02
LabSpend	**-0.06**	**0.08**	**-0.04**	**-0.03**
LibDemSpend	0.01	-0.02	**0.05**	-0.02
Constant	**-10.99**	**5.74**	3.79	**9.21**
R^2	*0.14*	*0.20*	*0.45*	*0.18*
Con–Lib Dem Contests				
Margin	**-0.16**	**-0.09**	**0.23**	-0.04
By-election	**-3.91**	0.47	**4.21**	0.52
Third/second	10.36	4.01	- 9.84	-2.65
LibDem target	**-1.69**	**-4.34**	**5.86**	**-1.06**
LibDem council	0.02	-0.01	**0.06**	0.05
ConSpend	**0.04**	**-0.06**	0.03	0.01
LabSpend	-0.01	**0.08**	**-0.06**	**-0.02**
LibDemSpend	**-0.04**	**-0.10**	**0.14**	-0.02
Constant	- 9.41	**18.55**	**-14.43**	**8.55**
R^2	*0.29*	*0.45*	*0.47*	*0.09*
Lab–Con Contests				
Margin	**0.11**	**-0.18**	**0.07**	-0.01
By-election	-0.61	-1.41	-1.31	-0.02
Third/second	**4.12**	1.33	**-5.51**	**-4.09**
LibDem council	0.06	-0.01	0.03	0.04
ConSpend	**0.03**	**-0.04**	**0.02**	**-0.02**
LabSpend	**-0.01**	0.01	-0.01	-0.01
LibDemSpend	**-0.02**	-0.02	**0.03**	-0.01
Constant	**-15.24**	**13.24**	-1.34	**9.04**
R^2	*0.44*	*0.22*	*0.16*	*0.08*

Note: Coefficients significant at the 0.05 level or better are in bold.

include Christchurch, Eastleigh and Newbury, all won by the Liberal
Democrats at by-elections in 1993 and 1994.

Most striking, however, is the role of local campaign spending. In all three
groups of constituencies, the more a challenger party spent, the greater the
increase in its votes, and the smaller the increase (or the larger the decrease)
in the shares of the vote for its rivals. In addition, campaign spending by
challenger parties helped reduce the level of abstention: the more challengers
spent on their campaign, the less abstention grew. By and large, however,

incumbent parties did not seem to benefit from their own campaign efforts. In Conservative–Labour, and Labour–Conservative seats, the local campaign seems to have been asymmetric, giving an advantage to challengers but not to incumbents. In this respect the effect of local campaigns in 1997 was similar to that in earlier elections (see Pattie *et al.*, 1995). In Conservative–Liberal Democrat seats, however, incumbent campaigning seems to have had rather more of an impact: the more the Conservatives spent there in 1997, the fewer votes they lost, and the fewer Labour gained.

Although most of these regressions indicate significant relationships which are in line with expectations, and show the impact of a spatially-differentiated campaign focused, in varying ways, on the marginal constituencies, few of them have large R^2 values: the nature of the local contest influenced the outcome, but rarely dominated it.

Some of the detailed outcome of 1997 general election was created by local scale variables, therefore, through carefully-orchestrated strategies focused on the key constituencies: the magnitude, if not the fact, of Labour's (and the Liberal Democrats') success depended in part on careful local campaigning. Labour and Liberal Democrat challengers were best able to mobilize voters in the marginal seats that they needed to win in order to ensure victory. The overall haemorrhage from Conservative incumbents was stemmed somewhat in more marginal seats but this was insufficient to ensure a fifth successive victory. Finally, the differential patterns of changing votes between the Conservative–Labour and Conservative–LibDem marginals suggests the presence of tactical voting on a considerable scale, a topic to which we now turn.

Tactical Voting

There was considerable discussion of tactical voting during the election campaign, most of it focusing on the desirability of supporters of a third-placed party (either Labour or Liberal Democrat in most cases) in a Conservative-held seat voting tactically for the second-placed challenger to try to oust the incumbent. It was not promoted by the party leaders nationally (though implicitly condoned at least by Paddy Ashdown), but much canvassed in many constituencies, not only by the parties themselves but also by *ad hoc* pressure groups.

The concept of tactical voting suggests that movements between parties (and in and out of non-voting) between elections varies according to which party is most likely to defeat the incumbent. We have estimated the inter-party movements in each constituency from a national flow-of-the-vote matrix.[6] We focus on the flows relevant to tactical voting in the three main constituency types, and the summary data (all flows are expressed as percentages of the original total – e.g. Conservative-to-Labour flows as a percentage of those

TABLE 6
INTER-PARTY VOTER MOVEMENTS IN CONSTITUENCY FLOW-OF-THE-VOTE MATRICES

From	To	Min.	Max.	Mean	SD
All constituencies					
Conservative	Labour	2.7	14.2	9.7	2.1
Conservative	Liberal Democrat	2.3	12.2	5.3	1.7
Labour	Conservative	0.6	4.8	1.8	0.6
Labour	Liberal Democrat	1.3	17.2	3.4	2.0
Liberal Democrat	Conservative	1.2	5.6	3.2	0.8
Liberal Democrat	Labour	3.1	27.5	17.3	4.7
Non-Voting	Conservative	3.9	19.6	12.1	3.4
Non-Voting	Labour	6.4	29.5	19.3	3.6
Non-Voting	Liberal Democrat	2.3	18.8	6.5	2.5
CL/CD		0.2	4.8	2.1	0.8
DL/LD		0.2	22.0	6.7	3.7
NVL/NVD		0.4	8.1	3.5	1.4
CD/DC		0.5	9.4	1.9	1.1
LC/LD		0.2	1.4	0.6	0.2
NVC/NVD		0.6	4.7	2.0	0.6
Conservative–Labour contests					
Conservative	Labour	6.1	13.0	10.4	1.1
Conservative	Liberal Democrat	2.3	8.7	4.3	0.8
Labour	Liberal Democrat	1.3	5.0	2.5	0.5
Liberal Democrat	Labour	11.9	27.5	20.7	2.7
Non-Voting	Labour	12.0	29.5	22.5	2.2
Non-Voting	Liberal Democrat	2.9	10.3	5.6	1.1
CL/CD		1.2	4.8	2.5	0.6
DL/LD		2.6	22.0	8.8	3.1
NVL/NVD		1.9	8.1	4.2	1.0
Conservative–Liberal Democrat contests					
Conservative	Labour	2.7	12.1	7.3	1.8
Conservative	Liberal Democrat	3.2	12.2	6.9	1.7
Labour	Liberal Democrat	1.8	17.2	5.6	2.5
Liberal Democrat	Labour	3.1	23.6	12.3	4.1
Non-Voting	Labour	6.4	24.3	16.8	3.7
Non-Voting	Liberal Democrat	4.1	18.8	9.5	2.5
CL/CD		0.2	3.3	1.2	0.5
DL/LD		0.2	13.0	2.9	2.1
NVL/NVD		0.4	5.5	2.0	0.9
Labour–Conservative contests					
Conservative	Liberal Democrat	2.6	9.2	5.0	1.1
Labour	Conservative	0.7	2.8	1.4	0.3
Labour	Liberal Democrat	1.5	4.8	2.7	0.6
Liberal Democrat	Conservative	1.4	5.6	2.7	0.6
Non-Voting	Conservative	4.5	17.5	9.3	2.1
Non-Voting	Liberal Democrat	2.9	9.7	5.3	1.2
CD/DC		0.5	5.6	2.0	0.9
LC/LD		0.2	1.4	0.5	0.2
NVC/NVD		0.8	4.7	1.8	0.5

who voted Conservative in 1992) are in Table 6.

Across all 639 constituencies, for example, an average of 9.7 per cent of 1992 Conservative voters shifted their support to Labour in 1997, with a range from 2.7 to 14.2, whereas an average of 5.3 shifted their allegiance to the Liberal Democrats (range 2.3–12.2). In Conservative-held seats where Labour was in second place, however, the respective means were 10.4 and 4.3, whereas in those where the Liberal Democrats occupied second place they were 7.3 and 6.9. On average it seems, where Labour had the best chance of defeating the Conservatives more Tory defectors voted Labour in 1992, whereas where the Liberal Democrats had the best chance, fewer defected to Labour and more to the main challenger. Similarly, many fewer 1992 Labour supporters shifted their allegiance to the Liberal Democrats where Labour was second than where the Liberal Democrats were and more 1992 non-voters shifted to Labour in the Conservative-Labour contests than in the Conservative-Liberal Democrat contests.

If tactical voting operated to favour the second-placed candidate, then the relative balance of flows should favour that person. In the Conservative-held seats, therefore, we look at three ratios:

• CL/CD – the ratio of 'defectors' from the Conservatives to Labour and to the Liberal Democrats (the larger the ratio, the greater the relative shift to Labour);

• DL/LD – the ratio of Liberal-Democrat-to-Labour movements to Labour-to-Liberal-Democrat flows (the larger the ratio, the greater the relative shift to Labour); and

• NVL/NVD – the ratio of 1992 non-voters moving to Labour to those moving to Liberal Democrat (the larger the ratio, the greater the relative shift to Labour).

In all three cases, Table 6 shows that the ratios were on average much larger in the Conservative–Labour contests than in the Conservative–Liberal Democrat contests: where Labour was in second place it was a much greater net beneficiary of the inter-election flows than was the case where the Liberal Democrats were second in the 1992 estimated result. For the Labour–Conservative contests, where there may have been tactical voting by Conservative and Liberal Democrat supporters seeking to prevent a Labour victory, three similar ratios were computed:

• CD/DC;

• LC/LD; and

• NVC/NVD.

We conducted regression analyses to see if there were systematic variations in the relative volumes of flows, consistent with the general hypothesis that there should be more tactical voting where it has the greatest chance of success – in the more marginal constituencies. Eight independent variables are used: seven are defined above – Margin, LibDem target, LibDem council, By-election, ConSpend, LabSpend and LibDemSpend; the eighth is the ratio between the votes for Labour and Liberal Democrat in 1992 (for the contests against a Conservative incumbent) and that between the 1992 shares of Conservative and Liberal Democrat (where Labour is the incumbent).

The fitted regressions produce results consistent with expectations, with one major exception (see Table 7).[7] In the Conservative–Liberal Democrat contests, the closer the margin the larger the ratios, and hence the greater the net flows to Labour, although less so in the Liberal Democrat target seats: Labour benefited most from tactical voting (by dissident Conservatives, by previous non-voters, and by former Liberal Democrat supporters) the closer the contest in a seat. On the face of it, this seems rather counter-intuitive, with Labour doing better in seats where the Liberal Democrats were close behind the Conservative incumbent. However, flows to Labour in Conservative–Liberal Democrat seats were also higher where the ratio of Labour to Liberal Democrat share of the 1992 vote was larger (i.e. where Labour came a close third to the Liberal Democrats' second at the previous election). It seems, therefore, that even though Labour was not the obvious tactical choice, the party still benefited in 1997 where the Conservatives were being challenged strongly by the Liberal Democrats and where the Liberal Democrats themselves were being challenged strongly by Labour. The overall swing to Labour throughout the country was large enough to override the fine calculations of tactical voters in these circumstances. It is likely that, with Labour riding high in the opinion polls for many months before the election, many tactical voters' deliberations would take into account the possibility that Labour would overtake the Liberal Democrats in Conservative–LibDem marginals: in these circumstances, voting Labour in a Conservative–LibDem marginal may still have been a sensible tactical vote!

In the Conservative–Labour contests, on the other hand, margin was not significantly related to all three flow ratios. However, the greater the ratio of Labour's 1992 vote share to that of the Liberal Democrats (and hence the further Labour was ahead of the Liberal Democrats in the seat), the greater the flows of support to Labour in 1997, relative to flows to the Liberal Democrats.

The final block of regressions in Table 7 indicates that there was also tactical voting in Labour-held seats by those opposed to that party. Thus the closer the margin, the smaller the flow of Labour 'defectors' to the Conservatives rather than the Liberal Democrats and the larger the flow of former non-voters in the same direction, and also the smaller the flow from a

TABLE 7
REGRESSION ANALYSES OF TACTICAL VOTING CROSS-FLOW RATIOS

Conservative–Labour Contests

	DL/LD	CL/CD	NVL/NVD
Margin	-0.054	-0.010	-0.005
Lab/LibDem92	**-0.682**	**-0.118**	**-0.122**
LibDem target	-4.440	**-0.951**	**-1.011**
By-election	-0.646	-0.113	-0.071
LibDem council	-0.007	-0.122	-0.002
ConSpend	0.015	0.003	0.007
LabSpend	**0.055**	**0.012**	**0.004**
LibDemSpend	**-0.054**	**-0.010**	**-0.011**
Constant	**6.411**	**2.036**	**2.299**
R^2	*0.24*	*0.25*	*0.23*

Conservative–Liberal Democrat Contests

	DL/LD	CL/CD	NVL/NVD
Margin	**-0.066**	**-0.015**	**-0.024**
Lab/LibDem92	**1.871**	**0.546**	**0.920**
LibDem target	**-1.373**	**-0.374**	**-0.639**
By-election	0.545	0.008	0.013
LibDem council	-0.004	-0.002	-0.003
ConSpend	-0.003	-0.001	-0.002
LabSpend	**0.025**	**0.006**	**0.011**
LibDemSpend	**-0.058**	**-0.014**	**-0.023**
Constant	**6.056**	**1.930**	**3.250**
R^2	*0.51*	*0.57*	*0.57*

Labour–Conservative Contests

	CD/DC	LC/LD	NVC/NVD
Margin	**0.022**	**0.003**	**-0.012**
Con/LibDem92	**-0.221**	**0.043**	**0.147**
LibDem target	**2.161**	-0.129	-0.435
By-election	-0.203	0.057	0.194
LibDem council	-0.002	-0.009	0.001
ConSpend	0.001	0.003	0.002
LabSpend	0.001	0.001	-0.001
LibDemSpend	**0.013**	**-0.002**	**-0.007**
Constant	**1.758**	0.539	**1.820**
R^2	*0.41*	*0.41*	*0.41*

Note: Coefficients significant at the 0.05 level or better are in bold.

1992 Conservative vote to 1997 support for the Liberal Democrats, relative to flows in the opposite direction. In addition, Conservative candidates benefited more from those flows the more secure their second place relative to the third-placed candidate.

In all three groups of seats, local campaign spending by Labour and the Liberal Democrats helped encourage tactical shifts in their favour. In part, that is a function of whether the Liberal Democrats targeted a seat: where they did, they tended to benefit. But it is also a function of the general level of campaign spending in each seat. The more Labour spent in its local campaigns, the more votes it won from the Liberal Democrats, the Conservatives and previous non-voters in Conservative–Labour and Conservative–Liberal Democrat contests: Similarly, in all three groups of seats, the more the Liberal Democrats spent on their campaigns, the more votes they won from the Conservatives, Labour and previous non-voters.

Tactical voting was a significant element in the 1997 election, therefore. Where the Liberal Democrats campaigned strongly – in their target Conservative-held seats – they benefited substantially from it, especially if the Labour challenger was in a poor third place, and where Labour had a good chance of unseating the Tory incumbent (whether it was well-placed as the runner-up in 1992 or in third position relative to the Liberal Democrats) it too garnered significant numbers of tactical votes, as did Conservative candidates where they were running second to Labour incumbents.

The Final Equation

To explore the relative importance of the regional, inter-constituency and local scale variables, we have conducted final sets of regressions expanding on those in Table 5. After experimentation we included variables relating to:

- the local conditions in each seat;
- the five inter-constituency scale factors; and
- the regions.

Many were excluded as insignificant in all regressions, and Table 8 gives the final versions, showing the significant variables in each and including no variable that was not significant in any of the twelve. Compared to Table 5, most of the R^2 values are very substantially larger, especially for the change in Labour share of the vote.

The nature of the local contest was widely significant, indicating the importance of the local tactics of the two opposition parties in the election: the general pattern replicates that in Table 5. Local campaign spending in particular stands out as an important feature in the local geography of the vote.

But of particular interest are the inter-constituency and regional scale variables, indicating that the outcome had some broader geographical lineaments too. In the Conservative–Labour contests, for example, the pattern of change in the Labour vote was significantly related to three of the five factors. Finally, at the regional scale there was a considerable number of significant coefficients for the regions in two of the three contest types – the exceptions being in the seats defended by Labour (where the only regional patterns were in changes in Conservative vote). In the Conservative–Labour and Labour–Conservative contests, the Conservative vote held up relatively well (*ceteris paribus*) in a number of the 'northern' and Midlands regions, and Labour did relatively badly in some.

So Why Was It a Landslide?

So far, our attention has entirely focused on the pattern of voting in 1997. The outstanding features of the election outcome were not only the very substantial net change in support for the two main parties, however, but also the massive majority which Labour won, much greater than the Conservatives achieved when they had a similar percentage of the votes cast at each of the three previous contests. For Labour, the 1997 result produced a landslide in terms of seats won – a new geography.

Table 9 illustrates the extent of that landslide and the new geography of representation that resulted. Especially noteworthy is the changing pattern of Conservative membership of the House of Commons. After the 1992 election every one of the 22 regions returned at least one Conservative MP: after the 1997 election nine regions (including all five in Scotland and Wales) had no Conservative member. Within northern England, the Tories lost 36 of their 53 seats, including all nine in West Yorkshire and 9 of the 13 in the rest of the north-west (Lancashire and Cheshire other than Greater Manchester and Merseyside). The party now has only two MPs from the northern conurbations (both in Greater Manchester). In the three Midlands regions, too, the complement of Conservative MPs fell very sharply, from 62 to 28: it lost around one-quarter of its votes there, but some 55 per cent of its seats – a figure more than matched in Outer London, where its vote share fell from 49 to 34 (i.e. by 30 per cent) but its MPs from 35 to only 9 (a 75 per cent drop). Labour, as a consequence, substantially increased its representation in a number of regions – by over half in the rest of the west Midlands (outside the metropolitan county), the East Midlands, East Anglia and the whole of southern England except Inner London (where it already held 20 of the 27).

Why was the Labour performance in terms of votes so magnified in terms of seats? The first-past-the-post system is notoriously fickle in the allocation of seats relative to votes overall, and the biases within the system are very sensitive to the particular distribution of votes across the constituency template. They come about because of differences between constituencies in the number of electors, the proportion of the votes cast won by 'third' parties (and their success in converting them into seats), the proportion of the electorate who abstain, and the winning party's majority. In most post-war elections, and particularly after the periodic reviews conducted by the Boundary Commissions, these factors have tended to cancel each other out, but the 1997 election saw bias reach an unprecedented level.

Following Brookes (1960), we define bias as the additional number of seats which one party would have won rather than the other had it obtained the same

TABLE 8
THE FINAL REGRESSION EQUATIONS ON CHANGE IN PARTY SHARES OF VOTES AND IN
ABSTENTIONS

	Conservative– Labour seats				Conservative– Liberal Democrat seats			
	C	L	LD	A	C	L	LD	A
Margin	-0.07	–	0.10	–	-0.14	–	0.18	-0.05
By-election	-2.82	–	–	–	-3.97	–	5.64	–
Third/second	2.56	9.01	-14.67	–	–	–	–	–
LibDem council	–	–	–	–	–	-0.04	–	–
LibDem target	–	-7.75	7.80	–	–	-3.65	4.52	-1.08
ConSpend	0.04	–	–	–	–	–	–	–
LabSpend	-0.03	0.06	-0.04	-0.03	–	0.07	-0.05	-0.02
LibDemSpend	–	–	0.04	-0.02	-0.04	-0.09	0.14	–
Factor								
Financial	–	-0.82	1.14	–	–	-2.29	1.73	-1.15
Suburban	–	-0.91	0.62	–	–	–	1.33	–
Retirement	–	–	-0.52	–	–	–	–	–
Urban	-0.53	0.78	–	–	–	–	–	–
Coalfields	–	–	–	–	1.31	-1.60	–	–
Region								
Strathclyde	–	–	–	-3.87	–	–	–	–
EC Scotland	–	–	–	–	–	–	–	–
Rural Scotland	–	–	4.01	-4.19	–	–	–	–
Industrial NE	–	–	–	–	–	–	–	–
Rural north	–	–	–	–	–	–	–	–
Merseyside	–	2.98	–	-2.90	–	-8.84	10.59	–
Gtr Manchester	–	–	–	–	–	–	–	–
Rest of NW	1.88	–	–	–	4.63	–	–	–
W Yorks	3.09	-3.40	–	–	–	–	–	–
S Yorks	–	–	–	–	–	-11–35	15–73	–
Rural Wales	–	–	–	–	–	-10.43	–	-3.66
Ind Wales	3.28	-3.36	–	–	–	–	–	–
W Midlands C	2.99	-3.27	–	–	–	–	–	–
Rest W Mids	3.75	–	–	–	2.61	-3.88	–	–
East Midlands	–	-1.82	–	–	–	–	–	–
East Anglia	–	–	–	–	–	-2.62	–	–
South-west	–	–	–	–	–	-3.59	–	–
Wessex	2.54	–	–	–	2.02	–	–	-0.84
Inner London	3.02	-3.05	–	3.34	–	–	–	–
Outer London	–	2.14	-2.04	–	–	–	–	1.61
Outer met	–	–	–	–	–	–	–	–
Constant	-14.02	7.17	6.69	8.06	-9.59	20.46	-16.26	8.91
R^2	0.47	0.53	0.59	0.29	0.40	0.59	0.54	0.27

TABLE 8 (continued)

| | Labour–Conservative | | | |
	C	L	LD	A
Margin	0.14	-0.13	0.08	–
By-election	–	-2.57	-1.61	–
Third/Second	4.41	–	-7.11	–
LibDem Council	–	–	–	–
LibDem target	-5.27	–	4.55	–
ConSpend	0.04	-0.04	–	–
LabSpend	–	–	–	–
LibDemSpend	–	-0.03	0.04	–
Factor				
Financial	–	–	0.73	-0.85
Suburban	–	–	–	–
Retirement	–	–	–	–
Urban	–	–	1.36	–
Coalfields	–	0.60	-0.35	0.39
Region				
Strathclyde	–	–	–	–
EC Scotland	5.21	–	–	–
Rural Scotland	5.67	–	–	-7.35
Industrial NE	–	–	–	–
Rural North	–	–	–	–
Merseyside	–	–	–	–
Gtr Manchester	3.61	–	–	–
Rest of NW	3.57	–	–	–
W Yorks	5.05	–	–	–
S Yorks	–	–	–	–
Rural Wales	–	–	–	–
Ind Wales	–	–	–	–
W Midlands C	3.67	–	–	–
Rest W Mids	–	–	–	–
East Midlands	–	–	–	–
East Anglia	–	–	–	–
South-west	–	–	–	–
Wessex	–	–	–	–
Inner London	–	6.61	–	–
Outer London	–	7.81	–	–
Outer met	–	–	–	7.18
Constant	-20.15	11.59	1.68	5.66
R^2	*0.66*	*0.49*	*0.33*	*0.33*

TABLE 9
THE DISTRIBUTION OF SEATS WON BY PARTY AND REGION

	Conservative		Labour		Liberal Democrat		SNP/PC	
	92	97	92	97	92	97	92	97
Strathclyde	1	0	30	31	0	0	0	0
EC Scotland	2	0	16	17	0	1	0	0
Rural Scotland	7	0	5	8	8	9	3	6
Rural Wales	5	0	7	11	1	2	4	4
South Wales	2	0	21	23	0	0	0	0
Rural North	16	11	11	15	1	2	0	0
Industrial NE	3	0	24	27	0	0	0	0
Merseyside	4	0	12	15	0	1	0	0
Gtr Manchester	7	2	17	22	1	1	0	0
Rest of NW	13	4	15	24	0	0	0	0
W Yorkshire	9	0	14	23	0	0	0	0
S Yorkshire	1	0	14	14	0	1	0	0
W Midlands Con.	11	4	18	25	0	0	0	0
Rest W Midlands	22	10	7	18	0	1	0	0
E Midlands	29	14	14	29	0	0	0	0
East Anglia	19	14	3	8	0	0	0	0
South-west	12	5	1	4	3	7	0	0
Wessex	29	17	3	11	3	7	0	0
Outer south-east	52	31	2	16	0	7	0	0
Outer metropolitan	62	42	1	20	0	1	0	0
Outer London	35	9	12	33	0	5	0	0
Inner London	6	2	20	24	1	1	0	0

proportion of the national vote, assuming a uniform swing between the two main parties across all constituencies and no change in the performance of other parties or in the level of abstentions (Rossiter *et al.*, 1997b). At the time of the 1992 election there was a consistent and significant bias favouring the Labour party, when with a lead of some 7.6 per cent over Labour there was a net disadvantage to the Conservatives of 26 seats. Furthermore, the closer the parties came together – towards an equal share of the vote with 39 per cent each – the greater Labour's advantage; if a uniform swing across all constituencies had led to each party having 39 per cent of the votes cast, then Labour would have had a 38-seat advantage over its main opponent.

The redrawing of the constituency map in the Boundary Commissions' fourth periodic review changed the situation somewhat, and we have calculated the likely biases if the 1992 general election had been held in the new constituencies (using the estimation procedure described in Rossiter *et al.*, 1997a). Redistricting in Britain tends to favour the Conservative Party, primarily because it provides the opportunity to minimize that part of the bias arising from inequalities in constituency electorates, which reflect migration patterns away from the less affluent parts of the country. The fourth review was no exception and the pro-Labour bias in the system was reduced by around 15 seats (from 26 to 13 on a 7.6 percent Conservative lead and from 38 to 21 assuming equal vote shares).

Bias on this scale is commonplace, but the 1997 election transformed the situation: if Labour and Conservative vote shares had been reversed, following a uniform swing across all constituencies, then the latter would have won 68 fewer seats. Labour's advantage would have been even greater if the two parties had been closer together in the distribution of votes, again assuming a uniform swing: indeed, if they had obtained the same vote share Labour would have won 82 more seats than the Conservatives.

We can decompose these biases, in a modification of Brookes' method, to show why Labour benefited so much. We identify six main sources of bias:

- *Variations in constituency electorate size due to national quotas* – because constituencies are on average much smaller in Scotland and Wales than in England, the party that does better in the two former countries is likely to win more seats for the same number of votes than the one whose best performance is in England.
- *Variations in constituency electorate size within countries* – constituencies vary in size within each of the three countries, and the party which performs better in the smaller constituencies will again tend to win more seats for the same number of votes.
- *Abstentions* – the larger the number of abstentions in a constituency the smaller its effective size, thereby conferring an apparent advantage in seats on the party which wins where turnout is lower.
- *Minor party votes* – for similar reasons, the larger the number of votes cast for other 'third' parties, the lower the number of votes needed to win a constituency.
- *Minor party victories* – however, if minor parties succeed in polling enough votes to deprive a party of the seat, then the bias operates in the other direction.
- *Efficiency* – a party which has large numbers of 'wasted' votes in seats it does not win, or 'piles up' votes by amassing large majorities in the seats that it does win, tends to gain fewer seats relative to its proportion of the votes cast than one which wins by relatively small majorities in most cases – the latter's votes are more efficiently distributed.

Table 10 shows these biases for the actual 1992 election results, the 1992 results had the election been fought with the same seats as 1997, and the actual 1997 election results, comparing the biases under the actual result with what would have happened if the Conservatives and Labour had achieved the same percentage of the votes cast. The clear message from these data is that Labour has gained very substantially between 1992 and 1997. It continues to benefit from the smaller seats in Scotland and Wales and, although the

TABLE 10
DECOMPOSING THE SOURCES OF BIAS IN THE ELECTORAL SYSTEM

	1992 result	1992 in 1997 constituencies	1997 result
Actual result			
Type of bias			
National quotas	12	13	11
Intra-national variations	28	4	13
Abstentions	19	21	25
Minor party votes	-28	-28	-33
Minor party victories	12	10	20
Efficiency	-12	-3	42
Total	26	13	68
Result if Conservative and Labour had equal vote shares			
Type of bias			
National quotas	12	13	11
Intra-national variations	29	4	13
Abstentions	19	21	24
Minor party votes	-30	-30	-36
Minor party victories	20	18	33
Efficiency	-7	0	48
Total	38	21	82

Note: A positive value indicates a bias towards Labour; a negative value indicates a bias towards Conservative. Total bias does not simply equal the sum of the individual elements because of interactions between them.

substantial advantage from being strong in the smaller (mainly inner city) constituencies was largely removed by the Boundary Commissions' redistricting exercise (Johnston *et al.*, 1996), this has been partially reversed by subsequent population movements. Labour also continues to benefit from differential rates of turnout, while the historic advantage accruing to the Conservatives from the large number of 'wasted' minor party votes has been significantly reduced by the greater success of those parties in securing enough votes to achieve victory. The big shift, however, is in the efficiency factor. A slight Conservative bias of three seats in 1992 has been transformed into a pro-Labour bias of 42 in 1997. Labour did not continue to build up large majorities in its safe seats, nor did it win lots of votes in Conservative safe seats. Rather, Labour increased its vote enough to win seats in the places where it mattered most.

The implication of these calculations is that the electoral system is now massively biased in Labour's favour. But the calculations assume uniform swing, an assumption which, as we have already seen, was not realized in 1997. Clearly, if the Conservatives were able exactly to reverse the swing in each constituency, then the efficiency element of bias would all but be eliminated. Nevertheless these figures are extremely significant and two interpretations are possible. First, it may be that the Conservatives have indeed suffered a long-term reverse in a large number of hitherto marginal seats. Under this scenario, the pro-Labour bias in the electoral system is real and it may take many years before seats such as Brighton Pavilion and Basildon, now apparently 'safe' Labour seats with majorities over 25 per cent, revert to the Conservative fold. Alternatively, it may be that the increasing attention paid to target seats has produced a greater volatility in their electorates. Under this interpretation the unprecedented scale of bias largely reflects a change in the 'rules of the game' resulting from Labour's targeted campaign in 1997 (plus the parallel campaign by the Liberal Democrats). Establishing the correct interpretation is a task for future research – and elections – but what is clear is that the local geography of Labour's campaign success in 1997 was crucial to its overall goal of not only winning more votes but also winning many more seats and escaping from its northern and inner-city ghettos into which it had retreated in the face of Thatcherism during the 1980s. It has now forced the Tories into a similar ghetto, in England's suburbia and rural areas, and it will take a substantial targeted campaign for it to escape from those areas in 2002 and 2007.

Conclusions

The 1997 general election produced one of the largest landslides in twentieth-century British politics. But it was built on the existing foundations of the country's electoral geography. Labour's success did not change basic underlying patterns at either the regional or the inter-constituency scale. The relative topography of the national electoral map did not change, though the baseline did. To that extent, the 1997 general election was fought on, and left behind, the same electoral terrain as previous contests.

Clearly, however, while the relative topography of the electoral map remained as before, the absolute topography changed substantially. Our analyses show that local scale variations in how the parties campaigned and in how voters responded to particular electoral conditions played an important part in creating the detail of the new electoral map. The Liberal Democrats' seat-targeting efforts paid off handsomely, for instance, giving them their best ever representation in Parliament (and the best representation for a third party since before the Second World War), even though their overall share of the vote fell slightly. But even where seats were not targeted, effective local campaigns (especially by Labour and the Liberal Democrats where they were the challengers) brought dividends in 1997.

Part of the impact of local campaigns by opposition parties seems to have been to encourage another source of local scale variations, tactical voting. Many voters in 1997 clearly wanted to unseat members of the governing Conservative party, and were willing to vote for the opposition candidate best placed to do so – with sometimes spectacular effect (as in the defeat of Michael Portillo, Secretary of State for Defence, in Enfield Southgate). To reiterate, the local geography of the election (both in terms of the opposition parties' campaigns and of voters' actions to unseat Conservative MPs) was crucial to the scale of New Labour's victory, and to the depth of the Conservatives' defeat.

The hill that the Conservative party needs to climb in order to win next time is high and steep. As our analysis of electoral bias shows, Labour now enjoys a large advantage as a result of the workings of the first-past-the-post system. It remains the case, however, that the New Labour landslide was built on the same old electoral geography.

ACKNOWLEDGEMENTS

Much of the work for this article was funded by the ESRC (grant numbers R 000 22 2170 and H 304 25 3001) and this is gratefully acknowledged: some of the data were obtained from the Data Archive at the University of Essex. All census data are Crown Copyright.

NOTES

1. All of our analyses exclude two constituencies: Tatton, where the Labour and Liberal Democrat candidates withdrew and the incumbent Conservative lost to an independent fighting on an 'anti-sleaze' ticket; and West Bromwich West, where the incumbent Speaker was not opposed by any major-party candidate. The boundaries of most constituencies were changed between 1992 and 1997 as a result of the Boundary Commissions' fourth periodic reviews. To measure change between the two elections, therefore, we have estimated what the result would have been in the new constituencies if they had been used for the 1992 contest, using a regression-based model incorporating regional-, inter-constituency- and local-scale variables (Rossiter *et al.*, 1997a). Though different from those produced for BBC/ITN/PA (Rallings and Thrasher, 1995), they are at least as reliable as a basis for assessing inter-election change (see Curtice and Steed, 1997).
2. Because the Census is only taken on a decennial basis, we have to assume that the relative values of the 12 independent variables remain constant across the 639 constituencies.
3. At the time of writing, we had data on campaign spending for 572 constituencies: the following analyses are restricted to this set unless stated otherwise.
4. Labour's targets included most of the marginal seats in which the party was the challenger. Hence we have not included a dummy variable for Labour target (since it would be strongly related to marginality).
5. Where there were two tiers of local government in a locality, we used the smaller scale.
6. The constituency flow-of-the-vote matrices were estimated using the well-tried entropy-maximizing procedure (see Johnston, 1985; for more details on the 1992–97 matrix, see Johnston *et al.*, 1997).
7. Because we are using data on campaign spending, our analyses are restricted to the 572 constituencies for which these are currently available.

REFERENCES

Bogdanor, V. (1983) *Multi-Party Politics and the Constitution*. Cambridge: Cambridge University Press.

Brookes, R.H. (1960) 'The analysis of distorted representation in two party, single member elections', *Political Science* 12: 158–67.

Curtice, J. and M. Steed (1982) 'Electoral choice and the production of government', *British Journal of Political Science* 12: 249–98.

Curtice, J. and M. Steed (1997) 'The results analysed', in D. Butler and D. Kavanagh (eds) *The British General Election of 1997*, pp.295–326. London: Macmillan.

Denver, D. and G. Hands (1997) *Modern Constituency Electioneering: Local Campaigning in the 1992 General Election*. London and Portland OR: Frank Cass.

Johnston, R J. (1983) 'Spatial continuity and individual variability', *Electoral Studies* 2: 53–68.

Johnston, R.J. (1985) *The Geography of English Politics: the 1983 General Election*. London: Croom Helm.

Johnston, R.J. (1991) *A Question of Place? Exploring the Practice of Human Geography*. Oxford: Blackwell Publishers.

Johnston, R.J. and C.J. Pattie (1991) 'Tactical voting in Great Britain in 1983 and 1987: an alternative approach', *British Journal of Political Science* 21: 95–108.

Johnston, R.J. and C.J. Pattie (1997a) 'The region is not dead: long live the region. Personal evaluations and voting at the 1992 British General Election', *Space and Polity* 1: 103–13.

Johnston, R.J. and C.J. Pattie (1997b) 'Uneven development and political behaviour: an analysis of regional variations in British public opinion in the mid-1990s', *European Urban and Regional Studies* 4: 347–64.

Johnston, R.J. and C.J. Pattie (1998) 'Feeling good and changing one's mind: longitudinal investigations of voters' economic evaluations and partisan choices', *Party Politics*, forthcoming.

Johnston, R.J., C.J. Pattie, and J.G. Allsopp (1988) *A Nation Dividing? The Electoral Map of Great Britain 1979–1987*. London: Longman.

Johnston, R.J., D.J. Rossiter, and C.J. Pattie (1996) 'How well did they do? The Boundary Commissions at the Third and Fourth Periodic Reviews', in I. McLean and D. Butler (eds) *Fixing the Boundaries: Defining and Redefining Single-Member Electoral Districts*. Aldershot: Dartmouth.

Johnston, R.J., C.J. Pattie, D.J. Rossiter, I. MacAllister, D. Dorling, and H. Tunstall (1997) 'Spatial variations in voter choice: modelling tactical voting at the 1992 General Election in Great Britain', *Geographical and Environmental Modelling* 1: 153–77.

Jones, K.,R.J. Johnston, and C.J. Pattie (1992) 'People, places and regions: exploring the use of multi-level modelling in the analysis of electoral data', *British Journal of Political Science* 22: 343–80.

Kellner, P. (1996) *Can the Feelgood Factor Save the Tories?* London: UBS Ltd.

Key, V.O. Jr. (1955) 'A theory of critical elections', *Journal of Politics* 17: 3–18.

McAllister, I. and D.T. Studlar (1992) 'Region and voting in Britain, 1979–1987: territorial polarization or artifact?', *American Journal of Political Science* 36: 168–99.

Miller, W. L. (1977) *Electoral Dynamics*. London: Macmillan.

Miller, W.L., G. Raab, and K. Britto (1974) 'Voting research and the population census 1918–1971: surrogate data for constituency analyses', *Journal of the Royal Statistical Society A* 137: 384–411.

Pattie, C.J., E.A. Fieldhouse, and R.J. Johnston (1993) 'Plus ça change: the changing electoral geography of Great Britain, 1979–1992', in D. Denver, P. Norris, D. Broughton and C. Rallings (eds) *British Elections and Parties Yearbook 1993*, pp. 85–99. London: Harvester Wheatsheaf.

Pattie, C.J., E.A. Fieldhouse, and R.J. Johnston (1994) 'The price of conscience: the electoral correlates and consequences of free votes and rebellions in the British House of Commons, 1987–1992', *British Journal of Political Science* 24: 359–80.

Pattie, C.J. and R.J. Johnston (1995) 'It's not like that round here: region, economic evaluations and voting at the 1992 British general election', *European Journal of Political Research* 28:

1–32.

Pattie, C.J. and R.J. Johnston (1998) 'The role of regional context in voting: evidence from the 1992 British General Election', *Regional Studies*, forthcoming.

Pattie, C.J., R.J. Johnston, and E.A. Fieldhouse (1995) 'Winning the local vote: the effectiveness of campaign spending in Great Britain, 1983–1992', *American Political Science Review* 89: 969–86.

Pattie C.J., P.F. Whiteley, R.J. Johnston, and P. Seyd (1994) 'Measuring local campaign effects: Labour party constituency campaigning at the 1987 General Election', *Political Studies* 42: 469–79.

Price, S. and D. Sanders (1995) 'Economic expectations and voting intentions in the UK, 1979–1987: a pooled cross-section approach', *Political Studies* 43: 451–71.

Rallings, C. and M. Thrasher (1995) *Media Guide to the New Parliamentary Constituencies.* London: Press Association.

Rossiter, D.J., R.J. Johnston, and C.J. Pattie (1997a) 'Estimating the partisan impact of redistricting in Great Britain', *British Journal of Political Science* 27: 319–31.

Rossiter, D.J., R.J. Johnston, and C.J. Pattie (1997b) 'Redistricting and electoral bias in Great Britain', *British Journal of Political Science* 27: 466–72.

Russell, A.T., C.J. Pattie, and R.J. Johnston (1996) 'Partisan preferences, regional patterns and the 1992 and 1997 general elections in Great Britain', *Environment and Planning A* 28: 191–8.

Sanders, D. (1994) 'Economic influences on the vote: modelling electoral decisions', in I. Budge and D. McKay (eds) *Developing Democracy,* pp.79–98. London: Sage.

Sanders, D., H. Ward, and D. Marsh (1987) 'Government popularity and the Falklands War: a reassessment', *British Journal of Political Science* 17: 281–313.

Seyd, P. and P. Whiteley (1992) *Labour's Grass Roots: The Politics of Party Membership.* Oxford: Clarendon Press.

Taylor, P.J. and R.J. Johnston (1979) *Geography of Elections.* London: Penguin Books.

New Labour, New Tactical Voting?
The Causes and Consequences of
Tactical Voting in the 1997 General Election

Geoffrey Evans, John Curtice and Pippa Norris

The outcome of the 1997 election broke a number of records. More Labour MPs (419 including the Speaker) were elected than ever before, surpassing even the party's victory in 1945. More Liberal Democrat MPs (46) were elected than at any time since 1929, more than doubling their numbers compared with 1992 and giving the party the kind of breakthrough of which the former SDP/Liberal Alliance had dreamed. Meanwhile the Conservatives were left with fewer seats (165) than at any time since the Liberal landslide of 1906.

Yet if we look at the outcome in terms of votes the performance of neither Labour nor the Liberal Democrats was at all historic. At 44.4 per cent, Labour's share of the vote was lower than at any election between 1945 and 1966. Its lead over the Conservatives was less than that secured by the Conservatives themselves over Labour in 1983. Meanwhile, the Liberal Democrats suffered their third successive drop in support. At 17.2 per cent, their performance was the second worst since the party resumed fighting elections on a nation-wide basis in 1974.

Evidently the Labour landslide and Liberal Democrat revival of 1997 were as much a product of the operation of the single-member plurality electoral system as an indicator of the strength of their electoral support. Had the movement of votes since 1992 been uniform across the country as a whole, Labour would have secured a majority of 131 rather than 179. The Liberal Democrats, meanwhile, would have won just 28 seats rather than 46, leaving the Conservatives with no fewer than 208 seats rather than 165. One reason for this divergence appears to have been the degree of tactical (otherwise known as strategic) voting. A significant number of voters appear to have been willing to support whichever of the main opposition parties was best able to defeat the local Conservative.

Tactical voting between Labour and the Liberal Democrats is therefore central to understanding and explaining the outcome of the 1997 general election. Moreover, the analysis of tactical voting has significant implications for our understanding of theories of voter choice and party strategy, in Britain and elsewhere. This article therefore sets about two tasks. First, it establishes whether there was any change in tactical voting between 1992 and 1997 by examining both the pattern of constituency election results and individual-level survey data from the 1997 British Election Study. In particular, we assess whether these two very different sources confirm that there was an increase in the amount of tactical switching between Labour and the Liberal Democrats. Second, we consider what might account for any observed changes by evaluating the plausibility of several theories of tactical voting – theories which emphasize the importance of changes in the motivation of voters, party mobilization, the information environment, and party competition respectively. We conclude by considering briefly some of the implications of our findings.

Data

This article draws primarily on two distinct sources of information. The first is analysis of the election results at constituency level. This allows us to assess the apparent incidence of tactical voting, taking into account the variable electoral geography of Britain. The second is analysis of individual-level survey data from the 1997 British Election Cross-section Study. This allows us to examine voters' own reports of having voted tactically rather than simply inferring its existence from constituency-level patterns. This survey is the largest and most representative of a number of studies conducted as part of the 1997 British Election Study (BES) and is therefore the one best-suited for examining a relatively rare phenomenon (see Galbraith and Rae, 1989; Heath *et al.*, 1991; Johnston and Pattie, 1991; Evans, 1994) such as tactical voting.

The British Election Cross-section Study interviewed a random sample of 3,615 respondents throughout Great Britain, including 882 respondents in Scotland, an over-sampling designed to make it possible to analyse the distinct political situation there. This represented a response rate of 62 per cent. The interviews, conducted face-to-face using computer-assisted interviewing, lasted one hour on average; in addition 85 per cent of respondents completed a self-completion supplement of 20 minutes' length. Approximately 90 per cent of the fieldwork was completed within six weeks or so of the election. The results in this article are based on a provisional weighting of the data which, *inter alia*, downweights Scottish respondents so that they form the same proportion of the sample as they do of the electorate.

The Incidence of Tactical Voting in 1997

The first indication of the incidence of tactical voting in 1997 that we examine is the pattern of the constituency results.[1] Table 1 analyses the average change in party support between 1992 and 1997 according to the tactical situation in

TABLE 1
CHANGE IN SUPPORT (%) BY TACTICAL SITUATION

Tactical Situation	Con	Lab	LibDem	N
Lab seats; Con > 33.3%	-12.6	+ 9.6	- 0.3	(107)
Con-Lab seats	-12.6	+13.0	- 3.0	(181)
LibDem seats; Con > 33.3%	-10.6	+ 9.6	+1.6	(8)
Con-LibDem; Con lead < 30%	-11.8	+ 6.5	+1.9	(80)
Con-LibDem; Con lead > 30%	-13.5	+10.0	- 0.8	(60)
Three-way marginals	-11.6	+10.9	- 2.3	(18)

Source: Curtice and Steed (1997)

a constituency.[2] It strongly suggests that anti-Conservative tactical voting occurred on a significant scale. The table distinguishes six situations:

• *Lab-Con safe seats.* Seats where Labour were first and the Conservatives second in 1992, but where the Conservatives won at least a third of the vote in 1992. This is, in effect, our control group against which we compare what happened in other situations. Given both the result in these seats in 1992 and the evidence of the opinion polls that Labour was well ahead nationally, there was little reason to doubt that Labour would win locally again in 1997, and thus little reason why people should vote tactically. We exclude from this group those seats where the Conservatives won less than a third of the vote in 1992 because Conservative support systematically fell by less than the national average where they had previously polled below that threshold (Curtice and Steed, 1997).

• *Con-Lab seats.* Constituencies where the Conservatives were first and Labour second in 1992. These are seats where voters who were concerned to ensure the defeat of the local Conservative would have reason to support Labour rather than the Liberal Democrats.

• *LibDem-Con seats.* Constituencies where the Liberal Democrats were first and the Conservatives were second in 1992, and where the Conservatives won more than a third of the vote. Although these seats were already in Liberal Democrat hands, given that the polls put Liberal Democrat support nationally lower than it was in 1992, Labour supporters in these constituencies might feel they needed to vote Liberal Democrat in order to keep the Conservatives out.

• *Con-LibDem marginals.* Seats where the Conservatives were first and the Liberal Democrats second in 1992, and where the Liberal Democrats were both more than six per cent ahead of Labour and less than 30 per cent behind the Conservatives.

• *Con-LibDem safe seats.* Seats where the Conservatives were first and the

Liberal Democrats second in 1992, but where the Liberal Democrats were
more than 30 per cent behind the Conservatives.
• *Three-way marginals.* Seats where the Conservatives were first and the
Liberal Democrats second in 1992, but where Labour were less than six per
cent behind the Liberal Democrats and less than 36 per cent behind the
Conservatives. These were in effect 'three-way marginals' where both
opposition parties might claim to be better able to defeat the Conservatives.

We therefore make three distinctions among those seats where the
Conservatives were first and the Liberal Democrats second in 1992. Given the
position of Labour and the Liberal Democrats in the polls, people in these
constituencies may not have been convinced that a vote for the Liberal
Democrats was an effective means of defeating the Conservatives if the
Liberal Democrats were starting off a long way behind or if Labour were also
in close contention.

These different tactical situations exhibited very different patterns of party
performance. Consider, first, those seats where the Conservatives started off
first with Labour second. Labour's vote rose on average by over three points
more in these seats than in those seats where they were already first.
Meanwhile the Liberal Democrat vote fell by nearly three points more. It
would appear that in seats where Labour started second to the Conservatives,
around three per cent of those who turned out to vote opted for Labour rather
than the Liberal Democrats because they wanted to try to ensure the defeat of
the local Conservative.

Meanwhile, we see the very opposite pattern in those seats where the
Liberal Democrats were second to the Conservatives and less than 30 per cent
behind. Here the Liberal Democrat vote rose by two points against the
national trend, while Labour's vote rose by three points less than where it
started first. In these seats it looks as though around two to three per cent of
voters opted for the Liberal Democrats rather than Labour in order to try and
defeat the Conservatives. This was most evident where the Liberal Democrats
started off less than 15 per cent behind the Conservatives; in these seats the
Liberal Democrat vote rose almost everywhere. In contrast, where the lead
was between 15 per cent and 30 per cent their performance was more patchy.
And where the Liberal Democrats were even further behind or where Labour
were also in close contention, voters evidently did not see much reason to
make a tactical switch to the Liberal Democrats. Indeed in a number of three-
way marginals Labour seem to have been the beneficiaries of tactical
switching. Overall, it looks as though voters needed rather more persuasion
about the value of making a tactical switch to the Liberal Democrats than
simply the claim that they were in second place last time.

Because it looks at how votes changed between 1992 and 1997, this form
of analysis can only hope to identify apparent evidence of *new* tactical voting,

that is the decisions of voters to vote tactically who did not do so at the previous election. Of course there may also be voters who voted tactically in 1992, or even earlier, and who continued to do so in 1997. Even so, at first glance this analysis appears to suggest that such new tactical voting was widespread in 1997. Yet we should be careful. Even within those constituencies where conditions evidently facilitated tactical voting we have found that only two to three per cent of voters acted were new tactical voters. And these constituencies themselves constitute only around a third of the total number of 641 seats (see the entries in brackets in Table 1). Thus in practice these results imply that only little more than one per cent of all voters voted tactically in 1997, having not done so in 1992. In addition, we should remember that some of the switching from Liberal Democrat to Labour in Con-Lab seats in Table 1 may arise from the decisions of Labour supporters to stop casting a tactical vote for the Liberal Democrats because their preferred party had regained second place in 1992. The only significant net increase in tactical voting that is necessarily implied by Table 1 is in switching from Liberal Democrat to Labour.

Is this confirmed by our survey results? Here our estimates of tactical voting will include those who may already have voted tactically in 1992 and decided to continue doing so in 1997. In order to establish whether the data confirm our expectations from Table 1 we need to compare the results obtained by the 1997 cross-section survey with similar figures obtained in 1992. The main indicator of tactical voting in the BES series is a question which has been asked as part of the cross-section election study at each of the last four elections. It asks:

Which one of the reasons on this card comes closest to the main reason you voted for the Party you chose?
I always vote that way.
I thought it was the best party.
I really preferred another party but it had no chance of winning in this constituency.
Other (Please specify).

Voters are classified as 'tactical' if they choose the response '*I really preferred another party but it had no chance of winning in this constituency'*. They are then asked which party they 'really preferred', allowing us, using information on how they actually voted, to identify the direction of their tactical switch. Using this measure of tactical voting we find that in 1997 approximately ten per cent of voters can be coded as tactical, compared with nine per cent in 1992.[3] This is the highest level of reported tactical voting since the question was first asked in 1983 (Evans, 1994; Heath *et al.*, 1991).

Even so, the increase in reported tactical voting is no more (and no less) than the small one percentage point increase that we anticipated. Has the pattern of tactical voting also changed in line with our expectations? Do we find that more people switched between Labour and the Liberal Democrats? Table 2 shows the proportion of voters in both the 1997 BES cross-section study sample and the equivalent 1992 sample who said that they had voted tactically, broken down by the kind of switch that they made.[4] Comparing the two parts of the table, we can see that reported switching between Labour and the Liberal Democrats was higher in 1997 than in 1992. In 1992 only 1.5 per cent of voters reported making a tactical switch from the Liberal Democrats to Labour; in 1997 no less than 2.2 per cent did so. Similarly, the proportion saying they switched from Labour to the Liberal Democrats rose from two per cent in 1992 to 2.5 per cent in 1997. So, altogether, in 1997 1.2 per cent more voters reported switching between Labour and the Liberal Democrats than did so in 1992, again close to the estimate of one per cent more which we derived from the election results themselves.

TABLE 2
REPORTED TACTICAL VOTING IN 1992 AND 1997

(a) Preferred party and actual votes of tactical voters 1992
(% of voters)

	Con	Lab	LibDem	Other	All
			Actual vote		
Preferred party					
Con	–	*	0.7	*	1.3
Lab	*	–	2.0	*	2.3
LibDem	1.8	1.5	–	*	3.4
Other	*	*	*	–	0.8
All	2.1	2.3	2.9	0.4	7.7

(b) Preferred party and actual votes of tactical voters 1997
(% of voters)

	Con	Lab	LibDem	Other	All
			Actual vote		
Preferred party					
Con	–	*	0.5	*	1.0
Lab	*	–	2.5	*	2.8
LibDem	1.3	2.2	v	*	3.5
Other	*	0.9	*	–	1.4
All	1.8	3.4	3.2	0.3	8.7

Source: BES surveys
Note: * indicates less than 0.5 per cent.

The rise in Labour/Liberal Democrat switching is more than enough to account for the total reported rise in tactical voting between 1992 and 1997. Other kinds of tactical voting did not increase. Indeed anti-Labour tactical switching clearly declined. In 1997, only 1.8 per cent reported switching in one direction or the other between the Conservatives and the Liberal Democrats compared with 2.5 per cent in 1992.[5] Thus our two very different sources of evidence agree that there was a small rise in anti-Conservative tactical voting in 1997 compared with 1992 while other forms of tactical voting became, if anything, less common. On their own, both kinds of evidence may have their limitations; but the correspondence between their findings suggests that these limitations are not obscuring the truth. In 1997 tactical voting both became more common and changed its character.

The number of voters engaged in tactical voting is still small. They matter not because of their numbers but because of their impact. Curtice and Steed (1997) estimate that at least 25 and perhaps as many as 35 seats were lost by the Conservatives as a result of new tactical voting. Using a different method of estimation, Norris (1997a) suggests a very similar figure of 24. The two estimates are not only close to each other, but are far higher than those that have been made for the impact of tactical voting in previous general elections (see Curtice and Steed, 1992; Crewe *et al.*, 1992). Without tactical voting Labour would clearly still have won a decisive majority, but the strength of the Liberal Democrat parliamentary party would have been much reduced, and the Conservatives would have been significantly stronger. (Ironically, as Table 2 shows, the Conservatives continued to be net beneficiaries of tactical voting in terms of votes; but thanks to its geographical distribution they were clearly losers in terms of seats.) The 1997 British election clearly demonstrates how under the single-member plurality system, tactical switching by a very small number of strategically placed voters can have a very big impact on the outcome in seats.

Explaining the Rise of Tactical Voting

There are four possible explanations for this important development in British electoral behaviour. They emphasize the importance of changes in the motivation of voters, party mobilization, the information environment, and party competition respectively.

Changes in Voters?

Could it be that voters have simply become more willing to vote tactically? If people vote tactically, it suggests they are concerned instrumentally about the outcome in seats, and are willing and able to engage in a rational calculus to ascertain what might be the best way of achieving the outcome that they desire (Cain, 1978; Cox, 1997). Thus an increase in the incidence of tactical voting has been interpreted as evidence that people have become more rational and less influenced by partisan loyalties than they were in the days of *The American Voter* (Campbell *et al.,* 1960) or *Political Change in Britain* (Butler and Stokes, 1974). Why should voters have become more rational? The most commonly proffered explanations have been rising levels of education and the expansion of mass communications, which together have supposedly led to the growth of an informed, participant citizenry (Dalton, 1996; Inglehart, 1997). Such citizens are thought to be more willing and better able to make the calculations needed to act strategically.

If this process accounted for changes since 1992, however, then we should expect to find a general increase in tactical voting *of all kinds* – between Liberal Democrat and Conservative as well as between Liberal Democrat and Labour. But as we have seen this was not what happened. Only a very specific form of tactical voting was more prevalent in 1997, that is switching between Labour and the Liberal Democrats. This suggests that we need to look at the context in which voters made their decision in 1997 rather than at the motivations that they brought to the ballot box.

Changes in the Information Environment?

Alternatively, what may have altered in 1997 is the information available to voters about the strategic situation in their constituency. One potentially important piece of information provided by the media consists of the results of opinion polls. The 1980s saw national opinion polling reach saturation levels, while polls conducted in individual constituencies also became common. However, thanks to doubts about the accuracy of opinion polls, especially after the debacle of the 1992 election (Market Research Society, 1994), fewer polls were commissioned in 1997 than previously. Despite the campaign being a record six weeks in length, only 43 national polls were published compared with 57 in 1992 (Crewe, 1997). Moreover these polls were given less prominence when they were reported. Meanwhile, the publication of local opinion polls had already peaked in 1987 when at least 78 single constituency polls in 52 seats were commissioned. In 1997 in contrast only about 29 single constituency polls were conducted in 26 seats. There is, then, little reason to believe that voters were better informed by the opinion polls in 1997 than previously.[6]

Increased Mobilization?

But we should remember that political parties can also try to inform voters of the local tactical situation in their campaigning. And recent academic research has suggested that constituency campaigning may have a greater influence on electoral outcomes than had hitherto been appreciated (Denver and Hands, 1997; Pattie *et al.*, 1994, 1995). There is evidence that in the 1997 campaign both Labour and the Liberal Democrats prioritized, professionalized and centralized their strategic attempts to gain swing voters in marginal seats to a greater extent than ever before. For two years before polling day a Labour task force was designed to switch 5,000 voters in each of 90 target marginal seats. Those identified as potential Labour converts were contacted by teams of volunteers on the doorstep and by canvassing run from twenty telephone banks around the country, co-ordinated from Labour headquarters at Millbank Tower. The Liberal Democrats also concentrated their campaigning resources on their target seats to a greater extent than previously (Norris, 1997b). One of the features of this targeted campaigning was the highlighting in campaign literature and elsewhere of claims about the likely outcome for different parties. Thus we might anticipate that certain forms of tactical voting might have become more common in 1997 because parties themselves had made greater attempts to stimulate it. If the efforts associated with Labour and Liberal Democrat targeting proved effective, we would anticipate that more people should have voted tactically in the targeted constituencies than elsewhere. However, the evidence is decidedly mixed.

Targeting does appear to have encouraged tactical voting for the Liberal Democrats. Among those seats where the Liberal Democrats started within 30 per cent of the Conservatives, the Liberal Democrat vote rose by four per cent in those seats which it targeted, but fell by 2.3 per cent where it did not. Labour's vote meanwhile rose by only 4.4 per cent in seats that the Liberal Democrats targeted compared with 11 per cent elsewhere.[7]

But in Labour's case targeting does not appear to have stimulated a higher level of tactical voting – or indeed had any discernible impact at all. Table 3 compares Labour's performance in those of its target seats where the party started off second to the Conservatives with its performance in those places where it started off second but which it did not target. The analysis is undertaken separately for London, the rest of the south-east and the remainder of the country in order to take account of the generally higher swing against the Conservative government in London and the south-east. As can be seen,

TABLE 3
THE NON-IMPACT OF LABOUR TARGETING

Change in % voting Labour in:

	Target seats	Non-target seats
London	+15.9 (7)	+14.6 (26)
Rest of south-east	+13.7 (12)	+14.2 (29)
Elsewhere	+11.8 (53)	+12.3 (54)

Source: Curtice and Steed (1997).
Note: Table confined to those seats where Conservatives were first and Labour second.

Labour's performance in its target seats was little different from what happened in non-targeted seats. Voters apparently did not need mobilizing locally to be persuaded to vote tactically for Labour.

Moreover, if access to information was important in explaining the incidence of tactical voting in 1997, one might anticipate that more voters would have been inclined to vote tactically at the end of the election campaign than at the beginning. After all, election campaigns are the time above all when parties attempt to impart information to voters. Yet the evidence from another part of the 1997 BES, that of a panel of voters interviewed during the course of the campaign as well as afterwards and known as the British Election Campaign Panel Study, fails to support this expectation. The proportion of the panel saying that they were likely to vote tactically when they were first interviewed during the election campaign was, at 9.7 per cent, almost exactly the same proportion who eventually did so. Equally, there is no sign either of any increase during the course of the campaign in the willingness of Liberal Democrat voters in particular to make a tactical switch to Labour.

Changes in Party Competition?

The final possible explanation is that the rise in anti-Conservative tactical voting reflects changes in the appeal of the parties, in turn reflecting changes in their ideological positioning or their perceived competence. Previous research has suggested that people are most inclined to vote tactically if they strongly dislike one party while being relatively indifferent between the remainder (Heath et al., 1991; Niemi et al., 1992). This suggests that tactical voting might become more common either because electors become heavily disillusioned with one party and/or because they come to believe that there is little to choose between the remainder.

There is good reason to believe that this may have been the case in 1997. The outgoing Conservative government had, after all, been the most unpopular government in the history of opinion polling in Britain and it entered the election still in the electoral doldrums (Norris, 1997a). Meanwhile, the two main opposition parties had moved closer together ideologically. Labour had come to endorse a wide range of constitutional changes, many of which had been long-standing Liberal Democrat policy. At the same time, under the leadership of John Smith and Tony Blair, 'New Labour' shifted towards the centre on many social and economic issues (Smith and Spear, 1992; Norris 1997c), abandoning the old Clause 4 and ruling out any increase in income tax rates to finance increased social spending. Indeed, if anything the latter policy put them to the right of the Liberal Democrats who, as in 1992, advocated increasing income tax in order to spend more on education. Meanwhile, Labour's stance was echoed by the

Liberal Democrats. Ashdown moved his party from an official position of 'equidistance' between Conservative and Labour to one which ruled out the possibility of supporting a minority Conservative government while leaving open the possibility of a deal with Labour. Moreover, just before the election Labour and the Liberal Democrats concluded a formal agreement on how best to implement the wide range of constitutional changes that they now both favoured. In short, there is every reason to anticipate that many voters will have come to the conclusion that there was little to choose between the two opposition parties, while there was an awful lot to choose between either of them and the Conservatives.[8]

Our survey evidence certainly suggests that is precisely what happened. In both 1992 and 1997 we asked our respondents how much they were in favour of or against each of the main parties. As we can see from Table 4, the results obtained in 1997 were very different from those obtained five years earlier.

TABLE 4
FEELINGS SCALES BY PARTY PREFERENCE IN 1992 AND 1997

| | | | *Rating of :* | |
		Con	Lab	LibDem
Con supporters	1992	4.30	1.86	2.94
	1997	4.00	2.56	2.92
Lab supporters	1992	1.94	4.30	3.06
	1997	1.90	4.40	3.38
LibDem supporters	1992	2.74	2.61	4.18
	1997	2.37	3.28	4.19
All	1992	3.07	2.90	3.15
	1997	2.60	3.62	3.38

Source: BES surveys

Note: The table shows the average score given to the party named at the top of each column on a scale ranging from 1 (strongly against) to 5 (strongly in favour). A Conservative supporter is someone who either did not vote tactically and voted Conservative or someone who voted tactically and said the Conservatives were the party they most preferred. A similar definition applies to Labour and Liberal Democrat supporters.

The most striking change is in the views of Liberal Democrat supporters. In 1992 Liberal Democrat supporters were if anything slightly more opposed to Labour than they were to the Conservatives. By 1997 they were much more favourably disposed towards Labour. Moreover, with their opinion of their own party little changed, the gap between their feelings towards the Liberal

Democrats and their feelings towards Labour had narrowed significantly. The views of Labour supporters changed too. The average rating they gave to the Liberal Democrats rose by 0.32, greater than the 0.10 increase in the score they gave to their own party. In short, Labour supporters came to see less of a gap between Labour and the Liberal Democrats as well.[9]

Here, then, appears to be the most fruitful line of explanation for the rise in anti-Conservative tactical voting in 1997. As a result of the closer ideological proximity between Labour and the Liberal Democrats, together with the isolation and perceived incompetence of the Conservatives, more Liberal Democrat supporters were relatively indifferent between their own party and Labour, while disliking the Conservatives. Labour supporters were also somewhat less likely to feel that there was a big difference between their party and the Liberal Democrats. As a result both sets of supporters were more willing to make a tactical switch in order to help defeat a local Conservative MP.

If this is indeed a sufficient explanation then two other things ought also to be true. First, those who actually made a tactical switch should on the whole have been those who were indifferent between Labour and the Liberal Democrats while disliking the Conservatives. This proves to be so. Among those Liberal Democrat supporters who voted tactically for Labour, there was on average an 'approval gap' of only 0.40 between the Liberal Democrats and Labour, while the Conservatives were extremely disliked (a gap of 2.76). Equally, among Labour supporters who made a tactical switch to the Liberal Democrats, the 'approval gap' between Labour and the Liberal Democrats was just 0.49, while the gap from the Conservatives was again extremely large (2.75).[10]

The second thing that should be true is that for any given pattern of likes and dislikes, the probability that a voter cast a tactical ballot should have been the same in 1997 as in 1992.[11] In other words, among those who were relatively indifferent between Labour and the Liberal Democrats while disliking the Conservatives, the level of tactical voting should have been the same on the two occasions. This is largely what we find. In 1997 15 per cent of those who said they were in favour of both Labour and the Liberal Democrats (that is, gave the parties a score of four or five on our scale) and were against the Conservatives (giving them a score of one or two) voted tactically. This in fact is slightly below the equivalent figure of 19 per cent in 1992. What was different, as we would expect from Table 4, was that far more people belonged to this group. In 1992, only nine per cent of voters were in favour of Labour and the Liberal Democrats while being against the Conservatives; in 1997 no less than 22 per cent fell into that category.

So it seems that the secret to understanding why anti-Conservative tactical voting increased in 1997 lies not in the social psychology of voters but rather in the actions of the parties. Voters did not enter the polling station with a new set of motivations that meant they were more willing or able to vote tactically. Rather the messages they had received from the parties had changed. Their reaction to that change was in fact highly consistent with the way they have behaved in the past.

Conclusion

We have provided considerable support for two propositions. First, in 1997 more people voted tactically in order to try to defeat their local Conservative candidate than did so in 1992. These people were still small in number but in terms of seats they had a significant impact. Second, this increase happened not because voters brought different motivations to the ballot box than five years previously, or because they were more informed or more effectively mobilized, but rather because they believed that the parties had changed.

There are at least two important implications that flow from these conclusions, one political, the other theoretical. First, in the forthcoming debate about the future of the single-member plurality electoral system that has been promised by the new Labour government, one question we might ask of the existing system is whether it is desirable that the outcome of an election can be influenced to such an extent by the strategic manipulation of the few? Of course, we cannot assume that such patterns of tactical voting will necessarily be repeated in future; if the parties change by 2002 then so also presumably will the behaviour of voters. But the potential for such manipulation under the existing system has clearly been demonstrated.

Second, there is a tendency in the study of electoral behaviour to make inferences about the motivations of voters on the basis of evidence of changes in their behaviour. Thus, for example, voters may be deemed less willing to be loyal to a political party because they change their voting behaviour more often. Here we have demonstrated why such reasoning is potentially misleading. The act of voting is not simply the result of what the voter brings to the ballot box; rather it is the product of an interaction between parties and voters. With changing party images comes a changing set of tactical choices. We should not be surprised that 'New Labour' brought with it 'New Tactical Voting'.

ACKNOWLEDGEMENTS

We would like to thank our colleagues Anthony Heath, Roger Jowell, Lindsay Brook, Alison Park, Bridget Taylor and Katarina Thomson for their contributions to the research reported here. The 1997 British Election Study is generously funded by the Economic and Social Research Council (ESRC) in collaboration with the Gatsby Charitable Foundation. The Centre for Research into Elections and Social Trends is core-funded by the ESRC as part of its research centres programme. Much of the aggregate data analysis reported here was originally undertaken with Michael Steed for the 1997 Nuffield Election Study for which funding was provided by the Leverhulme Trust. None of the funders necessarily concur with any of the views expressed here, which are solely the responsibility of the authors.

NOTES

1. In this article we focus on tactical voting in Great Britain only. The BES does not extend to Northern Ireland, which has a completely different party system. Note also that the pattern of tactical voting in Scotland can be expected to be somewhat different because of the strength of Scottish National Party there.

2. The 1997 election was fought on new constituency boundaries. Our analysis relies on the estimates made by Rallings and Thrasher (1995) of what would have happened if the 1992 election had been fought on the 1997 boundaries.

3. These figures include respondents who did not choose this answer but volunteered other, apparently tactical, motivations for their vote. Such responses occurred in 0.3 per cent of cases in 1992 and 0.4 per cent in 1997. These respondents were not asked for their preferred party and are not included in the analyses which follow. People who reported voting against a particular candidate (0.7 per cent in 1992 and 1.2 per cent in 1997) are not counted as tactical here.

4. Excluded from the table are respondents who either refused to say who they had voted for or were unable to give the name of their preferred party, together with those who reported having voted for their preferred party despite giving a tactical answer to the 'reasons for voting' question. This explains why the sum of all the entries in the table for 1997 is 8.7 per cent rather than the ten per cent who said they voted tactically, and why the equivalent figure for 1992 is 7.7 per cent rather than nine per cent.

5. These observations – and others that follow – are also confirmed by an equivalent analysis of the 1997 British Election Campaign Panel Study, which administered after polling day the same questions about tactical voting to a sample of 2,047 respondents who had previously been interviewed on up to three occasions in the 12 months before polling day.

6. The well publicized *Observer/Scotland on Sunday* poll in 16 constituencies undertaken the weekend before polling day may have had a significant impact in a handful of constituencies, most notably in Hastings and Rye and in St Albans where, in contrast to the 1992 result, it suggested that Labour was better placed than the Liberal Democrats to defeat the Conservatives. But there were simply too few polls in too few constituencies for this to provide any general explanation of the rise in tactical voting.

7. The Conservative performance in contrast was almost identical in seats the Liberal Democrats did target and in those that they did not.

8. Compared with 1992, fewer Labour supporters were living in constituencies where their party was starting off third, while in contrast more Liberal Democrats were in that situation. But while this might help account for some of the increase in tactical switching from Liberal Democrat to Labour, it should have been accompanied by a reduction in tactical switching from Labour to the Liberal Democrats. As we have seen that did not happen. Moreover, the election results themselves suggest that Liberal Democrats living in constituencies where their preferred party started off third in 1992 as well as in 1997 were still more willing to vote tactically this time around.

9. Note also that Conservative supporters' dislike of Labour fell markedly between 1992 and 1997, giving them less reason to switch tactically to the Liberal Democrats in order to keep Labour out, a pattern which, as we saw earlier, was reflected in their behaviour.

10. Similarly, among Liberal Democrat supporters who voted tactically for the Conservatives, there was an 'approval gap' of only 0.33 between the Liberal Democrats and the Conservatives, while Labour were distinctly less popular (a gap of 1.34).

11. This assumes that the proportion of voters with any given pattern of likes and dislikes living in constituencies where it might make sense to vote tactically was not significantly different at the two elections.

REFERENCES

Butler, D. and D. Stokes (1974) *Political Change in Britain*. London: Macmillan.

Cain, B. (1978) 'Strategic voting in Britain', *American Journal of Political Science* 22: 39–55.

Campbell, A., P.E. Converse, S.E. Miller, and D.E. Stokes (1960) *The American Voter*. New York: Wiley.

Cox, G.W. (1997) *Making Votes Count*. Cambridge: Cambridge University Press.

Crewe, I. (1997) 'The Opinion Polls: Confidence Restored?', *Parliamentary Affairs* 50: 569–85.

Crewe, I., P. Norris and R. Waller (1992) 'The 1992 general election' in P. Norris *et al.* (eds) *British Elections and Parties Yearbook 1992*, pp.xv–xxxvi. London: Harvester Wheatsheaf.

Curtice, J. and M. Steed (1992) 'Appendix 2: The Results Analysed', in D. Butler and D. Kavanagh, *The British General Election of 1992*, pp.322–62. London: Macmillan.

Curtice, J. and M. Steed (1997) 'Appendix 2: An Analysis of the Results', in D. Butler and D. Kavanagh, *The British General Election of 1997*, pp.295–325. London: Macmillan.

Dalton, R.J. (1996) *Citizen Politics: Public Opinion and Political Parties in Advanced Industrialized Democracies*. Chatham, NJ: Chatham House.

Denver, D. and G. Hands (1997) *Modern Constituency Electioneering*. London and Portland OR: Frank Cass.

Evans, G. (1994) 'Tactical Voting and Labour's Prospects' in A.F. Heath, R. Jowell and J. Curtice with B. Taylor (eds) *Labour's Last Chance?*, pp.65–84. Aldershot: Dartmouth.

Evans, G. and A. Heath (1993) 'A tactical error in the analysis of tactical voting', *British Journal of Political Science* 23: 131–7.

Galbraith, J.W. and N.C. Rae (1989) 'A test of the importance of tactical voting: Great Britain, 1987', *British Journal of Political Science* 19: 126–36.

Heath, A., R. Jowell, J. Curtice, G. Evans, J. Field and S. Witherspoon (1991) *Understanding Political Change: The British Voter 1964–1987*. Oxford: Pergamon.

Inglehart, R. (1997) *Modernization and Post-Modernization*. Princeton: Princeton University Press.

Johnston, R.J. and C. Pattie (1991) 'Tactical voting in Great Britain in 1983 and 1987: An alternative approach', *British Journal of Political Science* 21: 95–128.

Market Research Society (1994) *The Opinion Polls and the 1992 Election*. London: Market Research Society.

Niemi, R., G. Whitten and M. Franklin (1992) 'Constituency characteristics, individual characteristics and tactical voting in the 1987 British General Election', *British Journal of Political Science* 22: 229–40.

Norris, P. (1997a) 'Anatomy of a Labour landslide', *Parliamentary Affairs* 50: 509–32.

Norris, P. (1997b) 'The Battle for the Campaign Agenda', in A. King (ed) *New Labour Triumphs: Britain at the Polls,* pp.113–44. Chatham, NJ: Chatham House.

Norris, P. (1997c) *Electoral Change Since 1945*. Oxford: Blackwell.

Pattie, C., P. Whiteley, R. Johnston and P. Seyd (1994) 'Measuring Local Campaign Effects: Labour Party Constituency Campaigning at the 1987 General Election', *Political Studies* 52: 469–79.

Pattie, C., R.J. Johnston and E. Fieldhouse (1995) 'Winning the Local Vote: The Effectiveness of Constituency Campaign Spending in Great Britain, 1983–92', *American Political Science Review* 89: 969–83.

Rallings, C. and M. Thrasher (1995) *Media Guide to the New Parliamentary Constituencies*. Plymouth: Local Government Chronicle Elections Centre.

Smith, M.J. and J. Spear (eds) (1992) *The Changing Labour Party*. London: Routledge.

Sex, Money and Politics: Sleaze and the Conservative Party in the 1997 Election

*David M. Farrell, Ian McAllister and
Donley T. Studlar*

'Sleaze' entered the lexicon of British politics in the mid-1990s. A number of events coincided to give the impression that certain prominent individuals in the Conservative government or parliamentary party were engaged in wrongdoing, either of a financial or a sexual nature. The issue of sleaze went wider than concerns about the behaviour of certain individuals, however. As Dunleavy and Weir (1995: 55) observe, sleaze 'married together quite disparate areas of near-wrongdoing across several parts of public life which had previously been considered entirely separately'. In their review of the subject, Dunleavy and Weir categorize the concept of sleaze into eight areas:

- alleged financial wrongdoing by ministers and MPs, shady deals and the misleading of others;
- the perception of a dramatic surge in lobbying and the intermediary role of certain MPs;
- the alleged packing of 'quangos';
- 'jobs for the faithful', and tactical use of the honours list;
- company directorships for retired ministers and senior civil servants;
- the murky world of party fundraising;
- unconventional sexual behaviour;
- salary increases for 'fat cats' in the privatized public utilities.

This article examines how the issue of sleaze affected the electoral performance of the Conservative Party. First, the next section sets out the context of sleaze as an issue leading up to and during the 1997 campaign. Second, focusing on two key aspects of sleaze – money (a combination of points 1 and 2 in the Dunleavy/Weir list) and sex (point 7) – we identify 24 Tory candidates whose election prospects could be said to have been affected by sleaze.[1] We test whether in fact this was the case, utilizing data on the characteristics of the constituencies produced by Colin Rallings and Michael Thrasher. Then we make use of BBC-NOP exit poll data to assess the indirect effects of sleaze on Conservative support more generally.

Sleaze as an Election Issue in 1997

In early 1994, Stephen Milligan, the Conservative MP for Eastleigh and Parliamentary Private Secretary to the Defence Procurement minister, was found dead after asphyxiating himself in bizarre circumstances involving a plastic binliner, an orange and ladies' underwear. A tragic and unfortunate death, its significance was that it occurred in the midst of a series of mishaps involving the sexual proclivities of Tory politicians. Among the more prominent of these events were the revelations that Transport minister Steven Norris had been involved in five extra-marital affairs and that Environment minister Tim Yeo and Keighley MP Gary Waller had fathered illegitimate children; Suffolk West MP Richard Spring's three-in-a-bed incident involving a Sunday school teacher; and a spate of gay affairs and assorted extra-marital relationships involving Tory MPs. By any standards, this was a long list of indiscretions. These sexual misdemeanours were not lost on the mass media. In their view, the Conservative Party of John Major was fair game, especially after Major's 1993 party conference speech in which he called for a campaign to 'get back to basics'.

There was also a steady stream of revelations about financial malpractices. First, there was the outcry in July 1994 over two Conservative MPs – Graham Riddick (Colne Valley) and David Tredinnick (Bosworth) – who had accepted £1,000 in return for asking parliamentary questions when approached by *Sunday Times* journalists posing as lobbyists providing cash for questions.

Second, in mid-October *The Guardian* published a story that two Conservative ministers had received cash (and other payments in kind) in return for asking questions and writing letters on behalf of Mohammed al-Fayed, the new owner of Harrods who was locked in a bitter dispute with the store's previous owner, Tiny Rowland, over the nature of the take-over. Al-Fayed was anxious to prevent the Office of Fair Trading from taking Rowland's side on the case by intervening to examine the take-over and the sources of al-Fayed's finance. He employed the services of a prominent Commons lobbyist, Ian Greer, whose *modus operandi* was to identify sympathetic MPs, nurturing them with appropriate sweeteners. Greer was able to accumulate a valuable list of Tory parliamentary sympathizers to the al-Fayed cause. Prominent among them, and the subjects of the *Guardian* story, were Tim Smith (MP for Beaconsfield and a Northern Ireland minister), and Neil Hamilton (MP for Tatton and a trade and industry minister). But, as would emerge later, the Greer list also included such luminaries as Sir Michael Grylls (Surrey North West; chair of the Conservative backbench trade and industry committee), Sir Andrew Bowden (Brighton Kemptown), Michael Brown (Cleethorpes), and Sir Peter Horden (Horsham).

The *Guardian* story provoked a flurry of activity: Tim Smith's resignation from ministerial office, the subsequent ejection of Neil Hamilton from his DTI position and the start of his hugely costly libel case against *The Guardian*, and John Major's decision to act. In October 1994 Major established the Committee on Standards in Public Life, chaired by Lord Nolan with a brief to investigate existing practices and bring forward specific proposals 'to ensure the highest standards of propriety in public life'. The Nolan Committee reported in May 1995 (for details, see Oliver, 1995; Rush, 1997) and after some heated debate, and further reflection by a select committee, the House of Commons agreed to most of its proposals, establishing a Parliamentary Commissioner for Standards, drawing up a code of conduct, and merging the Privileges and Members' Interests Committees into a new Committee on Standards and Privileges. Sir Gordon Downey, a former senior civil servant, was appointed as the first Parliamentary Commissioner (see Oliver, 1997).

Events had not stood still while the Nolan Committee was deliberating. *The Guardian* faced a spate of expensive libel suits from, among others, Hamilton, Greer, and, later, the Chief Secretary to the Treasury, Jonathan Aitken, who had been the subject of yet another *Guardian* story over a Paris Ritz hotel bill and compromising Arab contacts. Aitken had been forced to resign his ministry over the affair, and he vowed to clear his name.[2] It was Hamilton's case which attracted most attention and it required constitutional reform to allow him to waive his rights of parliamentary privilege before the case could proceed. Eventually the case collapsed in October 1996 (see Leigh and Vulliamy, 1997). Attention now turned to the role of Sir Gordon Downey, who was asked to investigate the accusations regarding al-Fayed and the cash-for-questions MPs. But before he could issue his full report John Major called the election, in March 1997.[3]

Despite this lead-up to the election, many observers were surprised that sleaze became a major campaign issue: for instance, the pre-election guide of neither the *Economist* nor *The Guardian* had sections on sleaze. Major had hoped to use the unprecedented six-week long election campaign to maximize his chances of making in-roads into the large and long-term Labour lead in the polls. His plans unravelled in hours once the accusations started (fuelled by the statements of opposition leaders) that by proroguing parliament early he had prevented the publication of the Downey report until after the election. Within days, selected parts of the Downey report were leaked to *The Guardian*. Partially in consequence, sleaze was headline news on virtually every day during the first two weeks of the campaign (Deacon *et al.,* 1997). What also served to keep sleaze high on the agenda was a series of colourful stories about the sexual proclivities of certain Conservative candidates, and the controversy over Neil Hamilton's nomination in the Tatton constituency.

Piers Merchant (Beckenham) was caught during the first few days of the campaign in a classic tabloid sting when he was photographed kissing a teenage club hostess on a sunny afternoon jaunt around his constituency. The woman claimed that they had been having an affair, an accusation hotly denied by Merchant, who resisted calls from senior Conservatives for his resignation.[4] Then came a series of embarrassing revelations concerning Conservative candidates in the Scottish constituency of Eastwood. The sitting MP, Allan Stewart, resigned as candidate after an accusation that he had committed adultery with a married woman; shortly afterwards he had a nervous breakdown. The person who was expected to replace him as candidate, Sir Michael Hirst (a former chair of the Scottish Conservative Party), quickly pulled out over speculation concerning an alleged gay affair.

Most attention and press vitriol was focused on Neil Hamilton and Tim Smith and whether they should run as Conservative candidates, given the speculation concerning their links with al-Fayed. Under pressure, Smith withdrew his candidacy, but Hamilton resisted the pressure to stand down, rejecting calls from senior Conservative politicians for his resignation and winning the support of his Tatton constituency party, who refused to accede to Central Office pressure. Labour and the Liberal Democrats withdrew their candidates, and former BBC correspondent Martin Bell ran as an independent candidate, challenging Hamilton.

In her detailed analysis of election media coverage Norris (1997) observes that the first third of the six-week campaign was dominated by sleaze. Neil Hamilton was second only to John Major in terms of coverage of prominent Tory candidates. It is difficult to disagree with Norris's conclusion that by dissolving parliament early, 'Major had blundered into creating a yawning news hole into which, like the White Rabbit, the Conservative party fell' (Norris, 1997: 135). We have identified a total of 24 Conservative candidates with question marks against their behaviour prior to the election (Table 1).[5] In addition, another seven Conservative candidates against whom allegations had been made opted (or were forced) to stand down and not contest the election.[6] Of the 24 Conservative candidates contesting the elections, allegations of financial malpractice had been raised against 14 of them, five with regard to the cash for questions affair. Eight of the MPs had attracted allegations concerning their sexual proclivities. The two remaining MPs, Michael Brown and David Mellor, managed to have allegations made against them on both financial and sexual grounds, Brown for cash-for-questions and an alleged homosexual relationship, Mellor for allegations that he received a free holiday paid for by a PLO representative as well as adultery.

The Voters' Verdict

The average Conservatives Party vote loss across all 641 constituencies in Britain was 11.4 per cent, or 11.8 per cent if we exclude Scotland, where no

TABLE 1
THE TORY 'SLEAZE' MPS

Name	Constituency	Nature of allegation	
		Money	Sex
Jonathan Aitken	Thanet South	Compromising Saudi connections, Ritz hotel bill	
Rupert Allason	Torbay		Alleged affair
Sir Andrew Bowden	Brighton Kemptown	Cash-for-questions	
Giles Brandreth	City of Chester	Treasury wrote off debt owed by his company	
Michael Brown	Cleethorpes	Cash-for-questions	Gay relationship
Alan Clark	Kensington and Chelsea		Adultery
Michael Colvin	Romsey	Undeclared consultancies	
Nirj Deva	Brentford and Isleworth	Greer donation for 1987 election campaign	
Alan Duncan	Rutland and Melton	'Underhand' procedures to purchase house	
Neil Hamilton	Tatton	Cash-for-questions	
Jerry Hayes	Harlow		Alleged homosexuality
Norman Lamont	Harrogate and Knaresborough	House of Fraser connection	
Barry Legg	Milton Keynes SW	Prominent financial difficulties	
Olga Maitland	Sutton and Cheam	Benefited from Greer commissions, controversial free Gibraltar holiday	
Gerald Malone	Winchester	Benefited from Greer commissions	
Michael Mates	Hampshire E	Accepted gift from fugitive businessman, undeclared consultancies	
David Mellor	Putney	Allegations of free holiday paid by PLO	Adultery
Piers Merchant	Beckenham		Teenage club hostess
Rod Richards	Clwyd NW		Alleged affair
Graham Riddick	Colne Valley	Cash-for-questions	
Richard Spring	Suffolk West		Three-in-a-bed
David Tredinnick	Bosworth	Cash-for-questions	
Gary Waller	Keighley		Illegitimate child
Tim Yeo	Suffolk South		Illegitimate child

Sources: Press reports.
Note: In many cases the listed MPs had sleaze allegations made against them which had yet to be proven.
Their inclusion is based on press reports and secondary literature.

Conservative candidate was at the centre of a sleaze allegation (Table 2). In the 24 constituencies where the Conservative candidate was the subject of an allegation, the loss was 14.0 per cent, suggesting that the electorate may have been influenced by the allegations appearing in the press. However, in the Tatton constituency, the withdrawal of the Labour and Liberal Democrat candidates in favour of the Independent candidate Martin Bell resulted in a massive fall of 24.7 per cent in the Conservative vote, potentially skewing the results for all 24 candidates. In fact, even if we exclude Tatton, the Conservative loss in the 23 constituencies where there was a three-party contest remains 13.5 per cent, still noticeably greater than for the rest of the country.

Only five of the constituencies registered a vote decrease for the Conservatives that was smaller than the average for England and Wales as a whole. In no fewer than 11 of the seats, the Conservatives loss was more than two percentage points higher than the English and Welsh average. In terms of outcome, the Conservatives lost 16 of the 24 seats, 11 of them to Labour, four to the Liberal Democrats, and one to an independent. In total, 9 per cent of the Conservative's total loss of 178 seats in the election occurred in constituencies with a sleaze allegation against the Conservative candidate. Superficially at least, sleaze would appear to have played an important role in the election.

In practice, however, changes in electoral support occur for a variety of reasons, of which the personal standing of the candidate is but one – and often one which is of minor importance compared to national considerations. Moreover, the boundary changes that took place in some constituencies between 1992 and 1997 make any precise estimates difficult. In fact, as Table 2 demonstrates, the vote loss by Conservative candidates in the 24 constituencies varied greatly – by more than 15 percentage points. To estimate the net effect of sleaze, we need to calculate what the Conservative vote in the constituency should have been – the vote that they would have received based on the social characteristics of the constituency – and subtract that from the vote that they did receive. The predicted vote is estimated from a regression equation including details of the class, social and ethnic composition of the constituency, which explains over 70 per cent of the variance in the Conservative vote on an aggregate basis.[7]

A comparison of the predicted vote with the actual vote that each Conservative candidate attracted shows that the net electoral effect of a sleaze allegation, while some variation remains, is much reduced (Figure 1). The top left-hand corner of the graph shows those candidates where their predicted vote was greater than their actual vote: in other words, they performed worse than would otherwise have been expected. The bottom right-hand corner shows the candidates who performed better than expected, attracting more

TABLE 2
THE ELECTION RESULT FOR THE 24 CONSERVATIVE CANDIDATES

Candidate	Con vote change	Con	Lab	Lib Dem	Result
Neil Hamilton	-24.7	37.5	n.a	n.a	Lost to Indep
Piers Merchant	-17.7	42.5	33.4	18.1	Retained
Olga Maitland	-17.4	37.8	15.5	42.3	Lost to Lib Dem
Michael Colvin	-17.2	46.0	18.6	29.4	Retained
Roderick Richards	-16.0	32.5	37.1	12.8	Lost to Lab
Alan Duncan	-15.6	45.8	29.0	19.2	Retained
Alan Clark	-14.6	53.6	28.0	15.3	Retained
Michael Brown	-14.6	33.4	51.6	11.4	Lost to Lab
Tim Yeo	-14.0	37.3	29.3	27.7	Retained
Jerry Hayes	-13.9	32.1	54.1	9.5	Lost to Lab
Andrew Bowden	-13.9	38.9	46.6	9.7	Lost to Lab
Nirj Deva	-13.8	31.8	57.4	8.2	Lost to Lab
Graham Riddick	-13.4	28.6	36.2	19.8	Lost to Lab
Norman Lamont	-13.4	38.4	8.7	51.5	Lost to Lib Dem
David Mellor	-13.3	38.9	45.7	10.8	Lost to Lab
Barry Legg	-13.1	33.5	53.8	11.9	Lost to Lab
Richard Spring	-12.9	40.9	37.1	14.0	Retained
Michael Mates	-12.6	48.0	17.1	28.1	Retained
Jonathan Aitken	-11.9	39.8	46.2	11.7	Lost to Lab
David Tredinnick	-11.0	40.6	38.7	17.8	Retained
Gary Waller	-10.7	36.7	50.6	9.8	Lost to Lab
Gyles Brandreth	-10.5	34.2	53.0	9.5	Lost to Lab
Rupert Allason	-10.4	39.5	14.9	39.6	Lost to Lib Dem
Gerry Malone	-9.6	42.1	10.5	42.1	Lost to Lib Dem
Mean	-14.0	38.8	35.3	21.0	
(England and Wales)	(-11.8)	(31.9)	(45.8)	(17.2)	

Source: 1997 Constituency File.
Note: Change in the Conservative vote between the 1992 and 1997 general elections. Labour and the Liberal Democrats did not contest the Tatton constituency, held by Neil Hamilton.

votes than they would otherwise have expected based on the characteristics of the constituency.

    Using this model, two candidates stand out: Alan Clark, who won Kensington and Chelsea, and Graham Riddick, who lost Colne Valley. Clark achieved a spectacular victory, gaining nearly 18 per cent more votes than would otherwise would have been expected. He was a prominent ex-minister whose adulterous behaviour, as recounted in his own *Diaries* (1993) as well as by others, was removed from immediate concern. He had declined to run in 1992 (on grounds unrelated to these revelations), and in making a comeback in 1997, he was selected as the Conservative candidate for a new, presumably safe, constituency. His wife had also stood by him; thus he may have been viewed by many as more 'rougish' than morally corrupt. Riddick's

FIGURE 1
ACTUAL AND PREDICTED VOTES FOR THE 24 CONSERVATIVE CANDIDATES

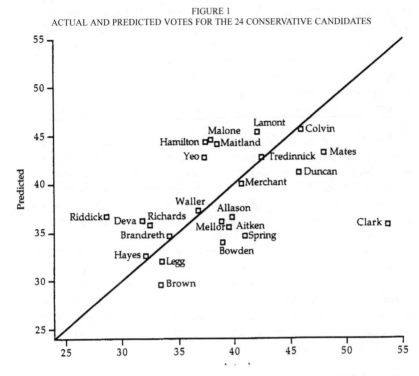

Source: 1997 Constituency File.
Note: The predicted vote is based on a regression equation predicting the Conservative vote
          from the social structural characteristics of the constituency. See footnote 7 for details.

vote share, on the other hand, was 8 per cent lower than it otherwise should
have been.

The variations between the other 22 candidates are much more modest.
Apart from Alan Clark, the best performance was by Richard Spring, who
gained just over 6 per cent more votes than he might otherwise have expected.
The worst performances, apart from Riddick, came from Neil Hamilton in
Tatton, whose vote was 6.8 per cent less than expected – a substantial
difference, but nevertheless a major improvement on the actual vote loss of
24.7 per cent – and Olga Maitland in Sutton and Cheam, who had 6.7 per cent
less than would otherwise have been expected.

While other factors may have been important, these results enable an
estimate to be made of the impact of the sleaze allegations on the loss of the
16 constituencies. If we compare the predicted Conservative vote with the
actual results for the major parties shown earlier in Table 2, the net effect of
sleaze was the loss of four seats. Other things (including sleaze) being equal,

the Conservatives should have retained Graham Riddick's seat of Colne Valley, Olga Maitland's seat of Sutton and Cheam, and Gerry Malone's seat of Winchester. Instead, the first was lost to Labour and the second two to the Liberal Democrats.[8] Tatton is a separate case because it was not contested by Labour or the Liberal Democrats. However, if they had contested the seat, it is likely that Neil Hamilton would have been returned since his vote was only 6.8 per cent lower than it otherwise would have been in a straight three-party contest.

Which of the two major sleaze allegations were voters more likely to punish: sexual perfidy or financial misdemeanour? Judged across the English and Welsh constituencies and controlling for social structure, incumbency and turnout differences,[9] financial sleaze allegations appear to have been punished by voters, while sexual allegations appear to have been rewarded. Conservative candidates with financial allegations against them polled 1.2 per cent of the vote less than expected, while those with sexual questions against their name actually polled the same proportion more than expected. However, most of this latter effect is attributable to the spectacular performance of Alan Clark; if we exclude his constituency from the analysis, sex allegations, on average, cost candidates 1.4 per cent of the vote. In other words, notwithstanding Alan Clark's electors in Kensington and Chelsea, financial and sexual scandals were of about equal importance in the minds of voters, although neither resulted in any major shifts in votes.

Voters' Perceptions of Sleaze

Sleaze, of course, was not just an element influencing the outcome in the constituencies where Conservative candidates had allegations against them, it was also a factor across the electorate as a whole. Norris (1997) concludes from her study of press coverage during the election that sleaze accounted for a total of 12 per cent of all policy coverage. How many seats did the Conservatives lose across the electorate as a whole through perceptions of widespread sleaze, even though the local Conservative candidate did not have any allegations against them? We can make these estimates using a BBC-NOP exit poll, which asked the respondents how decisive a range of issues were in determining how they voted.[10]

Of the four major issues asked about in the BBC-NOP survey – the economy, education, income tax and sleaze – the Conservatives were least trusted to deal with sleaze (Table 3). The Conservatives were just one percentage point behind Labour as the preferred party in dealing with the economy, and 8 per cent behind Labour on income tax. However, on education, only 25 per cent of voters preferred the Conservatives, and on sleaze, 22 per cent thought that the party could be most trusted to take the right decisions. The Liberal Democrats appeared to do particularly well on

TABLE 3
PARTY MOST TRUSTED BY VOTERS (COLUMN %)

Party most trusted	Trust on			
	Economy	Education	Income tax	Sleaze
Conservative	42	25	35	22
Labour	43	47	43	47
Liberal Democrats	15	28	22	31
Total	100	100	100	100
(N)	(2174)	(2128)	(2079)	(1986)

Source: 1997 BBC-NOP Exit Poll.
Note: The question was: 'Which party do you trust most to take the right decisions about... ?'

anti-Conservative views on sleaze: they were seen as the preferred party by 31 per cent of voters, presumably a reflection of the fact that sleaze allegations had also affected Labour MPs.

Did voters' preferences about which party was most effective in dealing with sleaze actually affect the outcome of the election? The main characteristic of the 1997 general election was the large number of defections from the Conservatives. The BBC-NOP exit poll shows that of those who voted for the Conservatives in 1992, only 68 per cent remained loyal to them in 1997: of the remainder, 13 per cent defected to Labour, 12 per cent to the Liberal Democrats and 7 per cent to other candidates. By contrast, Labour retained the support of 87 per cent of their 1992 supporters. The Conservatives, then, lost around one out of every three of their 1992 supporters, while attracting negligible numbers of defectors from the other major parties.

To estimate the extent to which defectors from the Conservatives were motivated by the four issues, Table 4 presents the results of a logistic regression analysis, predicting defection on the basis of which party respondents preferred on each of the four issues; the Conservative Party is the excluded category. The results show that, for 1992 Conservative voters defecting to Labour, it was their trust in Labour to deal with the issue of education that most motivated them; paradoxically, they actually had less trust in Labour to deal with the economy than the Conservatives. Among this group, there was significantly more trust in Labour to deal with the sleaze issue than the Conservatives. Sleaze was also an issue for 1992 Conservative voters defecting to the Liberal Democrats; they trusted the Liberal Democrats to deal with sleaze, but ranked Labour as little different from the Conservatives on the issue. For these voters, sleaze ranked third in importance in their defection, after education and the economy.

TABLE 4
PREFERRED PARTY AND CONSERVATIVE DEFECTION

Conservative defectors

	All		to Labour		to Lib Dem	
	Est	*(SE)*	*Est*	*(SE)*	*Est*	*(SE)*
Economy						
Labour	-0.82**	(0.22)	-0.69*	(0.30)	-1.70**	(0.55)
Lib Dem	-0.28	(0.23)	-1.10	(0.59)	-0.04	(0.30)
Education						
Labour	1.10**	(0.26)	2.50**	(0.45)	0.89	(0.51)
Lib Dem	1.00**	(0.25)	1.20*	(0.52)	1.90**	(0.43)
Income Tax						
Labour	0.07	(0.25)	-0.20	(0.34)	-0.36	(0.50)
Lib Dem	-0.14	(0.25)	-0.96*	(0.48)	0.34	(0.35)
Sleaze						
Labour	0.43	(0.27)	0.81*	(0.41)	-0.16	(0.54)
Lib Dem	1.00**	(0.23)	0.47	(0.40)	0.91**	(0.36)
Constant	-2.80		-4.40		-4.30	
Pseudo R-sq	0.07		0.12		0.24	

Source: 1997 BBC-NOP Exit Poll.
Note: Logistic regression estimates showing parameter estimates and standard error predicting defection from the Conservatives. N = 1,947.

Sleaze, then, was important in motivating defection, but it was overshadowed by other issues, such as economic management and, most important of all, education. What was the cost of the sleaze factor to the Conservatives in terms of seats, in addition to the four seats lost as a direct result of allegations against individual MPs? Any estimates are obviously approximate, but based on the weight of the various factors in Table 4, about one in every five defections from the Conservatives was as a result of concerns about sleaze.[11] If the Conservatives had thus suffered one-fifth fewer defections, then the Conservative vote would have increased in net terms by about 2.5 per cent.[12] Translating that increase to the constituency level means that the Conservatives might have expected to win about 15 more seats than they actually did, exclusive of the four seats where there were sleaze allegations against Conservative MPs. The net effect of sleaze to the Conservatives in the 1997 general election was, therefore, a loss of about 19 seats. In a close election, this could have represented the margin between victory and defeat – after all, the Conservatives had a majority of 21 in the general election of 1992 – but, of course, the result of the 1997 election was not close.

Conclusion

Our analysis finds, then, that sleaze charges did damage the performance of Conservative candidates in the 1997 general election, but the effects were largely 'national' rather than candidate-specific. In placing these results in perspective, we find that there is surprisingly little systematic empirical research from any country on the electoral effects of corruption charges. The literature on this topic in the United States focuses on one particular election, the congressional election of 1992, and one incident of corruption charges, the House 'check kiting' (bank overdrafts) scandal of that year (Jacobson and Dimock, 1994; Stewart, 1994). The only two studies over time concerning US congressional elections are those by Peters and Welch (1980) and Welch and Hibbing (1997). Their research provides both similarities to and differences from our findings.

First, our results in terms of estimated vote loss are similar to the US aggregate data studies, which estimated that incumbents of both parties overall suffered between a 6 and 11 per cent loss in the years 1968–78 and a 9.3 per cent loss in the years 1982–90. Despite these substantial diminutions of electoral support, most candidates charged with corruption in the USA still managed to win, with only 25 per cent of the incumbents losing in the second time period examined. Nevertheless, this was a smaller incumbency return rate than among other US incumbents. Although a much larger proportion of 1997 corruption-tainted Conservative candidates lost (64 per cent), only four out of the 24 losses (or 17 per cent) can be attributed to the direct aggregate effects of corruption charges against Conservative candidates in 1997.

There are two major differences, however, between our results and those for the USA. First, the US studies found that 'morals' charges resulted in greater vote loss than other forms of corruption charges; in Britain in 1997 such complaints resulted in about equal damage to a candidate electorally, excluding the notable case of Alan Clark. This suggests that compromises with the collective principles of the public interest are considered to be as serious an offence by the British electorate, while US voters, with a campaign finance system which emphasizes the importance of money, find sexual deviations to be more deserving of electoral punishment. Until recently, however, almost all British scandals were concerned with sex, not money, while the opposite was closer to the truth in the USA (King, 1986). It may be that voters punish the types of scandals they are least familiar with in their particular polity.

A second difference derives from the fact that, unlike the US studies, we were able to analyse survey data on the subject of corruption. Even in circumstances such as 1992, in which there were over 50 congressmen charged with house bank violations, corruption charges in the US rarely reach the level of being 'national' issues associated with one party. In Britain in 1997 sleaze was a national, party-related issue. Thus we show that the Conservatives suffered electorally more from the issue nationally than did the candidates who were specifically charged. The opposite is the case in the US, whose individualistic political culture attributes blame for corruption to the candidate, and only rarely to a party as a whole across the country. In Britain in 1997, the number of cases of reported corrupt activities by Conservative politicians, and their prominence in the media, made the issue a national, collective one. In a political culture in which, despite some loosening of the ties recently (Cain *et al.*, 1987; Wood and Norton, 1992), voters still cast their ballots on the basis of party rather than candidate characteristics, the Conservatives as a whole suffered for the misdemeanours of their MPs more than the individual perpetrators (see also Clarke *et al.*, 1997). Being identified as 'the party of sleaze' was not the most important reason for the Conservatives' electoral defeat, but it was a contributing factor.

ACKNOWLEDGEMENTS

We are grateful to the following for advice and feedback: David Butler, Philip Cowley, Kevin Cox, John Curtice, David Denver, Patrick Dunleavy, Justin Harrison, Ron Johnston, Michael Marsh, Arlene McCarthy, Pippa Norris, Jorgen Rasmussen and Andrew Russell. Responsibility for any errors are ours alone.

NOTES

1. Given our focus on the financial and sexual activities of individual Conservative MPs, this article does not deal with the issues surrounding the Scott inquiry, which was established to investigate the Matrix Churchill affair. Also relevant, but not being considered here, are the Pergau Dam and Westminster council house sales affairs.
2. Aitken's libel suit was to collapse a few weeks after the 1997 election due to inconsistencies in his evidence.
3. The full Downey report, published several months after the election, was unequivocally to conclude that Hamilton and each of the other accused Conservative MPs had acted improperly.
4. The Merchant story re-emerged soon after the election and he resigned his seat. The Conservatives narrowly held the seat in the subsequent by-election.
5. Among other possible 'sleaze candidates' not being considered here are the following: David Willetts (Havant) who, as a government whip, had attempted an unsuccessful cover-up on Hamilton's behalf; and Nicholas Lyell (Bedfordshire NE) and William Waldegrave (Bristol West) who were both implicated in cover-up accusations investigated by the Scott inquiry.
6. Namely: David Ashby (Leicestershire NW), failed libel case concerning allegations of homosexuality; Hartley Booth (Finchley), failed to be re-selected, allegations regarding sexual predelictions; Sir Michael Grylls (Surrey NW), cash-for-questions; Sir Peter Horden (Horsham), House of Fraser connection; Steven Norris (Epping Forest), five cases of adultery; Nicholas Scott (Kensington and Chelsea), deselected after controversy over drunk driving incident; Sir Jerry Wiggin (Weston-Super-Mare), used colleague's name to put down parliamentary question on behalf of lobby organization. In addition, the following cases of candidates forced to retire during the campaign received some notoriety: Sir Michael Hirst

(former chair of the Scottish Conservative Party) resigned during the campaign over a 'past indiscretion' (relating to an alleged gay affair); Derek Laud, selected as Conservative candidate for Tottenham, resigned in the first week of the campaign – it later transpired he was due to appear in a New York court on drunk-driving charges; Tim Smith (Beaconsfield), cash-for-questions, resigned as a candidate during the campaign; and Allan Stewart (Eastwood), alleged affair with married woman, resigned as candidate during the 1997 campaign.

7. Four scales were derived by factor analysis, based on the socioeconomic characteristics of parliamentary constituencies. These were manual occupation (based on the proportions of skilled manual workers, professionals [-] managers [-], and partly skilled workers in the constituency); social deprivation (economically inactive, attending government training schemes, reporting illnesses, and unemployed); familism (pensionable age [-], working age, owning a house outright [-], and aged 25 to 39); and ethnicity (Indian, Pakistani and Bangledeshi, other non-white, and blacks). A sign in square parentheses indicates that the characteristic in question is negatively related to the overall scale. For details, see McAllister (1997).

8. After the election, Gerry Malone successfully challenged the legality of the Winchester result over the treatment of spoiled ballot papers. In the subsequent by-election, however, the original election result was confirmed with a resounding defeat for Malone.

9. The analysis excludes the Speaker's constituency and the Tatton constituency, both of which were not contested by more than one major party.

10. Unfortunately, the survey did not record the constituency that the respondents were interviewed in, which would have permitted an estimate to be made of the impact of sleaze in each of the 24 constituencies with a Conservative candidate facing such allegations. This would have complemented the aggregate level estimates.

11. This estimate is arrived at by calculating the ratio of the parameter estimate against the standard error in Table 4.

12. This assumes that of the 32 per cent of 1992 Conservative voters who defected, one in five did so because of sleaze. Re-estimating this for the Conservative percentage vote produces a figure of 2.5 per cent.

REFERENCES

Cain, Bruce, John Ferejohn and Morris Fiorina (1987) *The Personal Vote*. Cambridge, MA: Harvard University Press.

Clark, Alan (1993) *Diaries*. London: Weidenfeld and Nicolson.

Clarke, Harold, Marianne Stewart and Paul Whiteley (1997) 'New Models for New Labour: The Political Economy of Labour Party Support, January 1992–April 1997', paper presented at EPOP conference, University of Essex.

Deacon, David, Peter Golding and Mick Billig (1997) 'Between Fear and Loathing: National Press Coverage of the 1997 British General Election', paper presented at EPOP conference, University of Essex.

Dunleavy, Patrick and Stuart Weir (1995) 'Media, Opinion and the Constitution', in F. F. Ridley and Alan Doig (eds) *Sleaze: Politicians, Private Interests and Public Reaction,* pp.54–68. Oxford: Oxford University Press.

Jacobson, Gary C. and Michael A. Dimock (1994) 'Checking Out: The Effects of Bank Overdrafts on the 1992 House Elections', *American Journal of Political Science* 38: 601–24.

King, Anthony (1986) 'Sex, Money and Power', in Richard Hodder-Williams and James Ceaser (eds) *Politics in Britain and the United States,* pp.173–202. Durham, NC: Duke University Press.

Leigh, David and Ed Vulliamy (1997) *Sleaze: The Corruption of Parliament*. London: Fourth Estate.

McAllister, Ian (1997) 'Regional Voting', *Parliamentary Affairs* 50: 641–57.

Mortimore, Roger (1995) 'Public Perceptions of Sleaze in Britain', in F. F. Ridley and Alan Doig (eds) *Sleaze: Politicians, Private Interests and Public Reaction,* pp.31–41. Oxford: Oxford

University Press.

Norris, Pippa (1997) 'The Battle for the Campaign Agenda', in Anthony King (ed.) *New Labour Triumphs: Britain at the Polls,* pp.113–44. Chatham, NJ: Chatham House.

Oliver, Dawn (1995) 'The Nolan Committee', in F.F. Ridley and Alan Doig (eds) *Sleaze: Politicians, Private Interests and Public Reaction,* pp.42–53. Oxford: Oxford University Press.

Oliver, Dawn (1997) 'Regulating the Conduct of MPs: The British Experience of Combating Corruption', *Political Studies* 45: 539–58.

Peters, John G. and Susan Welch (1980) 'The Effects of Charges of Corruption on Voting Behavior in Congressional Elections', *American Political Science Review* 74: 697–708.

Rush, Michael (1997) 'Damming the Sleaze: The New Code of Conduct and the Outside Interests of MPs in the British House of Commons', *The Journal of Legislative Studies* 3: 10–28.

Stewart, Charles (1994) 'Let's Go Fly a Kite: Correlates of Involvement in the House Bank Scandal', *Legislative Studies Quarterly* 19: 521–36.

Welch, Susan and John R. Hibbing (1997) 'The Effects of Charges of Corruption on Voting Behavior in Congressional Elections, 1982–1990', *Journal of Politics* 59: 226–39.

Wood, David and Philip Norton (1992) 'Do Candidates Matter? Candidate-specific Vote Changes for Incumbent MPs, 1983–1987', *Political Studies* 40: 227–38.

Euroscepticism and the Referendum Party

Anthony Heath, Roger Jowell, Bridget Taylor and Katarina Thomson

Europe was a continuing source of headlines during the 1992 parliament, whether over the Exchange Rate Mechanism, the Maastricht treaty, BSE, quota-hopping, or the question of whether Britain should join a European currency. Throughout, it was a major source of division within the Conservative Party at Westminster, most notably at the time of the nine whipless rebels. Europe thus will certainly have made a major impact on the ungovernability of the Conservative Party, its public image of disunity, and hence on the general disillusion of voters with the government.

But Europe also seemed to have played a more direct role at the polls in 1997 with the votes won by the Referendum Party. The party was a creation of the late Sir James Goldsmith, who announced his intention to form it on 27 October 1994, although it formally came into being a year later in October 1995. It campaigned on the single issue of a referendum on Europe. It eventually published the text of its proposed question for a referendum, namely:

> *Do you want the United Kingdom to be part of a Federal Europe*
> *or*
> *Do you want the United Kingdom to return to an association of sovereign nations that are part of a common trading market?*

Sir James emphasized that his proposed referendum was quite different from those proposed by the Labour and Conservative parties, which dealt only with the question of joining the single European currency.

David Mellor memorably described Goldsmith's share of the vote in his constituency as 'derisory', but it could alternatively be viewed as the strongest-ever performance by a British minor party. It could well have contributed to the loss of some Tory seats. The Referendum Party contested 547 constituencies, standing aside only in seats where the incumbent MP had given explicit support for a referendum. They won a total of 3.0 per cent of the vote in those constituencies where they stood (while the UK Independence Party secured a further 1.1 per cent of the vote in the 194 constituencies where it stood). But the Referendum Party's appeal tailed off noticeably north of the Scottish border where it secured an average of just 1.1 per cent of the vote. As John Curtice and Michael Steed have suggested, this may reflect the rather higher level of support for Europe in Scotland, or perhaps a feeling that the party's anti-Europeanism was a form of English rather than British nationalism (Curtice and Steed, 1997). Its best performances were all in those parts of England where euroscepticism was at its highest, especially the south of England outside inner London, and in East Anglia where it averaged 3.9 per cent. It tended to do particularly well in constituencies with a large agricultural or elderly population, the former doubtless a reflection of the controversy surrounding European agricultural policy and the European response to BSE.

It was widely assumed at the time that these votes had largely come from the Conservatives and that they might have cost the Tories as many as 19 seats (since in 19 seats the Referendum Party share of the vote was larger than the majority over the Conservatives).[1] But it was also a remarkable phenomenon in its own right. The conventional wisdom is that foreign affairs play little role in domestic voting behaviour and that bread-and-butter issues tend to be decisive. But at face value it seems that nearly three per cent of voters did vote on the basis of a single non-economic issue.

In this article we ask the following questions:

• How widespread was euroscepticism in the electorate?
• Where did the Referendum Party's vote come from and what were its motivations? Was it a specific vote on the issue of a federal Europe? Or was it a more general vote of protest by disillusioned Tories on the right of the party for whom the Liberal Democrats or New Labour were even less attractive than the Conservatives?
• What were the consequences of the Referendum Party for the Conservative share of the vote and of seats? Would the Conservatives have been better off, as some urged, in moving to a more eurosceptic line? Would this have retained the Referendum Party voters? Or would these voters have defected anyway because of their general disillusion?

Data

Our data come from the 1992–97 British Election Panel Study (BEPS). The panel study is particularly valuable for a study of the Referendum Party for two reasons. First, it gives contemporary records of vote in 1992 and hence does not suffer the recall bias that affects other sources. Secondly, the panel enables us to look at attitudes and behaviour of eventual Referendum Party voters *before* the party was formed in October 1995. It thus allows us to tackle questions of causation, specifically the question of whether the formation of the Referendum Party made any difference, in a way that simply is not possible with a conventional cross-sectional survey.

The BEPS has followed up respondents to the 1992 British Election Survey. Respondents were reinterviewed in 1993, 1994, 1995 and 1996 and for the final time after the general election in 1997. The 1992 survey was carried out by face-to-face interview, as were the 1994 and spring 1995, 1996 and 1997 waves. The 1993 wave was a short postal one. There were also two short telephone waves in the autumns of 1995 and 1996. We draw primarily on the five face-to-face waves.

In the 1992 BES, 3,534 interviews were achieved, a response rate of 73 per cent. Of these original respondents 2,277 participated in the 1994 wave and 1,924 in the final wave after the 1997 general election. However, we should note that the original 1992 BES oversampled in Scotland in order to enable a detailed study to be undertaken of Scottish voting behaviour for the Scottish Election Study. Where the data are used as a British sample, as they are in this article, the Scottish oversample requires downweighting to form a representative British sample. The weighted N which we report in this paper for the 1997 wave is therefore 1,583. Since we are ultimately interested in how people voted in 1997, we restrict ourselves throughout to people who completed the 1997 wave of interviews. We should note, however, that the BEPS does not include young voters who entered the electorate after the 1992 general election (since they would have been excluded from the sampling frame for the 1992 BES).

Every effort has been made to maintain the panel, but clearly it has been subject to attrition and inevitably the attrition has been concentrated in certain groups rather than uniform across all groups. Wherever possible, therefore, we check our results against independent random samples (such as the 1997 BES), which have not suffered from this problem of attrition. Checking results against the 1997 BES is also important given the small number of Referendum Party voters in the panel study. In the final wave of the panel we have only 34 Referendum Party voters, and we therefore have to be very careful that our results are not due to sampling error. As well as carrying out tests of significance, we therefore also check our results against those found in the 1997 BES, which contains 58 Referendum Party voters. Since the BEPS and the BES are completely independent samples, checks of this kind give one much greater confidence in the results.

How Eurosceptic was the Electorate?

The attitudes of the British electorate towards the European Union (EU), perhaps like those of the Conservative and Labour parties, has been distinctly ambivalent. On the one hand, few people actually want to leave the EU, and in this respect there is very little popular support for a radical euroscepticism, such as that occasionally mooted by eurosceptics such as Norman Lamont. On the other hand, a large proportion of the electorate is uneasy about the moves towards integration implied by the Maastricht treaty, and (as elsewhere in Europe) doubts about European integration have been increasing since the treaty was signed. This is shown clearly in Table 1. We asked our respondents:

> *Do you think that Britain's long-term policy should be ...*
> *to leave the European Community,*
> *to stay in the EC and try to reduce its powers,*
> *to leave things as they are,*
> *to stay in the EC and try to increase its powers or*
> *to work for the formation of a single European government?*

As we can see from Table 1, in 1992 the electorate was fairly evenly divided between eurosceptics and europhiles, but by 1997 the balance had shifted decisively in a eurosceptic direction with 66 per cent wanting either to leave outright or to reduce EU powers.[2]

TABLE 1
EUROSCEPTICISM IN THE ELECTORATE (COLUMN %)

	1992	1994	1997
% agreeing that ...			
Britain should leave the EC	9	10	14
Reduce its powers	35	39	52
Leave as is	13	14	16
Increase its powers	29	21	9
Work for single European govt	11	11	5
Don't know	4	6	4
Replace pound	25	20	16
Have both ECU and pound	24	21	26
Only have pound	49	58	55
Don't know	3	2	3

Source: BEPS 1992, 1994 and 1997 waves.

Similarly, the electorate was distinctly eurosceptic, and becoming more so, on the issue of a single currency. We asked our respondents:

> *And here are three statements about the future of the pound in the European Community. Which one comes closest to your view?*
> *Replace the pound by a single currency,*
> *Use both the pound and a new European currency in Britain,*
> *Keep the pound as the only currency for Britain.*

As we can see from Table 1, even in 1992 keeping the pound on its own was the most popular of the three options, and by 1994 opinion had hardened somewhat.[3]

Euroscepticism, therefore, was on the increase over the course of the last parliament, and in this respect popular sentiment was moving in the direction of the Referendum Party and of the Conservative Party's right wing. Indeed, as we shall see, it seems to have been the only major issue where popular sentiment was moving in a right-wing direction.

To chart the public's changing attitudes towards major issues, and their changing perceptions of the parties' positions, we constructed a number of measures where respondents were asked to place themselves, and the parties, on 11-point scales running between two contrasting policy options. These measures have been the major tool in BEPS for understanding the changing impact of issues on the electorate. They covered European integration, the redistribution of income, the control of unemployment and inflation, tax cuts versus government spending, and privatization. The question wording of the end-points of these scales was:

> *Britain should do all it can to unite fully with the European Community* vs *Britain should do all it can to protect its independence from the European Community*

> *Government should put up taxes a lot and spend much more on health and social services* vs *government should cut taxes a lot and spend much less on health and social services*

> *Getting people back to work should be the government's top priority* vs *keeping prices down should be the government's top priority*

> *Government should nationalize many more private companies* vs *government should sell off many more nationalized industries*

> *Government should make much greater efforts to make people's income more equal* vs *government should be much less concerned about how equal people's incomes are*

The scales have been coded so that high scores represent right-wing positions.

Table 2 shows that only the issue of European integration has seen a substantial popular shift to the right.[4] On every other major issue, public opinion moved away from the Conservatives over the course of the 1992 parliament.

TABLE 2
RESPONDENTS' POSITIONS ON MAJOR ISSUES (MEAN SCORES)

	1992	1994	1995	1996	1997	Change
Europe	5.9	6.5	6.7	6.9	6.7	+0.8
Privatization	5.9	5.2	5.3	5.3	5.5	-0.4
Inequality	4.9	-	4.3	4.5	4.6	-0.3
Unemployment	3.6	3.8	3.7	3.5	3.7	+0.1
Taxes	4.1	4.5	4.1	3.9	3.8	-0.3

Source: BEPS

The fact that public opinion moved in different directions on the European question and on the standard bread-and-butter issues of unemployment or tax cuts suggests that they may have rather little in common. It may be misleading to think of euroscepticism as a right-wing issue in the same sense that we think of privatization as a right-wing issue.

This is indeed what we find. Factor analysis shows that public attitudes towards redistribution, privatization, unemployment and tax cuts form a relatively tightly-integrated group of issues where people's attitudes are highly consistent across all four issues. If someone adopts a right-wing stance on, say redistribution, there is a high probability that they will be right-of-centre on tax cuts, privatization and inflation as well. For this reason we can think of these issues as reflecting people's positions on a basic socialist/laissez faire dimension that underpins their specific issue preferences (see Heath et al., 1994).

Attitudes to Europe, however, do not map onto this socialist/laissez faire dimension in a straightforward way. They are not entirely unrelated, but there is much less consistency between people's positions on Europe and their left/right values than there is between their positions on the individual economic issues (see Heath et al., forthcoming).[5]

What this means is that people who share similar economic attitudes on privatization, inflation and so on may be fairly dissimilar in their attitudes to Europe. And this of course may explain why Europe has the potential to divide political parties. Since parties in Britain are fundamentally based on groupings of like-minded people on the socialist/laissez faire dimension, a cross-cutting issue like Europe is quite likely to be divisive – just as nuclear disarmament, another cross-cutting issue, divided the Labour party in the early 1980s.

To be sure, there are other issues, such as questions of abortion, divorce and the death penalty, which cross-cut the left/right dimension even more powerfully (see Heath *et al.*, forthcoming). But these are issues which British political parties have historically kept out of party politics. They are ones on which a free vote is typically permitted in the House of Commons, and hence their potential for creating internal party divisions has been limited. Europe and nuclear disarmament, however, are issues which fall half-way between the moral questions such as abortion and the death penalty and the economic questions of the left/right domain. Hence it is not so easy to keep them out of party politics. But nor is it easy to keep them within the conventional party framework, as perhaps the Referendum Party demonstrated among the electorate and the whipless rebels demonstrated in the House of Commons.

The Source of the Referendum Party Vote

It is the autonomy of the European question from the conventional left/right dimension that gives it its potential to divide the parties internally. Is this also a factor in the (relative) success of the Referendum Party in detaching voters from their usual party alignments, or were voters for the Referendum Party simply signalling a general right-wing protest against the Tories?

Voters for the Referendum Party were certainly not a cross-section of the electorate. They were predominantly people who had voted Conservative (and, to a lesser extent, Liberal Democrat) in 1992. Hardly anyone who had voted Labour in 1992 supported Goldsmith's party. This is shown clearly in Table 3, and although the number of Referendum Party voters in the BEPS is very small, we find the same pattern in the 1997 BES.[6]

TABLE 3
THE SOURCES OF THE REFERENDUM PARTY VOTE (COLUMN %)

| | 1992–97 panel | | 1997 BES | |
	Referendum Party voters	All	Referendum Party voters	All
Vote in 1992				
Conservative	64	41	61	35
Labour	9	31	11	34
Liberal Democrat	24	17	19	11
Other	0	3	4	2
Did not vote	3	8	6	18
Total	100	100	101	100
(N)	(33)	(1537)	(56)	(3615)

Source: BEPS 1992 and 1997 waves; BES 1997.

This evidence on the source of Referendum Party support does not on its own tell us that the formation of the party in 1995 actually took votes that the Conservatives would otherwise have won in 1997. These voters might have defected from the Conservatives whether or not Sir James Goldsmith had created his party. So what were the motivations of the Referendum Party voters? Was a vote for the Referendum Party specifically about Europe, or was it a more generalized expression of discontent among people whose right-wing sympathies made Labour unpalatable? In other words, was the Referendum Party a vehicle for right-wing disillusion with the Tories?

In order to get some insight into whether they would have defected anyway, we compare the attitudes of Referendum Party voters with those of Conservative loyalists and of Conservative defectors.[7] In Table 4 we show their attitudes on the five 11-point scales described earlier.

TABLE 4
POSITIONS ON FIVE ISSUES (MEAN SCORES)

	Referendum Party voters	Conservative loyalists	Conservative defectors	All
European integration	10.2	8.0***	7.1***	6.7
Taxes and spending	3.5	4.7**	4.0	3.8
Privatization	5.9	6.7	5.8	5.5
Unemployment	3.7	4.8*	3.8	3.7
Redistribution	5.3	6.4*	5.0	4.5
N (minimum)	32	340	240	1338

Source: BEPS 1997 wave.
Note: Significantly different from Referendum Party voters * $p < 0.05$; ** $p < 0.01$; *** $p < 0.001$

What we find is that Referendum Party voters were in fact highly distinctive in their attitudes towards Europe. Europe stands out as the only issue on which these voters were actually more extreme than the Conservative loyalists. On our European scale they placed themselves at an astonishing 10.2. Since the maximum possible score is 11, this shows how eurosceptic the Referendum Party voters felt themselves to be. Despite the small numbers, the difference between them and the Conservative loyalists is statistically significant. We can check these results from the 1997 BES and this confirms the story of Table 4.[8]

Moreover, the voters for the Referendum Party were distinctively right-wing only on Europe. On all other issues they were remarkably similar to the Tory defectors. This demonstrates once again how Europe cross-cuts the other economic issues. There is little congruence between the attitudes of the Referendum Party voters to Europe and their attitudes to the standard economic issues. Their extreme euroscepticism was not matched by an extreme free-market ideology. So in these other respects they were not perhaps natural Tories in 1992. Even back in 1992 their support for the Tories might have been conditional on the Tories' euroscepticism rather than on their general free-market policies.

We can use the panel to check whether these eurosceptic views were long-standing. In attitudinal research there is always the problem of establishing causal direction. We can never be sure, from a cross-section survey, whether people have brought their attitudes into line with their voting behaviour or the other way round. The strength of the panel design, therefore, is that we can check what these people felt about Europe long before the Referendum Party had been mooted. Because the 11-point scales were asked only of a half-sample in 1992, we use some of the other European questions. Table 5 shows the results.

TABLE 5
1992 ATTITUDES TO EUROPE (COLUMN %)

% agreeing	Referendum Party voters	Conservative loyalists	Conservative defectors	All
Britain should leave the EC /try to reduce its powers	64	57	47	42
Keep the pound as the only currency for Britain	58	55	50	49
Lots of good British traditions will have to be given up if we stay in the EC	66	40	37	39
If we stay in the EC Britain will lose control over decisions	84	56	48	51
Competition from other EC countries is making Britain more efficient	26	54	50	50
N	32	375	169	1540

Source: BEPS 1992 and 1997 waves.

Table 5 shows clearly that the Referendum Party voters were already distinctively eurosceptic in 1992, long before Goldsmith had formed his party. The causal priority of their European views is thus clear. It is also interesting that, in 1992, the eventual Referendum Party voters were more distinctive in their beliefs about the EU than in their policy preferences. They were, for example, distinctively pessimistic about the implications for British traditions and decision-making of continued membership of the EU, but they were not, at that stage, markedly different from Conservatives generally in their policy views about the single European currency or withdrawal. However, this changed over the course of the parliament and by 1997 their views on the policy issues had hardened.

By 1994 they had also clearly turned against the Conservative government. Throughout the panel we measured feelings towards the parties on five-point scales. We have coded these scales so that higher scores indicate more favourable attitudes.

TABLE 6
FEELINGS TOWARDS THE CONSERVATIVE PARTY (MEAN SCORES)

	1992	1994	1995	1996	1997	N
Referendum	3.6	2.4	2.2	2.6	2.7	32
Conservative loyalists	4.4	3.7	3.6	3.8	4.0	341
Conservative defectors	4.1	2.7	2.4	2.5	2.5	146
All	3.2	2.5	2.4	2.5	2.6	1367

Source: BEPS

Table 6 shows that Referendum Party voters had been relatively favourable to the Conservative Party in 1992, more so than the average member of our panel. But by 1994 these people who later voted for Goldsmith's party had already turned decisively against the Tories, their scores falling precipitately. By this stage of the parliament they were already very different from the Conservative loyalists and looked remarkably similar to the Conservative defectors. At this point, well before the Referendum Party had been formed, it looked highly probable that few of the Referendum Party's eventual voters would support the Conservatives again.

What was it that led them to turn against the Tories? Was it simply their record on Europe, or were other factors important too? There were in fact substantial numbers of other voters, especially of Conservative loyalists, who took up equally extreme views on European integration. Why did some of them but not others defect to the Referendum Party? To explore this we can compare the loyalists, defectors and Referendum voters on a range of measures of the Conservative government's record and image. We include in our analysis measures from the 1994 wave of BEPS of the government's record on the economy and the health service (which previous research has shown to be important) together with measures of the government's image. We also include the respondents' distance from the government on major policy issues such as Europe. The results of multivariate analyses are given in Table 7.

TABLE 7
LOGISTIC REGRESSION OF LOYALISTS, DEFECTORS AND REFERENDUM PARTY VOTERS

	Defectors versus loyalists	RP voters versus loyalists	RP voters versus defectors
Europe	-0.01	0.13**	0.10*
Taxes	0.02	-0.10	-0.08
Unemployment	-0.12***	-0.12**	0.02
The economy	0.01	-0.37	-0.38
The NHS	-0.36***	-0.09	0.24
Competence	-0.39	-0.24	0.35
Sectionalism	-1.09***	-1.25***	-0.27
Improvement (DF)	90.6 (7)	35.7 (7)	10.0 (7)
N	571	422	213

Source: BEPS 1992, 1994 and 1997 waves
Note: Significant coefficients * $p < 0.05$; ** $p < 0.01$; *** $p < 0.001$

In the first column we report the results of a logistic regression in which we contrast defectors with Conservative loyalists. In the second column we contrast voters for the Referendum Party with the loyalists. And in the third column we contrast Referendum voters with Conservative defectors.

The results are clear cut. The eventual defectors could already, in 1994, be distinguished from the loyalists by their positions on unemployment and inflation, their evaluation of the government's record on health and their perception of the government as 'good for one class' rather than 'good for all classes'. In general, the defectors were people who lay to the left of the Conservative party, towards the centre of the political spectrum; they evaluated the government's record on the NHS very unfavourably, and they felt that the Conservatives were a sectional party who were not looking after all groups in society equally.

The eventual voters for the Referendum Party also, with one crucial exception, showed the same profile. They too lay towards the centre of the left/right spectrum on unemployment and inflation, and they shared negative views about the government's sectionalism. The only respect in which they differed significantly from the defectors was in their attitudes to Europe, where they lay well to the right, both of the loyalists and of the defectors.

The natural interpretation of these results is that it was disenchantment with the government's policies and record that led both the defectors and the Referendum Party voters to abandon the government and that it was their attitudes to Europe which decided whether they abandoned them for a centre-left party or for a eurosceptic party. To be sure, even from a multivariate analysis such as this, we cannot definitively disentangle the causal processes involved. It is possible that it was the government's record over Europe that led to the general disillusion of the Referendum voters; it is logically possible that if, say, the government had not signed the Maastricht treaty, the Referendum Party voters would have taken more charitable views of the government's performance in other areas (such as the NHS) too. But while we cannot rule out this alternative interpretation, the similarity of the results for the Referendum Party and for the other Conservative defectors inclines us to the view that there were similar processes at work.

On our preferred interpretation, then, the formation of the Referendum Party made little or no difference to the Conservatives' share of the vote; it simply affected the distribution of the anti-Conservative vote between the opposition parties. If we repeat the analysis using 1997 rather than 1994 measures, the story is virtually unchanged. The creation of the Referendum Party did not materially affect the patterns displayed in Table 7 (and nor for that matter did three more years of Conservative government).

Some further evidence in line with our interpretation comes from the way our respondents voted in the 1994 European elections, which is reported in Table 8.

TABLE 8
VOTE IN THE 1994 EUROPEAN ELECTIONS (ROW %)

	Conservative	Labour	Liberal Democrat	Other	Did not vote
Loyalists	49	1	4	4	41
Defectors	13	10	19	3	56
Referendum	11	14	13	23	40
All	16	24	12	5	44

Source: BEPS 1992, 1994 and 1997 waves

Again, at this stage, the actual voting behaviour of the eventual Referendum Party supporters showed many similarities with that of the Conservative defectors, especially in their lack of support for the government. They did however display higher turnout in the European elections (no doubt reflecting their concern with Europe), and they also showed at that stage a propensity to support the minor parties rather than the main opposition parties (no doubt because the positions of Labour and the Liberal Democrats on Europe were even more distasteful to them than those of the Conservative government).[9]

So whatever put them off the Tories had already done so by 1994. In other words, the formation of the Referendum Party may well have made no difference to the Tories' loss of votes but simply capitalized upon existing disillusion.

Consequences for the Conservatives

As we noted earlier, there were 19 seats where the number of votes case for the Referendum Party exceeded the size of the opposition lead over the defeated Conservative. In addition there were another six seats where either the vote for the UK Independence Party alone, or the UKIP in combination with the Referendum Party also exceeded the Conservative majority.

Our data show clearly that the Referendum Party primarily gained votes from people who had voted Conservative in 1992. Table 3 suggests that just under two-thirds of Referendum Party voters had voted Tory in 1992. This therefore represents the upper bound for any estimate of how many might have supported the Conservatives again in 1997 if the Referendum Party had not been formed. Depending on what assumptions are made about how the remaining one-third divided, this means that eurosceptic candidates can have cost the Conservatives 18 seats at most (and perhaps as few as 13).

But our analysis in the previous section makes it very implausible that anything like two-thirds of the Referendum Party voters would actually have supported the Conservatives again in 1997 in the way they had done in 1992. As we have seen, they were just as disillusioned as other defectors with the Conservative government.

Unfortunately we have too few respondents in the panel to be able to determine how people with similar views behaved in the constituencies where Goldsmith did not put up a candidate. But we can look at what our respondents said their second choice of party would have been in 1997. The responses are shown in Table 9.

Table 9 reinforces our claim that the Referendum Party voters were very like the Conservative defectors, and it suggests that they would have divided their votes fairly evenly between the main parties. On this evidence, the effect of the Referendum Party was entirely neutral, and so if the upper bound is that

TABLE 9
SECOND CHOICE OF VOTE IN THE 1997 ELECTION (ROW %)

	Conservative	Labour	Liberal Democrat	Other	None/ NA
Loyalists	-	19	45	7	29
Defectors	31	15	26	4	24
Referendum	26	23	25	6	19
All	7	17	45	7	24

Source: BEPS 1992 and 1997 waves (excluding non-voters)

Goldsmith cost the Conservatives 18 seats, the lower bound is that it did not cost them any at all. However, the actual cost may well have been slightly more than this lower bound: the 1997 BES shows somewhat more second choices for the Conservatives and fewer for Labour. Thus in the BES 36 per cent of the Referendum Party voters gave their second choices to the Conservatives, 30 per cent to the Liberal Democrats, and 18 per cent to Labour. This suggests a very similar estimate to the one that Curtice and Steed (1997) reached on the basis of their analysis of the aggregate data. They concluded that 'there are just six seats where the presence of an anti-European candidate can be said to have cost the Conservatives the seat, of which two were the result of a UKIP rather than a Referendum Party intervention' (p.308).

Conclusions

Voters for the Referendum Party were remarkably eurosceptic but were unremarkable in most other respects. They show no sign of being right-wing on the economic issues of the left-right dimension and they were not consistently right-wing ideologues. Their vote does not therefore appear to have been either part of a specifically right-wing revolt against the Conservatives or a general diffuse protest vote. The fact that these voters chose the Referendum Party rather than any of the other options open to them was undoubtedly a result of their long-standing and specific concerns about Europe.

At the same time, however, data from the panel study shows that their disillusion with the Conservative party was also long-standing and was already evident at the European elections of 1994, well before the Referendum Party had been formed. In almost all respects, other than their attitudes to Europe, the eventual Referendum Party voters were remarkably similar to other defectors from the Conservatives and we therefore conclude that Sir James Goldsmith's formation of the party probably had little or no impact on the Conservative share of votes or seats, but simply redistributed the anti-Conservative vote away from the centre-left parties.

Our evidence also suggests that, had the Conservatives adopted a more eurosceptic line in order to appease Sir James Goldsmith, this would have been of little electoral advantage to them. The Conservatives were already well-placed on Europe, their perceived position being closer to that of the average voter than was that of any of the other major parties. A further shift towards euroscepticism would, if anything, have reduced the Conservatives' overall appeal. It would only have made sense if it would have won back the passionate minority who adopted extreme eurosceptic views. But on its own a changed policy on Europe might not have been sufficient to win back the voters who defected to the Referendum Party, since their disillusion with the Conservatives was more thorough-going. To become electable once more the Conservatives need to tackle the problems that worried both defectors and eurosceptics alike.

ACKNOWLEDGEMENTS

We wish to thank the ESRC for funding CREST and the British Election Panel Study. Philip Cowley made very helpful editorial suggestions and we are also indebted to our colleagues in CREST: John Curtice, Geoffrey Evans, Lindsay Brook, Pippa Norris and Mandy Roberts.

NOTES

1. Some Referendum Party supporters make even more extravagant claims. Lord McAlpine claimed in *The Times* (7 October 1997) that it is 'generally accepted' that the Referendum Party cost 40 Conservative MPs their seats.
2. We can check these findings from the 1997 BES. In the BES we find that rather more, 17 per cent, felt that Britain should leave the EU but rather fewer, 43 per cent, felt that Britain should try to reduce the powers of the EU.
3. The 1997 BES shows 16 per cent wishing to replace the pound, 20 per cent wishing to have both, and 60 per cent wishing to have only the pound.
4. The 1997 figures can be checked against the 1997 BES. The results for the BES are comfortingly close to the 1997 BEPS figures: 6.6 for Europe, 5.3 for privatization, 4.3 for inequality, 3.7 for unemployment and 3.7 for taxes.
5. Factor analysis of the five items used in Table 2 yields a single factor, but the loading for Europe, at 0.37, is much lower than those for the other items, which are all around 0.70. The same pattern holds in the 1997 BES.
6. As might be expected, there are some differences in the distribution of 1992 vote between the two sources. The panel shows a lower proportion of 1992 non-voters since non-voters are particularly likely to drop out of a political panel study. On the other hand, the 1997 BES shows a higher ratio of 1992 Labour to Liberal Democrats, almost certainly reflecting recall bias.
7. Loyalists are defined as respondents who voted Conservative both in 1992 and in 1997. Defectors are defined as people who voted Conservative in 1992 but then in 1997 either abstained or voted for a party other than the Conservatives or Referendum Party. The Referendum Party voters include all those who reported voting for the RP in 1997, irrespective of how they voted in 1992. Respondents for whom there were missing data on either the 1992 or 1997 vote questions are excluded, but the base includes non-voters.
8. In the 1997 BES the Referendum Party voters scored 10.0 on European integration, 5.4 on redistribution, 5.8 on privatization, 4.0 on taxes and spending, and 3.9 on unemployment.
9. Thus their average distance was 4.2 points to the right of the Tories, but 7.1 to the right of

Labour and 7.5 to the right of the LDs (whom they correctly perceived as being the most europhile of the three parties).

REFERENCES

Curtice, John K., and Michael Steed (1997) 'An Analysis of the Voting', in David Butler and Dennis Kavanagh (eds) *The British General Election of 1997*, pp.295–325. London: Macmillan.

Heath, Anthony F., Geoffrey Evans and Jean Martin (1994) 'The Measurement of Core Beliefs and Values: The Development of Balanced socialist/laissez faire and libertarian/authoritarian Scales', *British Journal of Political Science* 24: 115–32.

Heath, Anthony F., Bridget Taylor, Lindsay Brook and Alison Park (forthcoming) 'British national sentiment', *British Journal of Political Science*.

Split-ticket Voting at the 1997 British General and Local Elections: An Aggregate Analysis

Colin Rallings and Michael Thrasher

Split-ticket voting, the practice of electors casting a ballot for different parties on the same visit to the polling booth, has long been of interest to political scientists. First systematically studied in America in the wake of the contrasting Republican presidential and Democrat congressional successes of the Eisenhower period, the phenomenon has subsequently been identified and analysed in a wide range of countries.

In Britain, split-ticket voting has been largely ignored – not because the British electorate might be seen in some way as immune to its temptations, but because there have been so few instances of two different types of election occurring on the same day. As far as general elections are concerned it has happened just twice, in 1979 and 1997, when polling coincided with the annual local election contests. The 1979 experience spawned a small literature focusing on local/national variations in behaviour. Waller, for example, found that 'in general electors did not split their...votes in the borough constituencies in May 1979 [but] … in rural areas … the correlation between local and parliamentary results is much less close' (Waller, 1980). On the other hand both Game (1981) and Cox and Laver (1979) provide evidence of considerable split-ticket voting in urban England too. Nonetheless, the subject received scant attention from 'flagship' sources such as the 1979 Nuffield study (Butler and Kavanagh, 1980) or the report of the British Election Study (Sarlvik and Crewe, 1983).

In this article we wish to examine the evidence of split-ticket voting at the synchronous 1997 general and local elections. Are there differences in participation at the two types of election? Does split-ticket voting tend to favour particular parties in particular electoral contexts? Is it possible to identify and explain areas where voter behaviour appears to be atypical? Has split-ticket voting increased and/or become more widespread since 1979? To put the study and our findings in context, however, we begin by first reviewing some of the explanations and conclusions about split-ticket voting produced by international studies and then presenting a brief analysis of the extent to which British electors have opted for different parties when they have been able to cast more than one vote on the same occasion at local elections.

Previous Research

It is hardly surprising that the phenomenon of split-ticket voting has been extensively researched in the United States as it is not unusual for different parties to control the presidency and the Congress. At state level divided government is commonplace. During the 1950s it was estimated that one in eight voters engaged in split-ticket voting but more recent studies of presidential/congressional elections have found that ratio to be one in four or higher (Stanley and Niemi, 1990). Even that figure may be an under-estimate of the true picture. A study of ticket-splitting in Ohio state elections found that 54 per cent of voters cast a ballot for each of the main parties across five contests (Beck *et al.*, 1992). Outside the US other studies have encountered a similar growth in split-ticket voting. In Germany, for example, Jesse (1988) found that the practice had increased over the previous 30 years as the electorate became more accustomed to the electoral system. Voters' willingness to exploit certain characteristics of the electoral system also appears to lie at the heart of increased split-ticket voting in Australia (Bowler and Denmark, 1993).

Various theories have been advanced to help explain why voters appear more willing than before to divide their loyalty between competing parties. Chief among these is the fact that as voters identify less with one particular party so they become more volatile in their electoral behaviour. That volatility, once expressed by voters switching to a different party at different stages of the electoral cycle, has now advanced to the point where voters feel able to switch between parties at the same election. As Hadley and Howell argued (1979, 274), 'Ticket-splitting may well be the first step in dealignment.' That same process of weakening party identification has been encountered in various studies of voters in Britain, the latest estimate being that less than two-fifths of voters now identify with one of the two major parties (Brynin and Sanders, 1997). It would seem likely, therefore, that the decline in party identification should also result in a greater incidence of split-ticket voting in Britain.

Other key factors which have been presented as possible explanations for split-ticket voting include the effect that individual candidates might have upon voters. Where voters respond positively to a party's candidate for president, for example, congressional candidates from that same party may benefit from a so-called 'coat-tails' effect. Equally, a negative image of the presidential candidate might act to dampen enthusiasm for other candidates from that party. McAllister and Darcy (1992) found that split-ticket voters at the 1988 election were both less positive and less negative about presidential candidates and in such cases the 'coat-tails' effect would have less impact. Another relevant candidate characteristic is political incumbency. Incumbents are particularly successful at winning re-election to the House of Representatives and do appear to benefit from a bias amongst split-ticket voters. Beck *et al.* (1992) found that a candidate's visibility during an election was an important factor in attracting support from split-ticket voters and that incumbents normally enjoyed higher visibility than their rivals.

A further area for consideration in explaining split-ticket voting lies with the nature of the ballot paper itself and, more generally, the way in which the electoral system operates to translate votes into seats. Both McAllister and Darcy (1992) and Beck *et al.* (1992) found that ballot papers allowing voters a straight party choice showed less evidence of ticket-splitting than those ballots where candidates were arranged by office rather than by party. Bowler and Denemark (1993), in a study of single transferable vote (STV) elections to the Australian Senate, demonstrate the tendency for supporters of the major parties to transfer preferences to candidates from the minor parties. In their view this ticket-splitting is entirely consistent with continuing partisanship because, 'while voters may split their ballots and *appear* to stray from strict partisan loyalty they appear more often than not to remain loyal to the same ideological bloc' (Bowler and Denemark, 1993: 24). In the context of the 1997 British general election, therefore, we might expect to find few voters dividing their ballot between the two main parties but rather more willing to support different parties viewed as proximate ideologically.

Split-ticket Voting and Local Elections

Local voters in Britain have two types of opportunity to engage in split-ticket voting. The most common occurs where more than one councillor is elected in a single ward at the same time and voters thus have the opportunity to divide their ballot between competing parties which usually field as many candidates as there are vacancies. The evidence, however, is that the greater tendency is not to use all available votes rather than to split them between parties (Denver and Hands, 1975; Rallings, Thrasher and Gunter, forthcoming).

A second opportunity to test for ticket-splitting comes when elections for different local authorities are held on the same day and with electoral units sharing the same boundaries. We have identified a small number of cases where district council by-elections have been held on the same day as the regular, quadrennial county council elections and where county division and district ward boundaries are identical. Potential split-ticket voters in these areas could, theoretically, support one party at the county election and another at the district by-election. Table 1 shows the mean difference in absolute share between a party's vote in the county election and the corresponding district level by-election. Although the number of cases must caution us against generalization, the fact that the range of values and the standard deviations are consistently small does suggest that ticket-splitting at this level is not widespread.

TABLE 1
VARIATIONS IN PARTY SUPPORT AT COUNTY AND DISTRICT ELECTIONS

		Con	Lab	All/LD	Turnout	N
1985	mean diff	1.1	1.0	1.7	0.6	7
	stdev	0.7	1.2	2.1	0.5	
1989	mean diff	2.2	2.4	1.5	0.1	21
	stdev	1.4	2.0	1.6	1.1	
1993	mean diff	1.5	1.2	1.4	0.6	14
	stdev	1.7	1.5	1.3	0.4	

Surveys have found that many electors cannot identify the specific functions of county and district authorities and in such circumstances it is not surprising that they do not treat their two votes as though they were for different types of authority. In short, the electoral context is perceived to be the same – who do I want to represent me as a councillor? Who do I want to run the council? The difference in electoral context is likely to be much clearer as we turn to examine voting at the 1997 general election and the simultaneous local authority contests.

The 1997 General and Local Elections

As in 1979, the fact that the local and general elections were held on the same day did not provide quite the analytical feast that might have been hoped for. The local elections due on 1 May 1997 were for 34 English shire county councils, together with inaugural elections for 19 new unitary authorities and one substantially revised district council, and partial council elections for two previously established unitary authorities. This meant that only about half the total English electorate had local contests in their area – there were no elections at all in Scotland, Wales, London or metropolitan England – and that only in a minority of cases did local and constituency boundaries coincide. For although parliamentary constituencies use whole district council wards as their building blocks, county council electoral divisions are not themselves required to be amalgams of district wards and frequently cross constituency boundaries. Furthermore, not all the wards in a local authority area are necessarily contested at every electoral cycle. For example, although there were local elections in Bristol on 1 May, in not one of the city's four parliamentary seats were they due to take place in every constituent ward.

Within such constraints we have been able to compile two sets of data. First, there are 56 constituencies where a whole number of county divisions or unitary wards exactly match the parliamentary boundaries and where electors had two votes – one at the general election and one at the local election. In two additional cases, Harrogate and Knaresborough and Harwich, there are very small discrepancies in boundaries but we have included the constituencies because of their political interest in 1997. Second, there are 20 constituencies where unitary ward and constituency boundaries match, but where electors had up to three votes at the local election in addition to their general election vote. The existence of such multi-member wards makes analysis more difficult as parties sometimes do not field a full slate of candidates in each ward and electors are able to split their vote not only between the parliamentary and local contests but within the local election as well. For present purposes we have added together the votes of each party's best performing candidate in each ward for our comparison with the general election result and we have not attempted to calculate local turnout in such cases. The detailed information from these two types of constituency is set out in an appendix to this article.

Turnout

As in 1979 there is no indication of gross disparities in turnout at the two elections – the difference in average turnout being less than one per cent with a small standard deviation of 1.3 (see Table 2). Although normal local election turnout in Britain is little more than half the level common at general elections, the figures suggest no intrinsic reluctance to vote in local contests once the crucial decision actually to visit the polling booth has been made. In a minority of cases turnout at the local elections was the higher. Partly this can be explained by the fact that the local electoral register includes EU citizens, peers and the like who are disbarred from voting at general elections, but a number of electors must have cast their local election vote and then gone home. Some will have done so consciously, though others might have thought they only had one vote and cast it at the locals 'by mistake'. One electoral administrator put to us the possibility that because so many of the local contests were straightforward three-party fights between Conservative, Labour and Liberal Democrat with the general election ballot paper by contrast often being filled out by fringe candidates (a total of seven candidates in his constituency), electors might have been confused. In 1979 the reverse could have been the case, with more non-party local candidates and just 536 (as against 1363 in 1997) 'others' in English constituencies at the general election.

TABLE 2
LOCAL/GENERAL ELECTION VOTING COMPARISONS
(SINGLE MEMBER LOCAL ELECTORAL UNITS)

		Con	Lab	LD	Ref	Other	Turnout
Average*	Local	33.0	38.5	23.1	0.0	3.6	70.8
	General	34.8	42.3	16.8	3.2	1.5	71.7
n=58	Diff	1.8	3.7	-6.3	3.2	-2.2	0.9
Perfect	Local	34.3	37.7	27.4	0.0	0.7	72.3
competition	General	35.6	41.8	17.8	3.5	1.2	72.9
n=28	Diff	1.4	4.1	-9.5	3.5	0.5	0.6
Average with	Local	33.2	39.1	23.0	0.1	2.6	70.8
Ref cand	General	33.9	42.6	15.7	3.8	1.4	71.5
n=47	Diff	0.8	3.5	-7.3	3.7	-1.2	0.7
Average without	Local	33.6	38.9	23.6	0.0	3.8	71.4
Ref cand	General	36.4	41.0	20.7	0.0	1.9	73.0
n=10	Diff	2.8	2.1	-3.0	0.0	-1.9	1.6
Con/Lab	Local	37.8	41.1	18.8	0.0	2.3	73.8
	General	38.9	44.8	12.0	3.1	1.5	74.5
n=24	Diff	1.1	3.8	-6.8	2.9	-0.9	0.8
Con/LD	Local	37.5	24.4	33.9	0.0	4.3	73.0
	General	41.0	26.4	26.9	4.0	2.0	74.1
n=17	Diff	3.6	1.9	-7.0	3.7	-2.3	1.2
Con/Lab marg	Local	33.9	45.4	18.3	0.0	2.4	74.3
	General	35.5	50.2	10.8	2.2	1.5	75.1
n=14	Diff	1.6	4.8	-7.5	2.2	-0.9	0.8
Con/LD marg	Local	34.4	24.4	36.9	0.0	4.2	74.2
	General	37.5	24.8	32.0	4.1	2.2	75.2
n=7	Diff	3.1	0.4	-4.9	4.1	-2.0	1.0
Labour held seats	Local	23.5	56.0	18.3	0.0	2.2	68.6
	General	22.5	60.6	12.8	3.2	1.0	69.4
n=15	Diff	-1.1	4.6	-5.5	3.2	-1.2	0.9
LD local authority/	Local	37.7	22.8	37.5	0.0	2.1	73.7
largest party	General	40.8	25.1	28.8	4.0	1.8	74.4
n=13	Diff	3.1	2.3	-8.7	3.7	-0.3	0.7
Con incumbents	Local	37.4	35.2	24.9	0.0	2.5	73.6
	General	39.6	38.4	16.7	3.6	1.7	74.2
n=26	Diff	2.3	3.2	-8.2	3.6	-0.8	0.8

Notes: *Epsom and Ewell is excluded from the analysis in every category except this. A marginal
seat is one where the gap between the share of the vote for the first and second placed
parties in 1992 was less than 20 per cent.

General election participation tended to be higher, albeit never more than 4.3 per cent above local election levels, where the major parties did not field candidates in every local contest or where there remains a tradition of voting for non-party candidates in local elections. Yet in many of these cases we can find immediate evidence of split-ticket voting. In Wellingborough, for example, the Liberal Democrats fielded no candidates at all at the local elections, but their parliamentary candidate polled 5,279 votes from a standing start and only 1,028 more people voted at the general election than at the locals. In Bromsgrove, where the Liberal Democrats contested two of the ten divisions, just 495 more people voted nationally than locally, but the party's vote more than trebled from 1,951 to 6,200. There is no other explanation than that thousands of voters cast a ballot for different parties.

Patterns of Party Support

If turnout was similar at the local and general elections, much less consistency is evident in votes cast for the various political parties. On average both the Conservative and Labour parties recorded a higher level of support at the general election, as of course did the Referendum Party which fielded no local government candidates (see Table 2). On the other hand, the vote for independents and others and especially that for the Liberal Democrats was higher in the local contests. The average Liberal Democrat local vote was 6 per cent more than the party's general election vote in the same constituency, rising to an average of 9.5 per cent in those constituencies where all the parties fielded a full slate of local candidates. There was less gross variation in the vote of all parties in those constituencies in our sample which did not have Referendum Party candidates. An analysis of those constituencies with multi-member ward local elections yielded similar results.

It is of course a weakness of the aggregate data used here that they necessarily hide any counter-balanced switching by individuals. Nevertheless, we can be certain that in the sub-set of constituencies with perfect, noise-free competition nearly 10 per cent of electors voted for different parties at the two types of election. The evidence of research using survey data or actual ballot papers would lead us to expect that the true level of split-ticket voting in Britain in 1997 was perhaps twice this (Gitelson and Richard, 1983). In other words perhaps one in five of all electors faced with fully competitive contests at both the local and general elections could have cast them for different parties on 1 May.

Some indication of the overall flow of split votes may be gleaned from the results of a MORI poll conducted jointly for the Local Government Association and *Local Government Chronicle* a few days before the election. MORI found that at least 10 per cent of Conservative and Labour general election supporters intended to vote Liberal Democrat at the locals (Table 3).

This pattern accounts for the fact that the likely Liberal Democrat local vote was 7 per cent higher than the party's general election vote according to this survey, with the Conservatives down by 4 per cent and Labour by 5 per cent. Looked at the other way, whereas more than 90 per cent of respondents who intended to vote either Conservative or Labour at the local elections would also support that party at the general, fewer than three in five 'local' Liberal Democrats were likely to remain loyal, such 'deserters' favouring Labour over the Conservatives in the ratio 4:3. The survey also suggests that a clear majority of the small number of Referendum Party supporters in the sample were 'local' Conservatives.

TABLE 3
SUPPORT FOR PARTIES AT LOCAL AND NATIONAL LEVEL (COLUMN %)

Distribution of local election 'votes' by general election 'vote'

		General Election vote			
		Con	Lab	LD	Ref
Local election vote					
28	Con	79	2	2	58
42	Lab	3	84	10	16
23	LD	11	10	77	16
7	Ind	6	4	11	8

Distribution of general election 'votes' by local election 'vote'

		Local Election vote			
		Con	Lab	LD	Ind
General election vote					
32	Con	91	2	17	29
47	Lab	4	94	23	26
16	LD	1	3	57	26
3	Ref	4	1	2	16

Source: MORI for Local Government Association/Local Government Chronicle, April 1997.

While such data seem to be largely consistent with the average outcome in the full sample of constituencies, the variation in the amount and direction of split-ticket voting in different categories of constituency cannot be so easily explained. We have divided constituencies into a number of groups based on the electoral circumstances confronting voters when they went to the polling booth. The first comparison is between seats which the Referendum Party fought and those which they did not. In line with *a priori* expectations, the Conservatives received a greater increment in support from the local to the general election contest where there was no Referendum candidate (see

Table 2). Labour's vote was up on local election levels in both cases, but the average drop in Liberal Democrat share was significantly higher where there was a Referendum candidate than where there was not. In keeping with the traditional assumption that the Liberal Democrats remain the repository of elements of a floating protest vote, it could be that rather more of the party's local voters gave their general election vote to Referendum candidates than is consistent with the Liberal Democrats' policy stance as the most pro-European party

Next, it is possible to look at the different voting patterns in those seats held by the Conservatives but with a margin of less than 20 per cent over either Labour or the Liberal Democrats. In the Conservative/Labour marginals Labour's average general election vote share is almost 5 per cent above that in the locals, helped in considerable part by the Liberal Democrats losing nearly half their total local election vote in those constituencies. However, in the Conservative/Liberal Democrat marginals Labour's vote hardly varies at all, with the Conservatives appearing to benefit from a much smaller drop in total Liberal Democrat support. Although not all the Conservative/Liberal Democrat marginals in our sample were seats identified by the Liberal Democrats themselves as 'targets', the drop in vote between local and general election cost the party some additional MPs. In the somewhat wider group of constituencies where the Liberal Democrats either have majority control or are the largest party in the relevant local authority, there was even more evidence of contextual voting. In these cases the average Liberal Democrat general election vote was almost 9 per cent lower as electors chose different parties for the two types of contest.

We also identified seats where Conservative incumbents or ministers were seeking re-election. Their presence seemed to make little difference to the patterns of party support, except to provide further evidence of the likely churning of electors between parties. Indeed in these categories as in the others it is important to note the often quite high standard deviation and wide range in the difference between each party's local and general election vote in all categories of constituency. This suggests that there were few universal patterns in how votes were split and in particular that explanations should be sought through the closer examination of individual cases

The Evidence from the Results

Having looked at what happened in groups of constituencies defined by their prior electoral circumstances, we will now turn the inquiry round and look at variations in the results. We concentrate on those cases where there was 'perfect competition' at both local and national level.

The Conservatives' outstanding result was in Congleton, where their general election vote was 9.1 per cent higher than that in the locals, representing an increase of more than a quarter in their total vote. They were doubtless helped by having a well-known 'eurosceptic' candidate, Ann Winterton, and thus no Referendum Party opponent. The Liberal Democrats actually 'won' the constituency quite comfortably at the locals, but many of these supporters look to have defected to Winterton. There was almost no gross increase in Labour support. Not all eurosceptics were so fortunate. Michael Cartiss in Great Yarmouth was under threat from Labour rather than the Liberal Democrats and he benefited hardly at all from the squeezing of the already small Liberal Democrat vote. In Northampton North the Liberal Democrat vote was virtually halved, but Tony Marlow seems to have benefited from the fall-out less than his Labour opposite number.

There was a similar variation in performance where Conservatives were opposed by the Referendum Party. In Rushcliffe Ken Clarke failed to perform even as well as his Conservative county council candidates, with a drop in the Liberal Democrat general election vote helping Labour and, probably through churning among local Conservative and Liberal Democrat supporters, the Referendum Party. This pattern was also evident in the two seats which recorded the best Referendum Party result and which both happen to be in our sample. Michael Howard in Folkestone and Hythe also did a little worse than his local party and the somewhat lesser known Iain Sproat in Harwich suffered a yet larger fall. The result in Harwich should give pause to those who believe it is possible to identify seats where the Referendum Party cost the Conservatives victory. In fact Labour 'won' the local contests too and probably by a larger margin than is suggested by the figures in the appendix since some 3,500 rural electors, among whom Labour was likely to be a minority choice, are included in the local vote summary but are not in the Harwich constituency.

In a number of Conservative 'safe' seats with not dissimilar local election results the fall-out to the general election differs quite markedly. In crude terms Roger Gale in Thanet North benefited more than Labour from the drop in the Liberal Democrat local vote; in Hertsmere the gross Conservative vote hardly changed between the two elections despite a 9 per cent fall in Liberal Democrat support. The Conservatives retained the seats. In Castle Point, however, although the Conservatives 'won' in the locals, a subsequent 5 per cent fall in the general election votes cast for both them and the Liberal Democrats was enough to allow Labour through the middle and account for Robert Spink. Such differences are consistent not simply with split-ticket voting, but with different patterns of such behaviour in different constituencies.

In every constituency (except Torbay) where the Liberal Democrats fielded a full slate of local candidates the party's general election vote was less than the local vote. In seats such as Cheltenham and Winchester, benefiting like Torbay from the full deployment of the party's limited resources, the drop was very small, but in others like Cambridge, Gillingham and Pendle, where the party has a good local government base but has finished third at recent general elections, the decline was precipitate. In Cambridge, where the major parties were opposed by a single unsuccessful independent, 21,000 people voted Labour and just over 18,000 Liberal Democrat at the local elections. In the parliamentary contest, which actually attracted a slightly smaller turnout, Labour polled in excess of 27,000 and the Liberal Democrats fewer than 9,000. In Pendle, too, the Liberal Democrats slipped from a good second place locally to a poor third at the general election as their vote fell from nearly 16,000 to just 5,460. In Gillingham the Liberal Democrats quite comfortably 'won' the locals, but almost half that support haemorrhaged away at the general election to enable Labour to register an unlikely gain. Voters clearly saw no conflict in consciously supporting different parties according to the tier of government being elected: they were not necessarily driven by mere tactical considerations.

In four cases in our sample, and to a lesser extent, Labour local voters returned the favour. Labour's general election vote was lower than the local in Cheltenham, Torbay and Winchester and also in Harrogate and Knaresborough. The latter is a rare uncontentious example of tactical voting. Not only was Labour's share less than at the 1992 general election; the party's local support was cut into on 1 May in a greater proportion than in any other constituency, with most votes presumably cast for the Liberal Democrats in order to keep Norman Lamont out of the parliamentary seat. The exchange of votes between parties in safe Labour seats was comparatively minor, though in Durham, one of a number of northern Labour fiefdoms where the Liberal Democrats have cut into Labour local government support in recent years, many local Liberal Democrats appear to have plumped for Labour at the general election.

Comparing 1997 and 1979

Making direct comparisons of the incidence of split-ticket voting in 1997 and 1979 is complicated by a number of factors. The areas which had local elections on the two occasions only partially overlap – metropolitan borough contests were a key component in 1979 – and the pattern of party competition has changed radically since then. In 1979 the Liberals fought only slightly more than one in five seats in the English shire districts and there were three-party contests in fewer than half the metropolitan wards. As a result, the Liberal share of the vote then was a smaller proportion of the whole in the locals than at the general election where the party contested 414 out of the 424 seats in England with concurrent local elections. Data from the British Election Study suggest that split-ticket voting was widespread, but confirm that the Liberals did not record more support overall at the local elections (see Table 4). Where a direct comparison between similarly competitive local and national contests can be made, Waller is probably right that 'the Liberals did consistently better in the local elections', but lack of contestation alone must make one sceptical about Steed's claim that 'something of the order of a million people may have voted Liberal locally while on the same day choosing between a Callaghan and a Thatcher government' (Steed, 1979: 106). We calculate that in England outside London the Liberals received 3.4 million actual votes at the general election and 2.3 million at the locals – over a million fewer!

TABLE 4
SPLIT VOTING AT THE 1979 LOCAL AND GENERAL ELECTIONS

General election vote

	Con	Lab	Lib	Other	Total across	%
Local election vote						
Con	370	13	19	2	404	**42.8**
Lab	21	336	20	-	·377	**39.9**
Lib	22	20	61	1	104	**11.0**
Ind/Other	29	20	10	1	60	**6.3**
Total down		442	389	110	4	
%		**46.8**	**41.2**	**11.6**	**0.4**	

Total split votes (excluding local 'non-party' votes) = 118 or 12.5% of total.

Source: British Election Study 1979

In 1997 full party contestation was much more widespread. There were three-party contests in over 80 per cent of county divisions and the Liberal Democrats fielded at least one candidate in 78 per cent of unitary authority wards. We have calculated how many votes were cast for the various parties at both contests for 23 whole shire counties in England which had local elections on 1 May (see Table 5). The Conservative and Labour local vote totals are both substantially smaller than at the general election – as one would expect given the lack of complete candidatures – but the Liberal Democrats actually received nearly one-third of a million more votes. The previously cited MORI poll also suggests that there was more split-ticket voting in 1997. A greater proportion of the sample than in 1979 (15.7 per cent as against 12.5 per cent) reported an intention to switch their local and general election votes between parties, with local Liberal Democrats being the clear beneficiaries of this process (see Table 6). One feature that does not appear to have changed is that the Liberal Democrats like the Liberals occupy a position in the ideological middle. Votes are exchanged with both their political rivals whereas only very few electors split their vote between Labour and the Conservatives.

TABLE 5
LOCAL AND GENERAL ELECTION VOTING IN 23 COUNTIES, 1997

	Local election		General election	
	votes	%	votes	%
Conservative	3.30m	36.8	3.94m	37.9
Labour	2.92m	32.6	3.88m	37.3
Liberal Democrat	2.35m	26.3	2.04m	19.7

TABLE 6
SPLIT VOTING AT THE 1997 LOCAL AND GENERAL ELECTIONS

	General election vote						
	Con	Lab	Lib	Ref	Other	Total across	%
Local election vote							
Con	146	6	2	7	-	161	**28.4**
Lab	5	234	8	2	-	249	**44.0**
LibDem	20	27	65	2	5	119	**21.0**
Ind/Other	9	8	8	1	5	31	**5.5**
Green	2	2	-	1	1	6	**1.1**
Total down	182	277	83	13	11		
%	**32.2**	**48.9**	**14.7**	**2.3**	**1.9**		

Total split votes (excluding local 'non-party' votes) = 89 or 15.7% of total.

Source: MORI for Local Government Association/*Local Government Chronicle*, April 1997.

Conclusions

The results of the concurrent general and local elections held on 1 May 1997 provide important indicators of how contemporary electors behave when faced with making almost simultaneous voting decisions in different types of contest. Although recorded turnout varied little between the two elections, there was clear evidence of many individuals casting their available votes for different parties. Tabulations from constituency results show at least 5 per cent and up to 20 per cent of electors ticket-splitting in this way. The overall level of split-ticket voting appears to be higher than in 1979 according to both survey and aggregate data, in line with studies that have correlated an increase in its incidence with a decline in party identification.

The electoral context appears crucial in influencing voters. When they have been able to cast two council votes on the same day, few have opted to support different parties. However, when faced with a general election and a local election, it seems clear that many of them choose different parties according to the job that they believe needs to be done. They select 'horses for courses'. As a result of this process the Conservative and Labour parties fared better on average at the general election; the Liberal Democrat vote was consistently higher in the local elections. The Referendum Party general election vote appears from the aggregate data to have been made up largely at the expense of the Conservative and Liberal Democrat local vote. The relationship with the Conservatives is unsurprising; that with the Liberal Democrats is inconsistent in policy terms and demonstrates the continuing 'protest' element in Liberal Democrat support. In Conservative/Labour marginals Labour benefited from the Liberal Democrats losing almost half their total local election vote. In the Conservative/Liberal Democrat marginals the Liberal Democrat local vote declined by a lesser amount, but the greater proportion of it appears to have gone to the Conservatives. The Liberal Democrat local vote was significantly eaten into everywhere except in a handful of key party target constituencies. There was little evidence that incumbent, even nationally renowned, MPs performed any better than their local government colleagues, and often they did rather worse.

Although there were considerable inter-constituency variations within these broad patterns, few voters appear to have made the switch from Labour to the Conservatives or vice versa at the two elections. The simultaneous elections due to be held in Scotland and Wales in 1999 to elect both new national legislatures and continuing local authorities will provide a further test of the contingent loyalty to political parties now displayed by a significant proportion of the British electorate.

REFERENCES

Beck, P., L. Baum, A.R. Clausen and C.E. Smith (1992) 'Patterns and Sources of Ticket-splitting in Subpresidential Elections', *American Political Science Review* 86: 916–28.

Bowler S. and D. Denemark (1993) 'Split-ticket Voting in Australia: Dealignment and Inconsistent Votes Reconsidered', *Australian Journal of Political Science* 28: 19–37.

Brynin, M. and D. Sanders (1997) 'Party Identification, Political Preferences and Material Conditions', *Party Politics* 3.1: 53–77.

Butler D. and D. Kavanagh (1980) *The British General Election of 1979*. London: Macmillan.

Cox W. and M. Laver (1979) 'Local and National Voting in British Elections: Lessons from the Synchro-polls of 1979', *Parliamentary Affairs* 32: 383–93.

Denver D. and G. Hands (1975) 'Differential Party Votes in Multi-Member Electoral Divisions', *Political Studies* 23: 486–90.

Game, C. (1981) 'Local Elections', *Local Government Studies* 7: 63–8.

Gitelson, A. and P. Richard (1983) 'Ticket-Splitting: Aggregate Measures vs. Actual Ballots', *Western Political Quarterly* 36: 410–9.

Hadley, C. and S. Howell (1979) 'Partisan Conversion in the North East: An Analysis of Split-ticket Voting, 1952–1976', *American Politics Quarterly* 7: 259–82.

Jesse, E. (1988) 'Split-voting in the Federal Republic of Germany: An Analysis of the Federal Elections from 1953–1987', *Electoral Studies* 7: 109–24.

McAllister, I. and R. Darcy (1992) 'Sources of Split-ticket voting in the 1988 American Elections', Political Studies 40: 695–712.

Rallings, C., M. Thrasher and C. Gunter (forthcoming) 'Patterns of Voting Choice in Multimember Districts: The Case of British Local Elections', *Electoral Studies*

Sarlvik B. and I. Crewe (1983) *Decade of Dealignment*. Cambridge: Cambridge University Press.

Stanley, H. and R. Niemi (1990) *Vital Statistics on American Politics*, 2nd ed. Washington DC: Congressional Quarterly Press.

Steed, M. (1979) 'The Liberal Party' in H. Drucker (ed) *Multi-Party Britain*. London: Macmillan.

Waller, R. (1980) 'The 1979 Local and General Elections in England and Wales', *Political Studies* 28: 443–50.

APPENDIX

The party notionally holding each constituency is shown below the constituency name. In Conservative-held seats the second party is also identified and the margin of victory with 1 = majority less than 10 per cent; 2 = majority between 10 per cent and 19.9 per cent; 3 = majority between 20 per cent and 29.9 per cent; 4 = majority 30 per cent or more.

For each constituency we show the party vote shares and turnout in the local and the general election, the difference between the two, the number of wards contested by each party and the total number of wards in the constituency. The Referendum Party did not fight any local elections.

TABLE A1
CONSTITUENCIES WITH SINGLE-MEMBER DIVISION COUNTY/UNITARY ELECTIONS 1 MAY

Constituency		Con	Lab	LD	Ref	Oth	Tot wds	T'out
Ashford	Local	41.9	28.2	29.9	0	0.0		72.5
	General	41.4	31.7	19.7	5.8	1.4		74.2
Con/LD 4	diff	-0.5	3.5	-10.2	5.8	1.4		1.7
	wards	6	6	6		0	6	
Barrow	Local	34.4	55.1	9.3	0	1.2		72.1
and Furness	General	27.2	57.3	8.8	2.5	4.1		72.0
Lab	diff	-7.2	2.2	-0.5	2.5	2.9		-0.2
	wards	16	16	8		1	16	
Bassetlaw	Local	29.1	58.6	7.5	0	4.8		66.1
	General	24.7	61.1	10.3	3.8	0.0		70.4
Lab	diff	-4.4	2.5	2.8	3.8	-4.8		4.3
	wards	7	7	3		1	7	
Bedford	Local	29.2	41.6	28.5	0	0.6		73.5
	General	33.7	50.6	12.4	3.1	0.3		73.5
Con/Lab 1	diff	4.5	9.0	-16.1	3.1	-0.3		0.0
	wards	12	12	12		1	12	
Blaby	Local	40.1	32.3	20.5	0	7.0		75.0
	General	45.8	33.8	14.9	3.8	1.7		76.0
Con/Lab 4	diff	5.7	1.5	-5.6	3.8	-5.3		1.0
	wards	7	8	7		2	8	
Blyth Valley	Local	12.3	62.9	22.9	0	1.8		65.3
	General	13.3	64.2	22.5	0	0.0		68.8
Lab	diff	1.0	1.3	-0.4	0	-1.8		3.5
	wards	17	17	16		1	17	
Bognor Regis and Little-	Local	34.6	24.6	32.8	0	8.0		70.0
hampton	General	44.2	28.5	24.0	0	3.3		69.6
Con/LD 4	diff	9.6	3.9	-8.8	0	-4.7		-0.4
	wards	7	8	8		3	8	

TABLE A1 (continued)

Constituency		Con	Lab	LD	Ref	Oth	Tot wds	T'out
Bromsgrove	Local	52.1	41.2	3.8	0	2.9		76.3
	General	47.2	37.8	11.9	2.7	0.5		77.1
Con/Lab 3	diff	-4.9	-3.4	8.1	2.7	-2.4		0.7
	wards	10	10	2		2	10	
Broxtowe	Local	35.5	39.3	23.6	0	1.7		77.7
	General	37.4	47.0	11.9	3.6	0.0		78.3
Con/Lab 2	diff	1.9	7.7	-11.7	3.6	-1.7		0.6
	wards	8	8	8		4	8	
Burnley	Local	21.6	53.8	23.8	0	0.8		66.7
	General	20.2	57.9	17.4	4.4	0.0		66.9
Lab	diff	-1.4	4.1	-6.4	4.4	-0.8		0.3
	wards	6	6	6		1	6	
Cambridge	Local	24.0	40.2	35.1	0	0.7		72.7
	General	25.9	53.4	16.1	2.5	2.1		71.5
Lab	diff	1.9	13.2	-19.0	2.5	1.4		-1.2
	wards	12	12	12		1	12	
Canterbury	Local	38.2	27.9	30.0	0	3.9		72.2
	General	38.7	31.3	23.8	4.6	1.7		72.5
Con/LD 2	diff	0.5	3.4	-6.2	4.6	-2.2		0.2
	wards	6	6	6		6	6	
Castle Point	Local	45.1	40.3	14.4	0	0.2		71.6
	General	40.1	42.4	9.2	5.6	2.7		72.1
Con/Lab 4	diff	-5.0	2.1	-5.2	5.6	2.5		0.5
	wards	6	6	6		1	6	
Cheltenham	Local	34.4	14.7	50.9	0	0.0		75.0
	General	36.2	10.1	49.5	2.1	2.1		74.0
LD	diff	1.8	-4.6	-1.4	2.1	2.1		-1.0
	wards	11	11	11		0	11	
Chorley	Local	34.6	48.0	16.6	0	0.8		76.7
	General	35.9	53.0	8.5	2.3	0.3		77.3
Con/Lab 1	diff	1.3	5.0	-8.1	2.3	-0.5		0.7
	wards	6	6	6		6	6	
Congleton	Local	32.1	26.8	38.9	0	2.1		77.2
	General	41.2	27.5	29.7	0	1.5		77.6
Con/LD 2	diff	9.1	0.7	-9.2	0	-0.6		0.4
	wards	6	6	6		1	6	
Copeland	Local	35.0	59.2	5.8	0	0.0		75.5
	General	29.2	58.2	9.2	2.5	0.9		76.3
Lab	diff	-5.8	-1.0	3.4	2.5	0.9		0.8
	wards	12	12	4		0	12	

TABLE A1 (continued)

Constituency		Con	Lab	LD	Ref	Oth	Tot wds	T'out
Crawley	Local	33.5	53.9	12.4	0	0.2		72.1
	General	31.8	55.0	8.2	3.8	1.1		72.9
Con/Lab 1	diff	-1.7	1.1	-4.2	3.8	0.9		0.7
	wards	9	9	8		1	9	
Durham North	Local	14.2	68.3	16.2	0	1.3		68.4
	General	14.5	70.3	11.1	4.1			68.0
Lab	diff	0.3	2.0	-5.1	4.1	-1.3		-0.4
	wards	10	10	8		1	10	
Durham	Local	15.2	55.3	25.3	0	4.2		70.4
	General	17.5	63.3	15.3	3.5	0.4		70.8
Lab	diff	2.3	8.0	-10.0	3.5	-3.8		0.4
	wards	10	10	10		4	10	
Epsom and Ewell	Local	8.2	8.4	27.6	0	55.8		69.9
	General	45.6	24.4	22.9	4.4	2.8		74.0
Con/LD 4	diff	37.4	16.0	-4.7	4.4	-53.0		4.1
	wards	2	3	7		7	7	
Exeter	Local	24.7	38.0	24.6	0	12.6		76.0
	General	28.6	47.5	18.0	0	5.9		77.9
Con/Lab 1	diff	3.9	9.5	-6.6	0	-6.7		1.9
	wards	9	9	9		8	9	
Falmouth and Camborne	Local	23.1	31.6	28.1	0	17.2		72.6
	General	28.8	33.8	25.2	6.6	5.5		75.1
Con/LD 1	diff	5.7	2.2	-2.9	6.6	-11.7		2.5
	wards	13	15	15		11	15	
Fareham	Local	35.0	20.9	34.3	0	9.8		75.4
	General	46.8	27.0	19.6	5.6	1.0		75.9
Con/LD 4	diff	11.8	6.1	-14.7	5.6	-8.8		0.5
	wards	5	5	5		2	5	
Folkestone and Hythe	Local	39.5	23.6	35.8	0	1.1		70.9
	General	39.0	24.9	26.9	8.1	1.2		72.7
Con/LD 2	diff	-0.5	1.3	-8.9	8.1	0.1		1.9
	wards	6	6	6		3	6	
Gloucester	Local	31.1	43.8	25.0	0	0.2		72.9
	General	35.7	50.0	10.5	2.6	1.3		73.4
Con/Lab 1	diff	4.6	6.2	-14.5	2.6	1.1		0.6
	wards	12	12	12		1	12	
Gosport	Local	38.3	24.5	35.7	0	1.6		69.7
	General	43.6	30.7	19.6	5.3	0.9		70.3
Con/LD 4	diff	5.3	6.2	-16.1	5.3	-0.7		0.5
	wards	6	6	6		1	6	

TABLE A1 (continued)

Constituency		Con	Lab	LD	Ref	Oth	Tot wds	T'out
Gravesham	Local	37.7	49.6	12.7	0	0.0		76.1
	General	38.8	49.7	7.8	2.7	1.0		76.9
Con/Lab 1	diff	1.1	0.1	-4.9	2.7	1.0		0.8
	wards	6	6	6		0	6	
Great Yarmouth	Local	35.1	51.2	13.7	0	0.0		70.2
	General	35.6	53.4	11.0	0	0.0		71.3
Con/Lab 1	diff	0.5	2.2	-2.7	0	0.0		1.2
	wards	10	10	10		0	10	
Harrogate and Knaresb'gh	Local	35.3	14.8	44.9	0	5.1		n/a
	General	38.5	8.7	51.5	0	1.3		72.9
	(inexact)	diff	3.2	-6.1	6.6	0	-3.8	
Con/LD 2	wards	11	11	10		1	11	
Harwich	Local	38.2	39.8	22.0	0	0.0		n/a
(inexact)	General	36.5	38.8	13.2	9.2	2.4		70.6
Con/Lab 3	diff	-1.7	-1.0	-8.8	9.2	2.4		
	wards	6	6	6		0	6	
Hertsmere	Local	43.8	34.4	21.8	0	0.0		74.0
	General	44.3	38.2	12.8	3.4	1.3		73.9
Con/Lab 4	diff	0.5	3.8	-9.0	3.4	1.3		0.0
	wards	7	7	7		0	7	
Hull East	Local	15.5	67.5	16.1	0	0.9		58.4
	General	13.7	71.3	9.8	4.4	0.8		59.2
Lab	diff	-1.8	3.8	-6.3	4.4	-0.1		0.8
	wards	7	7	7		1	7	
Hull North	Local	16.4	61.4	22.3	0	0		56.7
	General	15.1	65.8	14.6	4.0	0.6		57.0
Lab	diff	-1.3	4.4	-7.7	4.0	0.6		0.2
	wards	7	7	7		0	7	
Ipswich	Local	35.6	52.4	12.0	0	0.0		70.5
	General	31.1	52.7	12.2	3.4	0.7		72.2
Lab	diff	-4.5	0.3	0.2	3.4	0.7		1.7
	wards	12	12	8		0	12	
N.W. Leics	Local	29.9	51.1	16.9	0	2.1		79.2
	General	31.0	56.4	8.6	4.0	0.0		80.0
Con/Lab 1	diff	1.1	5.3	-8.3	4.0	-2.1		0.7
	wards	8	8	8		1	8	
Maidstone	Local	41.8	21.4	34.7	0	2.1		70.1
	General	44.1	26.2	22.4	3.7	3.6		73.7
Con/LD 3	diff	2.3	4.8	-12.3	3.7	1.5		3.6
	wards	6	6	6		4	6	

TABLE A1 (continued)

Constituency		Con	Lab	LD	Ref	Oth	Tot wds	T'out
Mansfield	Local	23.1	59.7	17.2	0	0.0		69.2
	General	21.2	64.4	11.1	3.4	0.0		70.7
Lab	diff	-1.9	4.7	-6.1	3.4	0.0		1.5
	wards	8	8	8		0	8	
Mole Valley	Local	48.2	12.8	38.9	0	0.0		77.3
	General	48.0	14.8	29.3	4.5	3.5		78.4
Con/LD 3	diff	-0.2	2.0	-9.6	4.5	3.5		1.1
	wards	7	7	7		0	7	
North Norfolk	Local	29.3	27.7	28.4	0	14.6		74.5
	General	36.5	25.1	34.3	4.2	0.0		76.0
Con/LD 3	diff	7.2	-2.6	5.9	4.2	-14.6		1.5
	wards	8	10	9		10	10	
Northampton North	Local	28.5	46.7	24.2	0	0.6		68.7
	General	33.4	52.7	12.7	0	1.2		70.1
Con/Lab 1	diff	4.9	6.0	-11.5	0	0.6		1.4
	wards	12	12	12		2	12	
Oxford East	Local	21.1	46.4	19.0	0	13.5		68.5
	General	22.0	56.8	14.7	2.9	3.6		68.4
Lab	diff	0.9	10.4	-4.3	2.9	-9.9		0.0
	wards	12	12	12		12	12	
Pendle	Local	25.1	41.0	33.9	0	0.0		74.2
	General	30.3	53.3	11.6	4.9	0.0		74.6
Lab	diff	5.2	12.3	-22.3	4.9	0.0		0.4
	wards	6	6	6		0	6	
Runnymede & Weybridge	Local	48.2	28.8	17.0	0	6.0		67.7
	General	48.6	29.4	16.3	4.2	1.5		71.5
Con/LD 4	diff	0.4	0.6	-0.7	4.2	-4.5		3.8
	wards	6	6	5		3	6	
Rushcliffe	Local	45.0	31.4	22.7	0	0.9		78.3
	General	44.4	36.2	14.3	4.3	0.8		78.8
Con/Lab 4	diff	-0.6	4.8	-8.4	4.3	-0.1		0.5
	wards	9	9	9		1	9	
Shrewsbury and Atcham	Local	29.5	33.7	36.8	0	0.0		74.5
	General	34.0	37.0	25.0	2.4	1.6		75.2
Con/LD 2	diff	4.5	3.3	-11.8	2.4	1.6		0.7
	wards	13	16	16		0	16	

TABLE A1 (continued)

Constituency		Con	Lab	LD	Ref	Oth	Tot wds	T'out
Shropshire								
North	Local	34.3	31.2	31.6	0	2.9		70.5
	General	40.2	36.0	20.4	3.4			72.6
Con/Lab 3	diff	5.9	4.8	-11.2	3.4	-2.9		2.1
	wards	12	13	11		1	14	
Sittingbourne	Local	33.2	37.3	29.6	0	0.0		71.9
and Sheppey	General	36.4	40.6	18.3	2.3	2.4		72.3
Con/LD 3	diff	3.2	3.3	-11.3	2.3	2.4		0.3
	wards	5	5	5		0	5	
South								
Holland	Local	47.3	27.5	17.8	0	7.3		69.1
and The	General	49.3	33.3	15.6	0	1.8		71.9
Deepings	diff	2.0	5.8	-2.2	0	-5.5		2.8
Con/Lab 4	wards	10	10	10		4	10	
Spelthorne	Local	47.5	35.4	17.1	0	0.0		71.5
	General	44.9	38.2	13.1	2.9	0.9		73.6
Con/Lab 4	diff	-2.6	2.8	-4.0	2.9	0.9		2.1
	wards	7	7	6		0	7	
Thanet North	Local	39.9	35.9	23.2	0	0.9		70.8
	General	44.1	38.4	11.4	5.2	0.9		68.8
Con/Lab 4	diff	4.2	2.5	-11.8	5.2	0.0		-2.0
	wards	6	6	6		2	6	
Tunbridge								
Wells	Local	45.3	17.9	36.0	0	0.9		72.9
	General	45.2	20.4	29.7	3.8	0.9		74.1
Con/LD 3	diff	-0.1	2.5	-6.3	3.8	0.0		1.2
	wards	6	6	6		2	6	
Warwick	Local	37.1	35.1	21.3	0	6.6		74.5
and	General	38.9	44.5	11.9	2.5	2.4		75.1
Leamington	diff	1.8	9.4	-9.4	2.5	-4.2		0.7
Con/Lab 2	wards	13	13	13		10	13	
Warwickshire	Local	30.2	58.4	7.8	0	3.6		73.6
North	General	31.2	58.4	7.5	1.7	1.3		74.8
Lab	diff	1.0	0.0	-0.3	1.7	-2.3		1.2
	wards	12	12	6		2	12	
Welling-	Local	47.3	51.8	0.0	0	0.9		73.5
borough	General	43.8	44.2	9.4	0	2.7		74.8
Con/Lab 2	diff	-3.5	-7.6	9.4	0	1.8		1.4
	wards	12	12	0		1	12	
Winchester	Local	43.3	12.7	43.8	0	0.1		77.8
	General	42.1	10.5	42.1	2.6	2.7		78.3
Con/LD 2	diff	-1.2	-2.2	-1.7	2.6	2.6		0.5
	wards	6	6	6		1	6	

TABLE A1 (continued)

Constituency		Con	Lab	LD	Ref	Oth	Tot wds	T'out
Worcester	Local	38.8	44.6	16.6	0	0.0		72.8
	General	35.7	50.1	12.5	0	1.7		74.6
Con/Lab 1	diff	-3.1	5.5	-4.1	0	1.7		1.8
	wards	9	9	7		0	9	
Wyre Forest	Local	31.5	41.2	20.0	0	7.3		75.9
	General	36.1	48.8	8.0	3.6	3.6		75.3
Con/Lab 2	diff	4.6	7.6	-12.0	3.6	-3.7		-0.6
	wards	11	11	11		6	11	

TABLE A2
CONSTITUENCIES WITH MULTI-MEMBER WARD UNITARY COUNCIL ELECTIONS 1 MAY

Constituency name		Con	Lab	LD	Ref	Oth	Tot wds
Blackburn	Local	28.0	47.1	22.9	0	1.9	
	General	24.6	55.0	10.5	4.0	5.9	
Lab	diff	-3.4	7.9	-12.4	4.0	4.0	
	wards	11	15	15		2	15
Blackpool South	Local	35.9	55.9	7.3	0	1.0	
	General	34.4	57.0	8.6	0		
Con/Lab 1	diff	-1.5	1.1	1.3	0	-1.0	
	wards	15	15	3		2	15
Bracknell	Local	45.0	29.9	22.3	0	2.8	
	General	47.4	29.8	15.4	2.8	4.7	
Con/Lab 4	diff	2.4	-0.1	-6.9	2.8	1.9	
	wards	19	19	19		8	19
Gillingham	Local	30.8	31.4	37.5	0	0.3	
	General	35.9	39.8	19.0	2.9	2.3	
Con/Lab 3	diff	5.1	8.4	-18.5	2.9	2.0	
	wards	14	14	14		1	14
Halton	Local	21.4	64.7	14.0	0	0.0	
	General	17.7	70.9	7.3	2.3	1.8	
Lab	diff	-3.7	6.2	-6.7	2.3	1.8	
	wards	14	14	7		0	14
Maidenhead	Local	41.9	12.6	44.7	0	0.7	
	General	49.8	18.1	26.3	3.2	2.6	
Con/LD 4	diff	7.9	5.5	-18.4	3.2	1.9	
	wards	15	11	15		1	15
Medway	Local	37.9	47.6	13.4	0	1.2	
	General	36.9	48.9	10.2	3.2	0.9	
Con/Lab 2	diff	-1.0	1.3	-3.2	3.2	-0.3	
	wards	13	13	12		1	13
Nottingham East	Local	25.9	55.0	15.0	0	4.0	
	General	23.5	62.3	10.1	4.1	0.0	
Lab	diff	-2.4	7.3	-4.9	4.1	-4.0	
	wards	9	9	9		3	9
Nottingham North	Local	23.9	60.8	12.2	0	3.1	
	General	20.3	65.7	8.0	4.5	1.5	
Lab	diff	-3.6	4.9	-4.2	4.5	-1.6	
	wards	9	9	7		3	9
Nottingham South	Local	31.5	53.6	13.6	0	1.3	
	General	27.7	55.3	12.9	3.1	0.9	
Lab	diff	-3.8	1.7	-0.7	3.1	-0.4	
	wards	9	9	5		1	9

TABLE A2 (continued)

Constituency name		Con	Lab	LD	Ref	Oth	Tot wds
Peterborough	Local	35.7	43.0	9.2	0	12.1	
	General	35.2	50.3	10.7	1.9	1.9	
Con/Lab 2	diff	-0.5	7.3	1.5	1.9	10.2	
	wards	13	13	5		4	13
Plymouth Devonp't	Local	29.5	58.0	10.6	0	1.9	
	General	24.2	60.9	10.7	2.9	1.4	
Lab	diff	-5.3	2.9	0.1	2.9	-0.5	
	wards	8	8	4		1	8
Plymouth Sutton	Local	31.0	44.0	20.0	0	5.1	
	General	30.3	50.1	13.9	3.5	2.2	
Con/Lab 1	diff	-0.7	6.1	-6.1	3.5	-2.9	
	wards	8	8	8		5	8
Reading East	Local	30.5	33.6	33.1	0	2.8	
	General	35.2	42.7	18.5	2.1	1.5	
Con/Lab 3	diff	4.7	9.1	-14.6	2.1	-1.3	
	wards	11	11	11		3	11
Rochford and	Local	43.4	38.3	18.3	0	0.0	
Southend East	General	48.7	39.6	9.4	0	2.3	
Con/Lab 4	diff	5.3	1.3	-8.9	0	2.3	
	wards	7	7	7		0	7
Slough	Local	23.6	44.6	9.3	0	22.5	
	General	29.2	56.6	7.4	2.4	4.4	
Lab	diff	5.6	12.0	-1.9	2.4	-18.1	
	wards	11	12	8		12	12
Southend West	Local	34.8	19.8	42.6	0	2.7	
	General	38.8	22.8	33.1	3.7	1.6	
Con/LD 3	diff	4.0	3.0	-9.5	3.7	-1.1	
	wards	7	7	7		1	7
Torbay	Local	34.3	17.4	39.1	0	9.2	
	General	39.5	14.9	39.6	0	6.0	
Con/LD 2	diff	5.2	-2.5	0.5	0	-3.2	
	wards	9	9	9		5	9
Windsor	Local	41.7	16.6	30.6	0	11.1	
	General	48.2	18.3	28.7	3.3	1.5	
Con/LD 3	diff	6.5	1.7	-1.9	3.3	-9.6	
	wards	16	15	13		5	17
Wokingham	Local	41.6	13.6	41.7	0	3.0	
	General	50.1	16.8	31.4	0	1.8	
Con/LD 4	diff	8.5	3.2	-10.3	0	-1.2	
	wards	11	9	11		2	11

Between Fear and Loathing: National Press Coverage of the 1997 British General Election

David Deacon, Peter Golding and Michael Billig

When asked to explain his party's unforeseen defeat in the 1992 general election, the Labour MP Gerald Kaufman speculated that the British electorate had been caught 'between fear and loathing' and that, in the event, fear of the unknown had exceeded contempt borne of familiarity. In 1997 it would seem that Kaufman's analysis no longer applies: Labour's crushing victory clearly revealed an electorate no longer hamstrung by the prospect of change. However, in our view the phrase still retains some relevance, in this case as a way of characterizing the disposition of large sections of the national press throughout the 1997 campaign.

This may seem a strange claim to make, as an orthodoxy has quickly emerged – firmly subscribed to by the new government – which posits that one of the most notable features of the election was a major realignment in press opinion behind Labour, and that this probably played a significant part in the outcome. Certainly, an examination of the stated party affiliations of newspapers at the end of the campaign shows that 11 of the 19 national titles endorsed Tony Blair, delivering his party over 60 percent of press support in circulation terms. This contrasts dramatically with previous elections – in every post-war contest the Conservatives have commanded a clear majority of press support, and in 1992 70 percent of press opinion endorsed the Major government.

In this article, however, we argue that the 'reversal model' of press affiliation that this and other more anecdotal evidence implies at once oversimplifies and overestimates the changes that occurred. Furthermore, if unchallenged, it may create misconceptions about the likely nature of press influence in the election.

This perspective can only be gained by looking beyond the political machinations that led several papers to declare a shift in their allegiance – although the reasons for this change have an undeniable fascination (Deacon et al., 1997) – and focus instead upon the actual substance of press coverage. Towards this end, this article presents findings from a detailed content analysis of media reporting during the 1997 election, which was commissioned by, and reported in, the *Guardian* newspaper throughout the campaign. The content sample covered the last five weeks of the formal campaign period (31 March – 30 April 1997), and involved the analysis of election coverage in the main national newspapers, terrestrial television and radio news programmes.[1]

Our article examines the *interpretative* and *evaluative* features of press reporting in the 1997 campaign. This conceptual distinction was developed by the authors in previous research (see Golding, 1990; Deacon and Golding, 1994) and provides a convenient way of differentiating the contours of coverage. In conventional terms the adequacy of reporting is judged by its fairness, objectivity, and impartiality as an account of some event or person. Is the report pro or anti some party, policy or initiative? This is the *evaluative* dimension, but it is only one vector. We also need to consider what topics are rendered visible, named and promoted in coverage. This is the *interpretative* dimension and simply asks what is an issue – in this case, the election – seen to be about? We begin our analysis of national press coverage by addressing this important dimension of political coverage.

Interpreting the Campaign

Our discussion of the interpretative features of press coverage focuses on two related questions: how much newspaper attention in general was paid to the election during the campaign (i.e., how important was it seen to be as a composite 'issue'?); and, within these parameters, what were seen as the most important topics for consideration? For the latter question, we not only explore the extent of interpretative variation between different press sectors (broadsheets, middle-range tabloids and other tabloids), but also in comparison with broadcast coverage. This additional perspective is important because, although everybody recognizes the *evaluative* differences between press and broadcast coverage (in their mode of address, stylistic conventions, political motivation, etc.), far less attention has been paid to the extent of their *interpretative* distinctiveness. Is it meaningful to study the issue agendas of the press in isolation, or should we recognize that newspapers are simply part of a broad media consensus as to what the most important electoral issues are?

How Much Coverage?

The 1997 general election had one of the longest formal campaigns in recent times and one of the most drawn-out preludes. The pre-election phoney war started well back in 1996 and politicians and media alike had been on a war footing for many months. Whatever the political reasons for this tortuous shadow boxing, the sheer length of the hostilities presented a considerable challenge for journalists. How could they maintain a sense of interest and

FIGURE 1
PERCENTAGE OF NEWS SPACE (PER WEEK) COVERING ELECTION RELATED ISSUES

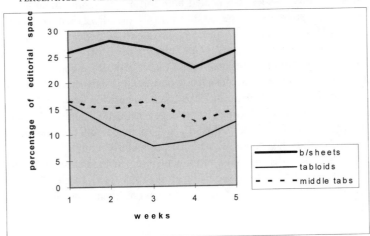

drama in a campaign that had been so long anticipated, had dragged out for so long, and that had all the signs of being a one-horse race?

Figure 1 compares the average proportion of available news space[2] allocated to the 1997 election by different press sectors in the last five weeks of the campaign. Two main points stand out. Firstly, as the campaign hotted up, press interest cooled down. By the second week, tabloid attention started to decline, and only increased significantly as the contest reached its conclusion. The broadsheets and the middle-range tabloids maintained a broadly consistent level of interest for slightly longer, but by the penultimate campaign week their attention too flagged appreciably. Secondly, the proportion of attention given to the election varied according to the amount of editorial space available. Broadsheets dedicated by far the greatest percentage of their (greater) news space to the election, while the popular tabloids dedicated the least of the little they have. The middle-range tabloids fell between the two.

These findings suggest that there were differing perceptions about the newsworthiness of the election across the national press. But beyond these fundamental interpretative judgements, what specific issues excited greatest press attention, and did this agenda vary in comparison with other media sectors?

Issue Prominence
A simple comparison of the most prominent overall topics in press and broadcast coverage suggests that there was a close congruity between them. Following previous campaigns, attention to the form, conduct and outcome of

the electoral process itself (e.g. opinion polls, party events, spin doctors, general 'horse race' issues) dominated both forums, being the main topic in 31 per cent of press items and 33 per cent of broadcast items. This was followed by 'Europe' (press: 15 per cent, broadcast:16 per cent), 'sleaze'(10 per cent: 7 per cent), 'education' (7 per cent: 6 per cent), 'taxation' (6 per cent: 6 per cent) and 'constitutional issues'(4 per cent: 8 per cent).

Furthermore, there was a consistency between media sectors in deciding what the election was *not* about. In 1997, 'social security', 'health', 'Northern Ireland', 'employment', 'crime', 'local government', 'housing', 'race', 'privatization', 'business', 'arts/media', and 'defence' all but fell off the media map,[3] as did 'the economy', which is particularly remarkable when one considers that this was the most prominent issue in broadcast and tabloid coverage of the 1992 election (see Billig *et al.*, 1993: 113). Evidently there is far greater media mileage in a full blown recession than a steady economic recovery.

TABLE 1

COMPARISON OF THE MOST PROMINENT ISSUES (BY WEEK) IN PRESS AND BROADCAST ELECTION COVERAGE

	'Election process'		'Europe'		'Sleaze'	
	press %	b/cast %	press %	b/cast %	press %	b/cast %
wk 1	27	27	5	1	18	15
wk 2	24	28	10	13	**20**	**13**
wk 3	**35**	**21**	**29**	**40**	4	5
wk 4	33	32	19	17	2	0
wk 5	**41**	**62**	14	**5**	4	0

	'Education'		'Taxation'		'Constitutional issues'	
	press %	b/cast %	press %	b/cast %	press %	b/cast %
wk 1	9	4	**11**	**20**	**3**	**14**
wk 2	3	3	9	7	3	6
wk 3	8	7	1	1	2	4
wk 4	7	10	4	2	6	5
wk 5	5	2	5	3	8	9

Notes: One main issue was coded per news item. Twinned cells printed in bold indicate a statistically significant variation ($p<0.05$) using the chi-squared test. Percentages are separate and do not add up to 100 'Wk 1' = 31/3/97 to 4/4/97; 'wk 2'=7/4/97 to 11/4/97; 'wk 3'=14/4/97 to 18/4/97; 'wk 4'=21/4/97 to 25/4/97; 'wk 5'=28/4/97. Base numbers of items for percentages are: Press (weeks 1 to 5) 448, 390, 420, 364, 241; Broadcast (weeks 1 to 5) 110, 141, 121, 134, 102.

However, despite this consensus as to the main parameters of electoral debate, there were also areas of significant variation between press and broadcast reporting. This becomes clear when one looks beyond an aggregated perspective of issue-prominence, and explores the rise and fall of individual issues as the campaign unfolded. Table 1 presents in rank order the changing degrees of press and broadcast media attention given to the six most prominent issues during the last five weeks of the campaign.

The prominence of 'election process' and 'Europe' issues in press and broadcast coverage show a pattern of initial convergence and eventual divergence. In week 3, the proportion of 'election'-focused coverage temporarily reduced in broadcast media, and increased in the press. But in the final days of the campaign, this coverage increased exponentially in broadcast media, and far exceeded the proportion of attention in the press. In terms of coverage of 'Europe', attention peaked and declined in a similar way, but the issue received significantly greater prominence in broadcast media in week 3 and significantly less in week 5.

In contrast, attention given to 'sleaze' and 'education' showed only momentary divergences across media sectors. The only statistically significant variation occurred in week 2, where the proportion of press coverage of 'sleaze' increased as broadcast interest started a terminal decline. With 'taxation' and 'constitutional issues' there were initial, significant divergences that quickly disappeared. In the first week of the sampling, both issues received considerably more attention in broadcast coverage, but this soon reduced into line with the lower levels of press interest.

Apart from highlighting moments of independence in press and broadcast electoral agendas, these data demonstrate how issues moved in and out of focus as the election progressed. For example, the dominance of 'sleaze' in weeks 1 and 2 was usurped by 'Europe' in week 3. Furthermore, they reveal how all but one of the issue categories became comparatively marginalized by the latter stages of the campaign. As decision time arrived, coverage of the election process itself started to clog available news space like pond weed.

Of course, these distinctions between press and broadcast agendas are very general, and raise the further question as to whether there were any interpretative variations within each grouping. Interestingly, there were no significant fluctuations between broadcast programmes in their interpretations of the key electoral issues, even when separated on a week-by-week and issue-by-issue basis. However, within press coverage there were occasionally wild discrepancies (see Table 2). The most noticeable example of this came in the changing amount of coverage given to 'election process' issues. In the popular tabloid and middle-range tabloid press, this coverage fluctuated greatly in prominence, collapsing in the second week, recovering in the third and fourth, and then tailing off in week 5. In contrast, the broadsheets retained

TABLE 2
COMPARISON OF THE MOST PROMINENT ISSUES (BY WEEK) ACROSS PRESS SECTORS

| | 'Election process' | | | | 'Europe' | | |
	B/sheets %	Tabloids %	Mids %		B/sheets %	Tabloids %	Mids %
wk 1	29	21	24		5	6	3
wk 2	**32**	**7**	**12**		11	6	12
wk 3	36	35	30		**27**	**25**	**37**
wk 4	32	31	38		20	16	20
wk 5	**49**	**23**	**32**		13	13	17

| | 'Sleaze' | | | | 'Education' | | |
	B/sheets %	Tabloids %	Mids %		B/sheets %	Tabloids %	Mids %
wk 1	16	22	20		7	14	13
wk 2	**14**	**37**	**28**		2	4	7
wk 3	4	6	4		**6**	**19**	**6**
wk 4	1	3	24		6	8	13
wk 5	4	0	7		4	6	7

| | 'Taxation' | | | | 'Constitutional issues' | | |
	B/sheets %	Tabloids %	Mids %		B/sheets %	Tabloids %	Mids %
wk 1	12	6	10		4	0	1
wk 2	**6**	**13**	**18**		5	0	0
wk 3	1	0	1		3	0	1
wk	4	6	4		8	3	2
wk 5	5	8	2		9	4	7

Notes: One main issue was coded per item. Percentages are separate and do not add up to 100. Twinned cells printed in bold indicate a statistically significant variation (p<0.05) using the chi-squared test. 'Wk 1'= 31/3/97 to 4/4/97 to 4/4/97; 'wk 2'= 7/4/97 to 11/4/97; 'wk 3'= 14/4/97 to 18/4/97; 'wk 4'= 21/4/97 to 25/4/97 to 25/4/97; 'wk 5'= 28/4/97 to 30/4/97. Base numbers of items for percentages are: Broadsheets (weeks 1 to 5) 296, 258, 281, 241, 152; Tabloids (weeks 1 to 5) 81, 71, 69, 67, 48; Middle-market tabloids (weeks 1 to 5) 71, 61, 70, 56, 41.

a more consistent level of attention to this topic between weeks 1 and 4, and increased this coverage greatly in the last week.

With coverage of 'Europe' and 'sleaze' the distributions are more consistent, but there were significant differences in the amount of attention given to these issues at particular moments. The peak of interest in 'Europe' in the third week of the sample was most evident in the middle-range tabloids, revealing their entrenched eurosceptic concerns[4], whereas the aggregate increase in press attention to 'sleaze' in week 2 previously noted in table 1 was driven by the growing fixation of the tabloids and, to a less extent, the middle-range tabloids. In contrast, the broadsheets, like the broadcasters, by that time had decided it was time to move on.

With 'education' and 'taxation' coverage there were momentary periods of variation: 'Education' flared up as a popular tabloid issue in week 3, and 'taxation' drew significantly greater coverage in the middle range and popular tabloids during week 2. 'Constitutional issues', meanwhile, were almost the sole preserve of the broadsheets, only scraping into the popular press frame in the very last stages of the campaign.

So what are the broader implications of these areas of interpretative variance between press and broadcast media, and between press sectors? The first point is that much of the media's election reporting covered difficult political terrain for the Conservative Party, particularly during the earlier stages of the campaign. In the first two weeks, political sleaze – an issue which almost solely implicated the Tories – was to the fore, only to followed in the third week by 'Europe', the issue that had divided the party from top to bottom over previous years. A closer analysis of the sub-themes of Europe coverage during the election show that the dominant European press topic was 'Tory divisions over Europe', being a prominent theme in 9 percent of all press items. In comparison, 'Labour divisions over Europe' were the focus of only 0.8 percent of items. At the same time, more expedient topics for Conservative spin-doctoring, such as the economy and employment, were completely marginalized, as were areas of potential difficulty for Labour (e.g. 'constitutional reform'). Of course, in making this point we are aware that these basic measures tell us nothing about how particular issues were dealt with by the media. Nevertheless, defining the terms of an argument is a crucial stage in any electoral battle, and on this score the Conservatives were conspicuous losers.

Secondly, there is no evidence that interpretative agendas of the press varied according to their stated party preferences. For example, despite the fact that both mid-market papers included in the analysis backed the Conservatives, they showed no inclination towards playing down difficult issues for the Major government. Indeed, they increased their attention to the sleaze issue in week 2, in contrast to declining levels of broadcast and broadsheet interest, and played a key role in forcing 'Europe' into the forefront of the media agenda in week 3.

We now turn our attention to the second vector of coverage mentioned in the introduction: the *evaluative* dimensions of press reporting of the 1997 campaign.

Evaluating the Parties

The obvious starting point for considering press evaluations is to examine the direct editorial statements made by the papers about their political preferences. In doing so there is a need to look beyond simple declarations of party preference and consider in a more detailed way the nature of support being given. Certainly, the press take these position statements very seriously themselves, and are very concerned about the nuances of their endorsement.

Tabloid Press Editorials

In the 1997 election all of the popular tabloids declared for Labour. However, on closer examination this apparent consensus begins to fragment. Predictably, the Mirror group titles (the *Daily Mirror, Sunday Mirror* and *People*) offered strident and unconditional support for New Labour and launched vitriolic attacks on the Conservatives. By comparison, the editorial endorsements offered by 'the converts' (the *Sun*, the *News of the World* and the *Daily Star*) were far more guarded. For example, a close analysis of the two-page editorial that accompanied the self-styled 'historic announcement' that 'The Sun Backs Blair' (18 March 1997) was permeated by reservations. According to this statement, the paper's shift had been mainly motivated by personality rather than policy considerations:

> The Tories have all the right policies but all the wrong faces. In Tony Blair, Labour has the face that fits – and many of the Tory policies. If it works, Clony Blair has hijacked it (18 March 97: 6).

The editorial ended by attacking the social chapter as 'the biggest Trojan horse imaginable', and warning that 'when we think [Labour] are wrong, we will shout so loud we will deafen them' (ibid.).

To a large extent, the sour and reluctant tone of this initial editorial can be explained by internal politics at News International, where Rupert Murdoch had imposed the political shift in spite of the views of senior editorial staff (*Guardian*, 23 March 1997: 23). As the campaign progressed, there was a noticeable thawing in the paper's editorial stance, and on the day of the election it ran a front page editorial that repeated on six occasions 'Britain deserves better. And Blair WILL make it better' ('It Must Be You', 1 May 97: 1). But, here again, it is not difficult to discern clear tensions in the paper's position. For example, early on in the editorial it is stated:

> Like us, [Blair] has grave fears for the fabric of the country and the quality of life of millions of people – families, children, the sick, old people, the poor. Fairness, social justice, equality and opportunity are not just politicians' buzzwords. They are REAL issues that affect REAL people (ibid.).

just as one begins to think that one is half way through a Fabian society leaflet, the argument suddenly shifts:

> Blair has some fierce battles ahead. He must take on Europe. He must face down the unions who wrongly reckon they are owed a pay-off, he must stamp on anyone in his Cabinet whose natural instinct might be to

solve a problem by throwing taxpayers' money at it. The party that founded the welfare state must be the one that tames a beast that is galloping out of control (ibid.).

These sorts of themes were echoed in the editorial proclamations of other tabloid converts. All agreed on the importance of maintaining a strong market-based, anti-union, eurosceptic, anti-welfarist, low-taxation approach to government, and all specifically identified a debt of gratitude to Thatcherism:

> [The Conservatives] created an affluent, strike free society able to compete in the modern world. Margaret Thatcher gave us back our pride, a belief in the enterprise culture (THERE'S TONY ONE WAY TO GO, *Daily Star*, 30 April 1997: 8).

Mid-Market Tabloid Editorials

In direct contrast to the popular tabloids, all of the mid-market papers endorsed the Conservative party in their final editorials (*Daily Mail, Mail on Sunday, Daily Express, Sunday Express*). Yet, here again, there were signs of bets being hedged.

At the start of the campaign there was some speculation that the *Daily Mail* would follow the Sun at least half way across the Rubicon and abstain from endorsing any political party in the election (*Guardian*, 24 March 1997: 2) In the event, it continued to support the Conservatives, citing Europe as its principal reason. On the penultimate day of the campaign the paper plastered a Union Jack over its entire front page alongside the stark comment:

> There is a terrible danger that the British people, drugged by the seductive mantra 'It's time for change', are stumbling, eyes glazed, into an election that could undo 1,000 years of our nation's history (*Daily Mail*, 30 April 1997: 1).

In the detailed editorial inside, the paper claimed a Labour landslide could 'sign Britain's death warrant as a free and sovereign nation state' (THE BATTLE FOR BRITAIN, 30 April 1997: 8). Blair was also criticized for supporting the social chapter and other employment directives and for not fully purging his party of its high-taxation, anti-entrepeneurial tendencies. But if New Labour bore the brunt of the thrashing, the Conservatives were also dealt some hefty blows:

> Let us say here that the Daily Mail holds no torch for this Conservative administration. It is ... John Major's incompetence as the nation's Chief Executive that has really marred his administration. To be blunt, he has been an ineffectual leader.

The *Mail on Sunday*'s editorial judgement (A QUESTION OF TRUST, *Mail on Sunday*, 27 April 1997: 32) was less scathing about John Major (acknowledging his 'remarkable' tenacity), was more convinced about the extent of Labour's reconstruction, and was far less fixated with the issue of Europe (although a strong eurosceptic stance was evident). Ultimately the paper claimed its decision to stay with the Conservatives was prompted by a series of unanswered questions about New Labour and an instinctive feeling that 'there is a better case – on balance – for trusting John Major' (*ibid.*). This issue of trust was also a prominent theme in the *Sunday Express*'s pre-election declaration, which asserted that 'If it is a choice between John Major and Tony Blair's well-drilled army, then we believe that John Major's rabble has its heart nearer to the right place' (IF YOU WANT A STEADY HAND GUIDING BRITAIN, VOTE FOR MAJOR, *Sunday Express*, 27 April 97: 24).

Of all the mid-market tabloids, only the *Daily Express* presented an unconditional and constructive case for voting Tory in its final editorial, citing OECD figures to demonstrate the strength of the economic recovery under the Conservatives and concluding that 'If the Labour party is prepared to give the Tories credit for transforming the British economy, it would be churlish for the rest of us to do any less' (*Daily Express*, 30 April 1997: 10).

Broadsheet Editorials

Of all press sectors, the broadsheet 'quality' papers revealed the greatest diversity in political affiliation. The Conservatives commanded support from three titles (the *Daily Telegraph*, *Sunday Telegraph* and *Sunday Times*), Labour were endorsed by five (the *Guardian*, *Observer*, *Independent*, *Independent on Sunday* and *Financial Times*), and one paper abstained from declaring a preference for a specific political party (*The Times*).

As with the Mirror group's support for Labour, the *Daily Telegraph* and *Sunday Telegraph*'s endorsement of the Conservatives was entirely predictable. Certainly, both papers remained conspicuously unmoved by the siren songs of New Labour. As the *Telegraph* put it, in Kipling-esque tones:

> It is true that Labour show some signs of understanding that Tory economic policies work, but they do so only in the way in which a savage, finding a watch in the desert, recognizes that it is a sophisticated object. They do not know how to operate it... Voting is a serious matter. If you vote Labour, you can't be serious. Vote Conservative (*Daily Telegraph*, 30 April 1997: 20).

By comparison, the final *Sunday Times* editorial was more equivocal in its support for the Major government. Full tribute was paid to Blair's leadership qualities and the internal reforms he had instituted, and the Conservatives' divisions and improprieties were trenchantly criticized, but in the end it adjudged that the stronger eurosceptic tendencies of the Tories (Europe being, in its view, the only issue that really distinguished the two parties), made them the least risky option.

Of the broadsheets that backed Labour, all but the *Financial Times* were certain about the need to depose the Tories and that the Liberal Democrats had a crucial future role to play alongside a new Labour government. On the latter point, there were subtle but clear differences between these four papers. The *Independent* and the *Independent on Sunday* intimated that while New Labour were their practical choice, the Liberal Democrats were their 'ideal world' preference. In contrast, neither the *Guardian* nor the *Observer* gave any sense of preferring Liberal Democratic radicalism over New Labour pragmatism. Although they commended the Liberal Democrats on many of their policies, and advised readers to vote for them where it made tactical sense, they were more fulsome in their praise for New Labour and more excited at the transformations in prospect. As the penultimate *Guardian* editorial put it:

> Tomorrow gives the progressive movement in the country its biggest and most exciting opportunity in a generation (30 April 1997: 20).

One uniting theme shared by all four papers was their strong pro-European sympathies. The *Financial Times* also took this stance, and backed Labour solely on the basis of it. Of all the Labour-supporting broadsheets, the *FT* was most unsure about Labour's broader credentials, and only endorsed the party, as it put it, 'by default':

> This does not amount to anything like an enthusiastic endorsement. The closer Mr Blair has come to power, the less impressive he has appeared (EUROPE IS THE ISSUE, *Financial Times*, 29 April 1997: 28).

Europe was also the defining consideration for *The Times*, albeit from a diametrically opposed perspective. Rather than declaring for any party, the paper urged voters to support local politicians with the most impeccable eurosceptic credentials. Consequently, the paper endorsed a plethora of political candidates, from Conservative, Labour, Liberal Democrat and Referendum parties, which it listed on the day of the vote on a constituency-by-constituency basis (PRINCIPLE NOT PARTY: A VOTE FOR MEMBERS WHO WILL DEFEND PARLIAMENT, *The Times*, 30 April 1997: 22).

The 'Opinion Continuum'

This review of national press opinion shows that categorizing the political preferences of newspapers simply on a party-by-party basis masks a diverse range of distinctive political positions. Whereas some papers endorsed their choice categorically, others adopted a more equivocal stance. Furthermore, papers gave very different reasons for their support. For example, the *Observer* backed Labour out of excitement at what it perceived to be a progressive, pro-European, social democratic agenda, whereas the *Sun* backed Blair on the basis of his strong leadership, public appeal, eurosceptic potential and apparent acceptance of Thatcherite orthodoxies.

For these reasons, we believe it is better to conceive of national press editorial opinion as falling at different points on a continuum between the two main parties, rather than categorizing support on an 'either/or' basis (see Figure 2). This allows us to appreciate how much press opinion in the 1997

FIGURE 2
THE 'OPINION CONTINUUM: NATIONAL PRESS EDITORIAL STANCES
IN THE 1997 GENERAL ELECTION

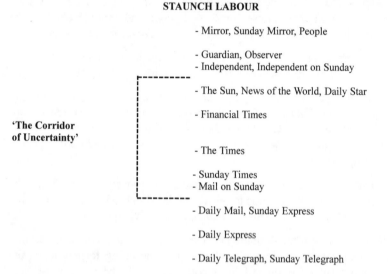

STAUNCH LABOUR

- Mirror, Sunday Mirror, People

- Guardian, Observer
- Independent, Independent on Sunday

- The Sun, News of the World, Daily Star

- Financial Times

'The Corridor of Uncertainty'

- The Times

- Sunday Times
- Mail on Sunday

- Daily Mail, Sunday Express

- Daily Express

- Daily Telegraph, Sunday Telegraph

STAUNCH CONSERVATIVE

campaign tended towards the centre, falling into an area we label here 'the corridor of uncertainty'.[5] Papers categorized in this section may have displayed differing levels of commitment and agnosticism about their chosen party, but all ultimately rationalized their choice through 'on balance' judgements rather than firm conviction. By recognizing the common ground shared by the flakier ends of Labour and Conservative press support, we can begin to appreciate the limits to the political conversions that occurred during the 1997 campaign. Although there was a clear swing towards Labour compared with 1992 (only the *FT* bucked the trend and moved back towards the Tories), these transitions all constituted movements either into the 'corridor of uncertainty' (the *Sun, Sunday Times, Mail on Sunday, News of the World*), or out of it (the *Independent, Independent on Sunday*). No title made the complete journey from one end to the other. In editorial terms, press opinion shifted rather than completely reversed.

There are dangers, of course, in relying solely on editorials to chart press partisanship, as we cannot be sure that what was *said* in leader articles is a reliable indicator of what was *done* in terms of routine news presentation. We also need to take a wider perspective on press evaluations throughout the campaign.

Bias in the news is notoriously difficult to define and, for this reason, analysts avoid using the term. However, we coded stories which were unambiguously favourable in tone or content to one of the main parties. These stories were judged to reflect, mainly or solely, the preferred 'frame' of one or other party simply because of the event they reported. Excluded from this count were stories that were roughly balanced, and also those which, despite containing a negative take on one party's position, were not positively presenting any other party position. This gave us a clear and tight assessment of evaluative trends in media coverage (see Table 3)

TABLE 3
'FRAMING' IN PRESS COVERAGE (ROW %)

	Conservative frame %	Labour frame %	Liberal Democrat frame %	Other frame %
Financial Times	20	24	1	7
Independent	17	22	9	8
Telegraph	23	19	4	4
Guardian	18	19	6	6
Times	23	21	6	9
Express	32	14	4	4
Mail	35	21	1	2
Star	31	31	4	3
Mirror	14	48	1	3
Sun	38	34	0	4

As a general rule, one would expect to find greatest balance in 'framing' in the broadsheet press, because of the clearer distinction made in these papers between editorializing and news reporting, and least balance in tabloids, where reporting is often more nakedly driven by partisan motives. The findings in Table 3 confirm the former assumption, as all broadsheets maintained a rough balance of positive stories across the major parties, regardless of their particular position on the 'opinion-continuum'. However, there were noticeable differences in the framing of different mid-market and popular tabloids, depending on their stated political affiliation. Among those tabloids that expressed a definite party preference in their editorials (the *Mail*, *Express* and *Mirror*) there was a clear privileging of their chosen parties' frame. But with those tabloids wandering 'the corridor of uncertainty' (the *Sun*, the *Daily Star*) there was a broad balance in their framing, with neither party gaining any clear evaluative advantage. Could it be that the political repositioning of these papers had also led to a road-to-Damascus-like conversion to the virtues of editorial balance, or is the evidence symptomatic of a different process? As we discuss in our concluding remarks, we are convinced the latter is the case.

Conclusions: Hollow-Centred Partisanship

Our discussion of national press coverage of the 1997 general election suggests several main points about press behaviour during this period. In general news terms, there is no doubt that the Conservative party had a difficult campaign, and the press played a major part in increasing their discomfort, particularly over sleaze and Europe. But these difficulties were mainly at the interpretative rather than evaluative level, for although the Tories signally failed to control the terms of press debate, they broadly achieved parity with Labour in presenting their views on the issues under discussion. In terms of editorial opinion, the Conservatives also suffered, but again perhaps not as greatly as some have assumed. Although the majority of editorial opinion, whether measured in terms of titles or readership, backed the Labour party, a large portion of this support was conditional and cautionary in nature. Certainly, while the Tories may have received a bad press from many of their previous cheerleaders in 1997, in no way can it be said to have approached the level of vitriol heaped on Labour in 1992. Labour's achievement in this election was in decommissioning the big guns of the Tory press rather than in turning their fire on their previous masters. Most tabloid partisanship in this election had a hollow ring.

Overall, for many newspapers, particularly those at the centre of the 'opinion continuum', the 1997 campaign was as much about disorientation as it was about reorientation: their fears about New Labour being counterbalanced by their loathing for an increasingly divided and directionless Tory party. This in turn seems to have generated a sense of *ennui* as the campaign progressed, as press attention fell in all sectors as the day of reckoning approached. For some, the 1997 election demonstrated the evil of two lessers.

Finally, although Conservative party affiliations may have wavered, conservative values – individualism, euroscepticism, anti unionism, antiwelfarism, etc. – remain engraved on the hearts of many papers. The fact that these can sit alongside an endorsement of Labour reveals more about the shift in the party-political landscape than it does about any transition in the core values of these influential opinion leaders. In 1997, the press may no longer be Conservative (with a capital C), but they remain highly conservative. We have witnessed a 'C' change, not a sea-change.

ACKNOWLEDGEMENTS

Our thanks to our coding team: Jackie Abel, Mark Harrison and Simon Cross.

NOTES

1. The newspaper sample comprised: the *Sun, Daily Mirror, Daily Mail, Daily Express, Financial Times, The Times, Guardian, Daily Telegraph* and *Independent*. The broadcast sample comprised: the BBC1 9pm news, ITN *News at Ten*, BBC2 *Newsnight*, Channel 4's 7pm news and BBC Radio 4's *Today* programme (7.30am – 8.30am). For logistical reasons (i.e. the *Guardian*'s copy deadlines), the sampling was circumscribed in the four respects.
    1. Only weekday election coverage was sampled.
    2. Not all editorial content in newspaper content was analysed. The study focused on front pages, all designated domestic news pages inside each paper, designated election segments and pages carrying leader editorials.
    3. The analysis focused on 'news' rather than 'feature' coverage.
2. Each election item was measured in cm^2. The coders then calculated what proportion of available coded editorial space in the newspaper the item covered (i.e., the base N was the total number of cm^2 on the number of pages sampled.
3. None of these topics individually received more than 4 per cent of either press or broadcast attention over the campaign period, and most attracted 1 per cent and less. The top six issues were the main topics in three quarters of the coverage in both media sectors.
4. During this week the *Daily Mail* took it upon itself to raise the issue of Europe in the campaign. At the start of the week it carried an approving story about 200 Tory MPs lining up against monetary union, and later in the week carried a front page editorial titled 'The Battle for Britain' in which it asserted there was 'a deafening silence at the heart of this election and its name is Europe' (*Daily Mail*, 16 April 1997:1)
5. Our thanks and apologies to Geoffrey Boycott, who first coined the term in an entirely different context.

REFERENCES

Billig, M., D. Deacon, P. Golding, and S. Middleton (1993) 'In the Hand of Spin Doctors: Television, Politics and the 1992 General Election', in N. Miller and R. Allen (eds) *It's Live, But is it Real?* London: John Libbey.

Deacon, D. and P. Golding (1994) *Taxation and Representation: the Media, Political Communication and the Poll Tax*. London: John Libbey.

Deacon, D., P. Golding, and M. Billig (1997) 'Losing Face or Loss of Faith? The Defection of the Conservative Press in the 1997 British General Election', *The Bulletin of the European Institute for the Media* 14 (2): 8–9.

Golding, P. (1990) 'Political Communication and Citizenship: the Media and Democracy in an Inegalitarian Social Order', in M. Ferguson (ed) *Public Communication: The New Imperatives*. London: Sage.

Does Negative News Matter?
The Effect of Television News on Party
Images in the 1997 British General Election

David Sanders and Pippa Norris

It is widely assumed that British voters obtain a considerable amount of their political information from television and that television news plays an important part in shaping their political and economic perceptions. In these circumstances it comes as something of a surprise to discover that there is no direct individual-level evidence to show that any such effects do indeed operate. This study seeks to address this shortcoming. It uses an experimental research design to assess the extent to which the political perceptions of a sample of 1125 UK voters tested during the 1997 general election campaign were affected by 'positive' and 'negative' party images presented in television news programmes.

As well as being of intrinsic importance to debates about the effects of television news, this focus on positive and negative news has more than passing relevance for the kinds of campaigning that political parties adopt. Evidence from the United States shows not only that American journalists have become more 'negative' in the way they approach the reporting of political stories (Patterson, 1993) but also that 'negative campaigning' has become much more prevalent in American elections (Ansolabehere and Iyengar, 1997). Given the tendency for the United States to export its cultural and political habits to the UK, it is conceivable that both negative reporting and negative campaigning will increase in Britain in the future. Although there are obvious differences between supposedly neutral news broadcasts and self-evidently biased exercises in party propaganda, any evidence about the relative roles played by positive and negative television images could have important implications for the likely success of the alternative strategies available to political parties.

Section 1 of this paper briefly reviews the existing evidence that links (or fails to link) television news coverage to British voters' perceptions and preferences. Section 2 summarizes our basic theoretical model and develops the specific hypotheses that we seek to test. Section 3 outlines the principles underlying our methodological approach. Section 4 reports our empirical findings. These show that voters' political perceptions *are* influenced by the content of television news and, in particular, that positive news images appear to exert more powerful effects than negative ones. The relationships that we report, though small, are sufficiently robust to withstand the application of statistical controls for a wide range of potentially confounding variables. Although our analysis measures only short-term responses to television news, the cumulative effects of repeated exposure to news broadcasts are likely to be considerable. Indeed, in the concluding section we discuss possible ways in which our findings can be linked to related data, covering both television news and public opinion, collected during the 1997 election campaign.

Previous Studies of Television News

Previous studies of British television news fall into three major categories. One strand of research, mainly involving researchers in the communications studies field, has focused primarily on the content of television news. The main research question considered has been the extent to which supposedly 'objective' broadcasts exhibit different sorts of political bias as a result of the 'news values' espoused by programme editors (Glasgow Media Group, 1976 and 1980). Although the studies in this field have revealed much about the way in which media agendas operate, they have not explicitly analysed the consequences for public opinion of the observed 'biases' in news coverage that they have identified. Indeed, they have not investigated the links between news content and public opinion at all.

A second area of research has involved the analysis of individual-level survey data from the various British Election Studies. Butler and Stokes (1974) first asked respondents about their television-watching habits in 1964 and the questions they posed have since been supplemented in subsequent BES surveys by questions about voters' perceptions of bias in the news coverage provide by BBC and ITN. The data thus obtained, however, have not provided much insight into the *effects* that television news might have on voters' political perceptions and preferences. Mughan (1996), for example, found that voters' perceptions of bias in news coverage were linked to their partisan identifications: party identifiers tended to believe that news coverage on both major channels was biased against 'their' party. However, this relationship in no way helps to 'explain' voters' partisan preferences. It merely indicates that partisan preferences affect voters' perceptions of television news content, not that content influences preferences. The key limitation of BES data in this context – and this is in no sense a criticism of the researchers involved – is that they contain no information either about which particular news programmes respondents have seen or about the *content* of those news programmes. In these circumstances, it is simply not possible to specify and test convincing causal models that seek to assess the effects of television news coverage on voters' perceptions.

A third strand of research has used aggregate-level time-series survey data in an explicit effort to consider the effects of television news coverage on public opinion. The only UK study so far conducted using this approach (Gavin and Sanders, 1996) focused on economic news and involved content-analysing news programmes on the major UK television channels over a 15-month period. Coverage, across a range of subcategories, was coded as being 'positive' (i.e. favourable to the government), 'negative' (unfavourable) or neutral. Weekly variations in the balance of coverage (positive *versus* negative) were compared with aggregate movements in voters' political preferences and economic perceptions. Although the study found significant relationships between the pattern of coverage over time and changes in public opinion, its conclusions were necessarily tentative. Aggregate-level analysis of this sort involves making quite strong (critics would say heroic) assumptions about what is going on at the individual level. In order to draw causal inferences about individual attitudes and behaviour, it must be assumed that 'the typical voter' is exposed each week to the balance of news coverage that is indicated by the aggregate-level coverage measure and that s/he responds to changes in that balance in a more or less consistent fashion. The limitations of these assumptions are self-evident. Aggregate-level correlations, since they reveal nothing about individuals, could be highly misleading. In common with individual-level BES data, aggregate data reveal nothing about which individuals have been exposed to which news programmes. Aggregate data also fail to specify which individuals – or even which sorts of individual – change their political preferences and perceptions over time. In principle, a strong aggregate time-series correlation between television coverage and changing preferences could be observed even in circumstances where the particular individuals who change their opinions have *not* been exposed to the television coverage that supposedly generates their changed opinions. People who watch long sequences of 'damaging' news about a particular party, for example, *could* be the very ones who reinforce their commitment to it – or even convert to it – rather than desert it. With aggregate-level data, we simply do not know if individual-level behaviour conforms to theoretical expectations.

All of these considerations about previous studies suggest a simple conclusion. If we are to establish how voters react to the content of television news, we need to adopt a rather different approach from those followed thus far. In order to conduct a 'critical' test of the effects of television news on voters' opinions, we need to know what preferences and perceptions an individual has before he or she is exposed to a particular set of news messages. We need to know the precise character of the messages to which the individual is then exposed. And we need to know what changes in preferences and perceptions this exposure in turn invokes. These requirements cry out for an experimental research design of the sort developed in the United States by Shanto Iyengar and his associates. The approach adopted here follows his classic experimental logic. Respondents completed a pre-test questionnaire and then were randomly assigned to separate groups. Each group was exposed to a distinctive 30-minute selection of video news and a post-test questionnaire then administered to each respondent. The purpose of the experiments was to establish the extent to which any changes between pre- and post-test responses varied according to the type of video footage that had been seen.

The Theoretical Model

The theoretical model that we employ here is so simple that we would not wish to dignify it with the label 'theory'. We make two core assumptions: that television news is an important source of political information for voters; and that voters modify their political attitudes and preferences in the light of information they receive about political parties. We assume further that, although significant and permanent changes in perceptions are likely to occur only after repeated exposure to new and potentially challenging information, small (and possibly ephemeral) changes in perceptions are likely to result from quite limited exposure to such information. We also assume that some voter types are more likely to change their perceptions than others – a point that we develop in hypotheses H3–H7 below.

Based on these assumptions, our pivotal hypothesis (H1) is that, *ceteris paribus*,

> *'Positive' television news coverage of a particular party will tend to create a more favourable image of that party among voters than 'neutral' coverage; 'negative' coverage will tend to produce a less favourable image.*

By 'positive' news, we mean items that present the party in question in a favourable light, such as reports that stress its unity, morale or success. By 'negative' items, we mean reports that portray a party in an unfavourable light, stressing its embarrassment, disunity, failure or disarray. By 'party image', which we measure on a ten-point scale described in section 3 below, we mean the overall impression – favourable *versus* unfavourable – that voters have of each major party.

Specifically, we test for the direct effects of four types of positive or negative coverage, producing four sub-hypotheses:[1]

> H1.1 *Positive coverage of the Conservative party will increase the Conservatives' party-image ratings.*

H1.2 *Negative coverage of the Conservative party will reduce the Conservatives' party-image ratings.*
H1.3 *Positive coverage of Labour will increase Labour's party-image ratings.*
H1.4 *Negative coverage of Labour will reduce Labour's party-image ratings.*

An obvious corollary to these hypotheses derives from the potentially 'zero sum' character of party politics. If positive coverage of one party increases that party's ratings, it may serve to reduce the ratings of others – to inflict 'collateral' damage on them. This produces H2.1 to H2.4.

H2.1 *Positive coverage of the Conservative party will reduce the image ratings of both Labour and the Liberal Democrats.*
H2.2 *Negative coverage of the Conservative party will increase the image ratings of both Labour and the Liberal Democrats.*
H2.3 *Positive coverage of Labour will reduce the image ratings of both the Conservatives and the Liberal Democrats.*
H2.4 *Negative coverage of Labour will increase the image ratings of both the Conservatives and the Liberal Democrats.*

These simple hypotheses, however, say nothing of the different tendencies of various sorts of voter to shift their party-image perceptions. In line with evidence reported by Iyengar and Kinder (1987), we expect to observe distinctive tendencies among three voter-types. Specifically, we would expect strong partisans, the politically well-informed and those who are interested in politics and current affairs to be less likely to change their pre-test to post-test responses than their respective comparator groups, the less partisan, the ill-informed and uninterested. This expectation derives from the fact that the partisan, the informed and interested are all likely to have thought seriously about political matters prior to being exposed to our experimental manipulations. They are concomitantly more likely to hold stable political views than their comparators. This in turn implies that we should observe smaller differences in their pre- and post-test party-image responses.

The effects of partisanship, knowledge and interest do not necessarily stop here, however. In addition to being less likely to change their party-image responses, it can be argued on *a priori* grounds that these groups are also *less likely to be affected by exposure to television news*; that is to say they are less likely than their comparators to be *affected* by our positive and negative experimental manipulations. The partisan, the informed and the interested are all less likely to be influenced by what they see and hear about party images in our video experiments – either because they have already made up their minds (the partisan) or because on many previous occasions they have been exposed to, and have taken note of, similar messages (the knowledgeable and the informed). Technically, these expectations imply that there should be interaction effects between partisanship, knowledge and interest, on the one hand, and video exposure, on the other: any observed effects of positive or negative video exposure should be weaker for the partisan, the knowledgeable and the interested than they are for comparator groups.

Two other sets of potential effects on voters' changing perceptions need to be considered. In addition to the purely experimental controls that we apply in H1 and H2, we are also in a position to apply non-experimental controls both for (a) the standard set of socio-demographic variables (age, gender, class and so on) that are normally found to exert significant effects on voters' political preferences and perceptions; and (b) respondents' television-watching habits. As a result of our experimental design, however, our hypotheses in both of these contexts favour the null. The experimental approach is predicated on the random assignment of subjects to test and control groups. If the stimulus (video exposure) genuinely affects the response (a shift in the respondents' party image), the *group* effect should be observable regardless of respondents' sociodemographic characteristics or television-watching habits because the test and control groups should contain roughly equal proportions drawn from all groups. At the individual level, we could, of course, simply assume that sociodemographic and television-habit effects do not confound any bivariate statistical relationships that we might observe between video exposure and changing party-images. We prefer, however, to conduct formal tests for any such possible effects. Specifically, we hypothesize that the observed relationship between positive/negative video exposure and pre- to post-test changes in party-image will not be confounded by the application of statistical controls for the effects of (a) the standard battery of sociodemographic variables or (b) respondents' television-watching habits.

Our final theoretical consideration also generates a null hypothesis. A standard problem that confronts any questionnaire-based assessment of attitude change – whether it involves pre-test/post-test comparisons of the sort developed here or panel data in which several months elapse between waves – is that some individuals' responses at different points in time are far more unstable across a range of different measures than the equivalent responses of other individuals. This raises the question as to whether some sort of correction for individual 'respondent instability' needs to be made before the consequences of measured change in the test items can be properly evaluated. We collected data on a sufficient number of measures in our pre- and post-test questionnaires to enable us to investigate precisely this sort of phenomenon. Specifically, we are able to make corrections for respondents' varying tendencies to provide unstable over-time responses to the nine-item battery of *party image* questions. We begin by calculating each respondent's average pre-test/post-test movement on all nine party-image questions. We can then measure the individual's shift on each party image variable as a *deviation* from his or her average movement score. It could be argued that this deviation score gives a more accurate representation of the extent to which each respondent has genuinely moved his or her position on each of the party-image questions that we are concerned to examine. In any event, given that this alternative way of characterizing change *can* be operationalized, it makes sense to see if it makes any difference to the substantive implications of the empirical findings that are reported here. Our expectation, however, is that the use of alternative, corrected, measures should make no difference to our empirical results.

The Experimental Research Design

During the 1990s experimental methods have gradually entered the standard repertoire of political research. Nevertheless, because this approach remains less familiar than survey analysis, we will outline our research design in some detail. In order to examine the effects of positive and negative news coverage on voters' perceptions, we carried out a series of experiments in a central London location (Regent Street). We included 1125 respondents in total, more than most experimental designs. Participants were drawn primarily from Greater London and south-east England. Respondents were not selected explicitly as a random sample of the British electorate, but they did generally reflect the Greater London population in terms of their social background and party preferences. We chose a busy central London location during the day to provide a diverse group of Londoners including managers, office-workers and casual shoppers. The generalizability of the results rests not on the selection of a random sample of participants, as in a survey design, but on the way that subjects were assigned at random to different experimental groups. Any difference in the response of groups should therefore reflect the stimuli that they were given rather than their social backgrounds or prior political attitudes.

One potential problem of experiments is that participants may alter their own behaviour given the artificiality of the research setting and their perceptions of the aims of the study. In order to counter this, respondents were told that they would be participating in research concerned with how people evaluate and understand television news. Prior to the experiment, we informed respondents (falsely) that we were primarily interested in whether young people and older people, or men and women, are interested in different stories in the news. We did not mention that the news would be about the election, which might well have discouraged participation by the politically apathetic, and we found that many participants believed we were carrying out television market research. We used a single-shot rather than a repeated design so that respondents would not become unduly conditioned by the research process itself.

Participants completed a short (15-minute) pre-test questionnaire about their media habits, political interests and opinions and personal background. They were then assigned at random to groups of 5–15 to watch a 30-minute video compilation of television news. Respondents subsequently completed a short (15-minute) post-test questionnaire. The experiments were carried out in April 1997 in the middle of the official general election campaign. This timing was deliberate: we wanted to examine the attitudes of participants who had been subjected to the intensive barrage of political coverage that characterizes television news during an election period.

The video compilations of news stories were chosen to represent a 'typical' evening news programme during the campaign. We drew on stories recorded from all the main news programmes on the terrestrial channels[2] from mid February until early April 1997. The videos all had the same format. They consisted of a 'sandwich', with ten minutes of identical, standard footage at the top and bottom of each programme and one of 15 different experimental video stimuli in the middle 'core'. Respondents were not told which video was being shown to which group or even that different videos were being watched by different groups of respondents.

To test for the effects of positive and negative news on subjects' perceptions of the political parties, we monitored the reactions of 240 participants who were divided at random into four treatment groups: positive Conservative, negative Conservative, positive Labour, negative Labour. We recognize the difficulty of objectively determining whether or not the content of a particular video selection is genuinely 'positive' or 'negative' in its portrayal of a particular party. Our decision rule as to what constituted positive, negative and neutral news coverage was that an item had to be coded as such by two independent coders.[3] In addition to the treatment groups, we also monitored the reactions of two control groups. The first was an *explicit* control group of 92 participants who were shown a non-political video 'core'. The second was an *implicit* control group whose 700 members were shown 'politically neutral' video footage relating to other experiments that we were conducting.[4] Given the similarities in the responses of these two preliminary control groups, the results reported here combine them into a single control group. Our simple expectation, reflected in hypotheses H1.1–H2.4, is that subjects in this overall control group did not significantly change their images of the major parties between the pre- and the post-test whereas subjects in the four test groups did.

Operational Measures

Measures of changes in party image. We designed the research to achieve conceptual replication of responses, that is, tests were repeated with conceptually similar but empirically different measures of the variables under scrutiny. We included nine related, BES-based, measures of party image in both the pre-test and the post-test. For each of the three major parties, we asked respondents to assess, on 0–10 scales, (a) how likely it was that they would vote for the party; (b) how much they liked the party; and (c) how highly they rated the (named) party leader. For each party, and for both the pre-test and the post-test measures, the three scales were averaged to produce a single party image index where a 0 score meant a respondent had a very poor image of the party and 10 meant a very good image. Calculating each respondent's 'change in party image' score was simply a matter of subtracting the pre-test score from the post-test score.

Measures of partisanship, political knowledge and political interest. For each party, the respondent's partisan commitment was measured using the pre-test score on the 'probability of voting for the party' scale referred to above: it was assumed that a higher pre-test score reflected a greater degree of commitment to the party; a lower score, a weaker degree of commitment. Political knowledge was measured from the responses to a five-item political quiz that had been included in the post-test questionnaire. Political interest was measured according to whether or not respondents expressed a strong interest either in current affairs or in political items of television news.

Measures of sociodemographic characteristics and television-watching habits. Previous research has shown that voting preferences (though not necessarily changes in preference) are linked to a range of sociodemographic and attitudinal characteristics (Butler and Stokes, 1974; Sarlvik and Crewe, 1983; Heath *et al.* 1985, 1991 and 1994). During the 1980s and early 1990s – though not, perhaps, in 1997 – Conservative support tended to be weakest, and Labour support strongest, among men, younger voters, manual workers, the unemployed, students, non-homeowners, non-graduates and voters from ethnic minorities (Brynin and Sanders, 1997). With the exception of age, which was measured as a continuous variable, these various characteristics were all measured as dummy variables so that they could be entered as independent variables in OLS regression equations. Finally, television-watching habits were measured as the average number of hours per week that the respondent watched television.

Results

Table 1 reports the pre- and post-test average scores on the main dependent variables of our study. The table also reports the average change that was observed on each variable between the pre- and post-test measurements. All the scales, including the three party-image indices, range from zero to ten.

TABLE 1
AVERAGE RATINGS ON PARTY-IMAGE VARIABLES AND INDICES, PRE-TEST AND POST-TEST
LEVELS, AND CHANGES

	Pre-test mean	Post-test mean	Mean change	N for mean change
Probability of voting Conservative	2.82	3.01	+0.21	945
Liking of Conservatives	3.19	3.32	+0.14	1082
Liking of John Major	3.86	3.84	-0.02	1084
Conservative party-image index	3.33	3.44	+0.11	916
Probability of voting Labour	5.67	5.50	-0.09	1003
Liking of Labour	5.30	5.29	-0.03	1085
Liking of Tony Blair	4.94	5.08	+0.13	1089
Labour party-image index	5.40	5.34	+0.01	969
Probability of voting Lib. Democrat	3.25	3.43	+0.20	889
Liking of Liberal Democrats	4.46	4.64	+0.13	1053
Liking of Paddy Ashdown	4.69	4.76	+0.04	1068
Liberal Democrat party-image index	4.13	4.30	+0.10	859

Note: All measures are based on 0–10 scale. The index score is the arithmetic average of the three other scores in each party grouping. It is measured only for those respondents who answered all three component questions. The average change figures are calculated only from those respondents who answered both pre-test and post-test questions.

The overall pattern of pre-test and post-test averages shows that Labour was the most popular party (post-test average index score = 5.34) and the Conservatives the least popular. The average *change* scores indicate that the Conservatives and the Liberal Democrats were both viewed marginally more favourably after our experimental manipulations than before them: the 'probability of voting' scores, the 'liking' scores and the 'party-image' indices all increased for both parties. Tony Blair's ratings also increased marginally, though this tendency was counteracted by small reductions in our respondents' 'liking' and 'probability of voting' for Labour: as a result, Labour's average party-image index score remained more or less constant. There are two obvious explanations for the general increase in Conservative and Liberal Democrat ratings. One is that this increased sympathy was somehow triggered by our participants' being reminded of the election campaign: all our videos began with the opening item from BBC1's *Nine O'Clock News* on the day that John Major called the election. Another possibility is that what we thought was generally neutral coverage in the common 'top' and 'bottom' of each video 'sandwich' was not in fact neutral but slightly pro-Conservative and pro-Liberal Democrat. We are not in a position to determine which, if either, of these explanations is correct (though we would prefer to believe the first). However, the fact that there is a slight 'inflation' of Conservative and Liberal Democrat scores does not in any sense damage either the character or the purpose of our experiments. What matters is whether there are any *treatment differences* in the average change scores; whether or not subjects who watched our test videos exhibit a different change profile from those subjects who watched a control.

Table 2 allows us to explore this question explicitly. It compares the average changes in our 12 party-image measures across five groups of respondents: the control group (who were shown neutral coverage); and those who were exposed to positive Conservative, negative Conservative, positive Labour and negative Labour coverage. The first point to note about the table is that, for the control group, all three party-image index scores show only small pre-test to post-test differences (+0.05 for the Conservatives, -0.02 for Labour and +0.04 for the Liberal Democrats). This suggests, notwithstanding our earlier comments about Table 1, that the overall coverage in the control videos *was* broadly politically neutral.

The scores relating to the Conservatives' component party-image variables show three statistically significant effects. Two of them relate to John Major's ratings. In line with H1.1, Major's ratings increased significantly among the group that were exposed to positive Conservative coverage (mean change = +0.43) compared to a small decline (mean change = -0.07) in the control group. Similarly (and in line with H2.4) Major's ratings also increased significantly among the negative Labour group (+0.33). The third significant change, however, is a clear anomaly in terms of our initial hypotheses. In direct contradiction of H2.3, those respondents who watched the positive Labour video significantly increased their liking for the Conservatives (mean change = +0.49, compared with +0.07 for the control group). Fortunately, this anomaly disappears when the more reliable Conservative party-image *index* is considered. Here, the control group registers an increase of 0.05 and only the positive Conservative group shows a significantly different change (a mean increase of 0.50), consistent with H1.1.

The Labour change scores in Table 2 exhibit a far simpler pattern. The only significant effects relate to the group exposed to the positive Labour video. As H1.3 predicts, this group's mean scores on 'probability of voting Labour', 'liking' for Labour, and the Labour-image index were all significantly higher than those for the control group. The Liberal Democrat results in Table 2 are somewhat more ambiguous. The positive Conservative and positive Labour videos both seem to have elicited increased 'collateral'

TABLE 2
DIFFERENCE OF MEANS TEST ON CHANGES IN PRE-TEST TO POST-TEST SCORES
ON 12 MEASURES OF PARTY IMAGE, BY VIDEO EXPOSURE

	Change in probability of voting Conservative	Change in liking for Conservatives	Change in liking for Major	Change in Conservative party image index
CONTROL mean	0.18 (510)	0.07 (585)	-0.07 (591)	0.05 (501)
POSCON mean	0.31 (55)	0.28 (61)	0.43*** (61)	0.50*** (55)
NEGCON mean	0.29 (65)	0.16 (68)	-0.06 (69)	0.14 (63)
POSLAB mean	0.20 (55)	0.49* (63)	-0.25 (63)	0.20 (53)
NEGLAB mean	0.20 (45)	0.20 (55)	0.33* (57)	0.20 (42)

	Change in probability of voting Labour	Change in liking for Labour	Change in liking for Blair	Change in Labour party image index
CONTROL mean	-0.14 (543)	-0.08 (590)	0.10 (594)	-0.02 (534)
POSCON mean	-0.27 (55)	-0.25 (59)	-0.10 (60)	-0.18 (54)
NEGCON mean	0.30 (54)	-0.07 (67)	0.31 (68)	0.20 (53)
POSLAB mean	0.29* (62)	0.59*** (63)	0.34 (62)	0.40*** (59)
NEGLAB mean	-0.14 (58)	0.33 (58)	0.20 (61)	0.07 (54)

	Change in probability of voting Lib Dem	Change in liking for Lib Dem	Change in liking for Ashdown	Change in Lib Dem party image index
CONTROL mean	0.22 (488)	-0.02 (571)	-0.03 (584)	0.04 (476)
POSCON mean	0.10 (52)	0.42* (59)	-0.23 (60)	0.07 (52)
NEGCON mean	0.26 (53)	0.25 (67)	0.10 (68)	0.19 (52)
POSLAB mean	0.02 (54)	0.44* (62)	0.02 (61)	0.17 (51)
NEGLAB mean	0.39 (46)	0.32 (55)	0.28 (56)	0.23 (42)

Notes: CONTROL refers to Control Group mean; POSCON refers to Positive Conservative Exposure mean; NEGCON refers to Negative Conservative Exposure mean; POSLAB refers to Positive Labour Exposure mean; NEGLAB refers to Negative Labour Exposure mean. Figures in brackets indicate the number of cases involved in the mean calculation. * denotes difference of means test significant at .05 level; ** significant at .02; *** significant at .01.

liking for the *Liberal Democrats* (see the significant column 2 scores in the Liberal Democrat section of the table). This suggests that positive television images of one party can increase respondents' sympathy for another, on the face of it a somewhat bizarre finding that contradicts H2.1 and H2.3. Note, however, that this effect does not extend to either the 'probability of voting Liberal Democrat ' or 'liking for Ashdown'. Indeed, the party-image index mean scores display no significant video exposure effects whatsoever.

The simple conclusion suggested by Table 2 is that, out of our initial set of H1 and H2 hypotheses, only H1.1 and H1.3 are supported by the data: *positive coverage clearly improves a party's image among voters.* This conclusion is based on the assumption that the index measures – since they are composites of three different indicators of party image – are the most reliable measures of opinion change. (Indeed, for the remainder of this paper we report only the results of models estimated using the three index measures). The only significant effects observed in the party-image index column are the increased Conservative image scores for respondents exposed to the positive Conservative video (H1.1) and increased Labour image scores for those who watched the positive Labour video (H1.3). Although most of the remaining relationships have the correct signs, none of them is statistically significant. This implies that, for the other H1 and H2 hypotheses, we should accept the null and conclude (a) that negative coverage does not adversely a party's image; and (b) that positive (or negative) coverage of one party does not appear to damage (or enhance) the image of its rivals.

This conclusion is reinforced by the results shown in Table 3. The table outlines three OLS regression models, one for each of the party-image index measures, using dummy variable predictors reflecting respondents' exposure (or not) to each of our four experimental manipulations. The base category is the control group who were exposed to politically neutral coverage only. Although the use of dummies in this way violates standard OLS assumptions, we use OLS here as a means of clarifying the overall pattern of effects rather than as a vehicle for obtaining good estimates of coefficients. The clear message of these results is that, yet again, it is *positive* news coverage of a

TABLE 3

DIRECT EFFECTS ON PARTY=IMAGE INDICES OF EXPOSURE TO POSITIVE CONSERVATIVE, NEGATIVE CONSERVATIVE, POSITIVE LABOUR AND NEGATIVE LABOUR

	Change in Conservative party-image index		Change in Labour party-image index		Change in Liberal Democrat party-image index	
	b	se	b	se	b	se
POSCON news	0.43***	0.13	-0.16	0.15	-0.11	0.24
NEGCON news	0.07	0.11	0.21	0.15	0.05	0.24
POSLAB news	0.13	0.13	0.41**	0.15	-0.19	0.24
NEGLAB news	0.13	0.14	0.09	0.15	0.18	0.26
Constant	0.07	0.03	-0.02	0.04	0.21	0.06
Corrected R2	0.01		0.01		0.00	
N	911		968		888	
Standard error of estimate	0.90		1.08		1.68	

Notes: POSCON news = Exposure to Positive Conservative News Coverage; NEGCON news = exposure to negative Conservative news coverage; POSLAB news = exposure to positive Labour news coverage; NEGLAB news = exposure to negative Labour news coverage. ** denotes coefficient significant at .01 level; *** at .001 level. Standard errors reported as se. Estimation by OLS.

party that is most likely to elicit an increase that party's overall image ratings; *negative* coverage of a particular party does not appear to have a damaging effect on that party's ratings.

TABLE 4
DIRECT EFFECTS ON PARTY-IMAGE INDICES OF EXPOSURE, CONTROLLING FOR
SOCIODEMOGRAPHICS, TELEVISION-WATCHING, POLITICAL INTEREST, POLITICAL
KNOWLEDGE AND INITIAL PARTISAN PREFERENCES

	Change in Conservative party-image index		Change in Labour party-image index		Change in Liberal Democrat party-image index	
	b	se	b	se	b	se
Exposure to POSCON Coverage	0.33**	0.13	-0.24	0.16	0.07	0.17
Exposure to NEGCON Coverage	0.09	0.13	0.23	0.16	0.18	0.17
Exposure to POSLAB Coverage	0.14	0.13	0.49***	0.16	0.10	0.17
Exposure to NEGLAB Coverage	0.16	0.15	-0.16	0.18	0.14	0.19
Male/not	-0.07	0.07	0.10	0.08	-0.02	0.08
Age (years)	-0.002	0.003	0.00	0.003	0.00	0.00
White/not	0.06	0.08	-0.14	0.09	0.01	0.10
Graduate/not	-0.14*	0.07	0.02	0.08	-0.02	0.09
Non-man. head of household/not	0.01	0.07	-0.06	0.09	-0.05	0.09
Owner-occupier/not	-0.12	0.07	-0.04	0.08	-0.32	0.09
Unemployed/not	-0.05	0.14	-0.01	0.16	-0.29	0.17
In paid employment/not	-0.02	0.11	0.00	0.13	-0.06	0.14
Student/not	-0.01	0.14	-0.08	0.16	-0.14	0.17
Interested in current affairs/not	-0.12	0.07	0.07	0.09	0.14	0.10
Interested in political news/not	-0.02	0.07	-0.07	0.08	0.06	0.09
Hours per week watch television	0.002	0.002	0.00	0.00	0.00	0.00
Conservative vote probability	0.00	0.01	-0.03**	0.01	0.01	0.01
Labour vote probability	-0.01	0.01	-0.07***	0.01	0.01	0.01
Lib. Democrat vote probability	-0.01	0.01	-0.01	0.01	-0.06***	0.01
Political Knowledge (0-5 scale)	0.02	0.02	0.01	0.03	-0.04	0.03
Constant	0.29	0.19	0.79	0.23	0.50	0.24
Corrected R2	0.04		0.05		0.03	
N	834		844		815	
Standard error of estimate	0.91		1.06		1.12	

Note: * denotes coefficient significant at .05 level; ** at .01 level; *** at .001 level. Standard errors reported as se. Estimation by OLS.

In addition to these relatively straightforward tests, we also estimated a series of models which allowed for the possibility that the party images of strongly partisan, politically interested and/or politically informed respondents were less likely to be affected by exposure to video news than their non-partisan, uninterested and uninformed counterparts. Although we do not report the results here, there were no systematic differences in the response patterns of these two groups.

Table 4 represents a more fully specified model of the effects of exposure to our experimental manipulations. It includes controls for the standard battery of sociodemographic characteristics and for the respondent's television-watching habits, as well as for partisanship, knowledge and interest. Two main conclusions are suggested by the table. First, the inclusion of additional controls does not in any way perturb the strong effects of exposure to the positive Conservative and positive Labour videos: the estimated coefficients on these variables remain large, significant and positive while the coefficients on the remaining exposure measures are still non-significant. Second, the sociodemographic and television-watching variables fail to demonstrate any consistent pattern of effect on the change indices. The model for Conservative party image suggests that graduates are significantly less likely to change their overall view of the Conservatives (b = -0.14), but this finding has no confirming counterpart in either the Labour or the Liberal Democrat equation.[5] The crucial point is that the sociodemographic and television-habit variables simply do not affect respondents' propensities to change their images of the three main parties. The critical driving factor that influenced our subjects' tendencies either to change their party-images or to retain them was whether or not they were exposed to our experimental manipulations. And what mattered, in particular, were the two manipulations that featured *positive* images of the Conservative and Labour parties.

TABLE 5
'CORRECTED' DIFFERENCE OF MEANS TEST FOR PARTY IMAGE INDICES

	Conservative image index	Labour image index	Lib-Dem image index
Control group mean (N=452)	+0.02	-0.04	+0.02
Positive Conservative exposure mean (N=51)	+0.34***	-0.30***	-0.04
Negative Conservative exposure mean (N=50)	-0.07	+0.03	+0.04
Positive Labour exposure mean (N=50)	+0.01	+0.14	-0.15
Negative Labour exposure mean (N=38)	+0.14	-0.23	+0.08

Note: mean pre-test to post-test change measures are corrected for the individual respondent's tendency to shift responses across the range of party-image variables. *** denotes comparison with control is significant at .001; all other control comparisons non-significant.

But what happens to our findings if corrections are made for individual subjects' pre-test/post-test 'response instability' as envisaged in our earlier discussion? Table 5 describes the effects on the mean changes in party image observed in our treatment and control groups, using our *corrected* measures of party-image. The results are certainly more ambiguous than the equivalent ones reported in Table 2. Exposure to the positive Conservative video continues to be associated with an improvement in the Conservatives' party image (mean change score = +0.34), but such exposure now also significantly *damages* Labour's image (mean change score = -0.30). The effects of the positive Labour and negative Labour videos on Labour's image both have the correct signs (the mean change score for positive Labour is +0.14 and for negative Labour is -0.23) but neither effect is statistically significant. In short, while the results shown in Table 5 broadly support our earlier conclusions using uncorrected data, the beneficial effects of exposure to the positive Labour video are not sufficiently strong to achieve statistical significance.

This qualification can be abandoned, however, in view of the multivariate results shown in Table 6. The models shown here replicate those estimated in Table 4, but on this occasion using corrected party-image measures. To be sure, there are some minor differences between the results in Table 4 and those in Table 6. For example, in Table 6, improvements in the Conservatives' party image are less likely if the respondent is interested in current affairs (b = -0.15) and more likely if the respondent is an avid television-watcher (b = +0.005). The only important difference between the two sets of results, however, is that exposure to the positive Conservative video continues to damage Labour's image (b = -0.29) as well as to enhance the Conservatives' (b = +0.27). This apart, the overall results are clearly consistent with our earlier observations: the sociodemographic variables do not exert consistent effects on changes in party-image; and exposure to positive Conservative and positive Labour news coverage yet again significantly enhances the respective images of those two parties.

An obvious question follows from the somewhat asymmetrical results that we have reported. Why should positive news have exerted such clear and consistent effects on our respondents' party-image perceptions while negative news appears to have had so little impact? Although we cannot answer this question definitely, we can explore the possible reasons for this asymmetry. One possibility relates to the timing of our experiments. Our fieldwork was conducted after a long period – covering most of the 1992 parliament – in which the two major parties had focused a significant part of their campaigning efforts on attacking their opponents. This in turn could have inured voters to the effects of negative political images to such an extent that they failed to respond to the negative images to which we exposed them: they would have needed a much more powerful negative stimulus to have produced a measurable response. If this were indeed the case, it would imply that negative campaigning perhaps contains within it the seeds of its own long-term failure: the more that voters are exposed to it, the less they are affected by it.

TABLE 6
DIRECT EFFECTS ON CORRECTED PARTY-IMAGE INDICES OF EXPOSURE, CONTROLLING FOR
SOCIODEMOGRAPHICS, TELEVISION WATCHING, POLITICAL INTEREST, POLITICAL
KNOWLEDGE AND INITIAL PARTISAN PREFERENCES

	Change in Conservative party-image index		Change in Labour party-image index		Change in Liberal Democrat party-image index	
	b	se	b	se	b	se
Exposure to POSCON Coverage	0.27**	0.11	-0.29**	0.11	0.01	0.12
Exposure to NEGCON Coverage	-0.07	0.11	0.07	0.11	0.01	0.12
Exposure to POSLAB Coverage	-0.03	0.11	0.22*	0.11	-0.19	0.12
Exposure to NEGLAB Coverage	0.11	0.13	-0.21	0.13	0.10	0.14
Male/not	-0.01	0.05	-0.05	0.06	0.05	0.06
Age (years)	0.00	0.002	-0.001	0.002	0.001	0.002
White/not	0.09	0.07	-0.12	0.07	0.04	0.07
Graduate/not	-0.07	0.06	0.06	0.06	0.02	0.06
Non-man. head of household/not	0.07	0.06	-0.06	0.06	-0.01	0.06
Owner-occupier/not	0.03	0.06	-0.14*	0.06	-0.16**	0.06
Unemployed/not	0.08	0.11	0.09	0.12	-0.17	0.12
In paid employment/not	0.03	0.09	0.00	0.09	-0.04	0.10
Student/not	0.17	0.11	-0.10	0.11	-0.07	0.12
Interested in current affairs/not	-0.15**	0.06	0.05	0.06	0.11	0.07
Interested in political news/not	0.00	0.06	-0.08	0.06	0.08	0.06
Hours per week watch television	0.005*	0.002	-0.003	0.002	-0.001	0.002
Conservative vote probability	0.004	0.008	-0.03**	0.01	0.02*	0.01
Labour vote probability	0.002	0.008	-0.04***	0.01	0.03***	0.01
Lib. Democrat vote probability	0.01	0.01	0.01	0.01	-0.02***	0.01
Political Knowledge (0-5 scale)	0.02	0.02	0.02	0.02	-0.03	0.02
Constant	-0.31	0.16	0.33	0.17	-0.02	0.17
Corrected R^2	.02		.05		.04	
N	797		797		797	
Standard error of estimate	.74		.78		.79	

Note: * denotes coefficient significant at .05 level; ** at .01 level; *** at .001 level. Standard errors reported as se. Estimation by OLS.

A second possibility is that British voters are more susceptible to positive news images precisely because they are generally so cynical about, and dismissive of, politics and politicians. Indirect evidence for this cynicism can be gleaned from Gallup's long-running time-series on voters' 'approval of the government's record'. These data show that, whichever party is in power, the vast majority of voters most of the time disapprove of what the government of the day has done.[6] In these circumstances of general cynicism, it is possible that positive news about a political party – any political party – represents more of a challenge to voters' existing mind-sets, thereby invoking more of a reaction in terms of changes in their party-image perceptions. Negative news images, on the other hand, since they conform with and confirm voters' prior dispositions, perhaps produce less of a response.

A third possible explanation for the asymmetrical effects of positive and negative news is that the images to which our respondents were exposed varied in intensity: the positive news stories included in our experiments were somehow more powerful than the negative ones. In compiling our videos, we obviously sought to ensure that such imbalances did not occur. Equally, however, we cannot be sure that that we eliminated them altogether. We can only assert that, in our view, there were no obvious differences in intensity between the positive and negative news videos that we employed. We are confident that our respondents genuinely reacted differently to positive as opposed to negative news items about the major political parties. Further research will clearly be necessary to establish the precise factors that underlie this finding.

Summary and Conclusions

The method that we have adopted here is based on the simple principle that a given experimental stimulus should produce an observable test response. We wished to know if voters' attitudinal responses varied systematically at the individual level according to the types of television news coverage they were shown. The very clear answer is that they do. Our analysis provides unambiguous experimental evidence that exposure to positive news coverage of a particular political party produces a clear and significant improvement in respondents' perceptions of that party's image. In contrast, exposure to negative news coverage elicits no consistent response.

Apart from this strong finding about the effects of 'positive' news coverage on voters' party-images, our analysis suggests a number of other conclusions. First, we find little evidence that positive or negative coverage of *one* party exerts 'collateral' effects on the images of *other* parties. In general, positive Conservative and positive Labour exposure, though they respectively helped the Conservatives and Labour, inflicted *no* collateral damage. The only exception to this pattern was when we used 'corrected' party-image measures. In this context, positive Conservative exposure did weaken respondents' images of Labour. Unfortunately, we are not in a position to determine whether the 'corrected' or the 'uncorrected' findings are the more appropriate; this remains a matter for future research into the question of response instability.

A second important conclusion is that more partisan, more informed or more interested respondents were no less likely than their respective comparator groups to change their assessments of the parties as a result of being exposed to positive or negative news. Finally, our findings about the role of sociodemographic characteristics and television-watching habits suggested that these variables not only failed to exert any clear effects on our respondents' changing party images but also failed to weaken the effects on positive and negative news coverage on those party images.

What, if anything, does all this tell us about the more general effects of television news on British public opinion? The cynical observer would almost certainly argue that, since we have 'merely' examined experimental effects, we still know precisely nothing about the effects of television news on 'real' voters 'in the real world'. Such a conclusion, however, would be both ill-advised and unfair. The value of the sort of research conducted here lies in the way that it relates to other projects which approach the same core materials from different perspectives. As we noted at the outset, aggregate correlations between television news coverage and voters' opinions have in the past been obliged to assume that exposure affects perceptions. We have been able to show that this is indeed the case. This in itself represents an important development for aggregate analysts. The fact that we have been able to demonstrate the existence of individual-level television news coverage effects, albeit in an experimental context, provides the necessary empirical underpinning for any analyses that seek to make use of the television coverage data that were systematically collected by Semetko and Scammel during the 1997 election campaign. Future attempts to relate these data to aggregate-level opinion poll data of the sort collected, on a daily basis during the campaign, by Gallup can be confident that their investigations are solidly grounded in a known, individual-level, relationship between coverage and party-image perceptions.

What we do not know, of course, is how enduring – or ephemeral – the changes in response that we have measured might turn out to be. The short-term changes that we observed were in fact quite considerable. The mean pre-test Conservative party-image score was 3.33. Our best estimate (from Table 4) of the effect of ten minutes of positive Conservative news coverage yields a coefficient of +0.33. This represents no less than a 9 per cent increase on the mean Conservative pre-test score. Remarkably, the equivalent calculation for the effects of ten minutes of positive Labour coverage produces the same estimated 9 per cent increase on the mean Labour pre-test score.[7] It seems highly unlikely that effects of this magnitude could last for very long. Equally, we have no way of determining, from our data, the rate at which they might discount over time. Our respondents were guaranteed confidentiality and anonymity, so we were unable to re-test them on a subsequent occasion in order to see if there might be any trace of the experimental effects that we observed. The only way of establishing the discount rates of any experimental effects would be for us to bite the 'experimental conditioning' bullet and construct a repeated-test research design. We certainly intend to do precisely this in our future work. For the moment, however, we have clear evidence that it is positive rather than negative television images that seem to best serve the electoral interests of the party concerned. Party managers, as well as news editors contemplating their own power, should take note.

NOTES

1. We originally intended to investigate the effects of two additional news categories: 'positive Liberal Democrat' and 'negative Liberal Democrat'. The Liberal Democrats, however, received such scant attention during the period sampled that few positive and almost no negative Liberal Democrat news items were identified. Both the positive and the negative Liberal Democrat hypotheses were subsequently dropped from our analysis.
2. The programmes sampled were *Nine O'Clock News* (BBC1), *News at Ten* (ITN), *Channel Four News* and *Newsnight* (BBC2).
3. We have every confidence, however, that similar codings would have been produced by other researchers. Full transcriptions of the content of the four videos concerned are available from the authors.
4. The results of these agenda-setting and time-balance experiments are reported in a companion paper (Norris and Sanders, 1997).
5. In these circumstances, it is tempting in any case to regard this single significant sociodemographic effect as a statistical artefact. Given the sheer number of coefficients estimated in Table 4, the chances of observing an .05 level coefficient, even if none of the exogenous variables genuinely affects the dependent variable, are high.
6. Between January 1964 and March 1997, for example, the average 'government's record' approval rating was only 31 per cent. This is considerably lower that the average popularity of the major parties. Over the same period, the average popularity rating of the governing party was 38.4 per cent.
7. The estimated coefficient for positive Labour coverage in the Labour image equation is +.49, which represents 9 per cent of the mean Labour pre-test score of 5.40.

REFERENCES

Ansolabehere, Steven and Shanto Iyengar (1997) *Going Negative*. New York: Free Press.
Brynin, Malcolm and David Sanders (1997) 'Party Identification, Political Preferences and material Conditions: Evidence from the British Household Panel Survey, 1991–92', *Party Politics* 3: 53–77.
Butler, David and Donald E. Stokes (1974) *Political Change in Britain: The Evolution of Political Choice*. London: Macmillan.
Gavin, Neil and David Sanders (1996) 'The Impact of Television News on Public Perceptions of the Economy and Government, 1993–1994' in David M. Farrell, David Broughton, David Denver and Justin Fisher (eds) *British Elections and Parties Yearbook, 1996*, pp.68–84. London: Frank Cass.
Glasgow Media Group (1976) *Bad News*. London: Routledge and Kegan Paul.
Glasgow Media Group (1980) *More Bad News*. London: Routledge and Kegan Paul.
Heath, Anthony, Roger Jowell and John Curtice (1985) *How Britain Votes*. London: Pergamon.
Heath, Anthony, Roger Jowell and John Curtice (1991) *Understanding Political Change*. London: Pergamon.
Heath, Anthony, Roger Jowell and John Curtice (eds) (1994) *Labour's Last Chance? The 1992 Election and Beyond*. Aldershot: Dartmouth.
Iyengar, Shanto and Donald R. Kinder (1987) *News That Matters*. Chicago: Chicago University Press.
Mughan, Tony (1996) 'Television Can Matter: Bias in the 1992 General Election', in David M.

Farrell, David Broughton, David Denver and Justin Fisher (eds) *British Elections and Parties Yearbook, 1996*, pp.128–42. London and Portland OR: Frank Cass.

Norris, Pippa and David Sanders (1997) *It Was the Media, Stupid: Agenda-Setting Effects During the 1997 British Campaign*, paper prepared for delivery at the 1997 annual meeting of the American Political Science Association, Sheraton Washington Hotel, 28–31 August 1997.

Patterson, Tom (1993) *Out of Order*. New York: Knopf.

Sarlvik, Bo and Ivor Crewe (1983) *Decade of Dealignment*. Cambridge: Cambridge University Press.

Triumph of Targeting? Constituency Campaigning in the 1997 Election

David Denver, Gordon Hands and Simon Henig

Although the use of the term 'targeting' with reference to election campaigning may be relatively new, the activity that it describes is not. Party organizers at regional and national levels have long realized that under the British electoral system the great majority of seats rarely change hands and have, therefore, attempted to concentrate the local campaign effort on what are variously called 'target', 'key', 'critical' or 'battleground' seats. Even in the 1950s and 1960s, when resources and attention were increasingly devoted to the national campaign, the parties were well aware that winning marginal seats was crucial to their chances of winning elections, and that additional local efforts in those seats might pay handsome rewards. Thus as long ago as the 1959 general election, the Nuffield study commented on 'the ruthless emphasis on marginal seats' (Butler and Rose, 1960: 135), and the study of the 1964 election reported that 'a much more explicit concentration on marginal seats was a feature of the campaign both for Conservatives and for Labour' (Butler and King, 1965: 216).

For a variety of reasons these attempts by the major parties to target their efforts on key constituencies were not always successful. Butler and Kavanagh, in their report of the 1983 election, pointed out that 'Parties have always had target seats, but this often meant little in practical terms' (Butler and Kavanagh, 1984: 212–3). Marginal seats might receive help with preparing election literature or be given some financial assistance, and volunteer workers from safe or hopeless seats would be urged to go to neighbouring marginal constituencies. Even such relatively modest measures were sometimes met with resistance from local party members, being seen as 'interference' by national headquarters, and, even where they were effective, constituency campaigns still remained just that – campaigns organized and run by constituency parties or associations, with some help and guidance from the centre.

From the late 1980s, however, a number of important changes in campaigning have taken place. There has been a reassessment of the significance of local campaigning and both local and national campaigning have become much more professional in all of the major parties. The combined result of these changes is that targeting has been transformed.

In part, the increased attention paid to local campaigning by the parties may have been encouraged by a change in academic assessments of the effectiveness of local campaigning. For much of the post-war period the dominant academic view has been that constituency campaigning makes little, if any, difference to constituency election results. This view is most closely associated with the Nuffield studies, but perhaps the most telling sign of its pervasiveness is the fact that constituency campaigning is never mentioned in the major British Election Study reports on voting behaviour at elections from 1964 to 1992. In recent years, however, a considerable body of evidence has accumulated which suggests that local campaigning can make a significant difference to how parties perform in elections (see, for example, Seyd and Whiteley, 1992; Pattie *et al.*, 1995; Denver and Hands, 1997a). The impact of this research on the parties' thinking is illustrated by the fact that the work of Denver and Hands is cited in support of Labour's 1997 campaign strategy in the party's most recent campaign manual (Labour Party, no date [1996?]: 6–7). (See also the Clare Short speech quoted by Whiteley and Seyd in this volume p.193.)

The increasing professionalization of campaigning has manifested itself in a variety of ways at the national level: greater use of opinion polling, reliance on professional advertising agencies, more emphasis on media management, and so on. Given the results of recent academic research, it is not surprising that, in addition, as campaign organizers have sought new ways in which they can influence election outcomes, their attention has turned to the local campaign. Hence there has been a renewed emphasis on targeting, but targeting now in a much more rigorous and far-reaching sense than that practised in the 1950s and 1960s. In their study of the 1992 election Denver and Hands showed that the parties' national campaign teams were giving much greater attention to constituency campaigns, especially in marginal seats (Denver and Hands, 1997a: 159–61). Targeting by Labour and the Liberal Democrats was effective in two senses. First, additional resources and effort were actually brought to bear in the targeted seats: campaigns were much stronger in marginal seats than in those which were safe or hopeless for the party concerned. Second, this targeting was reflected in the election results: measured in a variety of ways party performance was clearly better in seats in which stronger campaigns were mounted. In contrast, the Conservatives' efforts at targeting in 1992 met with much less success. They were clearly less able than the other parties to focus campaign resources and effort into the seats that mattered – in part because local Conservative associations have traditionally been more autonomous than the constituency organizations of the other parties, but also because associations in safe seats in 1992 were so well endowed with resources that it was easy for them to mount strong campaigns. Analysis of the results for the Conservatives failed to discover any positive relationship between constituency campaign effort and party performance.

It was evident well before the 1997 election that all three of the major parties would again focus a good deal of their effort on managing the local campaign, and it seemed clear that targeting would be carried to new heights. Our aim in this chapter is, first, to describe in detail the parties' targeting strategies in 1997, second to provide some evidence about the extent to which these central strategies affected the ways in which local campaigns were run, and finally to examine the impact of targeting on election outcomes. As we shall see, there is plenty of evidence to support our contention that in the 1997 election targeting was transformed.

Targeting Plans for 1997

Nowadays all of the major parties make extensive efforts to assist all of their local parties or associations to fight general election campaigns. Generally speaking they have to cater for three kinds of constituency. First, there are those in which the party organization is so weak that at best only a nominal campaign will be run. For all parties this includes seats which are hopeless prospects. In the case of Labour it would also include many traditionally safe seats – it is a sign of the decrepitude into which the party's local organization had fallen by the 1980s that many constituency parties in rock-solid city-centre seats had tiny memberships and neither the will nor the ability to mount an effective campaign. Second, there are those constituencies in which there is an active and perhaps strong local organization, but which are either safe enough not to be in danger of being lost or beyond the likelihood of capture on any foreseeable swing. These seats are not likely to affect the outcome of the election, and the campaign will go ahead with or without central prompting but, nonetheless, party headquarters are expected to provide a range of services to help the local effort – training, advice, access to cheap printing facilities, legal guidance, and so on. Thirdly, there are the key seats, usually around 100 for Labour and the Conservatives and around 50 for the Liberal Democrats. There is a realistic possibility of these changing hands and it is these constituencies which constitute the parties' lists of targets (which will overlap but not be identical). This is where we need to look for evidence of an effective targeting strategy. The parties seek to ensure that the best possible campaigns are mounted in these seats, and in practice that means well-organized and well-resourced campaigns, using the most up-to-date campaigning techniques – in particular making the most of computers, direct mail and telephone canvassing. But of course one would expect, and we find, rather different approaches from the three major parties as a consequence of the political positions in which they find themselves, their different organizational structures and their previous traditions of campaigning.

The Conservatives

The campaign strategists at Conservative Central Office began their planning for local campaigning in the 1997 election about a year after the 1992 election. They compiled a list of about 100 'battleground' seats. These were the seats which would determine whether the party remained in government or not. Given that it was already clear that the party was likely to be on the defensive in the next general election, most of them were Conservative-held, but a handful were held by one of the other parties. Although there were ongoing adjustments to the list in the light of constituency boundary changes and by-election losses, these seats were the focus of the party's preparations over the next four years and then of the party's local efforts during the campaign itself. The selection of this list of key seats, and the focusing of organization and resources on them, constituted the first level of the Conservative targeting strategy. The first priority was to ensure that each target constituency had a qualified agent in place. One of the Conservatives' main organizational advantages has traditionally been their large number of full-time agents, but in the early 1990s many constituency associations found themselves in financial difficulties and were unable to continue to pay an agent's salary. In a very significant development, Central Office stepped in to help with the appointment of agents in target seats, paying half, or usually more, of the salary. Local Conservative associations were traditionally very independent-minded and resistant to control from the centre, but these agents were on the central payroll and therefore more likely to be amenable to accepting a nationally-planned strategy. Further resources were also allocated – each target seat was given a new computer, and in addition an economical service for high-quality printing of election addresses and such like was made available to all seats. This substantial commitment of resources by the centre is a clear indication of the determination of Central Office to maximize the efficiency of the campaigns in the target constituencies. In order to explain and get support for the strategy and to ensure that local associations were getting on with their election planning, a series of regional meetings was held with the relevant candidates, association chairmen and agents. These meetings continued on a regular basis – twice a year at first and then more frequently – throughout the inter-election period.

But there was a second and radically new aspect to the Conservatives' targeting in the lead-up to the 1997 election. For the first time, the targeting strategy went beyond a focus on constituencies to focus on individual voters – indeed, the whole strategy was called 'Battleground Voters'. Central Office set out to build up a database of two million target voters – 20,000 from each target constituency. This was developed in a number of ways. To start with, there were the results of traditional doorstep canvassing, supplemented by an increased use of telephone canvassing – Central Office helped financially with the installation of telephone lines and provided training in telephone canvassing techniques. But then, in addition, a major effort was put into a series of mail surveys. Lists of potential or likely supporters were initially compiled from computerized electoral registers using geo-demographic data based on post codes and 'lifestyle' data supplied by commercial firms. Over a period of two-and-a-half years these voters were sent mail surveys designed to identify previous Conservative voters and possible future supporters, and also to get information about voters' concerns on the central political issues. Particular efforts were made to identify 'soft' Conservative supporters – those who had voted for the party in the past but were now worried about some aspects of the government's performance. This combination of canvassing and survey techniques allowed the database to be refined into what was potentially a very powerful electoral weapon. The main way in which it was used in the pre-election period was to send direct mail from the centre to target groups. Thus in September and November 1996 and in January 1997 Central Office sent out two million personalized letters to their target voters. In addition, however, candidates and party workers were expected to use the information available from the database and make special efforts to personally visit 'swing' voters and to respond to their particular concerns.

Thus, during the campaign itself, the Conservatives hoped to be in a position to mount strong and well-targeted campaigns in the constituencies. They had strengthened local organization and poured considerable resources into the target constituencies, and in addition they had a soundly-based list of target voters in each constituency who would be the main focus of local activity.

The Liberal Democrats

Given their comparative organizational and financial weakness, it is not surprising that the Liberal Democrats have not developed targeting to the same extent as their competitors. In the 1983 and 1987 general elections the cumbersome campaign structure of the Alliance meant that there was very little targeting of key seats. In 1992, however, the Liberal Democrats devised a system of 'layered targeting' in which seats were assigned to one of four categories, with most effort being put into those in the top category. Party organizers judged this strategy to be successful, and in preparation for the 1997 election more time and more resources were devoted to the targeted campaigning strategy. The process was started almost immediately after the 1992 election with 53 seats being selected for targeting – most of those that were already held, plus those which could be won on a 6.5 per cent swing.

Candidates in these seats were selected early and special training was given to agents. In addition, special advisers, or 'campaign consultants', were put in charge of clusters of key seats – from four to eight seats per person – to monitor progress and ensure that the necessary preparations were being made. By the time of the 1997 election there were seven such advisers.

As with the Conservatives, the list of Liberal Democrat targets was gradually amended in the light of boundary changes, and also as a consequence of by-election victories. A few constituencies were also dropped because they were unable or unwilling to do the necessary work. Unlike the other parties, however, the organization of the long campaign in target seats was devolved to the local level – at party headquarters only Chris Rennard, the director of campaigns, and a couple of helpers were involved. A set of objectives to be achieved between autumn 1994 and autumn 1996 was drawn up but, although headquarters made financial grants towards the costs of employing agents and helped with such matters as designing leaflets and voter survey forms, the emphasis was on training and encouraging people on the ground. Similarly, during the actual campaign there was no centrally organized telephone canvassing or direct mailing, although Paddy Ashdown's tours were carefully planned to ensure that, for the most part, he visited only target seats.

In general, however, it is probably fair to say that the Liberal Democrats were one election behind the other parties. They targeted their campaign on key seats more effectively than before, but unlike the Conservatives, they did not move on to targeting voters as well as seats. As national officers freely admit, the Liberal Democrats lack the necessary resources (and will continue to do so for the foreseeable future) to mount the high-powered targeting operations undertaken by the Conservatives and (as we shall now see) by Labour in 1997.

Labour

For the 1992 general election, the Labour Party mounted a substantial targeting operation, and party officials were in no doubt that it paid significant electoral dividends (see Hill, 1995). In preparation for the 1997 election an even greater effort was planned. Codenamed 'Operation Victory', the plan was highly sophisticated and extremely ambitious. The operation was launched relatively late, in the autumn of 1995, and as with the Conservatives, it involved targeting individual electors as well as key constituencies. At a superficial level Labour's targeting strategy might appear not to differ greatly from the Conservatives' effort, but when one goes into the detail, one is driven to the conclusion that in terms of its sophistication of conception, thoroughgoing attention to all aspects of the campaign, and sheer professionalism it was on an altogether different level.

National party officials drew up a list of 90 constituencies to be targeted – the 57 required for Labour to gain an overall majority, plus a further 22 marginals which would provide a comfortable majority and 11 which were notionally Labour-held under the new boundaries but where there was no current Labour MP. Wirral South was added to the list following Labour's win in the by-election there in February 1997. Labour's campaigns in these seats provided the focus of the party's efforts at all levels between late 1995 and May 1997. A key seats unit was formed to oversee and co-ordinate the campaigns, and great efforts were made to persuade local party workers to fall in with the strategy. Contrary to the usual secrecy about these things, the list of key seats was regularly sent to party members in order to persuade them to concentrate their efforts in 'the seats we need to win to get a majority' (Labour Party, 1997: 7). The remaining constituencies were designated 'majority' seats (whether they were held by Labour, the Conservatives the Liberal Democrats or nationalists). Here there was to be a 'high-profile, high-impact but low-energy and low-cost campaign designed to release resources to the campaign in the key seats' (Labour Party, no date [1996?]: 30). There was a great deal of emphasis on not using up resources unnecessarily in the majority seats, and very strong encouragement for volunteers from these seats to work for the campaign in their nearest key seat.

A long-standing problem for the Labour Party has been its relatively small number of full-time agents. As in 1992, this was overcome by appointing temporary special organizers to look after small groups of key seats. Now, however, this was done on a much larger scale, with as many as 100 special organizers being paid for from central funds, and by the time the official campaign started there was, more or less, one special organizer per key seat. Labour was as usual able to call on the support of its affiliated unions, but this was also done much more systematically and effectively than previously, with union joint co-ordinators being appointed in each of the key seats to help bring in resources and people. There was also the usual extensive effort in training volunteer agents and encouraging more extensive and more sophisticated use of computers.

But the central element in Labour's key seats strategy was mass telephone 'voter identification' (voter ID) – this being the new name for what had traditionally been known as canvassing – in the 18 months before the election. A target was set of contacting 80 per cent of the electorate in key seats, with the aim of achieving this by October 1996. To this end, telephone banks were established across the country, in regional and local party offices, and party workers from all constituencies used them to contact voters in the key seats. There was considerable pressure on constituency organizations to achieve this target, and progress was monitored at the centre on a three-monthly basis. Telephone 'canvassers' were provided with a script-cum-questionnaire and for each contact were asked to record the elector's party identification, vote in 1992, current vote intention, regularity of voting and answers to some other follow-up questions. This information permitted electors to be allocated to one of a number of categories – 'reliable Labour', 'weak Labour', 'undecided', for example – each with a number of sub-categories. The two most important groups to be targeted were 'switchers' (those who voted Conservative or Liberal Democrat but now identified with Labour) and first-time voters (aged 18 to 23) but, in addition, 1992 Liberal Democrats who preferred Labour to the Conservatives, and Labour identifiers who did not always vote received special attention.

The party's own figures for the mean number of electors per key seat in each of the target groups are shown in Table 1. The figures reveal that the numbers of identified 'switchers' were small – less than two per cent of the electorate. The numbers of first-time voters and weak Labour supporters were larger and, in total, an average of 15 per cent of the electorate in key seats fell into one of the categories to be targeted. Labour's constituency campaigning strategy was, therefore, focused not only on selected constituencies but on a small minority of electors within those constituencies. From the British electorate of about 42.6 million fewer than 925,000 were targeted (just over two per cent).

TABLE 1
MEAN NUMBER OF ELECTORS IN EACH TARGET GROUP IN LABOUR'S KEY SEATS

	Mean number per constituency	Mean % of electorate
Target Group:		
Con–Lab switchers	936	1.39
Lib Dem-Lab switchers	349	0.52
Lib Dems with Lab preference	1261	1.80
Other weak Labour	4985	9.29
First-time voters	2643	3.76

Source: Labour Party

Potentially at least, the highly detailed information resulting from the voter identification exercise provided the basis for a much more sophisticated approach to the mass electorate than had been possible before, notably in the use of direct mail. The use of direct mail for election campaigning originated in the United States but has expanded rapidly in Britain since the mid 1980s. Modern computer packages allow campaigners to produce what appear to be personal letters from candidates or party leaders to the voters and to tailor the message to the concerns of different groups of voters. All three parties have used direct mail (especially in by-elections) but the practice has been somewhat haphazard in general elections owing to a lack of detailed information about voters. Labour's voter ID work in key seats changed the picture dramatically in 1997. Labour campaign teams were now able to target direct mail to different categories of electors during the run-up to the election, and the plan was that 'switchers' should receive at least one direct mailing every week during the official campaign and also be personally contacted by the candidate. First-time voters received a number of direct mailings including a short video demonstrating that voting is easy, and even 'groovy'. One major advantage of this strategy was that there was no need for traditional doorstep canvassing during the election campaign (although key groups would be recontacted to confirm their support).

One further important element of Labour's targeting in 1997 should be commented on. The whole process was so thoroughly thought out and so tightly controlled from the centre that to a large extent the initiative in the constituency campaign had ceased to lie with the candidate or local party organizers. There was great emphasis on everyone marching to the same tune, everyone following the same script. In one sense, then, the local campaign had almost ceased to be local at all, and to be simply part of the larger national and nationally planned campaign. But there is another way of looking at this. Asked about the role of the key seat strategy in the party's overall campaign, one Labour official replied 'the key seat strategy was basically the centre of the campaign'. If this is correct, then what it implies is that there has been a significant shift of the centre of gravity of campaigning away from the national level and back towards the constituencies.

Modern targeting techniques have clearly been carried furthest by Labour, but certainly the Conservatives, and probably the Liberal Democrats too, are moving in the same direction. What our discussion so far suggests is that in the late 1990s there are three central aspects to targeting in election campaigns. First, there is the selection as targets of the key seats which are thought likely to be crucial to the outcome of the election, and the concentration of the party's resources and organizational expertise on the campaigns in these seats. Second, there is also now a focus on key voters – the relatively small number of voters in those key seats whose voting decision is likely to be crucial – using telephone canvassing and surveys to identify these voters and then using sophisticated direct mail and other techniques to get the party's message across to them. The third feature of modern targeting is perhaps the most significant, however. The initiative in organizing local campaigning appears to be moving from the constituencies to the centre (at least in key seats) and becoming an integral part of the party's overall (national and local) campaign. However, to plan a highly sophisticated targeting exercise is one thing – to put it into practice is another. We now consider the evidence about how effective the parties were in implementing their targeting strategies in 1997.

Campaigning in Target Constituencies

In 1997, then, all three of the major parties aimed to target their local campaigning more than ever before. There was, as we have suggested, a good deal of overlap in the parties' lists of key seats. Thus, of the 85 Conservative key seats which we have identified, 62 were also on Labour's target list, 15 were targeted by the Liberal Democrats and five by both. Of Labour's 91 targets 69 were also on the lists of one of the other major parties.[1] These figures imply that, in terms of local campaigning, the 1997 election battle was concentrated in a relatively small number of constituencies.

In this section we consider the extent to which the parties' attempts to target their campaigns on their key seats were effective. If they were, then we would expect to find that the campaigns in these key seats were markedly different from those in other seats. To explore this question we make use of a survey of election agents and organizers which we carried out immediately after the election and which was designed to provide information on various aspects of local campaigns in 1997. We received responses from 438 Conservative agents, 461 Labour and 412 Liberal Democrats, representing response rates of 68.5 per cent, 72.1 per cent and 64.5 per cent respectively. Of the Conservative responses, 64 were from target seats, while 65 of the Labour and 24 of the Liberal Democrat responses were from constituencies on their target lists.

It would not be very illuminating to compare local campaigns in target seats with those in constituencies which were very safe or hopeless prospects for the party concerned. We therefore selected from our responses a group of non-target seats for each party with which targets could be more meaningfully compared. In the case of Labour and the Conservatives the comparator non-target seats are those in which in 1992 the party had a lead of less than 20 per cent, or was no more than 20 per cent behind. Thus very safe and apparently hopeless seats are excluded. This gives 112 seats for comparison with Labour targets and 153 for comparison with Conservative targets. In the case of the Liberal Democrats 50 comparator seats were identified, comprising the six seats already held by the party but not on their target list and the 44 strongest non-target seats.[2]

As we have explained, the parties sought to concentrate their resources and their organizational expertise on their key seats, and Labour and the Conservatives also tried to target key voters in those constituencies. To the extent that this strategy was effective, therefore, we should expect to find significant differences in the types and strengths of campaigns mounted in target and non-target constituencies. We now consider the evidence, looking first at the most important of resources – volunteer workers – and then at the level and type of activity during the pre-campaign period, during the campaign itself, and on polling day.

Volunteer Workers

Although volunteer party workers are not foot-soldiers who can be ordered around by generals at party HQs, all parties seek to concentrate their available manpower in their key seats, in particular encouraging volunteers in safe or hopeless seats to work in neighbouring marginals. As Table 2 shows, in 1997 all three of the parties were relatively successful in this respect. The first two rows show the percentages of constituencies which reported receiving volunteers from other constituencies and those which sent people elsewhere. In each case target seats were much more likely to receive workers from, and less likely to send them to, other constituencies than were comparable seats. The Conservatives appear to have been least effective in organizing this exchange of manpower, however, while Labour was most effective – virtually all of Labour's targets received outside help. The third and fourth rows of the table show the average numbers of campaign and polling day workers. We asked agents to report how many people were working for the party in the constituency on an average day towards the end of the campaign and on

TABLE 2
VOLUNTEER WORKERS

	Conservative		Labour		Lib Dem	
	Targets	Non-targets	Targets	Non-targets	Targets	Non-targets
% seats received volunteers	56	17	98	9	67	16
% seats sent volunteers	2	18	6	60	4	54
Number of campaign workers (mean)	75	48	80	72	178	70
Number of polling day workers (mean)	164	116	250	150	302	145
N	64	153	65	112	24	50

Note: Here and in subsequent tables Conservative and Labour 'non-target' seats are those not targeted in which, according to estimates of voting in 1992, the party was either less than 20 per cent behind the 'winner' or less than 20 per cent in the lead. For the Liberal Democrats they are the 6 seats held by the party in 1992 but not on their target list for 1997, plus the 44 seats from which we received replies and in which they were closest to the winning party. The Ns in tables 2 to 6 are close to those shown here.

polling day itself. Again the target seats easily outscored the others, particularly on polling day, although in this case it was the Liberal Democrats who were most successful in targeting their efforts. They had more than twice as many campaign workers in their target seats as in comparable seats and more than twice as many polling day workers.

Pre-campaign Activity

As we have seen, all parties laid great stress on campaigning work done in the years before polling day. Labour's strategy involved an extensive voter identification campaign conducted largely by telephone, and this is reflected in the fact that 84 per cent of agents in Labour's target seats reported that 'a substantial amount' of telephone canvassing had been done before the campaign started, compared with 28 per cent in the non-target seats (Table 3). The Conservatives went about identifying key voters in a rather different way, relying to a large extent on mail surveys, though these were backed up with telephone canvassing. Even so, there is also a clear, if less marked, difference between their targets and non-target seats. The Liberal Democrats could not afford to organize telephone canvassing to anything like the same extent and, reassuringly, the figures confirm that this was not a significant element of their pre-election campaigns. We also asked respondents to indicate how far advanced they were in identifying potential supporters through canvassing when the date of the election was announced, using a scale ranging from 1 (not started) to 5 (fully prepared). In each case targets were clearly more prepared then non-targets with Labour target seats, on average, being almost fully prepared.

TABLE 3
PRE-CAMPAIGN ACTIVITY

	Conservative		Labour		Lib Dem	
	Targets	Non-targets	Targets	Non-targets	Targets	Non-targets
% did substantial amount of telephone canvassing	48	29	84	28	8	2
Identifying supporters	3.7	3.2	4.2	3.3	3.3	3.0

Note: The figures for 'identifying supporters' are mean scores on a scale running from 1 (not started) to 5 (fully prepared) measuring how far advanced preparations in this area were when the date of the election was announced.

Campaign Activities

Table 4 compares target and non-target seats in respect of seven campaign activities. We asked respondents how much telephone canvassing was carried out within the constituency during the campaign and the proportions doing a substantial amount are similar to those found for pre-campaign telephone

TABLE 4
CAMPAIGN ACTIVITIES

	Conservative		Labour		Lib Dem	
	Targets	Non-targets	Targets	Non-targets	Targets	Non-targets
% did substantial amount of telephone canvassing	42	28	80	36	8	2
% had telephone canvassing from outside constituency	31	7	88	4	22	17
% of electorate canvassed by phone (mean)	16	11	36	14	5	4
% of electorate canvassed on doorstep (mean)	30	29	29	33	36	21
% targeted leaflets	73	64	84	69	96	80
% did substantial amount of direct mail	52	35	79	39	48	16
Number of VIP visits (mean)	4.5	2.5	6.7	1.0	3.5	1.0

canvassing. Once again the Liberal Democrats appear to lag well behind the other parties, and although Conservative targets did more telephone canvassing than non-targets the biggest difference is found in Labour campaigns. The second row of the table shows the proportions of respondents who were aware of telephone canvassing of their constituency electorate having been organized from outside the constituency, by national headquarters or regional offices. Not surprisingly, more agents in Labour and Conservative target seats were aware of this happening than in non-targets, very many more in Labour's case. The figures for the Liberal Democrats are surprisingly large given that no telephone canvassing was organized at national level. It may be that in some areas more informal arrangements were in place which involved people in hopeless seats doing some telephone canvassing for those which were better prospects.

The difference made by Labour's canvassing (or 'voter ID') strategy in target as opposed to non-target seats are highlighted by the figures for the percentage of the electorate canvassed by telephone and in the traditional way – by knocking on doors. In Labour target seats more voters were canvassed by telephone than in non-target seats, whereas – indicative of a reliance on more traditional methods – slightly more voters were canvassed by knocking on doors in non-targets than in targets. There is little difference between

Conservative targets and non-targets while, as before, the figures show that telephone canvassing was rare in Liberal Democrat campaigns. In their case, the figure for doorstep canvassing is higher in target seats than in non-targets. Party campaign manuals urge their agents to produce and distribute leaflets aimed at particular groups of voters – first-time voters, women, OAPs, ethnic minorities and so on. As the data show, most campaigns do something along these lines, but the use of targeted leaflets is more common in key seats than in the non-targets. The same is true of the use of direct mail techniques. Almost 80 per cent of Labour targets did a substantial amount of direct mailing, as did more than half of Conservative targets – significantly larger proportions than in non-targets in both cases. The use of direct mail was less common in Liberal Democrat campaigns but again the technique was used more substantially in target seats than in non-targets.

One aspect of local campaign activity that can be controlled fairly directly from the centre is the programme of visits by party leaders and other VIPs to constituencies. We have noted in the past that such visits are not always welcomed by local campaign organizers (especially if the visitor is not the party leader) since they disrupt previously arranged schedules, raise security problems and involve finding something for the visitor to do. Nonetheless, in all parties, the programme of VIP visits is prepared well in advance by national officials in consultation with their regional colleagues. We asked respondent how many visits they had from 'leading national figures in your party' and the returns show clearly that, to a considerable extent, it was key seats which were targeted for such visits – especially in the Labour party, where target seats received an average of 6.7 visits as compared with an average of only one for the non-target seats.

Polling Day Activity

All previous campaign efforts reach a climax on polling day when the parties have to make every effort to ensure that their supporters come out and vote. Conventionally this is done by volunteers going round knocking on the doors of electors previously identified as supporters and encouraging them to go to the polls. Increasingly, however, parties find it easier to 'knock up' supporters by telephone. As Table 5 shows, large majorities of campaigns in key seats did some telephone knocking up (although we have no more detailed information other than that they contacted at least some of their supporters by telephone). Certainly, except for the Conservatives, telephones appear to have been used for this purpose much more frequently in target than in non-target seats. The table also shows that Conservative and Liberal Democrat target seats were much more likely to make use of computerized knocking up lists although, surprisingly, there was no difference between Labour's target and non-target seats in this respect. Finally, the table shows the mean percentage of the electorate covered by the polling stations at which the parties had number-takers, a good overall indicator of the strength of the polling day operation, and the differences between target and non-target seats are as expected.

TABLE 5
POLLING DAY ACTIVITY

	Conservative		Labour		Lib Dem	
	Targets	Non-targets	Targets	Non-targets	Targets	Non-targets
% contacted promises by telephone	88	76	84	34	63	38
% used computerized knocking up lists	75	49	63	63	67	50
% electorate covered by polling station operation (mean)	55	42	82	62	73	49

Electoral Effects

The evidence we have presented thus far suggests that the parties were certainly successful in producing markedly stronger campaigns, using more sophisticated campaign techniques, in their target seats. But finally we must ask whether, as a consequence, the parties performed better in these seats. Here, since we are dealing with actual results, we are able to consider all constituencies, not just those for which we have survey responses. This means that the analysis is based on 85 Conservative, 91 Labour and 48 Liberal Democrat targets. Comparator non-target seats are defined as before – giving 223 for the Conservatives and 159 for Labour – except that in the case of the Liberal Democrats 100, rather than 50, seats were selected for comparison.[3]

Table 6 shows differences in the results of the election, in terms of turnout and changes in vote shares, between target and non-target seats. First, it is worth noting that turnout was clearly higher in target seats – by 3.2 per cent in the case of the Conservatives, 4.4 per cent for Labour and 1.5 per cent for the Liberal Democrats. Moreover, where comparison with 1992 turnout is possible,[4] the data suggest that Conservative and Labour targeting efforts appear to have moderated the sharp decline in turnout which took place over the country as a whole. There is clear evidence, then, that the additional activities of the parties in target constituencies was effective in mobilizing voters to go to the polls.

TABLE 6
DIFFERENCES IN ELECTION RESULTS

	Conservative		Labour		Lib Dem	
	Targets	Non-targets	Targets	Non-targets	Targets	Non-targets
Turnout % 1997	75.0	71.8	74.7	70.3	74.8	73.3
Turnout change 1992-7	-5.4	-6.9	-5.6	-7.3	-5.6	-5.8
Change % Con	-12.2	-11.8	-12.3	-11.4	-12.0	-10.3
Change % Lab	+10.3	+9.6	+12.3	+10.8	+4.6	+9.3
Change % Lib Dem	-0.7	-0.8	-2.0	-2.2	+4.0	-2.4

Notes: These figures are based on all constituencies. The Ns for targets are Con 85, Lab 91, Lib Dem 48; for others – Con 223, Lab 159, Lib Dem 100. The figures for turnout change are based only on constituencies where boundary changes meant that the degree of change in the electorate was smaller than 10 per cent. In this case there are 44 targets and 107 non-targets for the Conservatives, 44 and 76 for Labour and 23 and 39 for the Liberal Democrats.

It is changes in party shares of votes that are of most interest to campaigners, however. In this respect Labour's targeting effort appears to have paid some dividends. Even though this was an election in which there was a strong tide moving in Labour's favour in all seats, the party's share of the vote increased more, and that of the Conservatives declined more, in seats targeted by Operation Victory than in the non-target seats. The Liberal Democrats also clearly did better in their target seats, where they increased their share by 4.0 per cent on average, than in the non-target seats, where they declined by 2.4 per cent. In addition, the Liberal Democrats also restricted the increase in the Labour vote in target seats to roughly half of the increase in the comparator seats. The figures for the Conservatives tell a different story, however. Mirroring the results of our research on the 1992 election, the Conservatives appear to have done slightly worse in their target seats than in the comparable non-targets while both Labour and the Liberal Democrats did slightly better.

This first consideration of the possible electoral effects of targeted campaigning is very rough, however. Changes in the parties' shares of the votes and turnout patterns may have been affected by considerations other than campaigning – personal incumbency and region, for example – and these need to be taken into account. In what follows we focus on changes in party support and we attempt to assess the effects of targeting by comparing the results of a series of regression models. For each party we first predicted change in share of vote on the basis of a series of dummy variables for personal incumbency[5] and region. We then added a dummy variable for target versus non-target seats and recomputed the equations. By comparing the two sets of equations we can determine whether the parties' performances in their target seats were significantly different from their results in comparable seats after taking account of other influences.

A summary of the results of this analysis is given in Table 7. For each party we show the results of the two regression models. The first equation for the Conservatives shows that their vote share declined by slightly less in seats where there was a Conservative incumbent. On the other hand, their vote share declined by more than average in the east Midlands, Greater London and the

TABLE 7
THE EFFECTS OF TARGETING

Conservative

	Equation 1	Equation 2	't' statistic
Incumbent	0.90**	1.07**	3.15
East Midlands	-1.51*	-1.48*	-2.14
Greater London	-3.67***	-3.72***	-6.05
South-east	-1.80**	-1.79**	-2.93
Target	n/a	-0.65	-1.90
adj. r2	0.198	0.205	

F-ratio for difference between equations = 3.61 p > .05

Labour

	Equation 1	Equation 2	't' statistic
Incumbent	-0.94	-0.17	0.76
Greater London	3.71***	3.86***	4.48
North	2.31*	-	-
Scotland	-1.91*	-1.86*	-2.00
South-east	2.22*	2.01*	2.07
Wales	-3.07**	-3.11**	-3.03
Target	n/a	1.49**	2.67
adj. r2	0.215	0.235	

F-ratio for difference between equations = 7.12 p < .05

Liberal Democrat

	Equation 1	Equation 2	't' statistic
Incumbent	5.24**	3.36*	2.04
North	-	-8.33*	-2.23
Target	n/a	6.62***	5.80
adj. r2	0.035	0.222	

F-ratio for difference between equations = 33.61 p < .001

Note: the figures shown are unstandardized regression coefficients ('b's). All the relevant variables were entered into each equation but, for the regional variables, only those with significant coefficients are shown. * = significant at .05 level; ** = significant at .01; *** = significant at .001.

south-east. After taking account of these patterns, the second equation shows that their was no significant difference between target and other comparable seats in the change in Conservative vote share. The regression coefficient for the additional dummy variable suggests that, if anything, the Conservative performance in their targets was slightly worse than in other seats, but it is not statistically significant. The F-ratio indicates that there is no significant difference between the two equations in terms of variance explained.

Personal incumbency did not affect Labour's performance significantly in 1997, but there were clear regional differences. Labour did better in Greater London, the north of England and the south-east, and worse in Scotland and Wales than elsewhere. Taking this into account, the second equation shows that Labour did better in their targets than in other seats – gaining a 'bonus' of 1.5 per cent in the change in their share of the vote. This difference between the two equations is statistically significant.

The first equation for the Liberal Democrats suggests that incumbency made a significant difference to the size of the change in their share of the vote but region did not. When the variable distinguishing target from non-target seats is introduced, however, the analysis suggests that they also did significantly worse in the north of England. More important from our point of view, however, is the fact that in this case target seats produced significantly better results than non-targets. The change in the Liberal Democrats' share of the vote was 6.6 per cent better than in comparator constituencies – a very substantial 'bonus'. Thus our analysis suggests that the Liberal Democrats reaped a substantial electoral benefit from their efforts to target a small number of seats. Labour's hugely complex Operation Victory produced a significant but relatively modest return, while the Conservatives still appear to have difficulty in using their resources to achieve effective constituency campaigning.[6]

Conclusion

The test of the effect of targeting on electoral outcomes which we have presented in the previous section is, of necessity, rather crude. We have simply investigated whether changes in the parties' shares of the votes differed in target and comparable non-target seats in 1997. Our results suggest that targeting seems to have been very successful for the Liberal Democrats and also paid off, though to a rather lesser extent, for Labour. In this analysis, however, we have taken no account of the actual intensity or strength of campaigning which will have varied within the target and non-target groups. Moreover, the selection of non-target comparator seats is, as we have explained, a somewhat arbitrary matter. We have reported elsewhere, however, other work showing that, for all parties, variations in campaign intensity in 1997 were associated with variations in party performance – the stronger the campaign the better the performance (Denver and Hands, 1997b). In the earlier sections of this chapter we have provided ample evidence to support the view that targeting was transformed in 1997, both in terms of the scope and ambitiousness of the major parties' plans and in terms of what was actually achieved. As we have seen, largely because of their much more slender resources, the Liberal Democrats lag some way behind the other two major parties. But for both Labour and the Conservatives the targeting of seats, and the concentration of resources on them, has become a central part of the overall campaign and both parties have now gone a significant stage further to target not just seats but also specific groups of voters. Particularly in the case of Labour, the whole targeting operation is now closely tied in with the overall campaign strategy, to the extent that, as we have suggested, the initiative in planning and directing the constituency campaign in key seats has moved to the centre – the local campaign is ceasing to be really local as the party's organizers seek to exercise ever greater control over all aspects of campaigning.

ACKNOWLEDGEMENT

The research on which this article is based was supported by the ESRC (grant reference number R000222027).

NOTES

1. Labour's list of target seats was widely circulated and, consequently, well-known. We have compiled the lists of Conservative and Liberal Democrat targets on the basis of information supplied by relevant national party officials and questionnaire responses from agents.
2. Inevitably the definition of comparator seats is somewhat arbitrary, but when we experimented with different definitions the results were substantially the same. In the case of the Liberal Democrats we chose 50 comparator seats because the number of comparators for the other two parties was approximately double the number of target seats for which we had responses.
3. As before, the number of Liberal Democrat seats chosen as comparators is fairly arbitrary, but varying the number did not significantly affect the results.
4. It is not possible to make a satisfactory estimate of 1992 turnout in constituencies where boundaries were substantially altered between 1992 and 1997.
5. Boundary changes also make the definition of incumbency more problematical than usual. We have defined candidates as incumbents if they were MPs contesting a seat where there were no boundary changes, or where at least 75 per cent of the electorate remained from their 1992 constituency.
6. We repeated the multiple regression analyses using as dependent variables the parties' shares of votes in 1997 and introducing share in 1992 as an additional control. This produced substantially the same results as those reported in Table 7.

REFERENCES

Butler, David and Dennis Kavanagh (1984) *The British General Election of 1983*. London: Macmillan.

Butler, D.E. and Richard Rose (1960) *The British General Election of 1959*. London: Macmillan.

Butler, D.E. and Anthony King (1965) *The British General Election of 1964*. London: Macmillan.

Denver, David and Gordon Hands (1997a) *Modern Constituency Electioneering*. London: Frank Cass.

Denver, David and Gordon Hands (1997b) 'Constituency Campaigning in the 1997 General Election: Party Effort and Electoral Effect', paper presented at the EPOP annual conference, University of Essex, September 1997.

Hill, D. (1995) 'The Labour Party's Strategy' in Ivor Crewe and Brian Gosschalk (eds) *Political Communications: The General Election Campaign of 1992*, pp.36–40. Cambridge: Cambridge University Press.

Labour Party (1997) *New Labour, New Britain*. London: Labour Party.

Labour Party (no date, 1996?) *General Election Handbook*. London: Labour Party.

Pattie, C.J, R.J. Johnston and E.A. Fieldhouse (1995) 'Winning the Local Vote: The Effectiveness of Constituency Campaign Spending in Great Britain, 1983–1992', *American Political Science Review*, 89 (4): 969–83.

Seyd, P. and P. Whiteley (1992) *Labour's Grass Roots: The Politics of Party Membership*. Oxford: Clarendon Press.

Labour's Grassroots Campaign in 1997

Paul Whiteley and Patrick Seyd

Without you there would have been no victory
Leaflet sent to all Labour Party members, June 1997

That this House notes the report on the General Election to the Labour Party NEC which points out that although the average swing to Labour nationally was 9.9 per cent, in Labour's 91 target seats it was 11.8 per cent; and therefore justifies the vast concentration of resources from Millbank Tower on these seats, but is concerned that the report omits to mention that in the 54 non-target seats which were won by the Labour Party without any centralised assistance from Millbank Tower the swing to Labour was 14.3 per cent.
Early day motion in the name of Ken Livingstone and eleven other Labour MPs, Order Paper, 31 July 1997

As the quotation from Ken Livingstone's early day motion in the House of Commons illustrates, the controversy over the role of local, as opposed to national, campaigning in influencing the outcome of a general election has clearly spilled over from the academic into the political arena. Of course Ken Livingstone was criticizing what he regarded as the over-centralization of campaigning in Millbank, whereas the academic debate on the role of campaigning has centred very much on the issue of whether or not the extensive campaign activity undertaken by party workers at the local level is a waste of time, at least in relation to influencing the vote.

Butler and Kavanagh have consistently put the case against the effectiveness of local campaigns in general elections. Writing in the 1992 Nuffield election study volume, they ask: 'Does the local campaign matter?' and then go on to conclude that 'It is hard to locate any evidence of great benefits being reaped by the increasingly sophisticated and computerised local campaigning' (Butler and Kavanagh, 1992:245).

The 1997 Nuffield election study echoes Ken Livingstone's early day motion, pointing out that the failure of Labour to achieve significantly different results in their target seats is further support for the view that local campaigns are by and large ineffective. Writing in the appendix to the 1997 study, while conceding that the Liberal Democrats may be an exception, Curtice and Steed argue that:

The 1997 election does not appear to support claims made that local campaigning can make a difference in respect of other parties performances too. The Labour Party targeted 90, mostly marginal Conservative constituencies. ... Yet ... the performance in these constituencies was very similar to that in other Conservative/Labour contests (Butler and Kavanagh, 1997: 312).

Similarly, in his review of the 1997 Nuffield election study volume, Crewe suggests that 'Millbank's ruthless concentration on Labour's 100 target marginals made not the slightest difference other than to deprive safe Labour areas of activists and any campaign to speak of' (1997: 45).

However, the evidence against this view is now fairly strong and it comes from a variety of different sources. Research which uses campaign spending as a surrogate for campaign activity shows that local campaigns have highly significant effects on turnout and voting behaviour (Johnston, 1987; Johnston *et al.*, 1989, 1995; Pattie *et al.*, 1995). Our own research using surveys of Labour Party members, which investigated their campaign activities over a period of five years, supports the same conclusions (Seyd and Whiteley, 1992; Whiteley and Seyd, 1992, 1994). Similarly, the work of Denver and Hands (1985, 1997), the most recent of which involves surveys of constituency agents from all the main parties, again argues that their are significant local campaign effects. It is clear, then, that the evidence from a variety of different sources confirms that local campaigns can have a significant influence on voting behaviour and turnout in general elections. Denver and Hands (1997: 305) sum up these findings in the following terms:

> This study of constituency campaigning in the 1992 general election has shown very clearly, we would suggest, that the easy generalisation made in many academic studies – that, in modern conditions, local campaigning is merely a ritual, a small and insignificant side show to the main event – is seriously misleading.

This gives rise to an apparent puzzle with regard to the 1997 election. If local campaign effects are important, and Labour targeted some 90 or so marginals, why wasn't there a bigger swing in these seats in comparison with other types of seats? The purpose of this article is, firstly, to address this puzzle, by focusing on grassroots campaign activity within the Labour Party during the general election. The question is addressed with the help of data from a new national survey of Labour Party members, conducted immediately after the 1997 general election. The survey makes it possible to measure fairly precisely the total amount of campaign activity undertaken by grassroots party members in the election.

A second key aim of the article is to examine the campaigning activities of the new members who have joined the party since Tony Blair became leader in 1994. The upsurge in party membership, which resulted from the extensive recruitment campaign initiated in 1994, might be expected to have changed the character of the Labour Party, and brought in members of a type which have not been recruited before. On the other hand, it may be that the new members are very similar to the existing party members in terms of their social backgrounds and rates of activism. The survey makes it possible to investigate this issue.

The article is divided into four parts. We begin with an overview analysis of Labour's campaign strategy, paying particular attention to the role of the grassroots party members in the campaign. This is followed by a section examining the campaign activities of Labour Party members, based on the results of the national survey of party members.[1] The third section examines the similarities and differences between long-standing party members and members recruited since 1994, when Tony Blair was elected as leader. In the final section, we draw some conclusions about trends in activism in the contemporary Labour Party.

The Labour Campaign and the Grassroots Party

After years of neglect, and following the surprise election defeat of 1992, Labour strategists began to see the electoral advantages of a revitalized grassroots party. In our book, published in 1992, we argued that the party could have done significantly better than the 31 per cent share of the vote that it obtained in the 1987 general election, if it had recruited more members to campaign at the local level. We concluded that 'the party could have obtained nearly 36 per cent of the poll if it had been about a third larger in size, assuming that the new members were as active as the old ones' (Seyd and Whiteley, 1992: 198).

Speaking from the platform on behalf of the National Executive Committee, Clare Short gave a report to the 1992 Labour Party conference on the general election campaign, in which she said:

> There is an important new book that I hope many comrades have looked at, by Patrick Seyd and Paul Whiteley, which is a study of Labour's grassroots and it shows very clearly that where we have a strong and active local party, we do better electorally. So the NEC intends, despite the financial difficulties that we face, to put a major effort into work that has been neglected in recent years to revitalize and strengthen our grassroots (Labour Party, 1992: 74–5).

The national party headquarters at subsequently set up a project for revitalizing the grassroots called 'Active Labour',[2] intended to guide local parties in reviewing organizational problems, setting up recruitment drives and motivating new members to join the party. It aimed to change the passive attitude to the recruitment and retention of members which had characterized the Labour Party for some time. The overall aim of the recruitment campaign was to rapidly increase the individual membership of the party, which would help with fund-raising and also achieve electoral benefits.

The effects of the new policy of actively recruiting members began to be felt by the time that Tony Blair became leader in 1994 and, in the event, the strategy turned out to be very successful. Writing some four years after Clare Short's statement, Peter Mandelson and Roger Liddle claimed that 'The British Labour Party has become the fastest growing political party in Europe. At over 363,000, the party has its highest level of membership since 1979.' (Mandelson and Liddle, 1996: 219). By 1997 the membership had reached 405,238 (*Observer*, 18 January 1998), a 40 per cent increase over the 1994 membership.

As the general election approached, the party prepared the ground for the campaign more thoroughly than ever before. A target group of 90 marginal constituencies was drawn up and these were provided with full-time organizers paid for by the national party. The plans for the campaign included extensive canvassing and leafleting, including much more telephone canvassing than before, the overall aim being to identify Labour sympathizers in the electorate during the long campaign before the general election itself was called.[3] A twinning arrangement was set up which linked Labour-held constituencies with target constituencies, and party members in the former were requested to concentrate their campaigning activities on the target seats. The targeting strategy was extended down to the constituency level, so that once sympathizers were identified, they were subsequently targeted for computer mailings of leaflets, including an eve-of-poll letter asking them to turn out and vote. The aim was also to target Labour sympathizers on polling day more intensively than ever before. More generally, the intention was to link the targeting strategy with the membership recruitment campaign, so that the work of mobilizing new members and revitalizing the party organization was carried on alongside the task of identifying Labour sympathizers in the electorate.

By the time that the short campaign began, a great deal of the groundwork had been laid for electoral mobilization on polling day. The overall strategic goal was to sustain levels of support achieved by the start of 1995, to maintain the strength of Labour Party identification among supporters, and to ensure the continuation up to polling day of the favourable impression of the party leadership and its policy goals among the electorate.

In the next section we go on to examine the scope and range of campaign activities at the grassroots level identified from the new survey of Labour Party members.

Campaigning at the Grassroots in 1997

The new Labour survey contained a battery of questions relating specifically to the activities of party members during the 1997 general election. The responses of party members to these questions, concerning the activities that they undertook during the short campaign and on polling day, appear in Table 1. The first part of this table focuses on activities undertaken mainly on polling day, and the second on recurring activities which take place throughout the election campaign.

TABLE 1
THE ACTIVITIES OF LABOUR PARTY MEMBERS DURING THE 1997 CAMPAIGN

	Yes %	No %		
Did Members:				
Display an election poster?	78	22		
Donate money to party election funds?	65	35		
Help run a party election day committee room?	17	83		
Drive voters to the polling station?	17	83		
Take numbers at a polling station?	26	74		
Remind voters on polling day to vote?	45	55		
Attend the counting of votes?	12	88		

	Not at all %	Once %	Twice %	Three or more occasions %
Did Members:				
Telephone canvass voters?	90	2	2	6
Canvass voters door-to-door?	76	4	4	17
Help with a fund raising event?	80	8	5	8
Deliver party leaflets?	52	8	9	31
Attend a party rally?	78	13	4	6
Help organize a street stall?	91	3	2	4
Help with party mailings?	79	5	4	11
Help with telephone fund-raising?	98	1	0	1

Note: Here and in subsequent tables N=5,761

Table 1 indicates that large majorities of Labour Party members displayed election posters and also donated money to the party for the campaign. These were easily the most popular grassroots activities, followed by the activity of reminding voters to turn out on polling day. The latter commonly involved knocking on doors to make sure that electors turned out, but it also refers to the act of reminding family, friends and neighbours to vote. Of the other traditional polling day activities, just under 20 per cent of party members helped to run a committee room or drove voters to the polls, and just over a quarter helped to take numbers at a polling station. Assuming that the total party membership on polling day was approximately 400,000, it can be inferred that about 100,000 of them were involved in campaigning on polling day itself.

The second half of Table 1 shows that about a quarter of the party members took part in door-to-door canvassing on at least one occasion, and around 10 per cent were involved in telephone canvassing. Delivering leaflets was easily the most popular activity, with some 48 per cent of the total party membership helping out on at least one occasion, and 31 per cent helping with deliveries on three or more occasions. This means that upwards of 200,000 people were involved in delivering leaflets during the campaign, and approximately 125,000 of them did it on several occasions. There were also significant groups of party members who attended party rallies (23 per cent), helped with mailings (20 per cent), and helped with fund-raising events (21 per cent).

TABLE 2
MEMBERS' PERCEPTIONS OF THE EFFECTIVENESS OF CAMPAIGN ACTIVITIES

Activity	Very Effective %	Effective %	Not Very Effective %	Not at All Effective %
Displaying election posters	23	54	21	2
Donating Money	41	52	6	1
Delivering Leaflets	27	56	15	2
Attending a rally	8	35	46	11
Canvassing door-to-door	32	49	17	2
Telephone canvassing	14	38	37	11
Running a committee room	22	52	22	4
Driving voters to the polling station	37	50	11	2
Reminding voters to vote	37	49	12	2
Helping with party mailings	22	62	14	2

Part of the reason for this pattern of responses relates to members' perceptions of the effectiveness of these activities. Respondent attitudes to the effectiveness of the various types of campaign activity is examined in Table 2, which shows that members thought that donating money was the most effective activity, with 93 per cent rating it very effective or effective. In contrast only 43 per cent thought that this was true of attending a party rally.

Other activities which rate almost as effective as donating money were canvassing door-to-door (81 per cent) and delivering leaflets (83 per cent). Members rated election day activities particularly highly, including the activities of 'knocking up' or reminding voters to vote (86 per cent), driving voters to a polling station (87 per cent) and helping to run a committee room

(74 per cent). They were a little more sceptical about telephone canvassing, but even here some 52 per cent rated it as being highly effective or effective.

TABLE 3
MEMBERS' PERCEPTIONS OF THE NATIONAL LABOUR CAMPAIGN

	Very %	Fairly %	Neither %	Fairly %	Very %	
Effective	80	18	1	1	1	Ineffective
Efficiently run	74	23	2	1	0	Badly run
United	62	33	3	1	0	Divided
Caring	31	40	19	7	2	Uncaring
Principled	36	37	11	12	4	Unprincipled
Positive	46	30	17	6	1	Negative
Left-wing	1	10	43	32	14	Right-wing
Modern	54	33	9	3	2	Old fashioned

In addition to rating the effectiveness of different types of campaign activities, members were asked to comment on the national Labour campaign, rating it in various ways with respect to its effectiveness, efficiency, and so on. These ratings appear in Table 3, and it can be seen that with a couple of exceptions, members rated the national campaign very highly. It was thought to be very or fairly effective by 98 per cent, very or fairly united by 95 per cent, and very or fairly positive by 76 per cent. However, it is also interesting that some 46 per cent of members rated it as being very or fairly right-wing, and some 16 per cent thought it was very or fairly unprincipled. Clearly, while attitudes to the national campaign were generally very favourable, there were some exceptions to this pattern.

Up to this point we can see that party members did a lot of work at the constituency level and that, on the whole, they were impressed by the effectiveness of the national campaign. However, as mentioned earlier, from the perspective of the campaign headquarters in Millbank, targeting was a key feature of the entire Labour campaign. But a key question is whether or not this national targeting strategy actually worked on the ground. If the party activists were asked to move to target constituencies, but did not actually heed the call, then it is hardly surprising that no difference in swings were observed between the target seats and other types of seats. In the event, the evidence from the survey supports this interpretation, as can be seen in Table 4.

TABLE 4
CAMPAIGNING IN OTHER CONSTITUENCIES

During the Election Campaign some party members were involved in campaigning work for a constituency party other than their own. How about you?

Were you requested to work in another constituency?
Did you work for another constituency party?

Requested	%	Worked	%
Yes	28	Yes	9
No	72	No	91

The results in Table 4 indicates that Labour's targeting strategy met with very limited success. Some 28 per cent of party members reported that they had been asked to campaign in another constituency, but only about 9 per cent of the members actually did work in a different constituency. Moreover, only just over 3 per cent of the members worked 'most' or 'all' of the time in that constituency. Thus it appears that while many members were aware of the national strategy of targeting marginal constituencies, only a few of them actually heeded the call and campaigned outside their own areas, and the great majority of these only put in a token appearance.

Thus Millbank ran a very effective national campaign, a fact appreciated by the overwhelming majority of party members. At the same time, however, party headquarters failed to motivate the members to campaign in the marginal seats, and thus the targeting strategy was not very successful. This may explain the puzzle: Labour did rather well in all types of seats because party members worked hard in all types of seats.

The relationship between activism and various social background and political characteristics is examined in Table 5, which gives an insight into variations in activity rates for different groups of party members. In this table the key election-related activities in the second part of Table 1 are aggregated for different sub-groups of party members, and the mean activity rates are displayed for those groups.[4]

The mean activity rate for all party members was just over 3.0. Such a score can, of course, be obtained in a number of different ways but an illustrative example gives a picture of the amount of campaigning done by the average party member. The frequencies with which members undertook various activities suggests that a score of 3.0 would be most commonly achieved by a member who delivered leaflets, canvassed door-to-door, and helped with party mailings, each activity being undertaken on one occasion only. Overall, then, it can be seen that the 'average' party member was fairly active during the election campaign.

TABLE 5
ACTIVISM AND CHARACTERISTICS OF MEMBERS

	Mean Activism Score		Mean Activism Score
All Members	3.07	In full-time education	3.50
		In full-time work	3.03
Aged under 26	3.50	In part-time work	3.65
Aged 26 to 45	2.96	Unemployed	3.52
Aged 46 to 65	3.46	Retired	2.76
Aged 66 plus	2.31	Voluntary worker	4.62
		Graduate	3.25
Male	3.13	Non-graduate	2.96
Female	2.94		
		left-wing	3.50
Salariat	3.10	centrist	2.94
Routine Non-Manual	3.25	right-wing	1.98
Petty Bourgeoisie	3.30		
Foreman and Technician	3.28	very strongly Labour	4.19
Working Class	2.75	fairly strongly Labour	2.09
		not very strongly Labour	1.36
		not at all strongly Labour	0.81
		Joined since 1994	2.13
		Joined before 1994	3.74

An examination of the mean activism scores for different subgroups of party members shows some interesting patterns. Young party members were significantly more active than their older counterparts, particularly the retired members. There is an interesting difference between activity rates for those aged under 26 in this survey compared with our earlier survey of Labour Party members. In the 1989–90 survey the middle-aged party members were significantly more active than the young members (Seyd and Whiteley, 1992: 99). In this case, however, it was the young party members who were the most active. It is noteworthy that Labour students, i.e., party members in full-time education, were significantly more active than average.

The data in Table 5 also show that men were slightly more active than women; members of the 'salariat' (middle class professionals) were more active than the working class; voluntary workers and part-timers were more active than full-time workers or the unemployed; and graduates were more active than non-graduates. These patterns have persisted over time, since they are very similar to the results of our earlier 1989–90 survey of Labour Party members (Seyd and Whiteley, 1992: 99). It is also evident that left-wingers were significantly more active than centrists or right wingers; the difference between left-wingers and right-wingers being particularly marked.[5]

However, a very large difference exists between members who are very strongly attached to the party and those who are not strongly attached; very strongly attached members, who made up about 50 per cent of the sample, were very much more active than the fairly strongly attached, or the not very strongly attached members. The sharp divide between the very strongly and the fairly strongly attached is particularly marked. The latter made up 43 per cent of the sample, and did not differ greatly in their activism rates from those who were not very strongly attached, or those who were not at all attached to the party. This finding is of particular importance for the future of grassroots campaigning since it is apparent that the strength of attachment of all party members has been declining over time. In our 1989–90 survey some 55 per cent of the respondents were very strongly attached to the party, and 38 per cent were fairly strongly attached (Seyd and Whiteley, 1992: 224). Thus just over five per cent of the members have shifted from the first to the second of these categories, which on the face of it does not appear a large proportion. But the sharp difference between the two categories in relation to their rates of activism, means that such a decline had an important effect on the overall rates of campaigning by grassroots party members; current Labour members are less likely to campaign than their predecessors. Of course the overall impact of this has been counteracted by the marked growth in membership in recent years, but it will nonetheless be a problem for the party in the next election if this decline of affective attachments continues.

One of the most intriguing findings in Table 5 relates to the members who have joined since Tony Blair became leader in 1994 (hereinafter the 'Blair members'). As mentioned earlier, the party embarked on an unprecedented expansion of its membership in 1994, which increased the membership dramatically by the time of the general election. One important and interesting question is whether or not these 'Blair members' differ from other members in their activism rates and we now investigate this issue.

The 'Blair Members'

Unlike members who joined earlier, many of the 'Blair members' joined in response to the unprecedented mobilization campaign which was launched in 1994 in order to increase the party membership significantly. Most of the members who joined the party before this time were 'self-starters', or individuals who joined as a result of their own initiative. Our earlier research showed that 79 per cent of the party members were 'self-starters', with only 21 per cent joining because they had been approached and asked to join (Seyd and Whiteley, 1992: 224). Clearly, the mobilization campaign greatly increased the number of members of the latter type who joined in this way.

It seems a plausible hypothesis that members who have been mobilized to join the party are less committed and are, therefore, less likely to be active than the 'self-starters'. The strongest version of this argument is that many of these are really only 'credit-card members': they donate money to the party but do little else.

There is significant support for this suggestion in Table 5, since it is noteworthy that the mean activism score for the 'Blair members' is just over half that of the traditional members. Since this is a particularly important question, we probe it further by re-analysing the data in Table 1, but this time dividing the responses into two groups: 'Blair members' and the others.

TABLE 6
CAMPAIGN ACTIVITY OF 'BLAIR' AND OTHER PARTY MEMBERS

	Yes		No	
	Blair %	*Others* %	*Blair* %	*Others* %
Did Members:				
Display an election poster?	72	82	28	18
Donate money to party election funds?	61	68	39	32
Help run a party election day committee room?	8	23	92	77
Drive voters to the polling station?	10	21	90	79
Take numbers at a polling station?	17	33	83	67
Remind voters on polling day to vote?	40	48	60	52
Attend the counting of votes?	7	15	93	85

TABLE 7
FREQUENCY OF UNDERTAKING CAMPAIGN ACTIVITIES

	Not at all		Once		Twice		Three or more Occasions	
	Blair %	*Others* %	*Blair* %	*Others* %	*Blair* %	*Others* %	*Blair* %	*Others* %
Did Members:								
Telephone canvass voters	93	88	2	2	1	2	4	8
Canvass voters door-to-door	86	70	3	4	3	4	8	22
Help with a fund raising event	87	74	7	9	3	6	3	11
Deliver party leaflets	63	43	8	8	8	10	21	39
Attend a party rally	83	74	11	14	3	43	3	8
Help organize a street stall	95	88	2	4	1	2	2	6
Help with mailings	86	75	5	6	3	5	6	15
Help with telephone fund-raising	99	98	0	1	0	0	1	1

The results in Tables 6 and 7 are striking. It is clear that the 'Blair members' are less active, and in some cases quite a lot less active, than traditional members, with respect to every type of activity. This is particularly true for election-day activities such as taking numbers at the polling stations, running a committee room, driving voters to the polls, and even displaying an election poster.

Moloney notes that many people join interest groups campaigning on issues such as the environment because they support the goals of those groups, but at the same time they want to contract-out their commitment to others (see Moloney, 1998 forthcoming). Thus they pay their dues, which allows them to experience a type of 'imaginary' participation in campaigns, while avoiding the costs in time and effort of working for an organization. If this idea is applied to the Labour Party it would imply that many of the new members joined in response to the mobilization campaign, with the aim of undertaking 'imaginary' participation by donating money, but doing little else.

There is a slight problem with applying this idea to the 'Blair members' since it implies that donating money is a substitute for being involved in conventional campaign activities. If this is true, then we might expect the 'Blair members' to give more money than the traditional members, the latter being willing to undertake the work of sustaining the party over time. The evidence in Table 6 is not consistent with that view; the 'Blair members' are not only less likely than traditional members to work for the party, they are also less likely to donate money. Differences in respect of recurring activities are shown in Table 7 and it is clear that 'Blair members' were significantly less active than members in general as far as canvassing, delivering leaflets, fund-raising and attending party rallies were concerned. Thus the pattern found for polling day activities is repeated for recurring activities.

Focusing on the two right-hand columns in Table 7, which show the proportions of members very actively involved in all types of campaigning, differences between 'Blair members' and others are particularly marked. Thus the 'Blair members' were only half as likely to do a lot of telephone canvassing, about half as likely to deliver leaflets and less than half as likely to attend a party rally as members in general; they were just over a third as likely to do a lot of door-to-door canvassing or to help with the mailing of literature; and they were only a quarter as likely to help frequently with fund-raising. In general, there are big differences between 'Blair members' and the rest with respect to high intensity campaigning.

With respect to the left-hand column in Table 7, which shows figures for the members who do nothing, again 'Blair members' are more likely to be in this category than their traditional counterparts, on every type of activity. The biggest differences relate to canvassing door-to-door, delivering leaflets and attending party rallies.

There are two possible explanations for these differences; one might be described as the *socialization* hypothesis, which suggests that the 'Blair members' are less active because they have only recently joined the party, and thus have not yet been fully socialized into the norms and values of the party, or fully integrated into the local party organization. As a result, they are likely to be less active than long-standing party members although the presumption is that eventually they will become as active as party members in general. It is not clear how long this socialization process will take, but it might be as much as the three years which separated the fieldwork date of the survey from Tony Blair's election to the leadership.

The second hypothesis, is referred to as the *recruitment* hypothesis, and suggests that 'Blair members' are fundamentally a new type of member who has been persuaded to join the party by the mobilization campaign referred to earlier, but in the absence of such an intensive campaign would not normally have joined. In other words, they may want to be 'imaginary' participants to a much greater extent than the traditional members.

In this interpretation the 'Blair members' are always going to be much less active than their traditional counterparts who joined in earlier times and so the gap between the two groups is likely to continue into the future. This implies that if the party continues to recruit more new members of this type and they become a larger proportion of the total membership, activism within the party organization is likely to decline.

To test these competing hypotheses definitively, we would need panel data which track the rates of activism of the two types of member over time. If we were able to return to the 'Blair members' in, say, three years time then at that point they should be as active as members in general, if the socialization hypothesis is correct. On the other hand, if they still continued to be relatively inactive then that would support the recruitment hypothesis. For obvious reasons, however, such data are not currently available.

A preliminary test of the hypothesis can be obtained, however, by comparing the 'Blair members' with party members who joined in the three years prior to the 1989–90 survey of Labour Party members. If the socialization hypothesis is correct, members who joined the party during the period 1986 to 1989 would also have been affected by this socialization effect, looked at from the perspective of 1990. If so, they would have been as active in relation to Labour Party members who joined before 1986, as the 'Blair members' are in relation to members who joined prior to 1994.

In the analysis of the 1990 Labour Party membership survey an activism scale was constructed from a battery of questions about members' activities over the previous five years (Seyd and Whiteley, 1992: 234). This activism scale included election-related activities such as delivering leaflets and canvassing, as well as donating money to the party and attending meetings. The analysis of this scale showed that the mean score for all party members at the time of the original survey was 21.[6] In our book, *Labour's Grass Roots*, we illustrated this in the following terms:

> He or she is very likely to have displayed a poster at election times and signed a petition sponsored by the party; quite likely to have given money occasionally to Labour Party funds, attended a party meeting or canvassed; and unlikely to have stood for office in the party or in a local election (Seyd and Whiteley, 1992: 97).

A re-analysis of the data from that survey shows that the mean activism score for members who had joined within the period 1986 to 1989 was 18, or about 85 per cent of the mean score of members who had joined before then. If we assume that this is all due to a 'socialization' effect, then it implies that the effect reduces party activity by approximately 15 per cent.

However, as Table 5 indicates, if the same analysis is repeated for the New Labour survey, the picture is very different. The mean activism score for the 'Blair members' is 2.13, or about 57 per cent of the mean activism score of 3.74, for the members who joined earlier. Putting this another way, the 'Blair members' are about 43 per cent less active than members who joined the party earlier. If we subtract the assumed socialization effect of 15 per cent from this figure, we can see that the 'Blair members' are some 28 per cent less active than members in general, even taking into account the socialization effect.

Even if the socialization effect has become more important recently, there is still a big gap between the activism rates of the 'Blair members' and the activism rates of their more long-standing counterparts. These results strongly suggest that Labour has been recruiting a new type of member since the mobilization campaign began and individual membership increased significantly from 1994. The 'Blair members' are less active than those of longer standing in all categories of activism, and this is particularly marked at the high intensity point on the activism scales.

Needless to say, this did not inhibit Labour's grassroots campaign in 1997, because the new members were an addition to the ranks of the existing party members. The party gained about 120,000 new members between the 1992 and 1997 general election campaigns, and so any decline in average levels of activism was offset by the fact that many more people became involved. However, if this trend towards a 'dilution' of activism continues and the new members continue to be significantly less active than the older members they are replacing, this will ultimately weaken activism in the grassroots party and the effectiveness of local campaigns in future elections. Given that Labour is in government and likely to neglect the task of building and sustaining membership over the next few years, and is also likely to experience a loss of members when it pursues policies which are unpopular in the grassroots party, this problem could be more serious by the time of the next election.

Conclusions

Earlier research, using a panel survey of Labour Party members over the period 1990 to 1992, suggested that the party grassroots was becoming significantly 'de-energized' over time (Whiteley and Seyd, 1998). This research showed that there was a decline in activism in both the Labour and Conservative parties, but that the decline was greater for Labour. The process was attributed to a number of political, cultural and sociological changes which have occurred in British society but chiefly it was the product of changing incentives for activism. Some of these incentives are private and relate to the desire to achieve elected office, or build a political career, or to mix with like-minded individuals. But they also relate to collective incentives concerned with policy goals, and expressive attachments to the Labour Party.

The earlier research showed that the decline in these incentives for participation could produce a 'spiral of demobilization' for the Labour Party in which electoral losses produced declining membership, which in turn produced more election losses. The present evidence indicates that while Labour's decision to reverse the decline and to recruit new members allowed the party to outcampaign the Conservatives at the constituency level in 1997 by a large margin,[7] this development may have exacerbated the decline in activism within the grassroots party in the longer run. This is because the 'Blair members' appear to be qualitatively different from their predecessors; they are less willing to do anything for the party, including donating money. If this situation persists then inevitably, as the 'Blair members' gradually become a majority in the party, the grassroots will be progressively de-energized over time.

The Labour Party is not of course a prisoner of these developments and the modernization process within the party organization continues even after the election victory of 1997. However, this modernization process must pay close attention to the task of stimulating incentives to participate which might include promoting policies supported by the grassroots party members, encouraging participation in local and regional government by promoting devolution, revitalizing local government and implementing organizational reforms which give members a real say in decision-making at all levels of the party. Without this, Labour faces the danger of becoming a party of 'inactive' activists, like the Conservatives (see Whiteley, Seyd and Richardson, 1994) – a development which contributed greatly to the electoral disaster which overtook the former governing party in May 1997.

NOTES

1. This was a two-stage stratified random sample of Labour Party members undertaken immediately after the 1997 general election. The first stage consists of a random sample of 200 constituencies in Great Britain, and the second stage aims to obtain average constituency samples of approximately 30 party members, giving an overall target sample size of 6,000. We contacted 9,197 party members and received 5,761 responses, which represents a response rate of 62.6 per cent.

2. The source of the information in this section is interviews with party officials at Labour Party headquarters at Walworth Road.

3. The term canvassing has disappeared from all the New Labour campaign material. It is now referred to as voter identification.

4. These scores are aggregated from the second group of eight activities in Table 1. The total activity score for a party member is the sum of the scores for each of these eight activities, with 'not at all' coded 0, 'once' coded 1, 'twice' coded 2, and 'three or more' coded 3. Thus an individual who canvassed voters once, delivered leaflets twice and attended a meeting once would score 4.

5. Ideology is measured along a nine-point left-right scale, with members being asked to assign themselves to a point along this scale (see Seyd and Whiteley, 1992: 241).

6. There were eight activities in the battery of questions, and the activism score was constructed by adding together the responses for each individual (not at all =1; rarely=2; occasionally=3; frequently=4). See Seyd and Whiteley, 1992: 95–7.

7. Our best estimate is that the Conservatives had about 350,000 members at the time of the general election. But only about a quarter of these are minimally active in contrast with about half of Labour Party members. Thus the Conservatives were outcampaigned by a significant margin in 1997. For a discussion of trends in Conservative party membership see Whiteley, Seyd and Richardson (1994: 222).

REFERENCES

Butler, David, and Dennis Kavanagh. (1992) *The British General Election of 1992.* London: Macmillan.

Butler, David, and Dennis Kavanagh. (1997) *The British General Election of 1997.* London: Macmillan.

Crewe, Ivor (1997) 'Mandy Won It, Not', *New Statesman*, 12 December: 44–5.

Denver, David and Gordon Hands (1985) 'Marginality and Turnout in General Elections in the 1970s', *British Journal of Political Science* 15: 381–98.

Denver, David and Gordon Hands (1997) *Modern Constituency Electioneering.* London and Portland OR: Frank Cass.

Johnston, Ronald J. (1987) *Money and Votes: Constituency Campaign Spending and Election Results.* London: Croom Helm.

Johnston, Ronald J., and Charles J. Pattie (1995) 'The Impact of Spending on Party Constituency Campaigns at Recent British General Elections', *Party Politics*, 1: 261–73.

Johnston, Ronald J., Charles J. Pattie and Lucy C. Johnston (1989) 'The impact of constituency spending on the result of the 1987 British General Election', *Electoral Studies*, 8: 143–55.

Labour Party (1992) *Conference Report 1992.* London: Labour Party.

Mandelson, Peter, and Roger Liddle (1996) *The Blair Revolution.* London: Faber and Faber.

Moloney, William A. (1998) 'Contracting Out the Participation Function: Social Capital and Checkbook Participation', in Jan Van Deth, Marco Maraffi, Ken Newton and Paul Whiteley (eds) *Social Capital and European Democracy.* London: Routledge (forthcoming).

Pattie, Charles J., Ronald J. Johnston and Edward Fieldhouse (1995) 'Winning the Local Vote: The Effectiveness of Constituency Campaign Spending in Great Britain, 1983–1992', *American Political Science Review* 89: 969–83.

Seyd, Patrick and Paul F. Whiteley (1992) *Labour's Grass Roots: The Politics of Party Membership.* Oxford: The Clarendon Press.

Whiteley, Paul F. and Patrick Seyd (1992) 'Labour's Vote and Local Activism', *Parliamentary Affairs* 45: 582–95.

Whiteley, Paul F. and Patrick Seyd (1994) 'Local Party Campaigning and Voting Behavior in Britain', *Journal of Politics* 56: 242–51.

Whiteley, Paul F. and Patrick Seyd (1998) 'The Dynamics of Party Activism in Britain: A Spiral of Demoblization?' *British Journal of Political Science* (forthcoming).

Whiteley, Paul F., Patrick Seyd and J. Richardson (1994) *True Blues: The Politics of Conservative Party Membership.* Oxford: The Clarendon Press.

Remodelling the 1997 General Election: How Britain Would Have Voted under Alternative Electoral Systems

Patrick Dunleavy, Helen Margetts, Brendan O'Duffy and Stuart Weir

There used to be a conventional wisdom among political scientists that electoral systems do not change in established liberal democracies:

> A major purpose of elections is to supply a stable institutional framework for expression of various viewpoints. Even if imperfect, a long-established electoral system may satisfy this purpose far better than could a new and unfamiliar system, even if it were inherently more advantageous. ... [M]ost of the long-established electoral systems do the job. Keeping the ills we know of may be better than leaping into the unknown (Taagepera and Shugart, 1989: 218, 236).

In Britain this attitude has shaped a conviction that change would not come, with lasting implications for the profession's intellectual and logistical preparedness for the new age in which we find ourselves. To take one small indicator, pointed out a considerable time ago, despite extensive ESRC funding of election studies and now two annual panel studies we have no regular or reliable data on over-time variations in the distribution of voters' second and subsequent preferences – a serious limitation if any new system of voting adopted for Britain involves expressing more than a single choice (Dunleavy, 1990: 462).

The current debate about electoral systems for Westminster elections revolves around four systems: the alternative vote (AV) and its variant the supplementary vote (SV); the additional member system (AMS); and the single transferable vote (STV). A fifth system, list PR, has been adopted for electing MEPs from 1999 onwards. In addition, some recent speculation about the Jenkins Commission on electoral reform has focused on possible combinations of a couple of methods known as 'AV plus' and 'SV plus' for electing the Commons. These options are both AMS systems where either AV or SV are used to elect a large majority of seats at the local level, but a minority of top-up seats are elected at regional level to secure a greater measure of proportionality. Three or more of these systems are likely to be in operation at some level in British politics by the time of next general election in 2002, and a referendum on keeping first-past-the-post or switching to an alternative system may by the same date have given a decision in principle to change the Westminster voting system. An outline of the previous history and current prospects of the rival systems is as follows. The properties of these systems are generally well known and a summary of their key features is given in the Appendix.

ALTERNATIVE ELECTORAL SYSTEMS

System and where it has been used

Application in Britain

Alternative Vote (AV)
• used in Australian lower House elections

• adopted in 1917 and 1931 by Labour and the Liberals for House of Commons elections: but proposals defeated in Lords and so not implemented
• currently backed by Labour people seeking only minimal change for Westminster elections (e.g. Peter Mandelson, Peter Hain)

Supplementary Vote (SV)
• simplified form of AV and French 'double ballot' system, only invented in 1991; not yet applied for legislative elections (but see Reilly, 1997)

• recommended by 1992 Plant Commission of the Labour party for Westminster elections
• strong possibility for London mayor elections (where AMS and STV are ruled out because there is only one possible winner)

Additional Member System (AMS)
• 'pure' form used in Germany and New Zealand
• similar 'mixed' systems adopted in Japan, Italy and Venezuela in 1990s

• a form of AMS will be used in Britain for the first time to elect the Scottish Parliament and Welsh Assembly
• main system backed by Labour electoral reformers (e.g. Robin Cook)
• acceptable to Liberal Democrats

Single Transferable Vote (STV)
• used in Eire and Malta;
• a form of STV is also used in Australian Senate elections

• most preferred system of Liberal Democrats
• ruled out by Labour's Plant Commission in 1992
• used in some Northern Ireland elections since the 1970s

List Proportional Representation (List PR)
• used in the majority of west European countries

• will be used in Britain for the first time in the 1999 elections to the European Parliament
• not proposed by any UK party for Westminster elections

The key role of social scientists, according to Lindblom and Cohen (1979) should be to inform 'ordinary knowledge' thinking especially about the key interactive systems by which liberal democracies are guided, in particular markets, elections and group processes. Much of the debate about electoral systems (even among political scientists) relies on extrapolation from foreign countries' experiences, plus theoretical exegesis and often strong normative position-taking. To do more we need to give the best feasible estimates of how alternative electoral systems would actually operate under specifically British conditions – the party system, the structure of social cleavages and the geographical distribution of social groups. A simulation approach offers the best hopes of achieving this difficult goal.

Our simulation approach developed over the two 1990s elections seeks to get as close as possible to how a new system might work via several innovations (see Dunleavy, Margetts and Weir, 1992a and 1992b; and Dunleavy *et al.*, 1997). These include:

- asking survey respondents to complete alternative ballots for the rival systems, immediately after they have voted in a general election (that is, within two to three days rather than the multiple weeks common with BES surveys). We believe that the provision of immediate stimulus material is a key element in persuading respondents to think through how they might vote under a different system;

- completing short interviews with a large enough sample to be able to capture the distribution of regional opinion accurately. In 1997 ICM Research interviewed a sample of nearly 8,447 people across 18 regions of Britain for the project, achieving a response rate of 82 per cent;

- combining regional responses for each type of voter and information from the general election on first preferences to extrapolate how second and subsequent preferences would be structured under the alternative voting systems at the level of local constituencies;

- creating appropriate constituency schemas for each alternative system, and re-running constituency contests using the counting processes relevant to each system. For our 1997 study we re-ran more than 1,430 separate constituency contests.

We believe that this approach uses the best current knowledge in political science to discover how the main contending systems would have operated under specifically British conditions in the two 1990s elections.

We should immediately note, however, that our study has some inescapable limitations. We briefly explained to respondents how to vote under each of our systems, but made no effort to explain how votes would be counted or with what characteristic outcomes. Hence this research (and any other research) cannot fully accommodate the dynamic changes likely if a new system were to be adopted. Equally our simulations involve making some assumptions – especially that voters for party A in constituency x will behave the same way as party A supporters among respondents whom we interviewed in the wider region z (including constituency x). Our regions are basically the same as government standard regions, but with the English metropolitan areas separated out from the more rural parts of the West Midlands, Yorkshire, and the north-west. In addition, however, we split up London (into a middle and a suburban zone), Scotland into three regions (Highlands, central, and southern Scotland), and Wales into two (mid and north Wales, and south Wales). Full details of our findings and methods are given elsewhere (Dunleavy et al., 1997) so we concentrate here on the top-line conclusions for each system in 1997.

Supplementary Vote and Alternative Vote

The basic rationale of both SV and AV is to broaden the basis of local support required to elect an MP. In 1997 under the plurality rule almost half of MPs (47 per cent) did not have majority support in their constituency (compared with 40 per cent in 1992) and this proportion varied sharply across the regions of Britain. In seven of our 18 regions (all safe Labour areas) over three-quarters of seats went to a majority winner, while in two more regions at least half of MPs could count on a majority. But in eight other areas fewer than half of MPs had this additional legitimacy. In the largest region by far, south-east England with 118 seats, only one in five MPs was backed by a majority of local voters in 1997, and in the second largest of our regions, south-west England with 50 seats, less than one MP in seven.

AV and SV count second or subsequent preferences in all cases where the leading candidate has only plurality support. In 1992 we ran a full AV test and found that both Conservative and Labour supporters give most of their second preference votes to the Liberal Democrats. But Liberal Democrat voters in 1992 split more in favour of the Tories than in favour of Labour, in virtually all regions except Greater London and the north. As a result, the constituency election outcomes changed in only 28 cases compared with the plurality rule. With offsetting switches of constituencies between the parties, the Conservatives would have ended up making net losses of 11 seats, and Labour a net loss of one seat. The Liberal Democrats would have gained 10 seats, and Plaid Cymru and the Scottish National Party one extra seat each (Dunleavy et al., 1992a: 5). None the less, these changes would have been sufficient to deprive John Major of his small majority, leaving the Tories one seat short of an overall majority but as the most likely party of government. Our analysis did not explicitly include an SV ballot in 1992, but we estimated that the difference between the systems would have been very small – in only one constituency would SV have produced a different winner compared with AV (Dunleavy et al., 1992a: 6).

In 1997 because the two systems are so similar in their operation we implemented an SV ballot paper in our main survey which went to nearly 8,500 respondents – and we confined our analysis of AV to our smaller nationally representative sample of 1,900 respondents. As with AV, the key influence on how a supplementary vote system works in practice is the interrelationship between voters' first and second preferences. Table 1 shows that on the SV ballot paper in 1997 Labour respondents gave strong support at the second-preference stage to the Liberal Democrats (up slightly from the 1992 AV ballot), while a tenth of Conservative voters gave their second preferences to the Referendum Party, weakening their transfers to the Liberal Democrats compared with 1992. But the really salient feature is the pattern of Liberal Democrat voters' second preferences, because they were the critical 'swing' component in many Conservative/Labour marginals in the 1997 election. The table shows that nearly half of all Liberal Democrats gave a second preference to Labour in 1997 (up from a third in 1992), while the proportion giving a second preference to the Tories declined by half from 38 per cent in 1992 to below a fifth in 1997.

TABLE 1
HOW RESPONDENTS SPLIT THEIR SECOND PREFERENCES ON THE SV BALLOT
BY FIRST PREFERENCE PARTIES IN 1997

| | First party supported | | | | |
| | Cons | Lab | Lib Dem | SNP/ PC | Ref |
Second party	%	%	%	%	%
Conservative	-	5	18	8	38
Labour	12	-	49	49	22
Lib Dem	51	57	-	28	21
SNP/PC	2	10	5	-	10
Referendum	11	7	2	3	-
Greens	3	5	10	0	5
No 2nd pref	22	20	12	12	4
N	2011	2943	1134	245	155

Notes: 'No second preference' includes respondents who marked a cross against the same party in both their first-preference and second-preference columns: it was explained to them that this choice would not count. The percentages in each party using this option were: Con 14; Lab 14; Lib Dem 9; SNP/PC 9; Referendum 0.

Undoubtedly the revolution in Liberal Democrat voters' attitudes towards embracing Labour reflected a strong 'time for a change' feeling, and an anxiety to get rid of the Tory government. But the growth of explicit Labour-Liberal Democrat co-operation before the general election must also have contributed to this extremely significant change, notably on constitutional reform where the Cook–Maclennan pact set out a joint programme of action in late March 1997. Labour had a lead of more than 25 per cent in Liberal Democrats' second preferences in 1997 in every region except the north, the north-west outside the conurbation area, and southern Scotland. In key areas where the Conservatives held on to most of their seats in 1997 this change was dramatic – for example, in the south-west region Liberal Democrats' second preferences for the Conservatives fell from 42 per cent in 1992 to just 8 per cent in 1997, and in the south-east from 41 to 15 per cent. These changes have immense consequences for the way that constituency results would shift under an SV system.

To simulate an SV outcome we looked at all 301 constituencies where the winning MP in 1997 had only plurality support, identifying the top two candidates who would go to the second stage of the count, and also those candidates who would be eliminated. We assumed that voters in a constituency for an eliminated candidate of party A would cast their second preference votes in line with the second preferences of party A supporters among our respondents in the region. The outcomes were dramatic. Across the country as a whole the Conservatives would have lost 55 seats, cutting their representation in Parliament to just 110 MPs, less than 19 per cent of seats in Britain compared with their vote share of 31.4 per cent (see Table 5, p.227). Such an outcome would be the most severe under-representation of the Tories in British history. The biggest reduction in Conservative seats would occur in the south-west, which was the most finely balanced three-party region in the real general election. SV would facilitate Lib-Lab co-operation there so effectively that Tory seats would be cut from 22 to just 5, while Liberal Democrat seats would more than double to 29 from 14 under the plurality rule. The other key area of multiple losses for the Conservatives was the south-east, where SV would transfer 13 seats, four to Labour and nine to the Liberal Democrats. Other changes would be on a smaller scale: for example, in the non-urban parts of the west Midlands, where three of the Conservative losses of five seats would go to the Liberal Democrats and two to Labour.

Under SV the Liberal Democrats would have won another 38 seats on top of their existing 46, a result very much in line with the AV results in 1992 when we take into account the large drop in Tory support five years later. With 13 per cent of Commons seats, the Liberal Democrats' historic under-representation would have been significantly cut back, and the party would have become firmly embedded as the majority party in the south-west region and a serious contender in the south-east. In other regions the party's gains would have less dramatic effects.

Under SV Labour would also have gained 17 more seats, buoyed up by extra transfers from supporters of eliminated Liberal Democrats, further boosting their already disproportionate majority, giving them over 68 per cent of British seats in Parliament on the basis of 44 per cent of the vote. The deviation from proportionality (DV) under SV would therefore *rise* appreciably from the level of 21 per cent under the plurality rule to 23.5 per cent (see Table 5). At a regional level the Labour Party's gains would be relatively small, adding one or two seats to its total in most areas, but with four extra seats in the south-east.

Turning to the alternative vote in 1997, it would operate in a very similar way to SV. We found that there were a few changes in how respondents completed our AV ballot in 1997, compared with five years earlier. As with the SV ballot the big shift was in Liberal Democrats' second preferences. Beyond that, the proportion of Tory voters with no second preference fell sharply from 28 per cent in 1992 to 19 per cent in 1997 (perhaps partly because of the Referendum Party), while among Labour voters the drop was from 23 to 16 per cent. Among supporters of the other parties there was less change. A distinctive feature of the AV system compared with SV is that respondents can, of course, indicate more than two preferences. However, in 1997 (as in 1992) the proportion of people who numbered more than two choices fell off very rapidly:

Choice indicated:	First	Second	Third	Fourth	Fifth
% of respondents	97	83	67	31	24

As in 1992 a majority of people indicated three preferences, but the proportion going further dropped off very sharply, while the pattern of responses at these later stages appeared rather random. Looking just at the first three preferences on the AV ballot paper (those most likely to express 'real' choices) shows a very similar pattern of support in 1997 to that of 1992, once allowance is made for the shift in first preferences away from the Conservatives and towards Labour. The Liberal Democrats were the primary beneficiaries at the second-preference stage, since they attract both Conservative and Labour respondents' second rankings.

We assessed AV's impacts by examining whether the tiny differences in second preferences from the SV ballot would have changed any of the SV simulation outcomes in any constituency but we could not identify any such cases. We also looked closely at the constituencies which would have changed hands under SV, and at those which came close to changing, to see if there were any cases where the step-by-step elimination of candidates from the bottom, used in AV, might have changed the candidates in the final run-off stage away from the top two candidates in first preference votes. We found several constituencies where results were close, but could not identify any cases where AV's elimination method would have made a difference to which candidates reached the last two in any constituency as compared with SV. Essentially, therefore, AV would have produced the same results as SV in 1997, so far as we could determine. This conclusion raises an interesting question about whether the multiple rankings of candidates under AV are really a worthwhile feature, compared with the simpler, and perhaps easier to explain, ballot paper and counting methods used in SV. Advocates of AV might argue, however, that no votes are 'wasted' under this approach, whereas in SV a voter who backs two 'no hope' candidates has no influence upon the election.

The fact that our SV (and AV) result is markedly *less* proportional than plurality rule has considerable significance. While the alternative vote in 1992 would have had a small net effect tending to produce a more proportional Parliament, five years later SV (and AV also) would have changed the outcome in 57 constituencies, considerably strengthening both Tory under-representation and Labour's majority. The convergence of Labour and Liberal Democrat supporters' second preferences explains why SV would have given extra muscle to the popular mood in 1997 to get the Major government out. In addition to the tactical voting already present in the general election results, SV would have enabled the Lab-Lib vote to operate as a fairly integrated bloc, commanding 62 per cent of first preferences across Britain, to the Tories' 31 per cent. These findings have already had a direct bearing upon the development of the debate about the electoral reform referendum. They have greatly weakened the case of those who argue that the supplementary vote (or the alternative vote) can meet the requirement of being a 'proportional system' eligible to be included in the voting systems referendum as the single alternative to the *status quo*.

The Additional Member System

If the British electorate were ever to endorse a shift from first-past-the-post to a proportional electoral method in a referendum sometime between now and 2002, then there must be very strong odds that the system in question will be some version of AMS. The system has already been adopted in both Scotland and Wales, and a specialized version is also planned to be used in the London Assembly elections (Dunleavy and Margetts, 1997). AMS is acceptable to Labour electoral reformers, and there has been a wider trend in many liberal democratic countries (notably New Zealand, Japan and Italy) towards 'mixed' electoral systems (Blais and Massicotte, 1996; Dunleavy and Margetts, 1995).

We modelled a 'pure' AMS system with a 50:50 split between local and top-up MPs by simply pairing together the existing constituencies, using their amalgamated voting data from the 1997 general election to provide a wholly reliable indicator of the partisan distribution of first preferences in the new local seats. (This is also the only version of AMS which could be implemented in time for the next general election in 2001 or 2002, since its local seats could be constructed by amalgamating current seats, without otherwise redrawing boundaries). Top-up seats were allocated within our 18 regions. In addition, we are able to extrapolate results for different mixes of local and top-up seats from the high quality information generated for a 50:50 schema, and for the 100 per cent local seats scheme under first-past-the-post.

We gave our respondents a two-ballot AMS form, where they marked an X for a constituency candidate and party first, and then marked an X for a party list to shape the allocation of top-up seats at regional level. Between 82 and 89 per cent of people chose the same party at constituency level as their general election vote – the main differences were that one in every 16 Tory and Labour supporters now backed a Liberal Democrat, while one in 8 Liberal Democrat voters switched to Labour. As in 1992, but even more strongly, when it came to the regional-level votes for parties Labour and, to a slightly lesser extent, the Conservatives were better at hanging on to their general election voters than were the Liberal Democrats, the Referendum Party or the SNP/PC. The main parties retained over four-fifths of their supporters, losing one in 12 to the Liberal Democrats. But on this ballot the Liberal Democrats and smaller parties lost between one in eight and nearly one in five of respondents who backed them in the general election to Tony Blair's ascendant Labour party, and a handful of votes to the Tories also. However, since Labour's support base is more than twice as large as the Liberal Democrats', the net effect of these various transfers is not very considerable. Labour support in our sample as a whole was actually higher at constituency level than in the party vote. As in 1992 it remains slightly perverse for the Liberal Democrats that their vote is higher in the constituency contests where their chances of success are less, but falls back somewhat at the regional level where most of their seats are likely to be allocated. British voters still associate the party with local-level activism and grassroots politics, but are vaguer about what it stands for in national politics.

In 1992 the double-sized AMS constituencies tended to accentuate patterns of regional dominance by the Conservatives in the south-east, East Anglia and the south-west, and by Labour in central Scotland – all these areas became virtually one-party zones at the local seats level. In 1997 Labour already held virtually every seat in five regions under the plurality rule – central Scotland, south Wales, the north, south Yorkshire, and middle London. Surprisingly only the first two of these would become exclusively Labour zones at the level of local seats under AMS. The Tories would manage to hang on to one of the enlarged local seats in the north and in middle London, and the Liberal Democrats one in urban Yorkshire. However, Table 2 shows that, overall, whereas in 1992 the AMS local constituencies were split fairly evenly between the Conservatives and Labour, in 1997 Labour's existing hegemony under the plurality rule would have been strongly reflected in the outcomes in AMS's local constituencies. As in the real general election the party would have won 65 per cent of the local seats on the basis of 44 per cent of the national vote.

TABLE 2
PARTIES' SEAT TOTALS UNDER THE ADDITIONAL MEMBER SYSTEM IN BRITAIN, 1997
GENERAL ELECTION

	Con	Lab	Lib Dem	SNP/ PC	Other
Local seats	91	204	14	4	0
Top-up seats	112	99	101	16	0
Total seats	203	303	115	20	0
Per cent of MPs	32	47	17	3	0
Per cent national vote	31	44	17	3	4

In the pure AMS system, however, winning local MPs is only half the story. The top-up MPs come into play, the aim being to redress any imbalances in local seat allocations and restore overall proportionality. In our 1992 study we showed that the main beneficiaries were the Liberal Democrats, who would have gained virtually all of their MPs at the regional top-up stage. But both Labour and the Conservatives would have won significant numbers of top-up MPs in 1992, in regions outside their heartland areas, where otherwise they can go largely unrepresented under the plurality rule. In 1997 this pattern altered, as Table 2 demonstrates. The Liberal Democrats again derived most of their AMS seats at the top-up stage, although they won considerably more local seats in their newly created bastions in the south-west, and even one or two double-size constituencies in the south-east. The Conservatives were also important beneficiaries at the top-up stage in 1997, however, winning nearly 40 extra seats compared with their real election total, and gaining more than half of their seats at the top-up stage.

Turning to the regional breakdown of the parties' local and top-up seats, a striking feature is that under AMS the Tories would have retained 12 seats in Scotland and eight seats in Wales. In fact, the Conservatives would have secured representation in all of our 18 regions under AMS – swapping their regional over-representation in the south-east, south-west and East Anglia for a much more balanced parliamentary party. Top-up seats would be the crucial mechanism for accomplishing this transformation of the Tories back into a 'one nation' party. By contrast, Labour in 1997 would have won a large majority of its seats in the constituency contests in every region except two (the south-east and south-west).

The pure AMS form was the only schema which we fully researched which would not have delivered a Labour majority in 1997, but instead would have required the formation of a coalition government. Labour would be far and away the largest party, but some 25 seats short of an overall Commons majority. AMS was also the only system which allocated seats fairly to both the Conservatives and the Liberal Democrats. It would thus be clearly consistent with the declaration in both the Labour and Liberal Democrat manifestos that the electoral systems referendum due to be held by 2002 will give UK voters a choice between the *status quo* and a single 'proportional' system.

The Single Transferable Vote

Few systems evoke such passionate attachment in their advocates as STV, a system which has conventionally been seen as certain to produce highly proportional results (for some contrary views see Gallagher, 1996). In our 1992 research, however, we demonstrated that, applied in mainland Britain, STV would have been considerably less proportional than pure-form AMS, significantly exaggerating Labour's representation compared with the Conservatives and producing an outcome with a DV score of over five per cent. The more 'unbalanced' configuration of electoral opinion in 1997 provides an ideal test of STV's robustness in producing seats outcomes which closely reflect parties' national vote shares.

The great attraction of STV is that it delivers (broadly) proportional outcomes with a definite constituency system, yet without the use of party lists. Every candidate must stand for election in a multi-member constituency and receive individual votes. Constituencies must have at least two seats, and may have as many as nine seats. The larger constituencies become, the more accurately STV will relate parties' share of the seats to their share of the vote. On their ballot papers voters rank candidates in order of preference 1, 2, 3, etc., as under the alternative vote, but with a much longer list of candidates, including several choices for each party. A unique feature of STV is that electors can vote for candidates of different parties in any combination that they choose. Voters' preferences completely determine how different candidates put up by each party are ranked, and which ones are successful.

The allocation of seats in STV begins by establishing a quota, calculated as the number of votes cast divided by one plus the number of seats to be filled. First preferences are counted and the candidate with most votes above the quota is elected. Any 'surplus votes' in excess of the quota level are redistributed by looking at the second preferences shown. The new totals of votes (that is, first preferences plus any redistributed second preferences) are examined, and the next highest candidate above the quota is elected: in turn that candidate's surplus votes are redistributed to second preference candidates. This process continues until all candidates with votes above the quota level are elected. Some of the seats in the constituency will remain unfilled at this stage. The STV system then switches over to the AV method of eliminating the bottom candidate, and redistributing their second preference votes. If another candidate has now reached the quota level they are elected and any surplus votes are redistributed: if no candidate still passes the quota level, the next bottom candidate is eliminated and their second preferences redistributed. This elimination and redistribution process continues until all the constituency seats have been filled by candidates remaining in the race passing the quota level.

We gave our respondents an STV ballot paper for a five-member seat, with at least 17 names on it, with four candidates each for the Conservatives, Labour and Liberal Democrats, four candidates for the SNP and Plaid Cymru in Scotland and Wales respectively, and one or two candidates for the Referendum Party, plus a range of other minority parties. Candidate names were drawn from actual people standing in the 1997 election for that party, with a mix including some well-known names, an equal balance of women and men, and the inclusion of some candidates with recognizable ethnic minority names where possible.

Only seven per cent of respondents who had voted in the general election made no response on the STV ballot paper; however, a further ten per cent filled in only one box out of the possible 17 on the ballot paper. In 1997 between half and three-quarters of respondents in all regions expressed multi-party preferences, an increase since 1992. The change was especially marked in the south-west, where multi-party preferences were given by 70 per cent of people compared with fewer than half five years earlier, and in East Anglia where multi-party preferences increased from 44 to 62 per cent.

As in 1992, a large majority of our 1997 respondents cast their first preferences on the STV ballot for the same party they supported in the general election, replicating very closely the pattern of responses we found in our 1992 survey. Conservative and Labour voters were the most loyal in their first choices, with around nine out of ten ticking a first preference from the same party on the STV ballot. Liberal Democrat voters were rather more prone to defect, with one-fifth choosing a different party in their first-preference choice. The nationalist parties were broadly comparable, but only three-fifths of the Referendum Party voters at the general election stuck by it on the STV ballot. As in 1992, when respondents made their second choices on the STV ballot, only two-thirds chose the same party they voted for in the general election, and this proportion declined gradually to just over half at the third-preference stage, and just below half at the fourth-preference stage. Most major party voters cast most of their preferences for the party they backed in the real election, but there was slightly greater 'cross-voting' in 1997 than five years earlier.

The proportion of 1997 voters giving a preference to a different party rose as people marked their second preferences. Conservative and Labour voters were the least likely to support two or more parties at this stage, while slightly more Liberal Democrat, Green and nationalist party voters 'defected'. On third and fourth preferences the 'defection' rate among all the parties became more similar, except that Labour voters were slightly more loyalist at this stage. Then as they reached their fifth choice, there was a sharp rise in the proportion of major party voters giving a preference to another party. At this stage, of course, even the most loyal voters run out of their own party's candidates to support.

The proportion of people making no response grew steadily from six per cent at the first-preference stage to 35 per cent expressing no fourth preference. However at the next stage there was a large jump, with 64 per cent of respondents who voted in the general election not expressing a fifth preference. This effect was due mainly to voters who are party loyalists having exhausted the candidates that they would vote for. A large majority of respondents stopped marking preferences after indicating five or fewer choices – the ballot paper made clear that the number of MPs to be elected was five. Conservative voters were least likely to continue expressing preferences.

Turning from how people chose between parties to how they selected individual candidates to support, many people clearly cast a 'loyalty vote', putting their preferences within a party in the same sequence as candidates were positioned on the ballot paper. As in 1992, ten per cent of all respondents cast a straight-run vote – giving their first four preferences to either the Conservatives, or to Labour, or to the Liberal Democrats, exactly in the order that the parties' candidates were arranged on the ballot paper. But this is a rather narrow conception of 'loyalty voting', since any minor deviation from the ballot paper order fails this test. A more general picture shows that in 1997 among Conservative, Labour and Liberal Democrat voters combined, 54 per cent gave their first preference to the first candidate in their party's column; 39 per cent gave their second preference to the second listed party candidate; 33 per cent gave their third preference to the third listed candidate; and 33 per cent gave their fourth preference to the fourth listed candidate of their party. These figures are again virtually identical to the pattern of responses in 1992. The primary influence on the number of votes a candidate received was their position on the ballot (although this could be a feature which is stronger in our method than in a real STV election, because our respondents had not been exposed to an election campaign held under STV).

To convert the STV ballot results into seats we first defined five-member constituencies (with a few areas having either four or six seats), produced by amalgamating existing Westminster constituencies on appropriate lines – such as, 'natural' community, partisan balance, conformity with local government areas, etc. (see Map 3 in Dunleavy, Margetts *et al.*, 1997). Our procedure is identical to that recommended in the Liberal Democrats' official submission to the Jenkins Commission, where they point out that STV could also be implemented in time for the general election in 2001 or 2002 by amalgamating constituencies without otherwise redrawing boundaries. In each new area we computed the total first preference votes for the parties in the real general election, and then assumed that each party's voters at the five-member seat level would express second and subsequent preferences exactly in line with our STV ballot results for that party's voters in the region as a whole. Using the profile of votes thus generated, we ran an STV contest for each of the 134 constituencies, using the STV election programme produced by the Electoral Reform Society. Since each such election had many rounds, this was a time-consuming process. Short of actually conducting an STV election, it is hard to see any feasible way in which a more accurate simulation could be conducted.

In 1992 this exercise showed that although Labour's share of the vote in Great Britain lagged behind the Conservatives by eight percent in the general election, an STV election would have given Labour virtually the same number of MPs in the House of Commons as the Conservatives. Labour under Neil Kinnock would have won 40 per cent of the seats in Great Britain on 35 per cent of the (first-preference) vote, while the Conservatives' share of seats was almost identical on 43 per cent of the vote. The Liberal Democrats would have under-performed slightly in terms of seats given their vote.

Table 3 shows results for 1997 which many STV advocates will find controversial. STV would have given the Conservatives many *fewer* seats than even under Britain's existing plurality rule elections – just 144 Tory MPs instead of 165 under the *status quo*. And Labour's huge majority would have been cut back, but not eliminated. With just over 44 per cent of the vote, Tony Blair would have been returned to Downing Street by an STV election with a convincing 53 per cent of the Commons behind him, and an overall majority of 43 over all other parties. Labour would be over-represented in Parliament by nine per cent, the Tories under-represented by the same amount. The Liberal Democrats also would have been somewhat over-represented (by three per cent), returning nearly three times as many MPs as under the plurality rule, and at least 15 more than they would gain under AMS or a pure proportional system.

Looking at the regional patterns under STV shows that in 15 of our 18 areas the Conservatives gained three to six seats fewer than a pure proportionality calculation would suggest they were due (and they were one to two seats down in the remainder). In the south-west region the Tories' share of first preferences suggested a proportional allocation of 19 seats (compared with their 22 seats in the general election); but under STV they elected only 13 MPs. They secured a first seat easily in the ten constituencies, but gained

TABLE 3
PARTIES' OVERALL SEATS ALLOCATION IN GREAT BRITAIN UNDER THE SINGLE
TRANSFERABLE VOTE (STV) IN 1997

	Con	Lab	Lib Dem	SNP/ PC	Oth	Total
STV seats outcome	**144**	**342**	**131**	**24**	**0**	641
Pure PR seats outcome	201	284	110	18	28	641
% STV seats	*23*	*53*	*20*	*3*	*0*	*99*
% votes	*31*	*44*	*17*	*3*	*4*	*99*
Deviation	*-9*	*+9*	*+3*	*0*	*-4*	

a second seat in only three cases, mainly because Labour and Liberal Democrat voters distributed many second or subsequent preferences between the two parties, and gave few to the Conservatives. So candidate eliminations always produced enough preferences for two Labour candidates to come up to quota. In fact in three south-west constituencies Labour subsequently achieved three seats in this fashion, just pushing out a Conservative or Liberal Democrat from gaining a second seat. In the south-east the Tories fared better, gaining second seats in 21 out of 24 constituencies, but in East Anglia they again got second seats in only two out of five constituencies, and in the London suburbs in only three out of eight constituencies. In multi-party areas of Scotland the party also did poorly, gaining only one quota across the six Highlands constituencies, although on a pure proportionality basis the Conservatives should have won six seats in the region.

Overall, once we allow also for the non-representation of any of the minor parties (which between them attracted 4.4 per cent of the vote in 1997), then the deviation from proportionality under STV in 1997 would have been 13 per cent, a level so high that it would be difficult to regard it as 'proportional'. There could consequently be a considerable difficulty for the Liberal Democrats in arguing that STV qualified as a 'proportional' voting system, and hence was eligible for inclusion in the election referendum promised in both the Liberal Democrat and Labour manifestos. At best the 1992 and 1997 evidence strongly suggests that STV is only a contingently proportional system – and a similar claim could easily be made (albeit implausibly) for the alternative vote or supplementary vote.

We should point out, however, that there is a difficulty in assessing deviation from proportionality under STV by measuring how seat shares differ from *first* preference shares, because of course STV counts multiple preferences as of equal value. So advocates could claim that the system is not under-representing the Tories in terms of *all* effective voter preferences (those that counted in allocating seats). On the contrary, STV is exactly reflecting the Conservative government's greater unpopularity when first, second and third preferences are all taken into account. The same effect occurred in both the other 'preferential' systems in 1997, the supplementary vote and the alternative vote, each of which would have delivered huge Labour majorities in 1997 – even though they had very modest effects in the different conditions of the 1992 election. However valid and important these arguments are, if most people in Britain give more weight to first preferences than to second and subsequent preferences, and hence to achieving a close fit between first preferences and seat shares, the problems for STV remain considerable.

The List PR System

This type of system is widely used in western liberal democracies. Parties offer a list of candidates to voters in a large multi-member constituency. Voters express a single preference *for a party*, and the seats in the constituency are then allocated to candidates from each party's list in proportion to their level of support. This approach has not been seriously advocated by any major group or organization in Britain for Westminster elections, but it is worth briefly considering it in comparison to STV and AMS especially. We did not gather survey evidence about how our respondents would complete a List PR ballot paper, but instead used real constituency votes to indicate first preferences, aggregating them up to the same five-member seats used in our STV simulation. This size is quite a small district magnitude for List PR, but there would be strong pressures in UK conditions to keep Westminster constituencies as small as possible.

The most important problem to be solved within any List PR system is to choose the rules which will precisely govern the way in which seats are allocated on the basis of votes, a problem which is made somewhat greater when the multi-member seats are not large. There are a number of formulae for working this out. Some rules favour large parties (like the Conservatives and Labour) against smaller parties (like the Liberal Democrats and nationalist parties). Others have reverse effects. We shall concentrate here on three better-known formulae for allocating seats which are widely used and shown in Table 4 (see Taagepera and Shugart, 1989: 29–35, for details of how each rule operates). The table shows some startling variations in the way that the different rules distributed seats between the parties in both general elections. In 1997 the d'Hondt formula gave Labour fully 50 more seats than another (largest remainder with a Hare quota). The variation in the Liberal Democrat seat totals was just as sharp, with the party getting more than 40 per cent more seats under its most favourable system (the Hare quota) as under its least favourable. By contrast the Conservatives won much the same number of seats under all three List PR systems. It would be pleasing if we could point to continuities in how List PR worked in 1992 and in 1997, but Labour did better with the Droop quota than the Hare quota in 1997, and vice versa in 1992. The Liberal Democrats fared best with the Droop quota by a wide margin in 1992, but five years later they would have gained 32 more seats under the Hare quota – reflecting their much stronger position in the south-west and south-east compared with the Conservatives. In both years, one form of List PR produced an exactly proportional outcome – but it was the Droop quota in 1992 and the Hare quota in 1997. The two less proportionate sets of rules in 1997 would have produced deviations from proportionality of up to seven per cent, an increase on 1992 reflecting primarily the higher vote given to small parties which did not win any seats.

TABLE 4
THE ALLOCATIONS OF SEATS UNDER LIST PR USING FIVE-MEMBER CONSTITUENCIES
(IDENTICAL TO THE STV CONSTITUENCIES)

	Con	Lab	Lib Dem	SNP/ PC	Other	Ref
Largest remainder with Droop quota	212	320	89	19	1	0
Largest remainder with Hare quota	205	295	121	19	1	0
D'Hondt system	205	345	72	19	1	0
Pure proportional result	202	285	110	16	1	17

Note: The 'pure proportional' figures assumes that each party wins exactly the same national share of seats as its share of the first preference vote, with no thresholds etc.

Conclusions

The evidence which we have considered, summarized in Table 5, throws considerable new light on how alternative electoral systems performed under British conditions in the 1990s.

- In 1997 and 1992 the most clearly and consistently proportional voting method was the additional member system (with half of the MPs elected locally, and half elected regionally using the top-up method). Variants of AMS which gave more local seats and fewer top-up seats would be less proportional. Applying the version of AMS to be used for the Scottish parliament would have left Labour just short of an overall majority, but with the Welsh version the party could have formed a single-party government.

- STV did not achieve any close fit between parties' seats and their first preference votes in 1997. And in both 1997 and 1992 STV produced an apparent over-representation of Labour in the Commons, for example giving Labour 53 per cent of seats in 1997 on the basis of 44 per cent of votes. In 1997 STV gave the Conservatives many fewer seats than their first-preference votes warranted.

• The supplementary vote and the alternative vote were markedly *less* proportional than first-past-the-post in 1997. In 1992 the results of both systems were slightly more proportional than first-past-the-post.

These findings also carry implications for how the major parties would have performed under alternative electoral systems in 1997, implications which are likely to weigh heavily in determining their attitudes towards electoral reform over the next four-and-a-half years, a critical period if the electoral reform referendum does indeed go ahead.

• Under any voting system taking account of voters' second or subsequent preferences, the Conservatives in the late 1990s would have fared worse than under the existing first-past-the-post electoral system. The Tories would have been severely under-represented by the single transferable vote (with only 144 seats), gaining fewer MPs than with first-past-the-post. And their number of MPs would have fallen to just 110 in 1997 under the supplementary vote or alternative vote (which are closely related systems).

• Labour would have formed a majority government under three alternative electoral systems in 1997.Under the supplementary vote or alternative vote Labour's majority would, indeed, have been greater than with first-past-the-post. Under the single transferable vote Labour would have had an overall majority of 44. But under the pure-form additional member system Tony Blair could have been short of an overall majority, and so have had to form a coalition government. Table 5 shows that a variant of AMS such as that to be used for electing the Scottish Parliament (53 per cent local, 47 per cent top-up seats) would also have necessitated a coalition government, but that a 66:33 split would have yielded an overall Labour majority of 21 seats.

• The Liberal Democrats would have gained a minimum of 84 seats under any alternative electoral system (up from 46 under first-past-the-post). Their maximum number of MPs would have nearly tripled to 130 under the STV system, which the party has historically advocated.

Our findings also have considerable implications for the electoral reform debate:

- The Labour and Liberal Democrat parties promised in their Joint Commission on Constitutional Reform report (27 March 1997) and in their election manifestos to hold a referendum in which UK voters could choose between keeping the *status quo* or endorsing 'a single proportional system' as the new method for Westminster elections. Only the pure-form additional member system operated in a fully proportional way in both 1997 and 1992.

- A referendum with STV as the 'reform' option could be problematic because it is not predictably a proportional system. Although it performed fairly well in 1992, the system would not have treated all parties fairly in 1997.

- A voting systems referendum with the supplementary vote or the alternative vote as the 'reform' option would seem straightforwardly incompatible with the election manifesto pledge. Both systems were less proportional than first-past-the-post in 1997.

Thinking through how these findings can be reconciled with political realities will be an important task both for the Jenkins Commission and for Labour and Liberal Democrat party managers once the commission has reported. Further work is likely to be needed to cope with ingenious permutations of the systems, such as the scenario floated in the *Independent* (23 September 1997) for using an AMS system, but with AV (or SV) employed for the local seats elections and a large majority of local seats, possibly on the lines of the Hansard Society's 75:25 scheme advocated in the mid 1970s. The attraction of such a scheme for Labour is that, if voters choose reform in the voting systems referendum, the AV element could be implemented for 2002, but the top-up seats would be created only for the subsequent election, following redistricting. We estimate that if people completed the local ballot in the same way that they filled in the SV ballot, while voting at the top-up stage as they did on the AMS ballot, then a scheme combining the two elements would have yielded results with a DV score of at least 13 per cent in 1997, virtually the same as the STV outcome. In 1992, with more balanced major party votes and the AV element acting as a stabilizing (rather than distorting) force, the scheme would have given a DV score around 6 per cent, slightly worse than STV's performance.

TABLE 5
COMPARING THE SEATS WON BY THE PARTIES IN BRITAIN UNDER ALTERNATIVE
ELECTORAL SYSTEMS, 1997

Voting Method	Con	Lab	Lib Dem	SNP/ PC	Oth	% DV
First past the post	165	419	46	10	1	21
Supplementary Vote	110	436	84	10	1	24
Alternative Vote	110	436	84	10	1	24
STV	144	342	131	24	0	13
AMS: Welsh version	191	340	93	17	0	9
AMS: Scottish version	198	319	105	19	0	6
AMS: 50/50 version	203	303	115	20	0	2
Pure proportionality	202	285	110	16	18	0

Finally, this study has some important implications for the way in which we undertake simulations in political science. The technical appendices to successive Nuffield election studies have used very crude approaches to simulation. For example, voting patterns on preferential systems (such as AV and STV) are estimated from answers to questions asking people their second preference party despite the fact that many more people will give a response to such a direct enquiry than will mark a second preference on an actual ballot paper. And while data on second preferences alone are sufficient to work out AV results quite accurately, they are wholly inadequate as a basis for estimating STV results without having a defined constituency schema and a full preference ordering for party voters in each region – because outcomes under STV often hang on the effects of small transfers of third or fourth preferences between eliminated candidates. It is also very important to use accurate regional data in estimating outcomes under all alternative systems, and not to try to use national opinion poll data for simulations, because it averages out very different regional patterns of voting. We believe that the earlier Nuffield election study estimates for the 1980s elections are very inaccurate, and we are absolutely certain that the same estimates for the two 1990s elections are badly wrong. For example, the seat projections for AV and STV for 1997 are based on a single question on a national survey asking directly about people's second preferences, and actually dating from September 1996, more than seven months before the general election took place (see Curtice and Steed, 1997). This question suggested that 62 per cent of Liberal Democrats would give Labour a second preference (we found only 49 per cent); and that 81 per cent of Labour supporters would give the Liberal Democrats a second preference (we found only 57 per cent). Little wonder, then, that an analysis based on these assumptions, using a national poll only and not including third or subsequent preferences for the STV ballot, misestimates AV outcomes by 44 seats in all, gets the party ordering wrong under

AV, estimates that the Liberal Democrats would do worse under STV than under AV (we found that the party gained 47 more seats under STV), and produces an STV outcome which is adrift by over 90 seats (*Economist*, 1 November 1997: 6). We hope to have shown that political science does not need to continue to operate with this level of inaccuracy in estimates. Systematically approaching simulation tasks can allow us to come much closer to a well-founded view of how alternative electoral systems would operate under the British party system and electoral conditions.

ACKNOWLEDGEMENTS

This paper reports some key 1997 findings of a larger research project, 'Modelling Alternative Electoral Systems in British Conditions in the 1990s', funded by the ESRC (Award Number N000222253) and by the Joseph Rowntree Charitable Trust. Full details of the 1997 results are given in our report *Making Votes Count: Replaying the 1990s General Elections under Alternative Electoral Systems* (London: Democratic Audit of the UK, 1997), available from Scarman Trust Enterprises, Exmouth House, 3–11 Pine Street, London EC1R OJH, price £12.50. Copies of our 1992 report, *Replaying the General Election of 1992* (London: LSE Public Policy Group, 1992) are still available from Public Policy Group, Government Department, LSE, Houghton Street, London WC2A 2AE, price £5.50. We would like to thank Nick Sparrow and Martin Boon of ICM Research for their help on the survey, and Nick Moon of NOP, Brian Gosschalk of MORI and Simon Osborne of BMRB International for polling advice. We are indebted also to Ivor Crewe, David Sanders and John Curtice who advised us on question-wording issues; Pippa Norris for help with 1997 electoral data; Lord Raymond Plant, Pat McFadden of the Policy Unit at 10 Downing Street, and Alan Leaman of the Liberal Democrats for interviews on political background; Jane Pugh of the LSE drawing office for invaluable help in mapping redesigned seats; and David Shutt, Steve Burkeman, and Lord Trevor Smith of JRCT and JRRT for their invaluable advice and committed support. The paper was also given to the Elections, Parties and Public Opinion Conference, University of Essex, 27 September, 1997: we thank the participants there for helpful comments.

REFERENCES

Blais, A. and L. Massicotte (1996) 'Mixed electoral systems: An overview', *Representation* 33: 115–19.

Curtice, J. and M. Steed (1997) 'Appendix 2: The results analysed', in D. Butler and D. Kavanagh (eds) *The British General Election of 1997*. Basingstoke: Macmillan.

Dunleavy, P. (1990) 'Mass political behaviour: Is there more to learn?', *Political Studies* 38: 453–69.

Dunleavy, P. and H. Margetts (1995) 'Understanding the dynamics of electoral reform', *International Political Science Review* 16: 9–29.

Dunleavy, P. and H. Margetts (1997) *Report to the Government Office for London: Electing the London Mayor and Assembly. London*: LSE Public Policy Group.

Dunleavy, P., H. Margetts and S. Weir (1992a) *Replaying the General Election of 1992: How Britain Would Have Voted Under Alternative Electoral Systems*. London: LSE Public Policy Group/Joseph Rowntree Reform Trust.

Dunleavy, P., H. Margetts and S. Weir (1992b) 'How Britain would have voted under alternative electoral systems', *Parliamentary Affairs* 45: 640–55.

Dunleavy, P., H. Margetts, B. O'Duffy and S. Weir (1997) *Making Votes Count: Replaying the 1990s General Elections under Alternative Electoral Systems*. London: Democratic Audit of the UK.

Gallagher, M. (ed) 'Special Issue: The single transferable vote', *Representation* 34, no. 3.

Lindblom, C. and D. Cohen (1979) *Useable Knowledge: Social Science and Social Problem-Solving*. New Haven, CT: Yale University Press.

Reilly, B. (1997) 'The Plant report and the supplementary vote: not so unique after all', *Representation* 34: 95–102.

Taagepera, R. and M. Shugart (1989) *Seats and Votes: The Effects and Determinants of Electoral Systems*. New Haven, CT: Yale University Press.

APPENDIX

THE MAIN FEATURES OF THE PLURALITY RULE AND FIVE ALTERNATIVE ELECTORAL SYSTEMS

System name:	Plurality rule ('first-past-the-post').
Voters fill in ballot paper by:	Marking an X against one candidate only.
Seats contested in:	Current 659 single-member constituencies.
Winning candidates must:	Get more votes than any other candidate in the constituency, a plurality (but not a majority)

System name:	Supplementary vote (SV).
Voters fill in ballot paper by:	Marking an X against their first preference candidate, and (if they want to) against a second preference candidate also.
Seats contested in:	Current 659 single-member constituencies.
Winning candidates must:	*Either* get majority (50.1 per cent) support from voters' first preferences *or*, be the leading candidate after redistribution of the second preferences of voters who did not back one of the top two candidates at the first preference stage.

System name:	Alternative Vote (AV).
Voters fill in ballot paper by:	Marking their ballot paper 1, 2, 3, etc. against candidates in the order of their preferences.
Seats contested in:	Current 659 single-member constituencies.
Winning candidates must:	*Either* get majority (50.1 per cent) support from voters' first preferences *or*, obtain majority support following one or more redistributions of the second or subsequent preferences of voters backing the bottom candidate; *or* be the leading candidate in a two-horse race after one or more such redistributions of second and subsequent preferences of voters backing the bottom candidate.

System name:	Additional Member System (AMS).
Voters fill in ballot paper by:	Marking an X against their first preference candidate or party at the local constituency level, and marking an X against their first preference party at regional level.
Seats contested in:	Half (or more) of seats are elected by plurality rule in single-member constituencies perhaps twice as large as current constituencies. The remaining seats are allocated at the regional level so as to 'top up' parties' seats, so that their share of MPs matches their share of votes.
Winning candidates must:	Be the leading candidate in one of the local constituencies, or be elected from the party list at regional level, either because their party has put them near the top of the regional list or (possibly) as one of the 'best losers' in the constituency competitions.

System name:	Single Transferable Vote (STV).
Voters fill in ballot paper by:	Marking their ballot paper 1, 2, 3, etc. against their most preferred individual candidates across any party or combination of parties.
Seats contested in:	All seats are elected in multi-member constituencies, around five times as large as current constituencies.
Winning candidates must:	Obtain a 'quota' of support so as to qualify for one of the seats in a constituency, a quota being a fifth of the votes plus 1.
System name:	List Proportional Representation (List PR).
Voters fill in ballot paper by:	Marking an X against one party (or party candidate) only.
Seats contested in:	All seats are elected in multi-member constituencies, at least five times the size of current constituencies.

Reference Section

This volume is now a *Review* of British elections and parties rather than a *Yearbook*, but we believe that the reference sections in previous editions have proved extremely useful sources for colleagues and that a reference section should continue to feature in the *Review*. Cumulative details of parliamentary by-elections, comprehensive figures for voting intentions in monthly opinion polls and details of local election results, for example, are simply not published elsewhere. These data, and the other information provided, take a good deal of digging out and – although many EPOP members are themselves inveterate fact gatherers – they are collected and presented in this section in a convenient form, thus saving the hard-pressed a good deal of time and effort.

We begin with a chronology of events during 1997 – undoubtedly a momentous year in British politics. As in all previous volumes, this has been expertly prepared by David Broughton. Since 1997 was a general election year, we provide details of the election results for the UK as a whole, as well as separately for England, Scotland, Wales, Great Britain and Northern Ireland – in particular giving full details of the minor parties which are usually simply lumped together as 'others'. The by-election section gives the result of the last by-election held under the Conservative government and the results of the first four which occurred after Labour came into office. The general election also affects the opinion polls section since, in addition to the usual figures, we give voting intention figures from all polls conducted during the campaign. Although they were somewhat overshadowed by the general election, local elections also took place on 1 May. We provide a summary account of these as well as a guide to the increasingly complex structure of local government in Britain and to the electoral cycles of the different types of local authority. Among the details for political parties we have not, on this occasion, given figures for party membership. Parties are unwilling or unable to provide up-to-date figures and it seemed unwise to provide estimates which may be very inaccurate. On the other hand, we have included more details on internal party elections.

We would like to thank those who have helped in the gathering and checking of the material in this section, especially David Broughton, Colin Rallings, Michael Thrasher, Mark Stuart and Simon Atkinson.

David Denver
Justin Fisher
Philip Cowley
Charles Pattie

1. Chronology of Events 1997

JANUARY

2.   Stephen Dorrell, the Health Secretary, suggested that the institutions of the European Union should be overhauled and that Britain's relationship with the EU should be re-negotiated. His remarks were widely interpreted as an attempt to improve his standing with the 'eurosceptics' within the Conservative Party.

5.   Conservative MP Jerry Hayes denied allegations that he had a homosexual relationship with an 18-year-old boy in 1991.

6.   Labour leader Tony Blair expressed support for a so-called 'zero tolerance' policy to deal with begging and petty crime.

7.   Of the 2.5 million television viewers who voted during a debate on the monarchy broadcast on ITV (*Monarchy – The Nation Decides*), 66 per cent were in favour of retaining it, although this figure was only 44 per cent in Scotland.

11.   Nine women were ordained as the first women priests in the Anglican Church in Wales in Bangor Cathedral.

15.   The government gave approval for the building of a second runway at Manchester Airport by the year 2000.

16.   The government became a minority administration after the death of Iain Mills, Conservative MP for Meriden since 1979, aged 56.

20.   Gordon Brown, the Shadow Chancellor, pledged that the Labour Party would not increase the basic rate (23 per cent) or the top rate (40 per cent) of income tax. He also said there would be no new commitments in the forthcoming Labour manifesto which would require additional spending.
      The government was no longer a minority administration after the death of Martin Redmond, Labour MP for Don Valley since 1983, aged 59.

22.   Michael Portillo, the Defence Secretary, announced that a new royal yacht, to replace *Britannia*, would be built at a cost of £60 million by the year 2001.

25.   Gordon Brown, the Shadow Chancellor, said that if a Labour government were elected later in the year, it would look to alternative ways of funding any replacement for the royal yacht.

28.   Lord Rippon of Hexham, Conservative MP for Hexham, 1966–87 and key negotiator of the UK's entry into the European Community, died aged 72.

29.   Toyota, the Japanese car manufacturer, entered the debate over the single European currency when its president reportedly warned that the company would shift its European investment from the UK to continental Europe if the UK stayed outside the single currency.

30.   The government announced the establishment of an independent Food Safety Council.

FEBRUARY

4.   Gordon Brown, the Shadow Chancellor, said that a future Labour government would introduce a one-year pay freeze for ministers, MPs, senior civil servants, military officers and judges.

5.   A midweek National Lottery draw was announced.

7.   The London to Glasgow West Coast main-line rail franchise, the largest under the rail privatization programme, was awarded to the Virgin Group.

14.   The *Daily Mail* published the pictures of five men on its front page whom it accused of the racist murder of Stephen Lawrence, challenging them to sue the paper if the accusation was wrong. A murder trial had collapsed in 1996 for lack of evidence but an inquest jury on 13 February had ruled that Lawrence had been unlawfully killed by white youths.

17.   In the House of Commons, an Opposition censure motion on the Agriculture Minister (Douglas Hogg) over his handling of the BSE crisis was defeated by 320 votes to 307 votes.

19.   Malcolm Rifkind, the Foreign Secretary, in a speech in Bonn, described the government as 'on balance hostile' to a single European currency.

Deng Xiaoping, paramount leader of China since 1978, died aged 92.

21.   The 'Bridgewater Three' who had been in prison for 18 years for the murder of newspaper boy Carl Bridgewater were released on bail by the Appeal Court after the Crown accepted that fresh evidence revealed fundamental flaws in the prosecution case.

26.   Gordon Brown, the Shadow Chancellor, announced that, if Labour formed the next government, he would establish a new monetary policy committee chaired by the governor of the Bank of England and a new council of economic advisors for the Treasury.

27.   Labour won the Wirral South by-election, with a 17.2 per cent swing from the Conservatives, producing a majority of 7,888 votes on a turnout of 73 per cent. The following day, John Major, the Prime Minister, admitted that 'if opinion does not change, then we are going to have a Labour government'.

MARCH

6.   An official internet web site on the British monarchy was launched by the Queen at a school in north London.

9.   Conservative MP George Gardiner, who had been de-selected by his constituency party in February 1997, announced that he had resigned the Conservative Party whip and had joined the Referendum Party.

13.   The prison ship *Weare* arrived in Portland Harbour in Dorset as one means of reducing prison overcrowding. Prison ships had not been used in the UK since the nineteenth century.

16.   Former Conservative Minister Alan Howarth, who joined the Labour Party in 1995, was selected as the Labour candidate for the safe seat of Newport East.

17.   John Major, the Prime Minister, announced that a general election would be held on 1 May 1997. This meant that Parliament would be adjourned on 21 March and formally dissolved on 8 April, thus preventing the publication of the report by Sir Gordon Downey, the

Parliamentary Commissioner for Standards into renewed 'cash for questions' allegations.

18.   *The Sun* announced its support for the Labour Party at the forthcoming general election.

19.   The report of the Parliamentary Ombudsman recorded a total of 1,920 complaints in 1996, with over half of them against the Child Support Agency.

24.   The former Scottish Office Minister Allan Stewart, stood down as a Conservative candidate at the forthcoming general election after newspaper allegations of an extra-marital relationship.

26.   The former Northern Ireland Minister, Tim Smith, resigned as the Conservative candidate for Beaconsfield at the forthcoming general election after admitting that he had received payments from business-man Mohammed al-Fayed, and that he had failed to declare them.
       Bomb explosions at Wilmslow in Cheshire were described as an IRA 'two-fingered insult to democracy' by Home Secretary Michael Howard.

29.   The chairman of the Scottish Conservative Party, Michael Hirst, resigned; on 30 March, a newspaper published allegations that he had had a homosexual relationship.

30.   John Major, the Prime Minister, promised to take stern action against those criticized in the Downey report.
       The new television station, Channel 5, began broadcasting.

APRIL

3.   Two separate bombs halted traffic on both the M6 and the M5 in the West Midlands. The IRA admitted responsibility for planting the bombs the following day.

5.   A spectacular bomb hoax took place which forced the abandonment of the Grand National horse race at Aintree in Liverpool. The warnings, using recognized IRA code words, forced the evacuation of 60,000 people and hundreds of horses. The race took place two days later.

6.   The BBC correspondent Martin Bell said he would stand in Tatton in Cheshire against Neil Hamilton as an 'anti-sleaze' candidate if Hamilton did not stand down; the Labour and Liberal Democrat candidates had agreed to withdraw in Bell's favour. On 7 April, Hamilton was confirmed as the Conservative Party candidate for the seat.

16.   John Major, the Prime Minister, made a television broadcast in which he appealed for support for his 'wait and see' policy on the question of any single European currency. On 17 April, Major said that Conservative backbenchers would be given a free vote if the Cabinet were to recommend that Britain should join any single currency.

21.   The President of the European Commission, Jacques Santer, was accused of interfering in the British general election campaign after he said that European integration would continue and that eurosceptics were 'doom merchants'.
        A series of bomb threats brought London to a virtual standstill during the morning rush hour. The threats closed most of the main-line railway stations, several underground stations and two of the airports serving the capital.

23.   A poll by ICM published in the *Guardian* reported that Labour's lead over the Conservatives had fallen to 5 per cent.
        Up to 1,000 lorries were forced to queue on the M20 in Kent after a blockade of three French Channel ferry ports by fishermen protesting against an EU ruling on the mesh sizes of fishing nets.
        Baroness Seear, deputy leader of the Liberal Democrats in the House of Lords since 1988, died aged 83.

28.   Lord Taylor of Gosforth, Lord Chief Justice 1992–6 and author of the report into the Hillsborough football disaster, died aged 66.

MAY

1.   The Labour Party won 418 seats in the House of Commons at the general election with 44 per cent of the votes. It was the largest majority ever held by Labour (178 seats) and the largest majority for a single party since 1924. The Conservatives won 165 seats with their lowest share of the vote since 1832, and in Scotland and Wales they won no seats. The Liberal Democrats won 46 seats. The turnout was 71 per cent, the lowest since 1935. The number of women elected

more than doubled to 120.

Local elections were also held for county councils and some unitary authorities in England.

2.   John Major resigned as leader of the Conservative Party.

The Labour Party leader Tony Blair was invited by the Queen to form a government and to become the youngest Prime Minister since 1812; he was officially sworn in as Prime Minister the following day.

3.   The former Deputy Prime Minister, Michael Heseltine, was admitted to hospital after an attack of angina. He said he would not be a candidate in the forthcoming contest for the leadership of the Conservative Party.

Sir John Junor, editor of the *Sunday Express* 1954–86 and newspaper columnist, died aged 78.

Katrina and the Waves won the Eurovision Song Contest in Dublin with *Love Shine a Light*. Britain had last won the contest 16 years ago with Bucks Fizz.

4.   Robin Cook, Foreign Secretary, announced that the new Labour government was signing up to the European social chapter on employees' rights.

6.   Gordon Brown, Chancellor of the Exchequer, relinquished the power to set interest rates to the Bank of England, giving the bank operational control of monetary policy.

7.   The composition of the new Labour government was completed, with more than 100 ministers, junior ministers, whips and senior law officers being appointed. Key portfolios were mainly given to ministers who had shadowed them in opposition, with the exception of the appointment of Frank Dobson as Secretary of State for Health rather than Chris Smith. The Cabinet included a record five women.

8.   The new Labour government held its first Cabinet meeting. Ministers agreed to forego the controversial salary increases which had been approved by the previous administration in July 1996. In addition, it was agreed that ministers would henceforth refer to one another by their first names rather than by their formal titles.

Sir Michael Shersby, Conservative MP for Uxbridge since 1972, died aged 64.

9.   Tony Blair, the Prime Minister, announced changes to Prime

Minister's Question Time in the House of Commons. The twice-weekly sessions each of 15 minutes on Tuesdays and Thursdays would be replaced by one single 30-minute session on a Wednesday afternoon.

13.   The official report of the inquiry into the fire in the Channel Tunnel in November 1996 was published. The report stated that Eurotunnel had failed to act on warnings of fundamental weaknesses in its safety systems.

14.   The state opening of Parliament took place. The Queen's Speech announced 26 bills and a number of white papers mainly designed to enact the key pledges of the new government. The programme included referendums on proposals for devolution to Scotland and Wales.

Betty Boothroyd, the Speaker of the House of Commons, said that any MPs who did not swear the oath of allegiance to the Queen (the two MPs from Sinn Féin – Gerry Adams and Martin McGuinness) would not be allowed to use the facilities of the House of Commons.

16.   Tony Blair, the Prime Minister, visited Belfast in an attempt to break the deadlock in the Northern Ireland peace process. He announced the re-opening of direct contacts between the British government and Sinn Féin.

The ban on trade unions at GCHQ in Cheltenham, imposed in 1984, was lifted.

18.   A police investigation was launched after allegations in the *News of the World* that a new Labour MP, Mohammad Sarwar, had bribed an opponent during the general election campaign; on 19 May, Sarwar issued a libel writ against the newspaper.

19.   Ann Widdecombe, the former prisons minister, criticized the former Home Secretary and candidate for the Conservative Party leadership, Michael Howard, over the sacking of the director-general of the Prison Service, Derek Lewis, in October 1995. She also claimed that Howard had misled Parliament about the earlier decision to remove John Marriott, the governor of Parkhurst prison, from his post.

21.   Sir Archie Hamilton was elected chair of the Conservative 1922 committee of backbench MPs.

22.   David Blunkett, the Education and Employment Secretary, announced that nursery school vouchers would be abolished from September 1997 and that free nursery places would be available for every four-year-old from September 1998.

28.   George Robertson, the Defence Secretary, announced a review of Britain's defence needs and the role of the armed forces.

29.   Tony Blair held talks with President Clinton at Downing Street.

JUNE

2.   In a speech, Tony Blair outlined plans to help unemployed people find work.
        Gordon Brown, Chancellor of the Exchequer, appointed four leading economists as members of the new monetary policy committee.
        The National Heritage Secretary, Chris Smith, ordered the directors of Camelot, the National Lottery operator, to forego their large pay rises and bonuses; on 6 June, the directors said they would donate some of the money to charity.
        Nearly 8 million people received a total of about £18.4 billion of free shares when the Halifax, the country's biggest mortgage lender, completed its transformation from a building society to a publicly quoted bank and began trading shares on the stock market.

10.   In the first round of the contest for the leadership of the Conservative Party, Kenneth Clarke won 49 votes, William Hague 41, John Redwood 27, Peter Lilley 24 and Michael Howard 23. Lilley and Howard withdrew from the contest.

11.   MPs voted to ban .22 pistols, making the ownership of all handguns illegal from the autumn of 1997.

16–17. At the European Council summit in Amsterdam, Britain negotiated the right to retain control over its own visa, asylum and immigration policies. This was Prime Minister Tony Blair's first meeting with his European Union partners.

17.   In the second round of the contest for the leadership of the Conservative Party, Kenneth Clarke gained 64 votes, William Hague 62 and John Redwood 38. Redwood was therefore eliminated from the contest.

18.   The Labour MP Bob Wareing was suspended by the Parliamentary Labour Party for allegedly failing to declare a financial interest in the House of Commons register.

19.   In the final round of the contest for the leadership of the Conservative Party, William Hague won 92 votes, while Kenneth Clarke won 70. Hague, at 36 years old, therefore became the youngest Conservative Party leader since 1783. Clarke refused Hague's offer of a position in the Shadow Cabinet.
        Tony Blair insisted that the Millennium Dome exhibition in Greenwich in south-east London would go ahead. Peter Mandelson, the Minister without Portfolio, was given the task of masterminding the project the following day as the 'Dome Secretary'.
        The longest trial in English legal history ended after 314 days when McDonald's won £60,000 damages from two environmental activists who were adjudged to have libelled the company. McDonald's legal bill was however estimated to be £10 million.

20.   Former Conservative Cabinet Minister Jonathan Aitken halted his libel action against the *Guardian* and Granada TV when the *Guardian* disclosed new evidence proving that parts of the testimony given by Aitken were false. On 24 June Aitken resigned from the Privy Council. Aitken faced the possibility of prosecution for perjury and perverting the course of justice.

25.   Prime Minister Tony Blair announced plans to begin detailed talks on the future of Northern Ireland in September with or without the participation of Sinn Féin. He said that he wanted the discussions to be completed by May 1998.

30.   The Prime Minister, the Foreign Secretary (Robin Cook) and the Prince of Wales attended ceremonies in Hong Kong to mark the return of the colony to China.

JULY

2.   The Chancellor of the Exchequer, Gordon Brown, presented his first Budget statement to the House of Commons. The package was described by Brown as a 'people's Budget for Britain's future'. The details of the long-promised 'windfall tax' on the privatized utilities were unveiled, more money was allocated to education and the health service and a fundamental overhaul of corporate taxation was announced.

The Parliamentary Commissioner for Standards (Sir Gordon Downey) published his 900-page report on allegations that MPs had accepted payments from Mohammed al-Fayed in return for furthering his interests through their activities in the House of Commons. The report found that five MPs (Neil Hamilton, Tim Smith, Sir Andrew Bowden, Sir Michael Grylls and Michael Brown) had accepted money from al-Fayed and failed to declare their interests.

10.   A rally against the proposed ban on fox-hunting was held in Hyde Park in London. An estimated 80,000 people attended, including William Hague, the Leader of the Opposition.
           The Orange Order decided to cancel four of the coming weekend's marches in Northern Ireland. This followed the violence the previous week in Drumcree after an Orange parade.

19.   The IRA announced the 'unequivocal restoration' of its August 1994 ceasefire, broken in February 1996, with effect from the following day.
           Sir James Goldsmith, business tycoon and founder of the Referendum Party, died aged 64.

22.   The government published a White Paper setting out its proposals for establishing an elected Welsh Assembly.
           Tony Blair, the Prime Minister, announced that the leader of the Liberal Democrats (Paddy Ashdown) and four senior colleagues would be invited to serve on a new Cabinet committee to discuss the constitution and other areas of 'mutual interest'. Ashdown insisted that his party would not be bound by collective responsibility and that the Liberal Democrats would continue to press the government from outside, especially on issues such as tax and spending.
           Vincent Hanna, broadcaster, died aged 57.

23.   The report of an enquiry into higher education headed by Sir Ron Dearing was published. The report said that there should be a higher level of investment in higher education, that limits on numbers entering higher education should be abolished and that students and graduates should make a greater contribution towards the cost of higher education. David Blunkett, the Education and Employment Secretary, said that maintenance grants would be replaced by increased student loans and there would be a means-tested parental contribution of £1,000 per year towards tuition fees from October 1998.

24.   The government published a White Paper setting out its proposals for a Scottish Parliament.

28.   The Labour MP, Gordon McMaster, was found dead. He left a suicide note, blaming several colleagues for spreading false rumours about his health and his sexuality.

        David Mellor, the former Conservative Minister and Chelsea supporter, was appointed to head a football task force charged with representing the interests of the fans.

29.   The government published proposals for a Greater London Authority with an elected Mayor.

31.   The Conservatives won the Uxbridge by-election, their first by-election victory for more than eight years. On a 55 per cent turnout, the Conservative majority over Labour increased by more than 3,000 votes.

AUGUST

2.   Alex Kitson, deputy general secretary of the Transport and General Workers' Union 1981–6 and member of the Labour Party's National Executive Committee 1968–86, died aged 75.

        Robin Cook, the Foreign Secretary, announced that he was leaving his wife of 28 years to live with his secretary (Gaynor Regan). Downing Street made it clear that there was no question of Cook's resignation over the matter.

3.   The government said that it favoured a £50 million refit for the royal yacht *Britannia* to be financed by the private sector.

5.   After allegations of a conflict of interest, the Minister for Trade and Competitiveness in Europe (Lord Simon of Highbury) said he would sell his £2 million portfolio of shares in British Petroleum.

19.   After an enquiry by the Chief Whip, the Labour MP for West Renfrewshire, Tommy Graham, was suspended from the Parliamentary Party for alleged 'verbal attacks' on colleagues and for bringing the party into disrepute.

23.   The Secretary of State for International Development (Clare Short) criticized the government of Montserrat for raising unrealistic expectations about the financial help available from the British

government in the wake of the eruption of a volcano on the island.

25–26.   In a series of newspaper articles and television interviews, David Shayler, a former MI5 agent, alleged that the service had kept secret files on a large number of prominent politicians, including Jack Straw, the Home Secretary, and Peter Mandelson, the Minister without Portfolio, as well as other politicians, trade unionists and journalists.

29.   Mo Mowlam, the Secretary of State for Northern Ireland, announced that the conditions had been met for the inclusion of Sinn Féin in the multi-party talks on the future of Northern Ireland which were scheduled to resume on 15 September.

31.   Diana, Princess of Wales, died aged 36 in the early hours of the morning from injuries sustained in a car crash in Paris. Campaigning in the Welsh and Scottish referendum campaigns was suspended.

SEPTEMBER

4.   The Royal Family returned from Balmoral and the Queen broadcast to the nation.

6.   The funeral of the Princess of Wales took place at Westminster Abbey. During the funeral service, the Princess's brother, Earl Spencer, delivered a tribute to his sister in which he attacked the press for hounding her. He also said that her blood family would ensure that her sons were raised as she would have wanted. After the funeral, a minute's silence was observed throughout Britain. The Princess was later buried in a private ceremony in the grounds of the Spencer family estate at Althorp in Northamptonshire.

8.   The annual Trades Union Congress (TUC) conference opened in Brighton.

9.   Sinn Féin leaders agreed to abide by the Mitchell principles of democracy and non-violence.

11.   A referendum was held in Scotland on the government's plans for devolution. The turnout was 60 per cent, of whom 74.3 per cent voted in favour of a Scottish Parliament and 63.5 per cent in favour of the Parliament having tax-varying powers.

The IRA said it had problems with some of the Mitchell principles. It ruled out any disarmament during talks and it rejected the principle of consent.

12.   The conference of the Green Party opened in Hastings.

15.   Substantive talks on the peace process in Northern Ireland opened at Stormont. None of the unionist or loyalist parties attended.

16.   Prime Minister Tony Blair announced that he would not be taking the £43,000 salary increase to which he was entitled from April 1998.

17.   A referendum was held in Wales on the government's plans for devolution. The turnout was 50 per cent, of whom 50.3 per cent voted in favour of a Welsh Assembly with an annual budget of £7 billion and the task of handling matters currently devolved to the Welsh Office in areas such as education, health, agriculture and planning.

19.   Six people were killed and more than 160 injured when a passenger train crashed into a freight train in Southall, west London. A seventh person died later.

22.   Viscount Tonypandy (George Thomas), Speaker of the House of Commons 1976–83, died aged 88.
        The Liberal Democrats' conference opened in Eastbourne. Party leader Paddy Ashdown claimed that 'I have bigger ambitions for the Liberal Democrats. ... I accept no glass ceilings for this party'.

23.   Unionist, loyalist, nationalist and republican leaders met face-to-face across the negotiating table at Stormont in Belfast. The Unionists argued unsuccessfully that Sinn Féin should be expelled from the talks.

24.   It was agreed at Stormont that the issue of decommissioning terrorist weapons would be dealt with by a new independent commission and that the substantive talks would concentrate upon constitutional issues.
        The Labour Party suspended the party memberships of nine senior members of Glasgow City Council at the centre of 'votes for trips' allegations. The party's national executive committee approved the establishment of a full investigation into the Labour group on the council and the local party in Glasgow.

The Scottish National Party (SNP) conference opened at Rothesay. National convenor Alex Salmond claimed that the SNP had the 'best opportunity in its history' to advance its cause.

25. The chairman of the Press Complaints Commission (Lord Wakeham) put forward proposals for a revised code of practice for newspapers to protect privacy and to prevent intrusive photography.
The Plaid Cymru conference opened in Aberystwyth.

26. The FT-SE index closed at a record high and sterling fell against the Deutschmark after rumours that the government was adopting a more positive approach to economic and monetary union.
The government and the Royal Family agreed to abandon plans to either re-fit or replace the royal yacht *Britannia*.

29. The Labour Party annual conference opened in Brighton. Peter Mandelson, Minister without Portfolio, failed to be elected to the party's national executive committee (NEC). He said that 'a taste of humility is good for everyone'.

30. Tony Blair, in his first speech to the Labour conference as Prime Minister, stated that he wanted to lead 'one of the great, radical, reforming governments of British history'.

OCTOBER

3. A. L. Rowse, historian, poet, authority on Shakespeare's Sonnets and author of more than 90 books, died aged 93.

7. The High Court ruled that the general election result for the Winchester constituency was void and ordered that a fresh election should take place. The result had been contested by the Conservative candidate, Gerry Malone, after he had lost to the Liberal Democrat Mark Oaten by two votes. Malone argued that procedural errors had occurred during the count involving the rejection of 55 votes.
The Conservative Party annual conference opened in Blackpool. Lord Tebbitt attacked 'multiculturalism' in Britain, while William Hague, the Party leader, spoke of 'patriotism without bigotry'.

10. In his leader's speech to the annual Conservative party conference, William Hague attacked the Labour government for lacking a 'moral compass' and for being a government whose very instinct was 'to

boss, meddle, to interfere and to control'.

13.   Tony Blair, the Prime Minister, met Sinn Féin leader Gerry Adams at Stormont in Belfast. It was the first meeting between a British Prime Minister and a Sinn Féin leader since David Lloyd George and Michael Collins signed the Anglo-Irish Treaty of 1921 which formally partitioned Ireland.

14.   Piers Merchant, Conservative MP for Beckenham, was forced to resign following renewed press allegations about his relationship with a former night club hostess. The allegations had first surfaced during the general election campaign but Merchant had retained the support of his local party and his seat.

Tony Blair, the Prime Minister, appointed Keith Hellawell, chief constable of West Yorkshire, as the country's first 'drugs czar'. The task involves advising the government on drug abuse, co-ordinating efforts against drug traffickers and influencing youth attitudes to drugs.

21.   Conservative MPs gathered in Eastbourne for a two-day 'bonding' session designed to create party unity. Former Prime Ministers John Major and Sir Edward Heath were not present; Nicholas Soames refused to attend 'on principle'.

23.   The Shadow Cabinet decided that no matter how successful the single currency might prove to be, the Conservative Party was committed to campaigning against EMU entry at the next election and perhaps beyond. This represented a clear hardening of the 'wait and see' approach adopted under John Major's leadership.

The Combined Loyalist Military Command, the umbrella group which had called the loyalist ceasefire in 1994, was formally disbanded, indicating a growing split between the main loyalist parties in their attitudes towards the multi-party peace talks in Northern Ireland.

25.   Four Labour members of the European Parliament (Ken Coates, Alec Falconer, Hugh Kerr and Michael Hindley) were temporarily suspended from membership of the European Parliamentary Labour Party for defying a new party code of practice forbidding public criticism of party policy.

27.   Gordon Brown, the Chancellor of the Exchequer, made a statement

to the House of Commons setting out the government's position on European economic and monetary union (EMU). Brown insisted that Labour was committed to taking the UK into a successful single European Currency (the euro) but he ruled out the country being in the first wave of those countries joining EMU on 1 January 1999. Brown also made it clear that there would be a referendum after any Cabinet decision to join.

29.   A Conservative spokesman on Northern Ireland, Ian Taylor, resigned from the Opposition front bench, describing the party's decision to commit itself to 'saving sterling' as 'false and dangerous'.

30.   Michael Heseltine attacked the Shadow Cabinet's decision on the single currency. Heseltine said there was going to be a single currency and the only issue was when Britain joined. Heseltine was appointed chairman of the pro-European Conservative Mainstream group, an umbrella group within the Party. Kenneth Clarke, the former Chancellor of the Exchequer, was also involved in the group.

NOVEMBER

5.   Tessa Jowell, Minister for Public Health, announced that the government was seeking an exemption for Formula One motor racing from an EU ban on tobacco advertising in sport. Questions were raised the next day when it emerged that Jowell's husband had been a non-executive director of a Formula One company until earlier in the year.

6.   The Bank of England raised interest rates to 7.25 per cent, a five-year high, provoking stern criticism from the CBI and the British Chambers of Commerce.

In its final report on the 'cash for questions' allegations surrounding former Conservative MP Neil Hamilton, the House of Commons Standards and Privileges Committee concluded that Hamilton's behaviour fell 'seriously and persistently' below the standards expected of MPs. Two Conservative MPs (Ann Widdecombe and Quentin Davies) objected to the decision not to hear further evidence. On 18 November, Widdecombe resigned from the committee, claiming that the committee had denied Hamilton natural justice.

The Paisley South by-election was held, following the suicide of MP Gordon McMaster in July. The Labour Party retained the seat but with a dramatic cut in its majority. The turnout dropped from 57 per cent at the general election to 44 per cent at the by-election.

Sir Isaiah Berlin, philosopher, historian of ideas and liberal thinker, died aged 88.

10.   The Labour Party revealed that it had received a substantial donation from Bernie Ecclestone, President of the Formula One Association, prior to the general election in May. The party refused to specify the amount.

Gordon Brown, the Chancellor of the Exchequer, announced a package of measures designed to prepare business for European economic and monetary union (EMU) in 1999, including allowing businesses to pay taxes and to set up bank accounts in the new currency.

The Confederation of British Industry (CBI) conference opened in Birmingham.

11.   Bernie Ecclestone revealed that he had donated £1 million to the Labour Party in January. Ecclestone insisted that he was not looking for any political favours in return for his money.

The Labour Party admitted that it had a £4.5 million overdraft after spending £27 million in the two years up to the May general election.

13.   The IRA rejected reports of mass resignations from its ranks. It insisted that it was united and committed to the Northern Ireland peace process.

16.   Tony Blair, the Prime Minister, claimed that the government had not been influenced by the donation to the party by Bernie Ecclestone. He insisted that he had done nothing wrong in meeting with Ecclestone on 6 October, a few weeks before the government decided to call for Formula One motor racing to be exempted from the tobacco advertising ban.

19.   The government announced that 500 paratroopers were to be withdrawn from Northern Ireland before the end of November and that daytime army foot patrols were to be ended.

20.   Two by-elections were held. The first, in Beckenham, followed the resignation of MP Piers Merchant. The Conservative Party retained the seat with a reduced majority. The second by-election took place in Winchester as ordered by the High Court in September. The by-election saw the Liberal Democrat Mark Oaten increase his majority

over the Conservative Gerry Malone from two votes to 21,556 votes.

21.   Peter Temple-Morris, a leading pro-European Conservative MP, was
        expelled from the Conservative Parliamentary Party after openly
        opposing the party's policy of not permitting sterling's membership
        of any single European currency for at least ten years. Temple-
        Morris's expulsion was criticized by Michael Heseltine as 'unwise'.

25.   Gordon Brown, the Chancellor of the Exchequer, unveiled plans for
        the biggest reform of the welfare state since its inception. The
        centrepiece was the welfare-to-work scheme, with other plans
        including giving low-income working families tax credits and
        examining the workings of the national insurance system for the low
        paid. The government also intended to embrace anti-pollution taxes
        after the December summit on the environment in Kyoto in Japan.
        Brown also announced that the forthcoming Budget would tackle tax
        avoidance and reform capital gains tax.

DECEMBER

1.   The government established an independent commission to
        recommend alternatives to the present first-past-the-post electoral
        system, chaired by Liberal Democrat peer Lord Jenkins. It also
        promised a referendum on the issue before the next election.

2.   The government's proposals for the new Individual Saving Account
        (ISA) were launched. The new account was intended as the successor
        to PEPs (personal equity plans) and TESSAs (tax-exempt special
        savings accounts) from 1999. The new account was given a £50,000
        ceiling, with the key objective of encouraging more people on low
        incomes to save.

3.   Jack Cunningham, Secretary of State for Agriculture, Fisheries and
        Food, announced a ban on the sale of beef on the bone, with effect
        from 16 December. The ban provoked fury from beef farmers, with
        protests designed to prevent the importing of foreign beef spreading
        to a number of ports.

7.   Geoffrey Robinson, Paymaster General, came under pressure to
        make a detailed statement about his financial interests in relation to
        offshore trusts given the apparent conflict between the Labour
        government's plans to restrict the use of offshore tax avoidance

schemes. He was backed by the Prime Minister.

Woodrow Wyatt, politician, journalist and chairman of the Tote, died aged 79.

10. A total of 47 Labour MPs defied a three-line whip and voted against the government in a vote in the House of Commons to cut lone parents benefits to new claimants. The vote came at the end of a day in which a junior minister resigned over the issue and three parliamentary private secretaries were forced from office.

11. The Prime Minister, Tony Blair, insisted that the government would not be deterred from its policy on welfare reform despite the rebellion by Labour MPs the previous day.

The Prime Minister, Tony Blair, held talks in Downing Street with Gerry Adams and five senior Sinn Féin figures. Blair and Adams had first met in October.

Security at the Maze prison near Belfast came under scrutiny when a republican prisoner, Liam Avril, successfully escaped. Mo Mowlam, Secretary of State for Northern Ireland, immediately ordered an inquiry.

The royal yacht *Britannia* was decommissioned in a ceremony in Portsmouth.

16. Mohammed Sarwar, the suspended Labour MP for Glasgow Govan, appeared in court in Glasgow on charges related to attempts to pervert the course of justice and contravention of the Representation of the Peoples Act in connection with electoral expenses.

19. The High Court ruled that the Westminster district auditor (John Magill) had acted lawfully in May 1996 when ordering that Dame Shirley Porter, former Conservative leader of Westminster City Council and her deputy, David Weeks, should be surcharged for their part in the 'homes for votes' scandal. The court ordered Porter and Weeks to pay a total of £27 million. They were refused leave to appeal against the ruling. The court also cleared three others of wilful misconduct.

The Leader of the Opposition, William Hague, married Ffion Jenkins in a ceremony at the Palace of Westminster. The couple had met during Hague's period as Secretary of State for Wales between 1995 and 1997 when Ms Jenkins was working as a civil servant in the Welsh Office.

21. Protesters chained themselves to the gates of Downing Street and

threw paint onto the street. Twelve disabled people, linked with the Disabled People's Direct Action Network, were arrested during the protest. Rumours had earlier circulated of suggestions by the Department of Social Security that benefits paid to disabled people should be cut.

Tensions within the Cabinet over the welfare cuts surfaced in a leaked memo from the Secretary of State for Education and Employment (David Blunkett) to the Chancellor of the Exchequer, Gordon Brown, in which Blunkett expressed 'grave anxiety' over the possible cuts in disability benefits. Such sentiments were reportedly supported by Deputy Prime Minister John Prescott and Frank Dobson, the Secretary of State for Health.

It emerged that a special Cabinet committee had been established to examine the possibility of replacing the House of Lords with an elected second chamber. This would go beyond Labour's manifesto pledge of removing voting rights from hereditary peers.

22.   Jack Cunningham, Secretary of State for Agriculture, Fisheries and Food, announced an £85 million package of aid to beef and hill farmers in order to help them absorb the cost of the beef export ban, the cost of BSE-related controls and cheap beef imports. He also announced the establishment of an inquiry into the handling of the BSE crisis.

27.   Billy Wright, one of the most notorious loyalist paramilitaries in Northern Ireland, was killed inside the Maze prison outside Belfast, apparently by two Irish National Liberation Army (INLA) gunmen from the roof of one of the prison's H-blocks.

29.   Mo Mowlam, Secretary of State for Northern Ireland, rejected calls for her resignation in the wake of the murder of Billy Wright. She announced the setting up of an inquiry into the incident to be led by the Chief Inspector of Prisons for England and Wales, Sir David Ramsbotham.

2. General Election Results

The following tables summarize the results of the 1997 General Election. The first provides details of all parties for whom votes and vote shares are reproduced here, together with the number of candidates fielded by each party. Thereafter there are figures for the number of votes received by each party, shares of the vote, mean vote share in seats contested, number of seats won and turnout. In each case data are given separately for the United Kingdom as a whole, Great Britain (England, Scotland and Wales), England, Scotland, Wales and Northern Ireland.

All data have been kindly provided by Colin Rallings and Michael Thrasher of the University of Plymouth and can be found, together with further details, in their comprehensive and authoritative compilation, *Britain Votes 6* (Ashgate, 1998).

TABLE 2.1 *Parties, Abbreviations and Candidates Fielded at the 1997 General Election*

Abbrev.	Party	Candidates
APNI	Alliance Party of Northern Ireland	17
BNP	British National Party	57
Conservative	Conservative and Unionist Party	648
DUP	Democratic Unionist Party	9
Green	Green Party	95
Labour	Labour Party	639
LibDem	Liberal Democratic Party	639
Lib	Liberal Party	55
MRLP	Monster Raving Loony Party	24
Nat Dem	National Democrat	21
NLP	Natural Law Party	197
PC	Plaid Cymru	40
PL	Pro-Life	56
Prog U	Progressive Unionist	3
Ref	Referendum Party	547
SDLP	Social Democratic and Labour Party	18
SF	Sinn Fein	17
SL	Socialist Labour	64
SNP	Scottish National Party	72
Soc	Socialist	24
Speaker	Speaker seeking re-election	1
SSA	Scottish Socialist Alliance	16
UKI	UK Independence Party	193
UKU	UK Unionist Party	1
UU	Ulster Unionist Party	16
WP	Workers Party	8

TABLE 2.2 *Number of Votes Gained at the 1997 General Election*

	UK	GB	England	Scotland	Wales	N.Ire.
APNI	62,972	-	-	-	-	62,972
BNP	35,832	35,832	35,181	651	-	-
Conservative 9,858		9,600,943	9,591,085	8,780,881	493,059	317,145
DUP	107,348	-	-	-	-	107,348
Green	63,991	63,452	60,013	1,721	1,718	539
Labour	13,518,167	13,518,167	11,347,882	1,283,350	886,935	-
LibDem	5,242,947	5,242,947	4,677,565	365,362	200,020	-
Lib	45,166	45,166	44,516	650	-	-
MRLP	7,757	7,757	7,553	-	204	-
NatDem	10,829	10,748	10,748	-	-	81
NLP	30,604	28,396	25,958	1,922	516	2,208
PC	161,030	161,030	-	-	161,030	-
PL	19,332	19,332	13,890	5,172	270	-
Prog U	10,928	-	-	-	-	10,928
Ref	811,849	811,849	746,624	26,980	38,245	-
SDLP	190,814	-	-	-	-	190,814
SF	126,921	-	-	-	-	126,921
SL	52,109	52,109	44,114	1,792	6,203	-
SNP	621,550	621,550	-	621,550	-	-
Soc	11,265	11,265	10,317	315	633	-
SSA	9,740	9,740	-	9,740	-	-
UKI	105,722	105,722	103,521	1,585	616	-
UKU	12,817	-	-	-	-	12,817
UU	258,349	-	-	-	-	258,349
WP	2,766	-	-	-	-	2,766
Total	31,286,284	30,495,522	26,058,712	2,816,748	1,620,062	790,762

Note: For details of party names, see Table 2.1.

TABLE 2.3 *Shares of the Vote at the 1997 General Election*

	UK	GB	England	Scotland	Wales	N.Ire.
APNI	0.20	-	-	-	-	7.96
BNP	0.11	0.12	0.14	0.02	-	-
Conservative	31.25	30.69	31.45	33.70	17.50	19.58
DUP	0.34	-	-	-	-	13.58
Green	0.20	0.21	0.23	0.06	0.11	0.07
Labour	43.21	44.33	43.55	45.56	54.75	-
LibDem	16.76	17.19	17.95	12.97	12.35	-
Lib	0.14	0.15	0.17	0.02	-	-
MRLP	0.02	0.03	0.03	-	0.01	-
NatDem	0.03	0.04	0.04	-	-	0.01
NLP	0.10	0.09	0.10	0.07	0.03	0.28
PC	0.51	0.53	-	-	9.94	-
PL	0.06	0.06	0.05	0.18	0.02	-
Prog U	0.03	-	-	-	-	1.38
Ref	2.59	2.66	2.87	0.96	2.36	-
SDLP	0.61	-	-	-	-	24.13
SF	0.41	-	-	-	-	16.05
SL	0.17	0.17	0.17	0.06	0.38	-
SNP	1.99	2.04	-	22.07	-	-
Soc	0.04	0.04	0.04	0.01	0.04	-
SSA	0.03	0.03	-	0.35	-	-
UKI	0.34	0.35	0.40	0.06	0.04	-
UKU	0.04	-	-	-	-	1.62
UU	0.83	-	-	-	-	32.67
WP	0.01	-	-	-	-	0.35

Note: For details of party names, see Table 2.1.

TABLE 2.4 *Mean Vote Share in Contested Seats at the 1997 General Election*

	UK	GB	England	Scotland	Wales	N.Ire.
APNI	9.15	-	-	-	-	9.15
BNP	1.42	1.42	1.47	0.62	-	-
Conservative 3.19		29.85	30.19	32.86	16.68	19.14
DUP	27.48	-	-	-	-	27.48
Green	1.38	1.38	1.43	0.84	1.08	1.30
Labour	45.81	45.81	45.10	46.22	54.43	-
LibDem	16.67	16.67	17.49	13.04	12.41	-
Lib	1.72	1.72	1.76	0.77	-	-
MRLP	0.67	0.67	0.68	-	0.48	-
NatDem	1.23	1.28	1.28	-	-	0.21
NLP	0.32	0.33	0.32	0.39	0.25	0.28
PC	10.61	10.61	-	-	10.61	-
PL	0.78	0.78	0.64	1.55	0.60	-
Prog U	9.40	-	-	-	-	9.40
Ref	3.04	3.04	3.37	1.05	2.73	-
SDLP	22.88	-	-	-	-	22.88
SF	15.94	-	-	-	-	15.94
SL	1.85	1.85	1.75	1.60	3.07	-
SNP	22.04	22.04	-	22.04	-	-
Soc	1.10	1.10	1.20	0.40	0.78	-
SSA	1.84	1.84	-	1.84	-	-
UKI	1.05	1.05	1.09	0.45	0.78	-
UKU	35.06	-	-	-	-	35.06
UU	37.45	-	-	-	-	37.45
WP	0.78	-	-	-	-	0.78

Note: For details of party names, see Table 2.1.

TABLE 2.5 *Seats Won at the 1997 General Election*

	UK	GB	England	Scotland	Wales	N.Ire.
Conservative		165	165	165	-	-
-						
DUP	2	-	-	-	-	2
Labour	418	418	328	56	34	-
LibDem	46	46	34	10	2	-
PC	4	4	-	-	4	-
SDLP	3	-	-	-	-	3
SF	2	-	-	-	-	2
SNP	6	6	-	6	-	-
UKU	1	-	-	-	-	1
UU	10	-	-	-	-	10
Independent		1	1	1	-	-
-						
Speaker	1	1	1	-	-	-
Total	659	641	529	72	40	18

Note: For details of party names, see Table 2.1.

TABLE 2.6 *Turnout at the 1997 General Election (per cent)*

UK	GB	England	Scotland	Wales	N.Ire.
71.4	71.5	71.4	71.3	73.5	67.1

3. Parliamentary By-elections 1997

There were five parliamentary by-elections during 1997 – the 18th and last of the 1992-97 parliament at Wirral South and the first four of the new parliament. These included the very unusual re-run of the general election contest at Winchester which arose from a successful election petition by the Conservative candidate. By-elections are numbered consecutively from the preceding general election.

18. WIRRAL SOUTH 27 February 1997 (Death of Mr. B. Porter)

Result

Candidate	Description	Votes
B. Chapman	Labour	22,767
L. Byrom	Conservative	14,879
F. Lucas	Liberal Democrat	4,357
R. North	UK Independence Party	410
H. Bence	Company Director	184
M. Cullen	Socialist Labour Party	156
P. Gott	Disillusioned Conservative	148
R. Taylor	Independent	132
A. Samuelson	Stop Conservatives Poncing on Tobacco Companies	124
G. Mead	Natural Law Party	52
C. Palmer	21st Century Foresters	44
F. Astbury	Thalidomide Action Group UK	40

Labour Gain from Conservatives: Majority 7,888

Turnout and Major Party Vote Shares (per cent)

	By-election	General Election	Change
Turnout	73.0	82.4	-9.4
Con	34.4	50.8	-16.4
Lab	52.6	34.6	+18.0
Lib Dem	10.1	13.1	-3.0

1. UXBRIDGE 31 July 1997 (Death of Sir M. Shersby)

Result

Candidate	Description	Votes
J. Randall	Conservative	16,288
A. Slaughter	Labour	12,522
K. Kerr	Liberal Democrat	1,792
Lord D. Sutch	Monster Raving Loony	396
J. Leonard	Socialist Party	259
F. Taylor	British National Party	205
I. Anderson	National Democrat	157
J. McCauley	National Front	110
H. Middleton	Original Liberal Party	69
J. Feisenberger	UK Independence Party	39
R. Carroll	Emerald Rainbow Islands Dream Ticket	30

Conservative hold : Majority 3,766

Turnout and Major Party Vote Shares (per cent)

	By-election	General Election	Change
Turnout	55.2	72.3	-17.1
Con	51.1	43.6	+7.5
Lab	39.3	41.8	-2.5
Lib Dem	5.6	10.9	-5.3

2. PAISLEY SOUTH 6 November 1997 (Death of Mr. G. McMaster)

Result

Candidate	Description	Votes
D. Alexander	Labour	10,346
I. Blackford	SNP	7,615
E. McCartin	Liberal Democrat	2,582
S. Laidlaw	Conservative	1,643
J. Deighan	Pro-Life Alliance	578
F. Curran	Scottish Socialist Alliance	306
C. Herriot	Socialist Labour	153
C. McLauchlan	Scottish Independent Labour	135
K. Blair	Natural Law	57

Labour hold : Majority 2,731

Turnout and Major Party Vote Shares (per cent)

	By-election	General Election	Change
Turnout	42.9	69.1	-26.2
Con	7.0	8.7	-1.7
Lab	44.1	57.5	-13.4
Lib Dem	11.0	9.4	+1.6
SNP	32.5	23.4	+9.1

3. BECKENHAM 20 November 1997 (Resignation of Mr. P. Merchant)

Result

Candidate	Description	Votes
J. Lait	Conservative	13,162
R. Hughes	Labour	11,935
R. Vetterllein	Liberal Democrat	5,864
P. Rimmer	Liberal	330
J. McAuley	National Front	267
L. Mead	New Britain Referendum	237
T. Campion	Social Foundation	69
J. Small	Natural Law	44

Conservative hold : Majority 1,227

Turnout and Major Party Vote Shares (per cent)

	By-election	General Election	Change
Turnout	43.7	74.7	-31.0
Con	41.2	42.5	-1.3
Lab	37.4	33.4	+4.0
Lib Dem	18.4	18.1	+0.3

4. WINCHESTER 20 November 1997 (Re-run election ordered by court following appeal by Mr. G. Malone)

Result

Candidate	Description	Votes
M. Oaten	Liberal Democrat	37,006
G. Malone	Conservative	15,450
P. Davies	Labour	955
R. Page	Referendum/UK Independence Alliance	521
Lord David Sutch	Raving Loony	316
R. Huggett	Literal Democrat	59
R. Barry	Natural Law	48
R. Everest	Euro Conservative	40

Liberal Democrat hold : Majority 21,556

Turnout and Major Party Vote Shares (per cent)

	By-election	General Election	Change
Turnout	68.9	78.7	-9.8
Con	28.4	42.1	-13..7
Lab	1.8	10.5	-8.7
Lib Dem	68.0	42.1	+25.9

TABLE 3.1 *Summary of By-election Results 1992–97*

		Change in Share of Vote			
Constituency	Turnout Change	Con	Lab	Lib Dem	SNP/ PC
Newbury	-11.5	-29.0	-4.1	+27.8	
Christchurch	-6.5	-31.5	-9.3	+39.7	
Rotherham	-27.6	-13.9	-8.4	+17.4	
Barking	-31.5	-23.5	+20.5	-2.5	
Bradford S	-31.6	-20.6	+7.7	+10.2	
Dagenham	-33.5	-26.4	+19.7	-3.1	
Eastleigh	-24.0	-26.6	+6.9	+16.3	
Newham NE	-24.9	-15.9	+16.6	-7.0	
Monklands East	-4.9	-13.8	-11.5	-2.0	+26.9
Dudley West	-34.8	-30.1	+28.1	-2.9	
Islwyn	-35.8	-10.9	-5.1	+4.9	+8.8
Perth and Kinross	-14.9	-18.8	+9.7	+0.4	+4.4
North Down	-26.7	-	-	-	
Littleborough & Saddleworth	-17.1	-20.9	+13.6	+2.2	
Hemsworth	-36.4	-9.8	+1.1	-3.6	
Staffordshire SE	-21.7	-22.2	+21.9	-4.9	
Barnsley East	-39.0	-6.9	-0.8	-0.2	
Wirral South	-9.4	-16.4	+18.0	-3.1	

TABLE 3.2 *Summary of By-election Results 1997–*

		Change in Share of Vote			
Constituency	Turnout Change	Con	Lab	Lib Dem	SNP/ PC
Uxbridge	-17.1	+7.5	-2.5	-5.3	
Paisley South	-26.2	-1.7	-13.4	+1.6	+9.1
Beckenham	-31.0	-1.3	+4.0	+0.3	
Winchester	-9.8	-13.7	-8.7	+25.9	

4. Public Opinion Polls 1997

Note: The distinction between 'adjusted' and 'unadjusted' results for voting intentions is becoming increasingly hard to make. NOP and ICM have weighted results – mainly by using previous vote – for some time. Now Gallup also adjust their results using a different technique. Only MORI provides figures as they have been traditionally calculated. Additionally, since the general election ICM have not published their unadjusted figures.

TABLE 4.1 *Voting Intentions (unadjusted) in Major Polls 1997 (per cent)*

Fieldwork	Company	Sample size	Con	Lab	Lib Dem	Other
Jan						
3–5	ICM	1201	29	50	17	4
11–15	Gallup	978	33	51	11	7
16	NOP	1591	31	54	12	3
24–28	MORI	1707	30	55	11	4
Feb						
31/1–2/2	ICM	1199	32	49	15	4
30/1–4/2	Gallup	1008	34	49	12	5
13	NOP	1576	30	49	13	7
21	NOP	1049	29	51	14	6
21–24	MORI	1940	31	52	11	6
Mar						
28/2–3/3	ICM	1201	27	51	15	7
28/2–4/3	Gallup	1000	28	54	13	5
n.a.	Harris	n.a.	32	53	10	5
15–17	Gallup	1045	29	57	10	5
14–17	Harris	1016	29	56	10	5
		General election: see Table 4.3				
June						
29/5–4/6	Gallup	996	23	59	13	5
20–23	MORI	1852	24	58	15	3
July						
2–3	Gallup	1045	23	61	13	3
25–28	MORI	1901	23	57	15	5
Aug						
31/7–6	Gallup	1023	25	58	12	4
21–25	MORI	1758	28	54	15	3
27–3/9	Gallup	1023	26	58	12	5
Sept						
26–29	MORI	1916	25	59	13	3
25–1/10	Gallup	1014	22	60	14	4

TABLE 4.1 (continued) *Voting Intentions (unadjusted) in Major Polls 1997 (per cent)*

Fieldwork	Company	Sample size	Con	Lab	Lib Dem	Other
Oct						
24–27	MORI	1772	24	60	12	4
Nov						
30/10–4	Gallup	1021	23	63	11	4
13–14	MORI	603	30	56	11	3
21–24	MORI	1879	24	56	16	4
27–3/10	Gallup	1011	21	57	17	5
Dec						
12–15	MORI	2122	26	55	15	4

Notes: The figures shown are 'unadjusted' voting intention percentages in that there is no weighting for vote in the 1992 election. Gallup results are normally reported to the nearest 0.5 but all such cases here have been rounded up.

TABLE 4.2 *Voting Intentions (adjusted) in Major Polls 1997 (per cent)*

Fieldwork	Company	Sample size	Con	Lab	Lib Dem	Other
Jan						
3–5	ICM	1201	31	48	16	4
Feb						
31/1–2/2	ICM	1199	32	48	15	4
21	NOP	1049	30	50	14	6
Mar						
28/2–2/3	ICM	1201	30	48	16	6
13	NOP	1596	27	52	13	8
14	NOP	1065	29	54	11	6
General election: see table 4.4						
June						
6–8	ICM	1202	23	62	14	2
27–8	ICM	1200	23	61	12	4
Aug						
8–9	ICM	1211	29	55	12	4
Sept						
5–9	ICM	1208	24	60	10	6
Oct						
6	ICM	1211	23	59	13	4
Nov						
7–8	ICM	1200	30	52	14	4
Dec						
5–6	ICM	1200	29	50	17	4

Note: NOP and ICM adjust their voting intention figures, taking account of past voting, and publish the resulting scores as their 'headline' figures.

TABLE 4.3 *Campaign Polls 1997 (unadjusted per cent)*

Fieldwork	Company	Sample size	Con	Lab	Lib Dem	Other
Mar						
19–21	Gallup	985	29	55	11	6
20–24	Harris	1096	30	54	11	6
21–24	MORI	1932	29	50	14	7
27–31	Harris	1091	28	52	14	6
29–31	ICM	1200	32	46	17	5
26–2/4	Gallup	1121	31	52	14	6
Apr						
1	MORI	1118	28	55	11	6
1–3	Gallup	1035	30	54	11	5
2–3	MORI	1069	30	55	9	6
2–4	ICM	1793	33	48	14	5
3	NOP	1575	28	52	12	8
4	NOP	1088	30	51	11	8
4–6	Gallup	1027	32	53	10	5
4–7	Harris	1138	28	52	14	6
6–7	ICM	1022	`34	46	15	5
7–9	Gallup	1019	30	53	11	6
8	MORI	1114	34	49	12	5
9–11	ICM*	1002	32	48	15	5
9–12	Gallup	1036	33	49	12	5
11	NOP	1595	28	48	17	7
11–14	MORI	1778	29	50	15	6
11–14	Harris	1136	31	49	13	6
12–15	Gallup	1025	30	51	12	6
13–14	ICM	1007	31	45	19	5
15	MORI	1137	32	49	13	6
16–18	ICM	1000	32	47	16	5
16–19	Gallup	1031	31	50	13	7
18	NOP	1595	31	45	17	7
18–21	Harris	1177	30	48	15	7
20–21	ICM	1004	37	42	14	6
20–22	Gallup	1129	30	51	12	7
22	MORI	1133	27	48	17	8
23–25	ICM*	1000	32	47	16	5
23–24	MORI	941	29	53	12	6
24	Gallup	1038	32	48	12	8
24–26	Gallup	1038	31	48	13	7
24–28	Gallup	1466	31	49	14	6
25	NOP	1588	29	47	16	9
26–28	Gallup	1344	29	51	13	6
27–29	Harris	1154	31	48	15	6
29	NOP	1093	28	50	14	8
29–30	MORI	1003	28	48	16	8
29–30	ICM	1555	33	43	18	6
29–30	Gallup	1739	33	47	14	6
Exit Polls						
May						
1	MORI	15761	30	46	18	6
	NOP	17073	29	47	18	6

Notes: The figures shown are unadjusted voting intention percentages after the exclusion of respondents who did not indicate a party preference. Gallup results are normally reported to the nearest 0.5 but all such cases here have been rounded up. * = panel survey.

TABLE 4.4 *Campaign Polls 1997 (adjusted per cent)*

Fieldwork	Company	Sample size	Con	Lab	Lib Dem	Other
Mar						
29–31	ICM	1200	32	46	17	5
Apr						
2–4	ICM	1793	33	48	14	5
3	NOP	1575	28	52	12	3
4	NOP	1088	30	51	11	8
6–7	ICM	1022	34	46	15	5
9–11	ICM*	1002	32	48	15	5
11	NOP	1595	33	49	12	5
13–14	ICM	1007	30	45	18	6
16–18	ICM	1000	32	47	16	5
18	NOP	1595	31	45	17	7
20–21	ICM	1004	37	42	14	6
23–25	ICM*	1000	32	47	16	5
25	NOP	1588	29	47	16	9
29	NOP	1093	28	50	14	8
29–30	ICM	1555	33	43	18	5

Note: * = panel survey

TABLE 4.5 *Voting Intentions in Scotland 1997 (per cent)*

	Con	Lab	Lib Dem	SNP
Jan	16	51	9	24
Feb	16	46	10	26
Mar (early)	17	52	9	20
Mar (late)	12	53	9	26
Apr	14	49	11	24
May	9	57	10	23
Jun	12	54	10	23
Jul	10	54	9	24
Aug	14	50	11	25
Sep	13	55	9	23
Oct	14	55	8	22
Nov	12	51	12	24

Note: System Three do not poll in December but have separate polls in early and late January. The January figure shown is the average of the two January polls. Rows do not total 100 because 'others' are not shown. In 1997 System Three also had two polls in March.

Source: System Three Scotland polls, published monthly in *The Herald* (Glasgow).

TABLE 4.6 *Monthly Averages for Voting Intentions 1997 (per cent)*

	Con	Lab	Lib Dem		Con	Lab	Lib Dem
Jan	31	53	13	Jul	23	59	14
Feb	31	50	13	Aug	26	55	13
Mar	29	54	12	Sep	24	60	14
Apr	-	-	-	Oct	24	60	12
May	-	-	-	Nov	25	58	14
Jun	24	59	14	Dec	26	55	15

Note: These are the simple means of unadjusted voting intentions.

TABLE 4.7 *Ratings of Party Leaders 1997*

	Major			Blair			Ashdown		
	Pos	Neg	Net	Pos	Neg	Net	Pos	Neg	Net
Jan	36	62	-26	67	26	+41	70	23	+47
Feb	36	59	-23	67	25	+42	63	23	+40
Mar	33	63	-30	67	21	+46	66	21	+45
Apr	33	60	-27	70	19	+51	67	18	+49
May									
Jun		Hague		82	10	+72	73	14	+59
Jul	40	37	+3	83	13	+70	76	16	+60
Aug	40	40	0	83	13	+70	74	18	+56
Sep	39	41	-2	76	20	+56	68	23	+45
Oct	20	60	-40	83	12	+71	76	15	+61
Nov	25	58	-33	78	17	+61	73	17	+56
Dec	24	60	-36	74	22	+52	79	13	+66

Notes: The figures are based on responses to the questions 'Are you satisfied or dissatisfied with Mr Major (Mr Blair) as Prime Minister?'; 'Do you think that Mr Blair (Mr Hague) is or is not proving (will or will not prove) a good leader of the Labour (Conservative) party?'; 'Do you think that Mr Ashdown is or is not proving a good leader of the Liberal Democratic Party?'. The difference between 100 and the sum of positive and negative responses is the percentage of respondents who replied 'Don't know'.

Source: Gallup Political and Economic Index

TABLE 4.8 *Best Person for Prime Minister 1997 (per cent)*

	Major/Hague	Blair	Ashdown	Don't know
Jan	28	39	14	19
Feb	28	39	13	20
Mar	25	41	12	22
Apr		Hague		
May	10	62	13	14
Jun				
Jul	11	61	15	14
Aug	11	59	15	15
Sep	12	63	13	11
Oct	8	67	11	14
Nov	8	60	15	16
Dec	8	59	16	17

Source: Gallup Political and Economic Index. The data are derived from the 'Gallup 9,000', which is an aggregation of all Gallup's polls in the month concerned.

TABLE 4.9 *Approval/Disapproval of Government Record 1997 (per cent)*

	Approve	Disapprove	Don't know	Approve–Disapprove
Jan	24	65	11	-41
Feb	26	63	11	-37
Mar	26	64	11	-38
Apr		General election		
May	76	13	11	+63
Jun	72	13	15	+59
Jul	68	22	11	+46
Aug	63	27	10	+36
Sep	71	18	12	+53
Oct	70	20	11	+50
Nov	61	27	12	+34
Dec	54	36	10	+18

Notes: These are answers to the question 'Do you approve or disapprove of the government's record to date?'. The data are derived from the 'Gallup 9,000'.
Source: Gallup Political and Economic Index.

TABLE 4.10 *Personal Prospective Economic Evaluations 1997*

	Get a lot better	Get a little better	Stay the same	Get a little worse	Get a lot worse
Jan	4	19	49	18	5
Feb	6	17	48	20	4
Mar	5	21	46	15	6
Apr	–	–	–	–	–
May	5	24	43	17	4
Jun	5	21	42	21	6
Jul	3	18	40	26	8
Aug	4	17	40	25	10
Sep	4	20	43	21	7
Oct	4	18	46	19	7
Nov	3	18	45	22	7
Dec	4	16	40	24	12

Notes: These data are based on the 'Gallup 9,000' and derive from answers to the question 'How do you think the financial situation of your household will change over the next 12 months?' Gallup no longer ask about personal retrospective evaluations (financial situation of the household over the last 12 months) or national evaluations (the general economic situation). Rows do not total 100 because 'don't knows' are not shown.
Source: Gallup Political and Economic Index.

TABLE 4.11 *Best Party to Handle Economic Difficulties 1997*

	Conservative	Labour	No difference	Don't know
Jan	36	45	9	10
Feb	38	47	6	9
Mar	35	49	6	10
Apr		General election		
May	28	58	5	10
Jun	34	54	5	8
Jul	30	58	4	8
Aug	33	55	5	8
Sep	27	61	4	8
Oct	27	61	4	8
Nov	28	58	6	8
Dec	29	55	8	8

Note: These are answers to the question 'With Britain in economic difficulties, which party do you think could handle the problem best – the Conservatives or Labour?' The figures are derived from the 'Gallup 9,000'.
Source: Gallup Political and Economic Index.

5. Local Elections 1997

Local elections in Britain are valuable indicators of the state of public opinion, have important effects on the morale of party workers and determine political control of local authorities. For these reasons the annual rounds of local elections attract increasing attention in the media, but interpretation of the results is complicated by the fact that the various authorities have different election cycles. Indeed, even keeping track of election cycles is currently not an easy task as piecemeal changes are being made to the structure of local government in England. A summary of the different types of authority that now make up the British local government system and their electoral cycles is as follows:

England
Counties (34)
All members are elected every four years. Elections were held in 1997 (on the same day as the general election) and the next round of elections is due in 2001.

Metropolitan Boroughs (36)
One-third of members are elected annually except in those years when there are county elections. Next elections are due in 1998.

Shire Districts with 'annual' elections (88)
Approximately one-third of members are elected annually except in those years when there are county elections. Next elections are due in 1998.

Shire Districts with 'all in' elections (150)
All members are elected every four years mid-way between county elections. Next elections are due in 1999.

London Boroughs (32)
All members are elected in another four-year cycle. Next elections are due in 1998.

Unitary Authorities (46)
'Shadow' authorities were elected in 1995, 1996 and 1997. The subsequent election cycle varies.

Scotland
Unitary Councils (32)
All members were elected in 1995 and the next elections will be in 1999.

Wales
Unitary Authorities (22)
All members were elected in 1995 and the next elections will be in 1999.

In 1997 there were no local elections in Scotland, Wales or London. There were elections for the 34 counties in England and partial elections for two established unitary authorities (Bristol and Hull). In addition, in 19 areas there were elections for 'shadow' unitary authorities which were to assume responsibility in April 1998. These were Blackburn, Blackpool, Bracknell Forest, Halton, Hereford, Medway Towns, Newbury, Nottingham, Peterborough, Plymouth, Reading, Slough, Southend, The Wrekin, Thurrock, Torbay, Warrington, Windsor and Wokingham. Also, in a departure from the normal cycle, a shire district council (Malvern Hills) was elected in its entirety due to an extensive boundary revision.

Election watchers in Britain owe a large debt of gratitude to Colin Rallings and Michael Thrasher whose indefatigable work in collecting and publishing authoritative local election results has smoothed the paths of many others. They have supplied the data presented in the following tables. Full details of the 1997 results, including individual ward results and commentary, can be found in their *Local Elections Handbook 1997* (Local Government Chronicle Elections Centre, University of Plymouth), obtainable from LGC Communications, 33–39 Bowling Green Lane, London EC1R 0DA.

TABLE 5.1 *Summary of 1997 Local Election Results*

	Candidates	Seats won	% Share of vote
Shire Counties (34)			
Turnout 73.2%			
Con	2051	873	36.9
Lab	2134	745	32.2
Lib Dem	1922	495	26.8
Other	707	90	4.1
Unitary Authorities (21)			
Turnout 69.7%			
Con	882	233	31.3
Lab	1011	549	40.2
Lib Dem	688	229	23.5
Other	232	33	5.0

Note: It is impossible to calculate gains and losses of seats due to extensive boundary changes.
Source: C. Rallings and M. Thrasher.

TABLE 5.2 *Monthly Party Vote Shares in Local Government By-elections 1997 (per cent)*

	Con	Lab	Lib Dem	Others	Number of Wards
Jan	23.8	27.5	46.7	2.0	9
Feb	29.4	29.7	33.5	7.4	18
Mar	31.7	48.0	16.6	3.7	16
Apr	28.1	38.9	28.1	4.9	14
May	27.4	47.9	21.1	3.6	56
Jun	30.8	40.6	27.6	1.0	16
Jul	29.6	43.2	24.0	3.2	54
Aug	35.0	44.0	18.7	2.3	14
Sep	28.9	34.8	28.9	7.4	38
Oct	27.5	44.2	19.2	9.1	37
Nov	32.3	37.2	25.6	4.9	25
Dec	32.4	38.7	24.1	4.8	14

Note: These figures relate to the results of local government by-elections in wards and electoral divisions contested by all three major parties.
Source: C. Rallings and M. Thrasher.

TABLE 5.3 *Quarterly Party Vote Shares in Local Government By-elections 1997 (per cent)*

	Con	Lab	Lib Dem	Others	Number of wards
Q1	28.9	36.3	30.3	4.5	43
Q2	27.7	46.6	22.2	3.5	86
Q3	30.2	40.1	25.1	4.6	106
Q4	30.0	40.8	22.3	6.9	76

Note: These figures relate to the results of local government by-elections in wards and electoral divisions contested by all three major parties.
Source: C. Rallings and M. Thrasher.

TABLE 5.4 *Seats Won and Lost in Local Government By-elections 1997*

	Con	Lab	Lib Dem	Others
Held	45	209	54	19
Lost	13	49	42	40
Gained	66	25	37	16
Net	+53	-24	-5	-24

Source: C. Rallings and M. Thrasher.

6. Economic Indicators

TABLE 6.1 *Unemployment, Retail Price Index, Inflation, Tax and Price Index, Interest Rates, Sterling Exchange Rate Index, Balance of Payments (Goods), Terms of Trade Index*

	UN	RPI	INF	TPI	%TPI	IR	SI	BP	TOFT
1993	10.3	140.7	1.6	131.4	1.2	5.50	88.9	-13,460	103.5
1994	9.3	144.1	2.4	135.2	2.9	6.25	89.2	-10,831	102.2
1995	8.2	149.1	3.5	140.4	3.8	6.50	84.2	-11,628	98.9
1996	7.5	152.7	2.4	142.4	1.4	6.00	86.3	-12,657	100.0
1997									
Jan	6.5	154.4	2.8	143.6	1.4	6.00	95.9	-742	101.6
Feb	6.2	155.0	2.7	144.2	1.3	6.00	97.4	-1,030	101.6
Mar	6.1	155.4	2.6	144.6	1.1	6.00	97.4	-1,015	101.5
Apr	5.9	156.3	2.4	143.8	1.5	6.00	99.5	-1,062	101.4
May	5.8	156.9	2.6	144.4	1.7	6.25	99.0	-858	101.3
Jun	5.7	157.5	2.9	145.0	2.0	6.50	100.4	-1,206	101.3
Jul	5.5	157.5	3.3	145.0	2.5	6.75	104.5	-686	101.3
Aug	5.3	158.5	3.5	146.0	2.7	7.00	102.5	-874	101.3
Sep	5.2	159.3	3.6	146.9	2.7	7.00	100.4	-1,284	101.7
Oct	5.2	159.5	3.7	147.1	2.9	7.00	101.1	-1,349	101.8
Nov	5.1	159.6	3.7	147.2	2.9	7.25	103.8	-1,576	101.9
Dec	5.0	160.0	3.6	147.6	2.8	7.25	104.4	-1,297	101.2

Notes: **UN** = Unemployment. Seasonly adjusted percentage of the workforce defined as unemployed. The current definition is used to estimate the whole series. **RPI** = Retail Price Index. All Items. January 1987=100. **INF** = Inflation rate and is the percentage increase in the RPI compared with the same month in the previous year. **TPI** = Tax & Price Index. 1987=100. **%TPI** = Percentage increase in the TPI compared with the same month in the previous year. **IR** = Interest rates based upon selected retail banks' base rates. **SI** = Sterling Exchange Rate Index. Compares the value of sterling with a range of other currencies. 1990=100. **BP** = Balance of Payments (goods) in £millions. **TOFT** = Terms of Trade Index. Price Index of exports as a percentage of the price index of imports.

Sources: Office for National Statistics – *Economic Trends, Monthly Digest of Statistics*

TABLE 6.2 *Gross Domestic Product, Real Personal Disposable Income Index, House Price Index*

	GDP	RPDI	HOUSE
1993	99.6	103.8	100.0
1994	103.5	105.1	102.5
1995	106.2	108.5	103.2
1996	109.6	112.3	106.9
1997			
Q1	111.8	113.7	111.9
Q2	113.0	118.5	114.2
Q3	113.9	116.9	120.0
Q4	114.5	119.0	119.1

Notes: **GDP** = Gross Domestic Product at factor cost, 1990=100. **RPDI** = Real Personal Disposable Income, 1990=100. **HOUSE** = Index of House Prices for all dwellings, 1993=100.

Source: Office for National Statistics – *Economic Trends*

7. Political Parties

THE CONSERVATIVE PARTY

Main Addresses
Conservative and Unionist Central Office
32 Smith Square
Westminster
London SW1P 3HH
Tel: 0171-222-9000
Fax: 0171-222-1135
http://www.conservative-party.org.uk

Scottish Conservative and Unionist Central Office
Suite 1/1
14 Links Place
Edinburgh EH6 7EZ
Tel: 0131-555-2900
Fax: 0131-555-2869

Other Addresses
Conservative Research Department
32 Smith Square
Westminster
London SW1P 3HH
Tel: 0171-222-9000
Fax: 0171-233-2065
Director: Daniel Finkelstein
Deputy Directors: Michael Simmonds

Conservative Political Centre
32 Smith Square
Westminster
London SW1P 3HH
Tel: 0171-222-9000
Fax: 0171-233-2065
Director: Michael Simmonds

National Union of Conservative and Unionist Associations
32 Smith Square
Westminster
London SW1P 3HH
Secretary: Chris Poole
Tel: 0171-222-9000
Fax: 0171-222-1135

One Nation Forum
32 Smith Square
Westminster
London SW1P 3HH
Tel: 0171-222-9000
Fax: 0171-222-1135
Chairman: Sir Neil Thorne

Board of Management

Lord Parkinson
Lord Bowness
Malcolm Chaplain
Sir Anthony Garrett
Sir Archie Hamilton
Robin Hodgson

Edward Macmillan-Scott
Graham Park
Lord Sheppard of Didgemere
John Taylor
Michael Trend
David Peniket

Officers

Party Chairman	Lord Parkinson
Deputy Chairman	Michael Trend
Vice Chairmen	Archie Norman (Party Reform)
	Peta Buscombe (Women)
	Alan Duncan (Communications)
	Christopher Chope (Local Government)
Chairman of the Party in Scotland	Raymond Robertson

Staff

Directors

Research	Daniel Finkelstein
Political Operations	Andrew Cooper
Fundraising/Treasurers	Tim Cowell
Campaigning	Sir Anthony Garrett
Finance (Acting Director)	David Peniket
Membership and Marketing	Stephen Gilbert

National Union Advisory Committees
Conservative Women's National Committee
Chairman: Caroline Abel Smith
Secretary: Mary Shaw

Young Conservatives' National Advisory Committee
Chairman: Andrew Griffiths

Conservative Trade Unionists' National Committee
Chairman: Derek Beard
Secretary: Susan Bray

National Local Government Advisory Committee
Chairman: Paul White
Secretary: David Trowbridge

Conservative Political Centre National Advisory Committee
Chairman: Graham Postles
Secretary: Alistair Cooke, Michael Simmonds

Association of Conservative Clubs
Chairman: Sir Marcus Fox
Secretary: Ken Hargreaves

Contest for the Leadership of the Conservative Party, 1997

Ballots of MPs

	Round 1 10 June	Round 2 17 June	Round 3 19 June
William Hague	41	62	92
Kenneth Clarke	49	64	70
John Redwood	27	38	
Peter Lilley	24		
Michael Howard	23		

The National Union undertook a process of consultation within the party, the results of which were presented to the 1922 Committee before each of the three rounds of the leadership contest.

	Conservative and Unionist Peers	MEPs	Chairmen, England, Wales and N. Ireland Constituencies	Chairmen and Area Chairmen Scotland	NU Executive and European Constituency Chairmen
Round One					
Kenneth Clarke	177	17	269	53	92
William Hague	45	0	178	10	45
Michael Howard	10	0	10	0	6
Peter Lilley	37	0	20	2	25
John Redwood	13	0	25	0	11
Turnout (%)	61.3	100.0	87.3	83.3	83.0
Round Two					
Kenneth Clarke	152	17	242	44	88
William Hague	59	0	223	15	70
John Redwood	20	0	28	2	16
Turnout (%)	50.2	100.0	85.1	79.4	80.2
Round Three					
Kenneth Clarke	145	17	235	43	111
William Hague	32	0	194	12	54
Turnout (%)	38.5	100.0	74.6	70.5	75.6

Source: The National Union.

THE LABOUR PARTY

Address
The Labour Party
Millbank Tower
Millbank
London
SW1P 4GT
Tel: 0171-802-1000
Fax: 0171-802-1234
http://www.labour.org.uk

Information
Tel: 0171-802-1212
Fax: 0171-802-1555

Officers and Staff

Leader	Tony Blair
Deputy Leader	John Prescott
General Secretary	Tom Sawyer
European Coordinator	Larry Whitty
Chief Party Spokesperson	David Hill
Election Campaigning	Peter Mandelson
Organization and Development	David Gardner
Policy	Matthew Taylor
Finance	David Pitt-Watson
Parliamentary Labour Party Secretary	Alan Haworth
Computers	Lesley Haswell
Women's Officer	Meg Russell
Senior Development Officer	Carol Linforth

National Executive Committee 1997–98

Chair	Richard Rosser
Vice-Chair	Clare Short
Treasurer	Margaret Prosser
Ex Officio Members	Tony Blair, John Prescott

Division 1 – Trade Unions

John Allen (AEU)
Derek Hodgson (CWU)
Maggie Jones (UNISON)
Frank Murphy (USDAW)
Richard Rosser (TSSA)
Margaret Wall (MSF)

Vernon Hince (RMT)
Diana Holland (TGWU)
John Mitchell (GMPU)
Steve Pickering (GMB)
Mary Turner (GMB)
Christine Wilde (UNISON)

Division 2 – Socialist, Co-operative and Other Organizations
Ian McCartney (Labour Clubs)

Division 3 – Constituency Labour Parties

Diane Abbott
Robin Cook
Ken Livingstone
Dennis Skinner

David Blunkett
Harriet Harman
Mo Mowlem

Division 4 – Women Members

Hilary Armstrong
Brenda Etchells
Clare Short

Margaret Beckett
Diana Jeuda

Youth Representative
Sarah Ward

Result of Elections to National Executive Committee 1997–98

Names asterisked were elected. Figures for 1996–7 are shown in brackets if applicable.

Trade Unions (Twelve places of which four must be women)

* Vernon Hince	3,405,000	(3,199,000)
* John Mitchell	3,390,000	(3,577,000)
* Diana Holland	3,385,000	(3,578,000)
* Mary Turner	3,384,000	(3,599,000)
* Maggie Jones	3,365,000	(3,556,000)
* Derek Hodgson	3,333,000	
* Frank Murphy	3,313,000	
* Margaret Wall	3,310,000	(3,519,000)
* Steve Pickering	3,299,000	(3,454,000)
* John Allen	3,263,000	(3,489,000)
* Richard Rosser	2,285,000	(2,842,000)
* Christine Wilde	2,770,000	(2,588,000)
Mike Leahy	1,061,000	(1,413,000)
Steve Kemp	174,000	(175,000)

Socialist, Co-operative and Other Organizations (One place)
* Ian McCartney   Unopposed   (35,000)

Constituency Labour Parties (Seven places of which three must be women.)

* Robin Cook	118,726	(109,801)	Alice Mahon	48,395	(32,462)
* David Blunkett	106,601	(94,096)	Lynette Jones	40,341	(31,353)
* Mo Mowlem	105,717	(68,271)	Jeremy Corbyn	39,565	(25,529)
* Dennis Skinner	100,268	(73,390)	Jean Bishop	26,802	(21,160)
* Ken Livingstone	83,669	(58,593)	Mary Hughes	26,743	
* Harriet Harman	80,498	(58,112)	Alan Simpson	25,940	(18,125)
* Diane Abbott	76,772	(54,800)	Marilyn Davis	14,782	
Peter Mandleson	68,023		Steve Merritt	14,158	
Peter Hain	65,816	(42,169)	David Brinton	13,208	

Women Members (Five places. Result announced in percentage terms)

* Margaret Beckett	20.71	(20.82)
* Clare Short	19.92	(18.64)
* Hilary Armstrong	18.60	(16.49)
* Diana Jeuda	16.78	(16.73)
* Brenda Etchells	16.54	(15.67)
Christine Shawcroft	7.44	(6.61)

Result of Elections to Constitutional Committee 1997–98
Names asterisked were elected.

Division 1 – Trade Unions
* Anne Gibson (MSF)	Elected Unopposed
* Derek Install (GPMU)	Elected Unopposed

Division 2 – Socialist Societies
No election this year

Division 3 – Constituency Labour Parties (%)
* Judith Blake	28.59
Emlyn Jenkins	24.68
W.D. Nock	24.60
Shirley Gadson	22.13

Division 4 – Women
* Dianne Haytor	Elected Unopposed

The Parliamentary Labour Party's Parliamentary Committee

4 officers of the PLP (ex officio)
Leader	Tony Blair
Deputy Leader	John Prescott
Chief Whip	Nick Brown
Chair	Clive Soley

6 elected Commons backbenchers
Jean Corston (Deputy Chair)
Charlotte Atkins
Sylvia Heal
Ann Clwyd
Chris Mullin
Llin Golding

4 ministers appointed by the PM
Ann Taylor	Leader of the House of Commons (ex officio)
Mo Mowlam	Secretary of State for Northern Ireland
Frank Dobson	Secretary of State for Health
Baroness Jay of Paddington	Minister of State for Health and Deputy Leader of the House of Lords

1 elected Lords backbencher
Lord Williams of Elvel

Formal right of attendance

Chief Whip in the House of Lords	Lord Carter
General Secretary of the Party	Tom Sawyer

The secretary of the committee is the secretary of the PLP, Alan Howarth (not the MP). The committee meets every week when the House is sitting, at 4.30pm on a Wednesday afternoon.

Parliamentary Committee Elections

Candidates elected

Jean Corston	165
Sylvia Heal	136
Ann Clwyd	116
Charlotte Atkins	109
Chris Mullin	105
Llin Golding	86

Candidates not elected

Robin Corbett	84
Ernie Ross	83
Andrew Mackinlay	67
Roger Stott	66
Roger Berry	59
Stuart Bell	52
Lynne Jones	52
Paul Flynn	50
Ken Livingstone	49
Terry Rooney	45
Alan Keen	37
Geraint Davies	33
John Marek	32
Lawrie Quinn	32
Jeremy Corbyn	31
Martyn Jones	21

A total of 330 MPs were eligible to vote; 281 ballot papers were issued; and 281 were returned, of which seven were spoilt. MPs had up to six votes, and had to vote for at least three women.

THE LIBERAL DEMOCRATS

Addresses
The Liberal Democrats
Party Headquarters
4 Cowley Street
London SW1P 3NB
Tel: 0171-222-7999
Fax: 0171-799-2170
http://www.libdems.org.uk

Scottish Liberal Democrats
4 Clifton Terrace
Edinburgh EH12 5DR
Tel: 0131-337-2314
Fax: 0131-337-3566

Welsh Liberal Democrats
57 St Mary Street
Cardiff CF1 1FE
Tel: 01222-382210
Fax: 01222-222864

Associated Organizations
Association of Liberal Democrat Councillors
President: William Le Breton
Chair: Sarah Boad
Tel: 01422-843785
Fax: 01422-843036

Association of Liberal Democrat Trade Unionists
President: Tudor Gates
Chair: Michael Smart
Tel: 01375-850881

Youth and Student Liberal Democrats
Chair: Ruth Berry
Tel: 0171-222-7999 ext. 587/8

Women Liberal Democrats
President: Diana Maddock
Chair: Justine McGuinness
Tel: 0171-222-7999 ext. 408

Ethnic Minority Liberal Democrats
Chair: To be elected
Tel: 0181-870-5348

Party Officers

Party Leader	Paddy Ashdown
President	Robert Maclennan
Vice-Presidents	Andrew Duff (England)
	Marilyne MacLaren (Scotland)
	Rev. Roger Roberts (Wales)
Chair of Finance	Tim Clement-Jones
Treasurer	Tim Razzall

Scottish Party

Leader	Jim Wallace
President	Roy Thomson
Convenor	Marilyne MacLaren
Chief Executive	Willie Rennie

Welsh Party

Leader	Richard Livsey
President	Lord Thomas of Gresford
Administrator	Judi Lewis

Federal Party Staff

Chief Executive	Elizabeth Pamplin
Press Officer	Elizabeth Johnson
Campaigns and Elections Director	Chris Rennard
Candidates Officer	Sandra Dunk
Policy Director	David Laws
Policy Officers	Christian Moon, Candida Goulden
International Officer	Kishwer Khan
Finance	Ken Loughlin, Steve Sollitt
Head of Membership Services	Keith House
Membership Finance Co-ordinator	Helen Sharman
Conference Organizer	Penny McCormack
Liberal Democrat News Editor	David Boyle

OTHER PARTIES

Scottish National Party (SNP)
6 North Charlotte Street
Edinburgh EH2 4JH
Tel: 0131-226-3661
Fax: 0131-226-7373
http://www.snp.org.uk
President: Winifred Ewing
National Convenor: Alex Salmond
Parliamentary Leader: Margaret Ewing
National Secretary: Colin Campbell
Director of Organisation: Alison Hunter
Communications and Research: Kevin Pringle
Chief Executive: Michael Russell

Plaid Cymru (PC)
18 Park Grove
Cardiff CF1 3BN
Tel: 01222-646000
Fax: 01222-646001
http://www.plaid-cymru.wales.com
President: Dafydd Wigley
Chief Executive: Karl Davies
Chair: Marc Phillips
Chief Whip: Elfyn Lloyd

Green Party
1a Waterlow Road
Archway
London N19 5NJ
Tel: 0171-272-4474
Fax: 0171-272-6653
http://gnew.gn.apc.org/greenparty
Chair: Jenny Jones
Press Officer: Peter Barnett

The Liberal Party
1a Pine Grove
Southport
Lancashire
PR9 9AQ
Tel: 01704-500115
Fax: 01704-539315
http://www.libparty.demon.co.uk
President: Michael Meadowcroft
Chair of National Executive: David Morrish
Secretary General: Nigel Ashton

Natural Law Party
Mentmore Towers
Mentmore
Buckinghamshire
LU7 0QH
Tel: 01296 662211
Fax: 01296 662486
http://www.natural-law-party.org.uk

Socialist Labour Party
9 Victoria Road
Barnsley
South Yorkshire
S70 2BB
Tel/Fax: 01226 770957
http://www.ifley.demon.co.uk/index.html

NORTHERN IRELAND

Ulster Unionist Party
3 Glengall Street
Belfast BT12 5AE
Tel: 01232-324601
Fax: 01232-246738
http://www.uup.org
Leader: David Trimble
Party Chairman: Dennis Rogan
Party Secretary: Jim Wilson

Democratic Unionist Party
91 Dundela Avenue
Belfast BT4 3BU
Tel: 01232-471155
Fax: 01232-471797
http://www.dup.org.uk
Leader: Ian Paisley
Deputy Leader: Peter Robinson
Party Chairman: James McClure
Party Secretary: Nigel Dodds
Press Officer: Samuel Wilson
General Secretary: Allan Ewart
Treasurer: Gregory Campbell

Social Democratic and Labour Party (SDLP)
121 Ormeau Road
Belfast BT7 1SH
Tel: 01232-247700
Fax: 01232-236699
http://www.sdlp.ie/sdlp
Leader: John Hume
Deputy Leader: Seamus Mallon
Party Chairman: Jonathan Stephenson
General Secretary: Gerry Cosgrove

Alliance Party
88 University Street
Belfast BT7 1HE
Tel: 01232-324274
Fax: 01232-333147
http://www.unite.net/customers/alliance
Leader: Lord John Alderdice
Party Chairman: Eileen Bell
General Secretary: David Ford
President: Addie Morrow

Sinn Féin
Belfast Headquarters
51-55 Falls Road
Belfast BT13
Tel: 01232-323214
Fax: 01232-231723

Dublin Office
44 Cearnóg Pharnell (Parnell Square)
Dublin 1
Republic of Ireland
Tel: (00) 3531-8726932/ 8726100
Fax: (00) 3531-8733441
http://www.sinnfein.ie/index.html
President: Gerry Adams
Vice-President: Pat Doherty
General Secretary: Lucilita Bhreatnach
National Chairperson: Mitchel McLaughlin
Six County Chairperson: Gearóid O hÉara
Director of Publicity: Rita O'Hare

8. National Newspapers

TABLE 6.1 *Circulation of National Newspapers*

Average net circulation

Newspaper	Jul 97– Dec 97	Jul 96– Dec 96	Jul 95– Dec 95
Sun	3,779,605	3,980,808	4,027,850
Daily Mirror/Daily Record	3,009,148	3,124,454	3,281,620
Daily Mail	2,237,949	2,090,803	1,876,011
Daily Express	1,202,291	1,195,069	1,261,977
Daily Telegraph	1,098,440	1,084,440	1,052,928
Times	792,151	790,857	668,756
Daily Star	619,553	671,494	663,048
Guardian	403,999	396,800	395,135
Financial Times	328,793	296,834	295,740
Independent	260,223	265,037	292,827
London Evening Standard	449,020	435,028	441,287
News of the World	4,425,708	4,505,632	4,690,563
Sunday Mirror	2,276,089	2,437,662	2,534,566
Mail on Sunday	2,219,430	2,105,566	2,040,758
The People	1,895,121	2,049,509	2,092,056
Sunday Times	1,343,324	1,325,021	1,252,774
Sunday Express	1,140,328	1,177,094	1,362,974
Sunday Telegraph	887,204	776,231	674,031
Observer	439,573	453,353	463,301
Independent on Sunday	287,543	287,282	326,675
Sunday Sport	275,246	259,366	289,702

Source: Audit Bureau of Circulations

NOTES FOR CONTRIBUTORS

The article should be submitted on hard copy and disk, accompanied by a brief abstract (c.150 words) and biographical notes, each in a separate file. All pages of the manuscript should be numbered, including those containing figures. The accuracy of the references is the sole responsibility of the author (follow Style Notes below).

FORMAT

Files should be saved in Rich Text Format, named for the author (Jones.rtf). The disk should be labelled with the name of the article, the author's name and the software system used (ideally IBM compatible).

Tables: Set page width to 108mm. Place table in the **text approximate position,** placing a page break at the top and tail: there is no need to include such guidance as '[INSERT TABLE 2 ABOUT HERE]'. **Do not use the 'Table' function** in the word processing package as this causes difficulties at production stage. Instead, use the tab function, as follows: set tabs for columns; align by decimal point; centre column headings. Set the font size of the table to 8pt. The table must fit **within type area 108mm x 175mm**. (Avoid landscape format if at all possible, but for wider tables, use landscape with maximum width 175mm). Tables should be titled and sources given.

Maps and Figures: Black and white only. Avoid tints, use solid white, black or open patterns (stripes, dots etc) instead. Provide a bromide, clearly labelled, and disk version. Titles and sources should be given, and permissions must be obtained by contributor.

STYLE

Font: Times New Roman 12pt. Headings: (1) Bold, (2) Italics, no underline, (3) Italics, no new paragraph.

Quotation marks: single in text throughout; double within single; single within indented quotations.

Spelling: use the -z- alternative (recognize) except where -yse (analyse); -our rather than -or (favour) except in proper names, e.g. Labour Party, if that is its formal title.

Capitalization: Use capitals sparingly, for titles (the Secretary-General; President Mitterrand) and for unique or central institutions (the European Commission, the International Atomic Energy Authority) but not for general or local organizations and offices (a government minister, the mayor, Brigham parish council). Capitalize Party in a title (the British Green Party), otherwise lower case. Lower case for the state and for the left and the right (but the New Left, the New Right). Capitalize -isms from names (Marxism), elsewhere lower case (ecologism). In general, lower case for conferences and congresses (the party's tenth congress was held in 1995).

Numbers: words one–ten, afterwards numerals 11, 12, etc; decimals preceded by a nought (0.4).

Dates: 12 July 1994. Abbreviate years: 1983–84; 1908–9; 1920–21; the 1930s (*not* 'the thirties').

Article: The manuscript should be referred to throughout text as an 'article', not a 'paper'.

REFERENCES:

Harvard-style references e.g. (Denver, 1990). References should be cited in the text thus: Denver (1990: 63–4), Denver and Hands (1985, 1990). Use '*et al.*' when citing a work by more than two authors, e.g. (Brown *et al.*, 1991). The letters a, b, c, etc., should be used to distinguish citations of different works by the same author in the same year, e.g. (Brown, 1975a, b).

References cited in the text should be listed alphabetically and presented in full, using the following style. All text references must be included in the list of references. Essential notes should be kept to a minimum and indicated by superscript numbers in the text and collected on a single page at the end of the text, before the references.

> **Articles in journals:** Anker, Hans (1990) 'Drawing Aggregate Inferences from Individual Level Data: The Utility of the Notion of a Normal Vote', *European Journal of Political Research* 18: 373–87.
>
> **Books:** Denver, David and Gordon Hands (1997), *Modern Constituency Electioneering*, London and Portland, OR: Frank Cass.
>
> **Articles in books:** Webb, Paul D. (1994) 'Party Organizational Change in Britain: The Iron Law of Centralization?', in Richard S. Katz and Peter Mair (eds) *How Parties Organize: Change and Adaptation in Party Organizations in Western Democracies*, pp.109–34. London: Sage.